BUSINESS STUDIES
FOR GCSE

BUSINESS
STUDIES
FOR GCSE

RENÉE HUGGETT

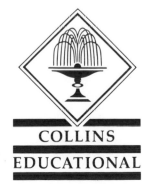

COLLINS
EDUCATIONAL

First published 1988 by Collins Educational, 8 Grafton Street, London W1X 3LA. Reprinted February 1989, October 1989.

ISBN 00 327461 6

Phototypeset by Tradespools Ltd, Frome, Somerset
Printed by Butler and Tanner Ltd, Frome, Somerset

The publishers would like to thank the following for permission to reproduce photographs:

Unit 1 – British Gas plc, Farmers' Weekly Library, Brenda Prince/Format; Unit 2 – Sheila Terry/Science Photo Library, Philips Electronics; Unit 6 – ASDA Supermarkets, Novosti Press Agency; Activities 1–6 – The Press Association Ltd; Unit 7 – Sally and Richard Greenhill, Brenda Prince/Format; Unit 12 – Civil Aviation Authority; Activities 9–12 – Barnaby's Picture Library; Unit 18 – ICI Corporate Slide Bank (×2); Activities 13–19 – Sally and Richard Greenhill; Unit 20 – Quadrant Picture Library; Unit 21 – Network, The Press Association Ltd; Unit 24 – Central Electricity Generating Board; Unit 25 – John Blake Picture Library, National Motor Museum; Unit 27 – Piers Cavendish/Reflex, Robert Harding Picture Library, ICI Petrochemicals and Plastics Division; Unit 29 – Science Photo Library; Activities 30–32 – Horner Collins and Kirvan, Philips Electronics; Unit 34 – Ardea London Ltd, Farmers' Weekly Library; Unit 35 – J. Walter Thomson; Unit 36 – British Gas plc; Unit 37 – The Press Association; Unit 39 – Iveco Ford Cargo, British Leyland; Activities 38–39 – Robert Harding Picture Library; Unit 40 – British Airways; Activities 40–42 – Solo Syndication (×3); Unit 44 – Permifique, Lustresilk; Unit 48 – National Motor Museum (×8), Art Director's Photolibrary; Unit 49 – Ace Photo Agency; Unit 50 – Hales Containers; Unit 54 – Northgate House Nursing Home; Unit 55 – British Telecommunications plc (×4); Activities 53–55 – National Trust Photographic Library; Unit 58 – Robert Harding Picture Library; Unit 61 – BPCC plc; Unit 63 – The Press Association; Unit 65 – Andrew Moore/ Reflex; Activities 62–67 – Solo Syndication (×2); Unit 68 – AA Picture Library; Unit 69 – Northumberland Water Authority, Sony Electronics; Unit 70 – Department of Trade and Industry; Unit 71 – Popperfoto; Unit 72 – Associated British Ports (Hull), Packshots Ltd; Activities 68–72 – The Design Council; Unit 73 – Popperfoto; Unit 75 – Network; Unit 78 – Chris Davis/Network; Unit 80 – *Town and Country Planning*; Activities 77–80 – Italian State Tourist Office (×2). All other photographs – Nance Fyson.

For permission to reproduce copyright material the publishers would like to thank the following:

ACAS, The Advertising Association, Barclay's Bank plc, British Amusement and Catering Trades Association, *British Business*, British Franchise Association, British Gas plc, British Rail Board, British Telecom, BTR Group plc, Centaur Communications Ltd, Central Electricity Generating Board, Central Statistical Office, Confederation of British Industry, The Consumers' Association, Co-operative Advisory Group, Co-operative Development Agency, *Daily Telegraph*, Department of Employment, Department of Environment, *Economic Review*, Excess Insurance Group, Export Network, Family Expenditure Surveys, The Farmers Publishing Group, Fastframe Franchises Ltd, FF Publishing Ltd, Ford Motor Company, *Franchise World*, Freight Transport Association Ltd, Global Holiday Services Ltd, Government Actuary Department, Gower Publishing Ltd, *The Grocer*, *The Guardian*, *Hampstead Advertiser*, Haymarket Publishing Group, Hospital Savings Association, IMAC Research, Imperial Chemicals Industries plc, *In Business Now*, *The Independent*, Institute of Management Services, Isle of Wight Development Board, Thomas Jourdan plc, Key Note, Lloyd's Bank plc, London Docklands Development Corporation, Luton Town Council, Mail Newspapers plc, Microlink, Midland Bank plc, The National Trust, News International, Ocean Publications Ltd, Pearson Group plc, *Public Service*, Road Haulage Association, RMC Group plc, Science Reference Library, Small Firms' Centre, Sir Frederick Snow & Partners, H.M. Treasury, Unilever, United Newspapers, 7-UP, West Somerset Free Press.

Illustrated by: Andrew Aloof, Ray Burrows, Jerry Collins, Illustrated Arts Ltd, Gillian Martin, Sally Neave, Jason Pizzey, Peter Schrank and Bill Stott.

Preface

THIS ENQUIRY-BASED BOOK, which provides a complete coverage of all the GCSE Business Studies syllabuses, is designed to encourage students to think and act like business men and women from the start by actively participating in a great variety of realistic situations. The whole range of business activity is dealt with — from the sole proprietor to multinationals.

Each of the 80 units starts with stimulus material about an essential business situation or problem which is very often presented in the form of a case study. Students' comprehension of the data is tested in the accompanying Study Points before they are asked to solve the problem, come to a decision or undertake some other form of business activity.

This stimulus material can be used in a variety of ways. It can form the basis for individual or group work, class discussion or, where essential concepts are more difficult to grasp, as reinforcement material after the text has been studied.

The text in each unit provides a many-faceted view of the topic under discussion. It is broken up into convenient sections, with important points and concepts itemised, to increase accessibility for the widest range of students. For the same reason, many charts, diagrams, graphs and illustrations are also included.

Key Terms, which could form an essential part of preparation for the examination, are highlighted in the text in bold type and then separately defined in a boxed area on each right hand page.

At the end of each unit, graded Check Points test the students' basic understanding of the text and, in some cases, lead on to further case studies or activities.

The Business Techniques sections in each unit provide another useful resource to increase students' skills. Some of them test students' verbal, numerical and graphical ability; others lead students out to research in the local environment; while some can be used as springboards for individual, group or class exercises.

Although the book is divided into the five main sections prescribed in the GCSE syllabuses, and structured logically within that framework, it is deliberately designed for the greatest flexibility in use.

Each of the 80 double-page spreads, which constitutes a unit, is self-contained; but the text in each unit contains cross references to previous and later units to make it easy for teachers to take any path through the book they prefer. This is also assisted by the comprehensive index which includes page references to all the Key Terms and many other important business terms and concepts.

The 19 Activities sections, which are included at logical points throughout the book, provide a multiplicity of further tasks which teachers can use in their own way to test the knowledge and skills that students have acquired in the preceding group of units.

The Activities sections include detailed coursework assignments which often range across a number of topics; groupwork assignments which allow each student to play a significant role; review points which check students' comprehension of the previous group of units; data response questions on material which is sometimes drawn from trade journals not easily accessible to the general public; structured essay questions and more case studies.

I should like to thank my many personal friends in the business world who gave me invaluable advice and information during the writing of this book.

Renée Huggett

Contents

People in Business

Aiding and Controlling Business Activity

External Environment of the Business

Business Opportunities

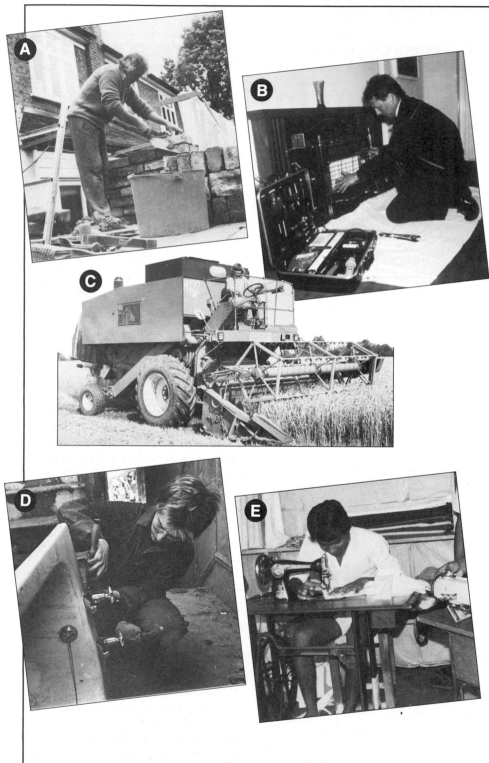

Basic needs

The business person is always looking out for chances to provide the **GOODS** and **SERVICES** which we all need. There are some things which we cannot do without. These five **BASIC NEEDS** are:

- food
- water
- shelter
- clothes
- warmth.

No human being could survive for long if these basic needs were not met. They are just as important for people in the developed societies of the western world as they are for the few tribal societies in remote corners of the developing world. Look at Figure 1.1, which shows the total amount spent by **CONSUMERS** (the people who buy goods and services) in this country. Which of the goods and services in the chart are meeting our basic needs? What percentage do we spend on basic needs?

Consumer spending 1985

		£ million
Food	FIG 1.1	29,950
Alcoholic drink		15,783
Tobacco		7,006
Clothing and footwear		14,894
Housing		31,711
Fuel and power		10,657
Household goods and services		14,607
Transport and communication		35,806
Recreation and education		19,593
Other goods and services		33,741
Total		213,748

Source: *United Kingdom National Accounts,* Central Statistical Office (1987)

Providing for our needs

One of the main differences between tribal societies and ourselves is that we let other people provide for most of our needs. In some tribal societies, women spend many hours gathering nuts and berries, while the men hunt wild animals. Most people in the western world rely on others to provide their food. The farmer grows wheat on his land. The grain is sold to

S T U D Y P O I N T S

1 What work are the people in the photographs doing?
2 What are the names of their jobs?
3 What needs are they providing for?
4 Which job do you think is the most useful to society?

a merchant, who resells it to a miller who makes the flour. This is then sold to a baker who makes the loaves of bread. Without their labour, there would be no bread for us to buy. Each of them makes a **PROFIT** on their part of the deal. Some of this money is invested in buying all the other goods, such as tractors, combine harvesters, milling wheels and dough-mixing machines, which are needed so that the process can be repeated again and again. These goods are called **CAPITAL**.

Production of a loaf of bread

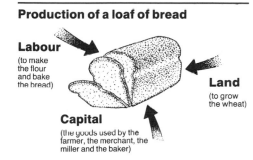

Labour
(to make the flour and bake the bread)

Land
(to grow the wheat)

Capital
(the goods used by the farmer, the merchant, the miller and the baker)

With all goods there is a chain of production similar to the one for bread. With services, there is a general dependence on other firms. The plumber, for instance, has to buy tools and equipment before he can do his work.

The whole of the business world is interdependent in this way. Money goes round and around from one person or firm to another to keep the economy working. People get a job – if they can – so that they will have enough money to pay for their needs. Business persons – and public bodies such as water boards – provide the goods and services which other people need and make a profit to pay for their own needs.

Providing for our wants

Some things we cannot do without; but there are others which we may not really need, but which are very pleasant to have. No-one really needs a car. You could live without one. However, travel is made much easier if you have one. Although most people would like a microwave or a freezer, you could live without one, as some people still do. A telephone isn't a necessity, but life can be much more difficult without one. In modern societies there are hundreds, if not thousands, of **WANTS** of this kind.

Business provides for these wants, as well as for our basic needs. (In fact, as we shall see in Unit 36, businesses can sometimes persuade us to want things that we don't really need, or to become aware of wants which we did not know we had.) Modern societies could not exist as they do today unless people's wants were always increasing. At the end of the Second World War, only rich people could afford to fly. Now that air travel is something nearly everyone can afford, lots of new industries have been created. Jobs have been provided for millions of people both in this country and abroad. Electronics has brought many new inventions into our homes from video recorders to compact disc players. As a result, many more skilled engineers have been needed to design and build these machines. In a similar way, computers have created a need for new skills which has brought about great changes in education and training. The world is always changing. The business person is always looking for new ways to meet new needs.

Bar charts

Business information is often expressed in the form of graphs. A bar chart shows how the sizes of different things compare to each other.

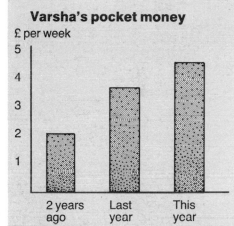

Varsha's pocket money
£ per week

Using the values from Figure 1.1, construct a bar chart showing the amounts spent by consumers on food, alcoholic drink, tobacco and clothing and footwear. You should round off the figures to the nearest thousand million and mark your vertical axis in divisions of £5,000 million.

C·H·E·C·K·P·O·I·N·T·S

1. What are the five basic needs?
2. What is the main difference between a basic need and a want?
3. For each of our basic needs, list three craftsmen, kinds of firms and organisations which are involved in providing it.
4. What other industries have been created or expanded as a result of air travel being made available to many more people?
5. Explain how a want can become a need in modern societies.
6. What kind of business would you set up to meet new needs? Give reasons for your choice.

K·E·Y T·E·R·M·S

GOODS Physical objects which can be bought at a price, e.g. a packet of crisps at 16p or so.

SERVICES Non-physical products, ranging from education to medical care and from tourism to entertainment, which are also bought, or paid for through taxes and rates, e.g. State education.

BASIC NEEDS Food, water, shelter, clothes and warmth; i.e. things which are essential for existence.

CONSUMERS People who buy goods or services for their own use.

PROFIT The difference between the selling price and the cost of production.

CAPITAL Man-made goods which are used to produce other goods and services.

WANTS Desires to obtain goods or services that one does not have.

Markets

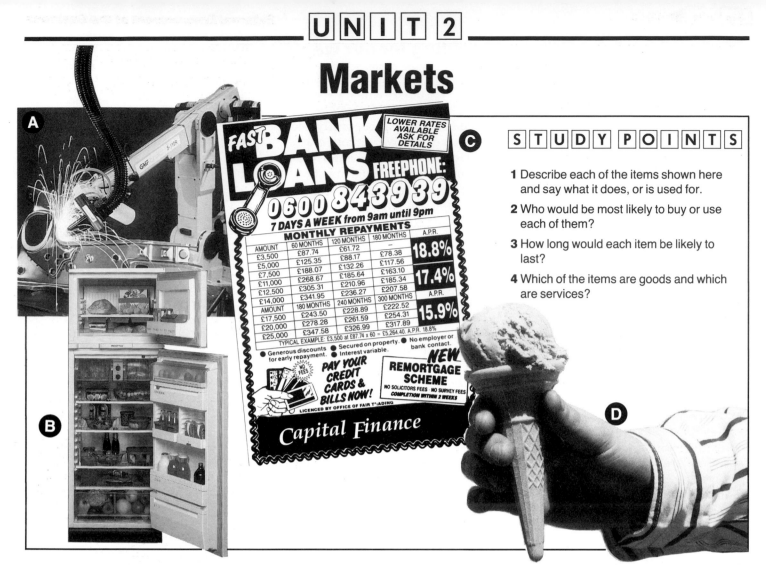

Buyers and sellers

The business person is constantly seeking markets for his or her **PRODUCTS**. In early societies, where even basic needs could not always be met, there was only one kind of market. Producers and traders went from town to town or set up their stalls at a suitable crossroad to sell their goods or services.

That kind of market still exists in modern societies. Consumers come from miles around to buy food, clothes, shoes and other goods in street markets. Most markets, however, do not exist in only one place. Buyers and sellers are scattered all over the country or even over the whole world. *A market brings buyers and sellers together so that an exchange of goods or services can take place at a price.* It can exist in a street market, in an auction room, or at Lloyd's in the City of London where brokers and underwriters meet to buy

and sell insurance. There are also many other kinds of markets which cannot be seen like a street market or Lloyd's. There is a market for cars, even though the buyers and sellers do not all come together in one place at one time. There is another for private education, television sets and so on.

The number of wants in modern societies are so many that there are thousands of different markets. Business persons have to choose their market carefully if they are to succeed. [See Unit 30.] First of all they must decide what type of market they are going to enter.·

Different types of market

There are four main types of market:

● The non-durable (non-lasting) consumer market exists to provide all the goods which people consume quickly.

● The consumer durable market deals in goods which last longer and which consumers will continue to use until they break or are replaced.

● The industrial market supplies goods to other manufacturers and producers, who may sell their finished goods to consumers or to still more manufacturers. (A small engineering firm, for instance, may make parts of an oil rig, which is used by a multinational oil company to produce oil, which is then refined and sold by a garage to the consumer.)

● The services market deals with non-physical products of all kinds which are needed by both consumers and businesses. This market, which is now the biggest and the one which is expanding most rapidly, deals in such things as hairdressing, insurance, transport and so on.

A market exists whenever some people want to buy and others want to

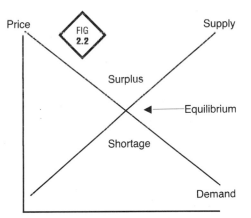

Markets FIG 2.1

Type of market	How long the product lasts	Examples of products
Non-durable consumer	Brief	Food, drinks, tobacco, newspapers, ice-cream
Consumer durable	Years	Electrical goods, clothes, cars, refrigerators
Industrial	Years	Ready-mixed concrete, industrial machinery, parts of large machines
Services	As long as need lasts	Education, loans, tourism

sell. If you made something – a dress, for instance – or offered a service – such as cleaning windows – and no-one wanted to buy, there would be no market. In a similar way, if people wanted to buy something, and there were no sellers, there would be no market either. (In that case, however, some keen business person would almost certainly start making the product if there were enough buyers for him or her to make a profit.)

Price

The price of goods and services is decided in the market. Basically, the price depends upon the **SUPPLY** (how many goods and services are available) and the **DEMAND** (how many buyers there are), though there are also many other factors involved [see Unit 33].

If supplies are bigger than demand, producers will cut back production and lower prices.

If demand increases, producers will increase production and put up prices.

When the amount demanded equals the amount supplied, the equilibrium price will be reached.

These **MARKET FORCES** can be seen at work most clearly whenever there is a face-to-face meeting between buyer and seller. A house owner may reduce the price of his or her house if there have not been many enquiries. In an auction sale, bidders drop out until only one is left, when demand is equal to supply.

These market forces can be expressed in the form of a graph:

FIG 2.2

Price / Supply / Surplus / Equilibrium / Shortage / Demand

Quantity demanded and supplied

Single line graphs

Single line graphs, like the one below, are used to give information about one item. Amounts are usually given on the vertical axis and time on the horizontal axis.

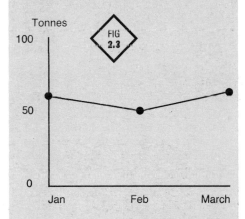

Tonnes / FIG 2.3

100 / 50 / 0 / Jan / Feb / March

Draw a single line graph showing the changes in the demand for the ice-cream produced by a manufacturer in the first six months of the year.

January, 60 tonnes;
February, 50 tonnes;
March, 65 tonnes;
April, 95 tonnes;
May, 75 tonnes;
June, 105 tonnes.

1 What is a market?
2 Why is the market so important for the business person?
3 Use the Yellow Pages to find two examples of each of the four main types of market.
4 How do markets help to fix prices? Give recent examples of how market forces have reduced or increased prices.
5 If you were setting up a business, state which of the four types of market you would go into. Give reasons for your choice.
6 Find out what kinds of services Lloyd's offers to businesses.

Types of Production

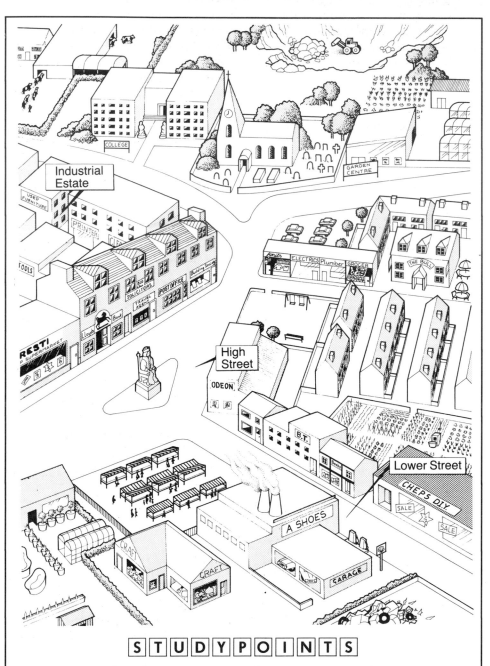

S T U D Y P O I N T S

(Look at the Key Terms on the opposite page first.)

1 Make three lists showing the primary, secondary and tertiary industries on the map above.

2 What kind of industry would you normally expect to find in a high street?

3 Why is primary industry usually found outside town centres?

4 Apart from secondary, what other kinds of industry would you expect to find on an industrial estate? Explain why these other kinds are also located there.

5 Find two examples of cities which once had big secondary industries in the middle of the city. What kinds of industry were once important in each of these city centres? Find out what kind of industry has often replaced them. What do you think are the reasons for the decline of the original industries?

When someone is starting a business and has studied the different markets, he or she will have to decide what kind of product or service they are going to sell.

With almost any kind of goods or service, three types of production are involved:

- **PRIMARY INDUSTRY**
- **SECONDARY INDUSTRY**
- **TERTIARY INDUSTRY**

Interdependence

It might seem that a tourist agency, which is in tertiary industry, has very little connection with either primary or secondary industry. Its main job is to book holidays and flights for customers. It doesn't grow anything or extract anything from the sea or land; and neither does it manufacture any goods.

However, it does depend greatly on other people or firms who do. Without its computers, it would do little business; but a firm in secondary industry had to make the machines. Other firms in secondary industry have to make the paper, the desks, the tables and all the other goods that the agency uses.

Without a supply of electricity, the agency's computers would not work. For this, the agency depends on miners in primary industry who extract from the earth the coal or uranium from which electricity is generated.

The agency is also dependent on other firms in tertiary industry – from the solicitor, who gives legal advice and the bank manager who provides loans to the window-cleaner who shines the plate-glass windows to attract customers.

Links in a chain

With services, there is a general interdependence with other types of industry; but with goods, the links are far more direct [see Unit 1]. There is a **CHAIN OF PRODUCTION** which links all three kinds of industry. The chain of production for a chair would be:

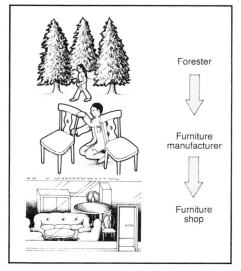

and for a hand-made woollen sweater:

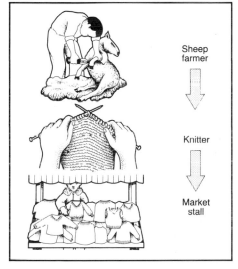

The more complex the product, the greater the number of chains involved.

Choosing a profitable industry

Business persons who can spot a gap in the market for goods or services will always be on to a winner. Over periods of time, some industries expand and others contract. It is no good going into a declining industry and hoping to make a profit, unless you have a really brilliant idea. So it reduces the risk to enter an industry which is booming, where the chances of success are high.

Look at Figure 3.1 which shows the amounts that various industries contributed to the GROSS DOMESTIC PRODUCT in 1975 and 1985. Which one showed the biggest proportional increase? Business people have to study information of this kind very carefully, before they decide which kind of industry is likely to be most profitable.

Gross Domestic Product by Industry	FIG 3.1	£ million	
		1975	**1985**
Agriculture, forestry and fishing		2,500	5,500
Energy and water supply		5,000	34,300
Manufacturing		27,600	76,800
Construction		6,300	18,700
Distribution, hotels and catering; repairs		11,900	40,400
Transport		5,300	12,900
Communication		2,500	8,000
Banking, finance, insurance, business services and leasing		10,000	42,500
Ownership of dwellings		5,600	17,800
Public administration, national defence and compulsory social security		7,300	21,600
Education and health services		9,000	26,200
Other services		5,000	18,000

Source: Central Statistical Office, *Annual Abstract of Statistics*, 1987

B U S I N E S S   T E C H N I Q U E S

Pie charts

Pie charts like this one are used to show the relationship of parts to the whole in graphic form. Use the figures in Figure 3.1 above to work out the total amount contributed by primary, secondary and tertiary industries to the gross domestic product in 1985. Calculate the percentage share of each (round the figures to the nearest whole number), and construct a pie chart to show the result.

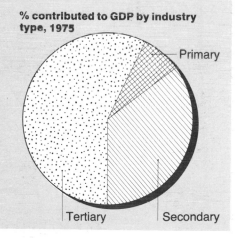

% contributed to GDP by industry type, 1975

K E Y   T E R M S

PRIMARY INDUSTRY Getting raw materials, such as oil, fish or coal, from the land or sea or using the earth to grow things such as crops or trees.

SECONDARY INDUSTRY Processing raw materials into finished goods.

TERTIARY INDUSTRY Providing a *service* to any branch of industry or direct to a consumer. This includes distributing and transporting goods.

CHAIN OF PRODUCTION The various stages, from raw material to finished product, through which goods pass before they are sold to a consumer.

GROSS DOMESTIC PRODUCT The total value of all goods and services produced by a country in a year.

C H E C K P O I N T S

1 What are the three main types of production? Give two examples of each.
2 What is a chain of production?
3 Draw charts showing the chain of production for a china cup, a plastic bag, a metal nail.
4 Why do you think all industries are dependent on each other?
5 Suggest reasons for the big increase (as shown in Figure 3.1) in financial services in the last 10 years.

International Trade

United Kingdom exports and imports by area

FIG 4.1

£million

| | Overall total | Developed countries | | | | | | Developing countries | | | |
		Total	European Community	Rest of W. Europe	N. America total	USA	Other	Total	Oil exporting countries	Other	Centrally planned economies
Exports by area											
1985	78,392	62,787	38,226	7,438	13,332	11,519	3,791	13,876	5,952	7,924	1,587
1986	73,009	57,709	35,004	6,963	12,128	10,380	3,614	13,139	5,495	7,644	1,727
1987 (1st quarter)	19,637	15,715	9,330	1,747	3,676	3,153	962	3,401	1,313	2,088	437
1987 (2nd quarter)	19,316	15,515	9,789	1,903	2,886	2,407	937	3,445	1,306	2,139	337
Imports by area											
1985	85,027	71,665	41,474	12,102	11,709	9,926	6,379	11,327	2,815	8,512	1,893
1986	86,066	73,285	44,506	11,864	10,054	8,468	6,861	10,514	1,877	8,637	1,856
1987 (1st quarter)	21,819	18,625	11,411	3,060	2,435	2,025	1,720	2,540	462	2,078	482
1987 (2nd quarter)	22,819	19,602	12,100	3,202	2,616	2,223	1,684	2,683	432	2,251	497

Source: *British Business*, 4 September 1987

Imports and exports

Britain has been a trading nation for many years. We cannot produce all the goods we need, so we have to buy some from abroad. To pay for these **IMPORTS**, we sell some of our products abroad – our **EXPORTS**. Some goods, such as cars, are imported and exported.

Keeping a balance

This trade in goods is known as **VISIBLE TRADE**. It is important that Britain exports as much as it can so that it can pay for all its imports. For many years Britain's **BALANCE OF TRADE** was always in the black, i.e. we had a surplus, or profit, on our visible trade. Raw materials, such as iron, and semi-manufactured goods, such as steel bars, were imported and processed into finished goods, to be sold abroad at a profit. The third line of Figure 4.2 shows that in recent years the balance of our visible trade has shown a deficit, or loss. We say it has gone into the red.

Since 1976 Britain has become a major oil exporter. We now export more oil than we import, giving us a surplus on our trade in oil which helps the balance on our visible trade.

Reasons for the decline

Britain used to be the 'workshop of the world', but between 1969 and

STUDY POINTS

1 Which of the goods seen in the picture above does the United Kingdom *export* or sell abroad? Which does it *import* or buy from foreign countries? Which are both imported and exported by the United Kingdom?

2 Look at Figure 4.1. Which area do we do the most trade with? What in your view is the reason for this?

3 Find out, a) where most of the developing countries are to be found, and b) examples of oil-exporting developing countries and developing countries which do not export oil.

4 If you were setting up as an exporter, which area shows the best general opportunities? Give reasons for your choice.

Balance of payments of the United Kingdom

FIG 4.2

£million

	1980	1981	1982	1983	1984	1985
Current account						
Visible trade						
Exports	47,422	50,977	55,565	60,776	70,367	78,051
Imports	46,061	47,617	53,234	61,611	74,751	80,162
Visible balance	1,361	3,360	2,331	−835	−4,384	−2,111
Invisibles						
Credits	41,008	56,635	64,592	65,224	76,737	80,608
Debits	39,440	53,836	62,986	61,225	71,141	74,895
Invisibles balance	1,568	2,799	1,606	3,969	5,596	5,713
Current balance	2,929	6,159	3,937	3,134	1,212	3,602

Source: Central Statistical Office, *Annual Abstract of Statistics 1987*

1985 our share of world exports dropped from 10 to 6 per cent. Some of the reasons why British business became less competitive are:

● Lack of long-term financial support for industry from governments and banks, so that firms cannot plan for the future.

● Low investment on modern equipment in factories.

● Weak management leading to poor relationships with trade unions.

● Low productivity.

● High unit costs because wages have risen faster than productivity.

● Unreliable delivery so customers turn to other countries.

● Poor design of British goods.

● Bad marketing of goods.

Some of these faults have been put right in recent years, but much still needs to be done if Britain is to avoid a process of deindustrialisation. This happens when the manufacturing industry becomes less important in comparison to other industries, such as service industries.

Sun-rise industries

Sun-rise industries is the term given to new industries, such as computers, space satellites or telecommunications, which replace declining industries like coal-mining or ship-building. Other countries, like Japan, have developed sun-rise industries much more than Britain. As a result, the balance on our visible trade has gone into the red. Without INVISIBLES, such as banking, insurance and tourism services, we would not be able to balance our books at all. If a foreign firm uses the services of a British bank, it pays a charge; this money coming into the country is a credit. If a British firm uses a foreign bank, the money that leaves the country to pay for the service is a debit. The difference between the total credits and the total debits is the

INVISIBLES BALANCE. Figure 4.2 shows that this is usually in surplus, which helps to make up for the loss on visible trade, and gave Britain a surplus on its BALANCE OF PAYMENTS from 1980 to 1985.

However, as the value of imports in 1986 was greater than the value of exports, there was a massive deficit of £8,463 million in our visible trade. The invisibles balance was a surplus of £7,483 million. As a result the balance of payments was £980 million in the red.

Although our invisibles usually help to keep us in the black, even they are not as healthy as they could be. Britain's share of world exports of services fell from 12 to 8½ per cent between 1969 and 1985.

Britain's books must balance if the country is to prosper. The money for this can only come from business, which is why we must compete successfully in international markets.

B U S I N E S S T E C H N I Q U E S

Free on board

The prices of exports are usually given as free on board, shortened to fob. This means that only the cost of transport to the port of shipment is included in the price; the buyer must pay all other transport costs.

What would be the total cost of a shipment of goods priced at £62,341 fob, if transport to the buyer's warehouse cost £2,122?

K E Y T E R M S

IMPORTS Goods and services which are bought from foreign countries.

EXPORTS Goods and services which are sold to foreign countries.

VISIBLE TRADE Trade between countries in goods (which can be seen).

BALANCE OF TRADE The difference in value between all the visible goods we export and import.

INVISIBLES Trade between countries in services (which cannot be seen).

INVISIBLES BALANCE The difference in value between all the services we sell to foreigners and buy from them.

BALANCE OF PAYMENTS The difference between the total a country pays to and receives from other countries.

C H E C K P O I N T S

1 What are exports? Give three examples of main British exports.
2 What are imports? Give three examples of goods that Britain needs to import.
3 What are the main reasons for losses on the British balance of trade?
4 What are invisibles? Why are they so important for the British economy?

Government Involvement

Central government income: by source

United Kingdom   Percentage and £ million

FIG 5.1	1961	1971	1985	1985
		(Percentages)		(£ million)
Taxes on income				
Paid by persons	27.9	31.9	24.1	35,286
Paid by corporations	10.7	7.4	11.4	16,673
Taxes on expenditure				
Customs and Excise duties (including VAT)	32.0	25.9	26.5	38,748
Other indirect taxes	3.2	6.2	3.0	4,484
National insurance and national health contributions				
Paid by employers	6.3	7.1	8.3	12,133
Paid by employees	7.2	6.6	8.0	11,645
Transfer payments	–	0.1	0.2	290
Rent, interest, dividends, royalties and other current income	6.7	8.0	8.0	11,718
Taxes on capital	3.3	3.3	1.5	2,154
Borrowing requirements	2.9	3.1	8.0	11,779
Other financial receipts	−0.2	0.4	1.0	1,542
TOTAL (=100%) (£ million)	7,941	20,413	146,452	146,452

Source: *United Kingdom National Accounts*, Central Statistics Office

UK public spending in real terms: by function

£ million (base year 1984–85)

FIG 5.2 Function	1980–81	1982–83	1984–85	1986–87
Defence	14,388	15,685	17,191	16,883
Overseas aid and other overseas services	1,938	2,264	2,747	2,387
Agriculture, fisheries, food and forestry	2,099	2,348	2,416	2,286
Industry, energy, trade and employment	7,440	7,115	8,889	6,037
Arts and libraries	713	750	782	765
Transport	6,115	5,771	5,521	5,306
Housing	7,308	4,100	4,333	3,558
Other environmental services	4,974	4,837	4,944	4,266
Law, order and protective services	4,894	5,397	6,001	6,132
Education and Science	17,099	16,990	16,989	15,955
Health and personal social services	18,194	18,810	19,601	20,065
Social security	31,086	36,513	39,320	40,365
Other expenditure	3,469	3,712	2,995	7,058
Privatisation proceeds	−521	−533	−2,091	−4,329
Total public expenditure	119,196	123,757	129,638	126,735

Source: *The Government's Expenditure Plans* (Cmnd 9702), HM Treasury

STUDY POINTS

1 From Figure 5.1 list the main sources of government income. Which source provided the most money in 1985?

2 a) Which source of government income has increased the most during the period 1961–1985? b) Which source has decreased the most in this time? c) Suggest reasons for these changes.

3 From Figure 5.2 which item of government spending has increased the most since 1980–81? What could be the main reason for the increase?

4 Make a list of the items of government spending in 1986–1987 with the biggest first. If you were the Chancellor of the Exchequer what changes would you make to the amounts spent, keeping the same overall total of £126,735 million.

Raising money through taxes

Although private businesses earn almost all of the country's money, the government decides how almost half of it should be spent. In 1985, it chose how to spend about 45 per cent of the gross domestic product (total value of all goods and services produced in the UK in that year).

The government raises money through **DIRECT TAXES** on individuals and businesses, **INDIRECT TAXES** on most goods and services and national insurance contributions, which are paid by both employers and employees. Then it decides – on behalf of the whole nation – how much money should be spent on defence, overseas aid, education, social security and all the other items listed in Figure 5.2.

Other government powers

The government's power does not stop there. It also controls and influences business in lots of other ways. As the Confederation of British Industry (CBI) has said in its *Business Manifesto*:

- The government provides much of the physical and social **INFRASTRUCTURE** which contributes to business performance.

- It provides most of the educational services and finances a large proportion of scientific research, particularly for new defence-related technologies.

- It provides support for the country's overseas trade.

- It makes large purchases of goods and services.

- It is the largest employer in the country, employing almost a fifth of the working population, and has a great influence – for better or worse – on industrial relations (how employees and employers get on with each other).

In addition, the government has a great influence on business by controlling interest rates and other financial aspects of the economy or business world [see Unit 73].

Who do you think should decide how the economy should be controlled and how resources should be divided out? Should it be businesses, consumers or the government – or a mixture of all three? If it is mixed, what should the proportions be?

Factors of production

Before these questions can be answered, it is necessary to consider certain economic facts. Although there may be no limit to wants, each country has only limited resources. All goods or services produced need an input of land, labour and capital. These resources are known as the **FACTORS OF PRODUCTION**. To these three factors, many economists now add a fourth – entrepreneurship. An entrepreneur is a business person who risks his or her money to organise a business producing goods or services.

The factors of production are scarce, so we cannot have all we want. We have to make a choice – or let business or the government make one for us. If we choose to have one thing, we cannot have another. If you, as an individual, choose to spend all your money on clothes, you couldn't afford to go to a disco. If we, as a nation, choose to spend more on housing, there will be less money available for education, roads, social security and other items. Economists call the value of this sacrifice – the thing which has to be given up – the **OPPORTUNITY COST**.

The opportunity cost of a sweater might be a visit to the disco. The opportunity cost of a new school might be two swimming baths. Look at your answer to Question 4 in the Study Points. What other choices were available? Did you make the best choice?

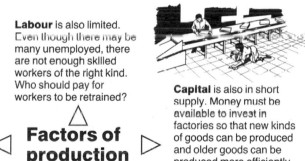

All of these resources are in short supply:

Land In the economic sense, includes the earth and oceans and everything which lives or grows on or in them. Also all the raw materials which come from them. Land is needed for houses, factories, roads and farms, but there is only a limited amount. The products of the earth and oceans e.g. coal, North Sea oil and fish are also limited.

Labour is also limited. Even though there may be many unemployed, there are not enough skilled workers of the right kind. Who should pay for workers to be retrained?

Capital is also in short supply. Money must be available to invest in factories so that new kinds of goods can be produced and older goods can be produced more efficiently. Who should decide how much should be spent?

Factors of production

Entrepreneurs who can start their own business and run it successfully, are always scarce. Those who can think of new ideas and beat foreign competitors are even more rare.

KEY TERMS

DIRECT TAXES Taxes taken by the government on income and wealth. For example, individuals pay income tax and firms pay corporation tax. These taxes are collected by the Inland Revenue.

INDIRECT TAXES Taxes and duties taken by the government on spending, such as VAT and duties on drink and tobacco. These are collected by Customs and Excise.

INFRASTRUCTURE The man-made environment such as roads, railways, housing and so on.

FACTORS OF PRODUCTION Land, labour, capital and entrepreneurship.

OPPORTUNITY COST The alternative which is given up when you choose one thing in business instead of another.

Calculating opportunity cost

A business person is faced with the choice of increasing the money he or she spends on advertising by £3,200, or buying four new computers at £800 each. If the person chose to spend more on advertising, what would be the opportunity cost?

CHECKPOINTS

1 What is a direct tax?
2 What is an indirect tax?
3 What percentage of the gross domestic product is spent by the government?
4 Give six ways in which the government controls or influences business. Which of these do you think is the most important from the business person's point of view? Give reasons for your choice.
5 Explain what is meant by opportunity cost.

Planned, Market And Mixed Economies

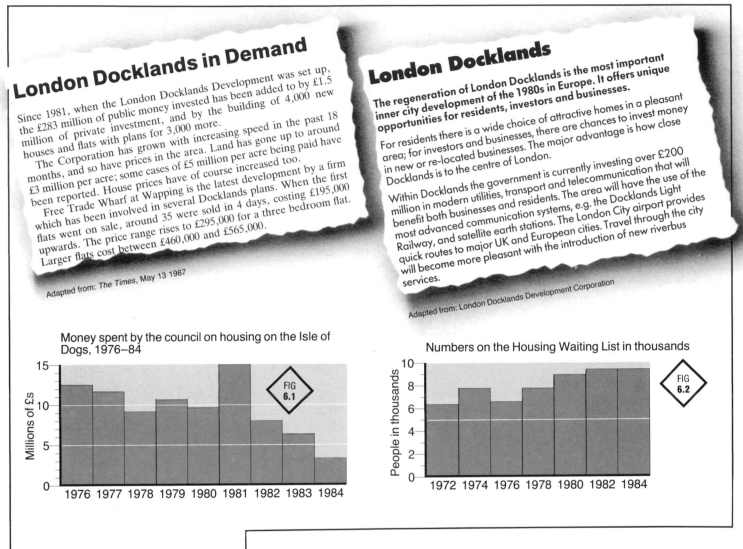

London Docklands in Demand

Since 1981, when the London Docklands Development was set up, the £283 million of public money invested has been added to by £1.5 million of private investment, and by the building of 4,000 new houses and flats with plans for 3,000 more.

The Corporation has grown with increasing speed in the past 18 months, and so have prices in the area. Land has gone up to around £3 million per acre; some cases of £5 million per acre being paid have been reported. House prices have of course increased too.

Free Trade Wharf at Wapping is the latest development by a firm which has been involved in several Docklands plans. When the first flats went on sale, around 35 were sold in 4 days, costing £195,000 upwards. The price range rises to £295,000 for a three bedroom flat. Larger flats cost between £460,000 and £565,000.

Adapted from: *The Times*, May 13 1987

London Docklands

The regeneration of London Docklands is the most important inner city development of the 1980s in Europe. It offers unique opportunities for residents, investors and businesses.

For residents there is a wide choice of attractive homes in a pleasant area; for investors and businesses, there are chances to invest money in new or re-located businesses. The major advantage is how close Docklands is to the centre of London.

Within Docklands the government is currently investing over £200 million in modern utilities, transport and telecommunication that will benefit both businesses and residents. The area will have the use of the most advanced communication systems, e.g. the Docklands Light Railway, and satellite earth stations. The London City airport provides quick routes to major UK and European cities. Travel through the city will become more pleasant with the introduction of new riverbus services.

Adapted from: London Docklands Development Corporation

Money spent by the council on housing on the Isle of Dogs, 1976–84

FIG 6.1

Numbers on the Housing Waiting List in thousands

FIG 6.2

S T U D Y P O I N T S

1 What is the major advantage of London Docklands?

2 Who has provided the most money for its development?

3 What has happened to the price of land?

4 a) What is the price range of flats in Free Trade Wharf? b) Who would be likely to buy them?

5 What has happened to the amount of money spent on council houses between 1976 and 1984?

6 Describe what has happened to the number of people waiting for houses between 1972 and 1984. What do you think is the reason for this?

Mixed economies

There are three main ways in which a nation can manage its economy. London Docklands is a good example of a **MIXED ECONOMY**. The government gave the go-ahead by setting up a public body, the London Docklands Development Corporation, in 1981. It also created an enterprise zone, or an area in which there are financial advantages for businesses.

These advantages might include:

● not having to pay rates until 1992;

● up to 100 per cent tax allowance for building;

● easier planning permission.

The government also provided money to create a modern infrastructure, or man-made environment, e.g. new roads and the Docklands Light Railway. When the **PUBLIC SECTOR** had provided the basic framework, it tried to persuade the **PRIVATE SECTOR** to invest money in the project.

In a mixed economy there are both private enterprise and government or state owned industries. For example, in Britain, the government controls some of the basic industries such as coal mining and steel production. It also controls the electricity and water supplies. This will not be true for much longer though, as the government plans to privatise (or sell off to private business) electricity and water supplies.

A typical supermarket in Britain

Planned economies

Another way of running the economy is the **PLANNED ECONOMY**, where business is financed and controlled by the State, or the government. The State decides how many factories should be built; where they should be situated; what they should produce and in what quantity; who should be employed there and how much they should be paid. Homes are built and managed in the same way, and so is the environment.

There are nations, such as China, Russia and other Communist countries with planned economies, where most major decisions are made by the State. Often, a five-year plan is drawn up so that the objectives are clear to everyone.

Until recently profit, in the western sense, did not exist in these countries. The economy, in theory, provided all the basic needs of the whole community.

By planning the use of limited resources, or supplies, Communist societies can achieve spectacular results in a few areas, as Russia has done in education and in space travel. China is still a developing country. In Canton, for instance, there are hardly any cars and some factories have no machinery, so that all the work is done by hand. Yet, by planning the use of resources in one area, China has managed to make nuclear weapons.

The GUM store in Moscow

Planned economies can be successful when there is a single agreed aim. During the Second World War, for example, Britain's economy was planned. People were told where to work; factories were given production targets to achieve; the government decided how much food each person should be allowed to buy.

The planned economy, however, is not so successful when wants are great, as they are in all parts of the world today. The State is too out of touch with the market and consumers'

needs. That is why most Communist countries are increasingly allowing market forces to work. Restaurants are run by private individuals; factories can plan their own production instead of being told what to do by the State.

Market economies

A third way of organising a nation's resources is the **MARKET ECONOMY**. With this system everything would be controlled by supply and demand, i.e. by market forces. There would be no government interference of any kind.

There are no examples of a true market economy. The United States comes closest, but even there the government has some say in how the economy is managed. For example, the government spends a greater percentage of its Gross National Product on defence than any other country in the world.

Percentages

The following formula is used to calculate a percentage (%):

$$\frac{\text{quantity of one item}}{\text{total quantity}} \times 100$$

The figures in *The Times* report on the opposite page show that £283 million of public money, and £1.5 million of private money, was invested in London Docklands. Calculate the percentage of public money involved in London Docklands development.

K E Y   T E R M S

MIXED ECONOMY An economy in which some resources are controlled by the State and some by private firms and individuals, i.e. where a public and a private sector exist.
PUBLIC SECTOR That part of the economy which is controlled by the government, local authorities and public corporations.
PRIVATE SECTOR That part of the economy controlled by private firms and individuals.
PLANNED ECONOMY A system in which the State plans and controls the whole economy.
MARKET ECONOMY A system in which the economy is governed by supply and demand without any interference by the State. No country in real life has a total market economy.

C H E C K P O I N T S

1 **What are the main features of the mixed economy?**
2 **Find four countries which have planned economies. How can these countries be described?**
3 **What are the main advantages and disadvantages of planned economies?**
4 **Why would it be impossible to have a total market economy?**

Activities

■ Review points

1 Explain why we cannot have all that we want.

2 What is a market? Why is it important for business?

3 Construct a table showing the main advantages and disadvantages of a) mixed and b) planned economies.

4 What is the main role of business in society?

5 Explain the following terms and what they mean for business and the whole economy: imports, exports, visible trade, invisibles balance, balance of trade, balance of payments.

6 What is meant by deindustrialisation? What are some of the main causes?

7 What is opportunity cost? Give an example of opportunity cost in a small business.

■ Essay questions

1 'The price of goods and services is decided by supply and demand.'
a) What is meant by 'supply' and 'demand'?
b) Using an example of one kind of goods and one kind of service, explain how the supply and demand of these might affect the price of each product.

2 a) Explain what is meant by i) a planned economy, ii) a free market economy and iii) a mixed economy.
b) What type of economy do we have in Britain?
c) Give examples of how things might be different in Britain if we had another kind of economy. Give reasons for your answers.

NEW BRITISH OIL BONANZA

Fuel giants are queueing to tap North Sea riches

Britain's oil industry is on the edge of a dramatic recovery that will continue well into the next century.

Big fuel companies are once again waiting to tap the wealth of the North Sea. Energy Secretary, Cecil Parkinson, seemed very confident as he told us yesterday that there are TEN applications on his desk for new drilling developments. Six are for oil, including the £350 million Kittiwake Project which will create thousands of jobs. The other four are for gas.

Rise

Most of these will be allowed to go ahead by the end of this year. This will start a new burst of exploration.

Mr Parkinson talked about the revival at the Offshore Europe Oil Conference in Aberdeen. This is held every two years and is one of the industry's biggest showcases; it attracted more than 1,000 organisations.

He said the industry had suffered a few set-backs over the last two years. However, the drop in prices was now over.

The good news was supported by the chief executive of the Scottish Development Agency, Iain Robertson, who predicted a steady rise in orders for British oil. Britain is the world's fifth largest oil producer.

Adapted from: *Daily Express*, 9 September 1987

1 How many new applications have been received to develop oil in the North Sea?

2 How much will the Kittiwake project cost?

3 What other applications have been received?

4 Where does Britain stand in the league of oil-producing countries?

5 What effect would an increased production of oil have on Britain's balance of trade?

6 What would be the effect on the balance of payments?

WHAT INDUSTRY WANTS

A wide range of business leaders were asked what plan they think the government should follow for success. Their replies are summed up here.

Business people themselves have the first responsibility for making the wealthier Britain which all political leaders say they want to see. This is an opinion shared by the Confederation of British Industry (or CBI), the Institute of Directors, the British Institute of Management and almost all the chairpersons and chief executives who replied to a survey last week in *The Sunday Times*.

However, they also agree that it is up to the government to provide the right situation and to help the UK to overcome the worst of its problems in competing with other nations. A list of these is given by the director-general of the CBI, John Banham. He lists five areas for special concern:

● A poor education system which doesn't produce enough engineers and scientists, and which allows 'too many young people to leave school unprepared for the world of work'.

● An under-developed network of roads, ports, air routes and communication methods.

● High taxes and business rates which change too often, i.e. are not stable.

● Money exchange rates which are not stable.

● Interest levels which are too high and often prevent many good business opportunities being followed up.

The same set of problems is seen everywhere, from the boardrooms of giant companies such as ICL, BP and British Telecom, to the new expanding businesses.

Sometimes it is the smallest and newest companies which are the most angry about these problems. Many say they are puzzled and annoyed at how difficult it is to find skilled and eager workers, even when they are keen to create jobs in areas of high unemployment.

Adapted from: *The Sunday Times*, 7 June 1987

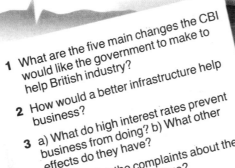

1 What are the five main changes the CBI would like the government to make to help British industry?

2 How would a better infrastructure help business?

3 a) What do high interest rates prevent business from doing? b) What other effects do they have?

4 Do you think the complaints about the education system are true?

5 Why are exchange rates important for business?

■ Coursework

1 Draw a map of a village, town or city that you know well, showing the location of primary, secondary and tertiary industry. Give reasons for the location of each type of industry. Identify any gaps in the market and suggest how these could be filled. Include these firms on the map and give reasons for your choice of location.

2 You are thinking of setting up an import/export agency in your area. Use your local knowledge and the Yellow Pages to find out the most suitable goods in which you could deal. Find a suitable location for the business and give reasons for your choice.

3 Keep a record of every item bought by members of your household over a week, and the cost of each item. Put these into two lists, one for basic needs (or things you can't do without) and the other for wants (or luxury items). Draw a piechart showing the proportion of money spent on each. Explain the difference in the size of the sections.

4 Find out from your local library or council details of some recent business planning applications in your area, including applications which have been approved and some which have been rejected. Suggest the reasons for the planning authority's decisions. If there was a completely free market economy in which all the plans could have gone ahead, what effects might this have had on a) the environment and b) the local economy?

Population Structure

Household projections by household type and age of head of household

England & Wales

FIG 7.1 Millions and *numbers*

Households (millions)	1983	1986	1991	1996	2001
Married couple households					
Head aged 15–29	1.3	1.2	1.3	1.1	0.9
30–44	3.7	3.7	3.7	3.7	3.8
45–64	4.4	4.2	4.2	4.4	4.5
65 or over	2.0	2.1	2.2	2.2	2.1
Total	11.4	11.3	11.3	11.4	11.4
One-parent households					
Head aged 15–29	0.2	0.2	0.3	0.2	0.2
30–44	0.6	0.6	0.7	0.8	0.8
45–59/64[1]	0.5	0.5	0.6	0.7	0.7
60/65[2] or over	0.3	0.3	0.2	0.2	0.2
Total	1.6	1.7	1.8	1.9	1.9
One-person households					
Head aged 15–29	0.4	0.4	0.5	0.5	0.4
30–44	0.4	0.5	0.7	0.8	1.0
45–59/64[1]	0.7	0.8	0.8	1.0	1.1
60/65[2] or over	2.8	3.0	3.2	3.4	3.5
Total	4.4	4.7	5.3	5.7	6.0
Other households					
Head aged 15–29	0.3	0.4	0.5	0.5	0.4
30–44	0.2	0.3	0.3	0.4	0.4
45–59/64[1]	0.2	0.2	0.2	0.2	0.2
60/65[2] or over	0.4	0.3	0.3	0.2	0.2
Total	1.2	1.2	1.3	1.3	1.3
All households	18.4	18.9	19.7	20.3	20.6
Average household size (*numbers*)	*2.65*	*2.59*	*2.50*	*2.46*	*2.44*

[1]45–59 for females 45–64 for males [2]60 or over for females 65 or over for males

Source: Department of the Environment

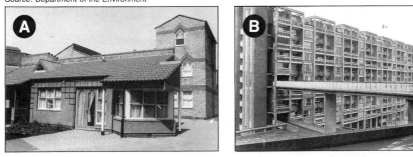

Elderly people by age group

England and Wales

FIG 7.2 Millions

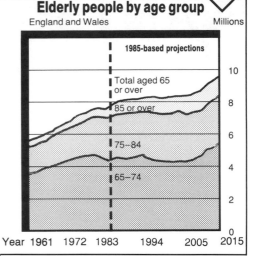

Source: Government Actuary's Department

How is the population made up?

The structure of the population – and forecasts about how it is likely to change – are of enormous importance for all businesses. For example, firms which produce goods or services for retired people must know the total number of senior citizens in the population. Without this knowledge, they would have no idea of the total size of the possible market for their products.

They would also want to know the number of people in various age groups, because this knowledge will help them to decide what products to make. The main wants and needs of a man of 65 might be quite different from those of a man of 85.

The sex of people is also an important factor. Men and women may want or need different goods and services. Information about numbers of each sex in different age groups can help firms decide which markets to enter.

The kind of household in which people live is another piece of important information. The needs and wants of an old married couple living together, an old person living alone and an elderly person living with a son or daughter would not necessarily be the same.

Knowing the areas of the country where most people live and to where they are likely to move can help a firm plan its sales and marketing policies

STUDY POINTS

Your firm is considering whether it should enter the market for building flats and houses for retired people. You are asked to write a report providing information on what the market for these homes might be in the 1990s.

1 Using figure 7.2, give information on how many people over 65 there are likely to be in the 1990s.

2 What proportion of this total are in the age groups a) 65–74, b) 75–84 and c) 85 or over?

3 Look at figure 7.1. How many households where the head of the house is 60/65 are there likely to be in the 1990s? What is the predicted average household size for the 1990s?

4 From the photographs, make a list of the advantages and disadvantages for old people of each of the two kinds of home.

5 Write the report and give your conclusions.

Distribution of wealth

Gross Domestic Product per head by region, 1985

FIG 7.3

Scotland 97.3

Northern Ireland 74.8

North 92.9

Yorkshire & Humberside 91.8

N. West 96.0

East Midlands 95.7

East Anglia 100.8

West Midlands 92.3

Wales 88.8

South East 114.8

South West 93.8

The numbers show regional Gross Domestic Product per head as a percentage of the national average. Regions with above average GDP per head are shaded.

Source: *Lloyds Bank Economic Bulletin*, May 1987

It also helps to know how the nation's income is spread out over the country, and which regions are richest or poorest. Figure 7.3 shows the gross domestic product, the value of goods and services produced in the UK each year, per person for each region. You can see from the map where the richer and poorer areas are. This information is used to help firms decide where they should concentrate their sales efforts. For example, if your products are expensive, luxury items, there may not be much point in trying to sell these in areas with little wealth. More detailed figures, which are readily available, show the average income of retired people and how they spend their money. Information

about other parts of the population can be obtained in the same way.

With all this information, a firm can draw up a basic marketing plan, showing where and how and to whom it will sell its products. Forecasts about future patterns allow the firm to calculate whether the market is likely to expand or contract and to make plans for the future.

The following table shows the number of children between 5 and 14 years old in the population between 1941 and 1985.

Number of children in the population between 5 and 14 years old

Year	Millions	Year	Millions
1941	6.8	1976	9.2
1951	7.0	1981	8.1
1961	8.1	1984	7.4
1971	8.9	1985	7.3

FIG 7.4

Source: CSO, *Social Trends*, 1987

You can see from the figures that the number of children in this age group

rose steadily from 1941, peaked in 1976 and is now dropping slowly. This information would be useful for many organisations, both in the public sector and the private sector. For example, education authorities need to know how many children in different age groups there will be in schools each year; businesses whose products are for children need to know which age group is best to aim at as their market.

The science which deals with the study of how population is made up and how it changes is called DEMOGRAPHY. From the business viewpoint, some of the most important aspects are:

- Total size of population
- The proportion in various age groups
- The balance between the sexes
- How households are made up
- Population movements between regions.

BUSINESS TECHNIQUES
Multiple line graphs

These graphs show the relationship between different sets of figures over periods of time. Time is represented on the horizontal axis or scale, and the figures on the vertical scale. A solid line should be used to join points on one curve and a line of dots and dashes for the other, as in Figure 7.5.

Use the information in Fig 7.1 to draw a multiple line graph comparing the number of one-parent households from 1983 to 2001 with a head of household of a) 15–29 and b) 30–44.

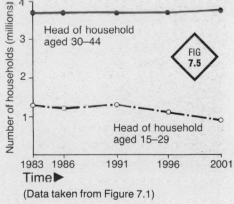

Married Couple Household

FIG 7.5

Number of households (millions)

Head of household aged 30–44

Head of household aged 15–29

1983 1986 1991 1996 2001

Time ▶

(Data taken from Figure 7.1)

KEY TERM

DEMOGRAPHY The science which studies the human population by collecting statistics or facts and figures and then studying them. Information is then provided on the total population, and different groups by age, sex, location and so on.

CHECKPOINTS

1 Why might a business need to know the numbers of males and females in the population?
2 List four other things about population which are of interest to businesses.
3 Imagine a population study has forecast that for the age group 6–10 years, the number of girls in

proportion to boys will increase in the next five years. How might firms make use of this information?
4 What kinds of demographic information would be of interest to: a) a manufacturer of baby foods, b) a leisure centre, c) a funeral director, and d) the Department of Education and Science?

Occupational Distribution

Employees in employment: by industry

FIG 8.1

United Kingdom   Thousands

	1971	1981	1985 Males	1985 Females	1985 Total
Agriculture, forestry, and fishing	432	352	253	85	338
Metal goods, engineering, and vehicle industries	3,705	2,919	2,073	539	2,612
Energy and water supply industries	797	709	531	82	613
Extraction of minerals and ores other than fuels, manufacture of metal, mineral products, and chemicals	1,278	934	651	148	799
Other manufacturing industries	3,102	2,367	1,237	885	2,122
Construction	1,207	1,138	849	121	970
Distribution, hotels, catering, and repairs	3,678	4,166	2,042	2,428	4,470
Transport and communication	1,550	1,423	1,035	269	1,304
Banking, finance, insurance, business services, and leasing	1,336	1,740	1,009	963	1,972
Other services	5,036	6,121	2,269	3,997	6,266
All industries and services	22,122	21,870	11,950	9,517	21,467

Source: Department of Employment

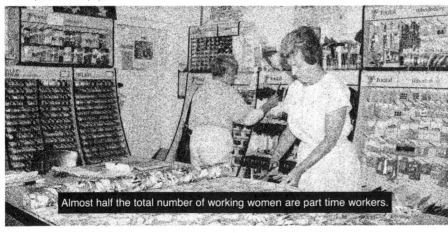

Almost half the total number of working women are part time workers.

STUDY POINTS

1 Look at Figure 8.1. Which industry employed a) the smallest number of females and b) the largest number of females in 1985?

2 Which industries employed more female than male workers in 1985? Suggest the main reasons.

3 Study Figure 8.1 and suggest industries where in your view there might be room for greater employment of women.

4 If more women decided to stay at home rather than go out to work, which industries would be most affected? What would be the likely effects on male employment as a result?

Changes in working patterns

In recent years, there have been dramatic changes in the occupational distribution of the population – the kind of work that is done and the kinds of people who do it. The main changes have been:

● A fall in the numbers employed in primary and secondary industry

● An increase in the numbers working in tertiary industry

● A rise in unemployment, particularly in certain regions and among young people

● An increase in the number of working women

● A rise in the total **WORKING POPULATION**.

These changes have had a great effect on the economy and on the whole of society.

Structural unemployment

Most job losses in manufacturing industry have occurred in the North and the Midlands through **STRUCTURAL UNEMPLOYMENT**. Factories have been closed, workers have been made redundant, and few new jobs have been provided. Meanwhile, the greatest growth in the service industries has occurred in the South. Many of the new sunrise industries are also located in the South. As a result, unemployment was higher in the North and the Midlands in 1987.

Mobility of labour

Lack of **MOBILITY OF LABOUR** has helped to keep the differences between the regions. Unemployed people in the North or Midlands were unable or unwilling to move south for a number of reasons:

- lack of low-price housing
- attachment to their home region, to relatives and friends
- cost of moving would be too expensive
- lack of retraining for new jobs
- lack of information about jobs available in other areas.

The government has tried to solve this problem of regional inequalities, the fact that some areas have more jobs and more wealth than other areas. However there has been little real success [see Unit 69].

More women working

In recent years there has been an enormous increase in the number of working women. One reason is that many shops prefer to employ women and girls as part-time workers. There has also been much growth in the number of home-workers, many of whom are women.

There are also deeper reasons. Women's views of themselves and their role in society have changed a great deal. Encouraged by the women's movement, they are no longer content to stay at home and do housework. They are much keener on a career and a life of their own. As a result, they are far more likely to go back to work after the birth of a child. The pressure to go on working is even greater when the woman earns more than her husband, or when, for example, the husband is unemployed. A few professional couples have deliberately chosen to delay having children, or to have none at all, for the sake of greater wealth. They are in the richest section of the population.

Baby boom

This increase in the number of women who work has helped to swell the total working population. There are other reasons for this rise. Between 1951 and 1966, there was a 'baby boom' in the United Kingdom, with more children being born every year. These children, who entered the labour market mainly between 1967 and 1982, also helped to increase the total working population. The laws of supply and demand meant that many of them were unable to find jobs, particularly in the North and in the Midlands where the traditional manufacturing industry had declined. This was one of the reasons for the growth in unemployment amongst young people. Another was the high wages that employers often had to pay young people.

The 'baby boom' is over. The number of births dropped dramatically between 1966 and 1981. Although it has risen slightly since then, it is not expected to reach the level of the Fifties and the Sixties again.

This demographic or population change could have a great effect on youth employment in the future. The number of young people aged 15 to 19 is predicted to fall by some two million over the next ten years. If the economy expands, firms will want to take on more young people. The laws of supply and demand could help to raise wages among young people.

Meanwhile, the number of retired people will increase in the future [see Unit 7]. There will be a much smaller number of young people to support a growing number of old people, who are no longer working and are therefore non-productive. These demographic facts may well cause economic problems in the future.

Percentage decrease

To find the percentage by which something has decreased between, say, 1971 and 1985, use the following formulae:

$$\text{total in 1971} - \text{total in 1985} = \text{decrease in number}$$

Then work out the decrease as a percentage of the original total:

$$\frac{\text{decrease in number}}{\text{original amount in 1971}} \times 100$$

Use Figure 8.1 to find the percentage decrease in the numbers employed in 'Other manufacturing industries' between 1971 and 1985.

CHECKPOINTS

1. What has happened to employment in the manufacturing and the service industries since 1971 (see Figure 8.1)?
2. Why has unemployment risen more in the North and the Midlands than in the South East?
3. Explain why more women have gone out to work in recent years.
4. What are the causes of unemployment among young people. What is likely to happen in the next ten years?
5. If in the future we have fewer young people and more old people, suggest what this might mean for the economy.

KEY TERMS

WORKING POPULATION The total number of people available for employment at any time, including the employed, the self-employed and the unemployed.

STRUCTURAL UNEMPLOYMENT Unemployment caused by the decline of traditional industries, and a lack of new industries to replace jobs lost.

MOBILITY OF LABOUR The ability, or willingness, of workers to move to new jobs in different parts of the country.

Activities

■ Review points

1 Explain how the occupational distribution of the population has changed in recent years.

2 Describe the factors which have led to a growth in the number of working women.

3 Describe how changes in the age structure of the population might affect a) what goods or services are needed and b) what job opportunities there are.

4 Give examples of four kinds of information about population structure which might be of interest to a business. For each example suggest what sort of business is likely to use the information.

1 What percentage of 16–17 year olds were in employment in 1931?

2 From the graph for 1981, say which area other than employment accounts for a large percentage of 16–17 year olds.

3 Why do you think the proportions of 16–17 year olds still at school or college, compared to those in employment, changed so much between 1931 and 1981?

4 Describe what changes occurred between 1931 and 1981 to the percentage of the population who were 'permanently sick or other inactive'.

5 Give possible reasons for this change.

Adult population – education and employment status: by age 1931 and 1981

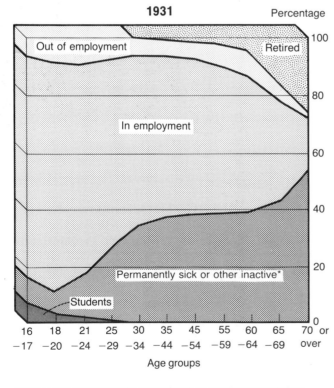

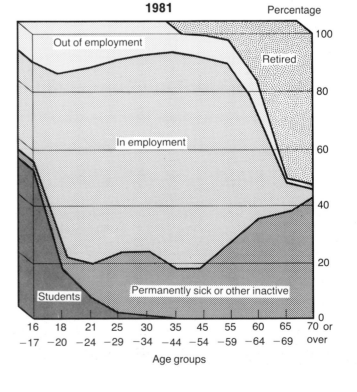

*Includes an unknown number of persons under retirement age in mental institutions and prisons who returned a previous occupation.

Source: Office of Population Censuses and Surveys

■ Case study

FOR THE LAST EIGHT YEARS, Ringland Newton have been building low-priced retirement homes for the over-65s. They have all been small, three-storey blocks of flats with one or two bedrooms. Each has a shared garden for which the residents pay a small charge for upkeep. Most of the blocks have been built on spare council land or on the edge of council car parks. This has helped to keep down costs, as most of the councils give a long lease of the building land at a low price.

The developments have been so popular that there is always a long waiting list. The main advantage for old people is that they can sell their house and buy a cheaper flat, making a large, tax-free profit. As the old people do not have to move out of their own area, they do not lose touch with their friends and/or relatives in the area.

Mr Brian Cooper, the new managing director of Ringland Newton, wants to change the company policy. At the last meeting with the other directors he presented figures showing that many business executives and self-employed people were now retiring earlier with golden handshakes, or large amounts of money from their firms, and large company pensions. He suggested that the firm should start building luxury blocks of apartments for the over-50s in the countryside, with leisure facilities such as restaurants, sun lounges, swimming pools, tennis courts and golf-practice ranges. The cost of producing these would be higher than the retirement flats in town, but so would be the profit.

The chairperson of the board of directors was against the scheme and wanted to continue with the firm's traditional policy of building low-cost flats in towns. Although the profits might be lower, so were the risks.

> Imagine you are a director of Ringland Newton. Write a report giving reasons for and against the new idea. What do you think the company's policy should be?

Equal rights campaign for part-time workers

USDAW is to start its most energetic campaign since the Shops Bill to fight for equal rights for part-time workers, announced deputy general secretary, John Flood, at the shopworkers' union annual conference in Blackpool this week.

In 1986 a quarter of the workforce was on short, or part-time, work, compared to 4% in 1952. This number is even higher in the retail business, 42% or 820,000 workers, he said.

The union is to continue trying to get more members in the part-time sector, not only because their needs are greater, but also because it has always been more difficult to get part-time workers to join the union, said John Flood at the conference.

'There are employers who are making offers that shopworkers cannot refuse. However we intend to list those greedy employers who are doing everything they can to rob part-time workers of their rights.'

He said the Government White Paper 'Building Business not Barriers' would leave a further 240,000 workers without employment rights. This would be done by changing the rules in areas such as unfair dismissal, sick pay, overtime pay and bonuses.

'Most of our part-time working members are women – over 85% in retail – and one in three have almost no employment protection rights,' he added.

Source: *The Grocer*, 2 May 1987

> 1 What proportion of the workforce was doing part-time work in 1986? How does this compare with 1952?
>
> 2 What percentage of the union's part-time workers in retail are women?
>
> 3 Why do you think there was such an increase in the number of part-time workers between 1952 and 1986?
>
> 4 What is meant by 'employment protection rights'?

Source: *Daily Telegraph*, 6 January 1988

£22-a-week paper jobs spurned

TEENAGERS in the South are turning down £22-a-week newspaper rounds—jobs which pay more than six times the rate available in poorer regions of the North and for which Northern youngsters are queueing.

Mr Joe Hill has been trying to add to his 20-strong team of boys and girls at his shop in Epsom, Surrey, for a month.

He blames the fact that other part-time work is easy to get and the area's general wealth for the lack of takers for one hour's work a day.

Mr Hill even has a 45-year-old man doing the work traditionally done by children keen to boost their pocket money.

Earnings are way above the going rate in the North.

Mrs Carol Hornby said her shop in South Shields, Tyne and Wear, paid 50p a round for either morning or evening papers and £1 on Sunday. "We have no problem getting people to do the job."

1 How much is a teenager paid per week for doing a paper round in the South and in the North?

2 Why is it difficult to get teenagers to do the work in the South?

3 From your own knowledge, what other differences are there between teenage life in the North and the South?

■ Essay questions

1 'Lack of mobility in labour helps to keep regional inequalities as they are.'
a) What is meant by 'regional inequalities'?
b) Give five reasons for lack of mobility amongst unemployed people.
c) How might lack of mobility in labour maintain the differences between one region and another?

2 a) What is demography?
b) Explain, giving examples, how a demographic study might be of use to a business.

■ Coursework

1 You are working for your local council which wants to attract foreign business to your area. Find out what advantages your area offers in terms of available labour, general facilities and investment. Design and write a display advertisement which describes to foreign business persons the advantages of moving into your area.

2 Interview some women of varying ages who have part-time or casual jobs. Find out: the reasons why they work part-time; what jobs they do; their rates of pay; what sort of conditions they work in; what they think of their jobs and so on. Look in your local library for a book about employment of women in the whole of Britain. Describe any differences between what you found out locally and the situation for the rest of the country. Give possible reasons for any differences.

3 You are setting up a club for young unemployed people. Find out what kinds of jobs, training and educational opportunities are available locally. Design a poster showing what is on offer. Think of some ideas for club activities which might increase the members' chances of finding jobs.

4 Find out what services, both public and private, are provided for old people in your area. You will need to interview some retired people, members of old people's clubs, social service workers, church organisations and other similar sources of information. Construct a chart which shows these services divided into categories, or types. Find one kind of service that old people might pay for which is not already on offer. Draw up a plan for a business to provide this service, and estimate how much it might cost. Write a letter to your bank manager asking for a loan; explain what capital you need and how it will be used.

5 Find out from local newspapers and the job centre what vacancies are available for men and women aged between 21 and 40. Write a report showing the kinds of jobs available in different business sectors. Use pie charts to illustrate your findings. Describe any local factors which might affect the kinds of jobs available. Explain why lack of mobility of labour might prevent some of the jobs being taken.

Business Structure and Organisation

Business Objectives

Ever since Tracey left school, she had wanted to have her own pottery. Instead of this she had been forced to take a job as a typist. After she got married, she started going to pottery classes in the evening, while her husband was playing squash.

Her pots were admired by everyone, including her husband, Bill. One evening, when she got back from her class, she told Bill that she would like to give up her job and start a pottery in the garage. He thought it was a good idea.

They worked out that, if Tracey gave up her job, she would save £250 a year on fares to work; £1,500 on child minder's fees; and another £500 on lunches and clothes for work that she would no longer have to buy. In addition, her tax bill would certainly be lower, perhaps by £1,000 a year. If she could make a profit of £3,250 a year, which didn't seem very much, they would be just as well off.

They decided to spend their savings of £1,000 on pottery equipment. Tracey worked hard and soon had a stock of pots to sell. That week-end, they took some samples round to local shops, but failed to get a single order. A craft fair was being held the following week-end, so Tracey hired half a stall for £15. However, she only sold £20 worth of pottery. Meanwhile, the household bills were mounting up. Tracey's wages had helped to pay these bills before she gave up her job.

Tracey went on with her business for two more months. Finally, she was forced to sell the pottery equipment at a loss and to take a job as a typist again. Tracey and her husband lost most of their savings, but things could have been far more serious. They did not get planning permission to start the pottery. If neighbours had complained to the council's environmental health officer about the noise or the increased fire risk, the council might have closed Tracey's business before it had even got started.

As well as this, Tracey failed to tell her insurance company that she was using a kiln in her garage. If it had caught fire and the blaze had spread to the house, she might have lost their home as well. The insurance company would almost certainly have refused to pay because it had not been told that the use of the garage had changed and there was now a greater risk of fire.

S T U D Y P O I N T S

1 What enquiries should Tracey have made before she started her business?

2 After she had started the pottery, what could she have done to make the business more likely to succeed?

3 If Tracey had opened the pottery in your area, what kind of pottery would you have advised her to produce? Explain your reasons.

Making a profit

The main aim of every business is to survive. The only way it can do this is to make a profit. Its **TURNOVER** – the goods or services it sells – must be bigger than its operating expenses – the day to day costs of running the business.

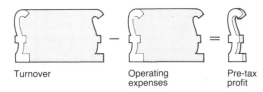

Turnover — Operating expenses = Pre-tax profit

If a business fails to make a profit, it will not have enough money to:

● pay all the wages; so it will lose workers
● pay its suppliers; so it cannot buy raw materials and services
● pay interest charges; so it cannot borrow money
● pay a **DIVIDEND** (a part of the profits) to its **SHAREHOLDERS** (people who own a share of the company); so the price of its shares will fall
● invest money to allow it to grow and expand; so it will not do very well against rival businesses.

If this situation continues for long, the firm will go out of business or be taken over by a more efficient company.

This basic law of survival applies to all firms in the private sector, both small businesses and huge **CONGLOMERATES** employing thousands of people. Look at the box on the opposite page, showing the 1986 figures for two companies. Work out for each company its pre-tax profits as a percentage of its turnover.

Planning ahead

To make sure that a business makes a profit, it must have clear aims or **OBJECTIVES**. The main objectives for businesses are:

● to make the main or core business more profitable
● to buy up new businesses which will produce further profits.

> **Company: Thomas Jourdan plc**
> Chairman and Managing Director:
> Archie McNair
> Turnover: £15.75 million
> Pre-tax profits: £2.06 million
> Products: Trouser presses, cots,
> cosmetic brushes, hosiery.

> **Company: BTR Group plc**
> Chairman: Sir Owen Green
> Turnover: £4019.2 million
> Pre-tax profits: £504.8 million
> Products: Construction, energy and
> electrical, industrial, transportation,
> health care, paper and printing, sports
> and leisure.

Listen to what the chairmen of the two companies above say. In his annual report for 1986, Mr Archie McNair wrote:

❛Last year the aim of the company was to expand in two main ways. First by being more profitable, and secondly by buying up other businesses. In 1986, even though no new business were bought, profits still increased. This was due to growth in our traditional businesses, together with the fact that we were able to increase the profitablity of the companies we bought in 1985.❜

BTR has expanded its activities into every continent and into most countries. The chairman, Sir Owen Green, wrote in his annual report:

❛1986 marked the twentieth year running in which we have greatly improved pre-tax profits. The success of the BTR Group comes from having a secure base made up of more than one type of business in lots of different countries.❜

These things apply to small businesses too. Before Tracey made a single pot, she should have made a thorough investigation of the *market* to find out what kinds of pottery were wanted. [See Unit 30]. Was it kitchenware; garden pottery; gifts or individual art items? This would have helped her decide what her core business would be. Then she should have set herself clear objectives. These should be:

● *Specific* Tracey should have decided what her competitive priorities (the things which are most important in competing against other businesses) were going to be. Was she going to concentrate for example on; lower prices, reliable products and deliveries, good quality, expensive pots with higher profits, or large numbers of cheaper pots with lower profits?
● *Practical* What was the best way to sell her goods; retail (selling in small numbers to individuals), wholesale (selling in large numbers to shops who then retail them), car

boot sales, fairs and exhibitions or local businesses such as cafés restaurants, public houses etc.?

● *Measurable* in terms of money and number of pots being made.
● *Easy to explain* to the bank manager to get a loan, to employees and so on.

As well as long-term objectives, short-term aims, for the next month, or six months or a year, are also important.

BUSINESS TECHNIQUES
Company logos

A logo is a symbol, a letter or a small drawing representing a business. It is used on the letters it writes and on its products. Find three examples of company logos. How are the logos used to represent the companies they belong to? Design a logo for Tracey's business or for a business you would like to set up yourself.

(BTR Group plc)

KEY TERMS

TURNOVER The total sales of a business during a set perod, usually a year.

DIVIDEND A small part of the profits of a company which is paid each year to all the shareholders.

SHAREHOLDERS Individuals who buy a number of shares or parts of a company, and have a right to share the company profits each year.

CONGLOMERATE A very large company made up of a variety of businesses producing different kinds of goods or services.

OBJECTIVES The aims which a business sets for itself so that it can measure how successful it has been in reaching its targets.

CHECKPOINTS

1　What is the main aim of every business in the private sector?
2　What would happen to a business which failed to make a profit?
3　Say in your own words why it is important for any business to have clear objectives.
4　Describe the main objectives of the two firms in the box above.
5　Why do you think both long-term and short-term objectives are needed?

Growth and Expansion

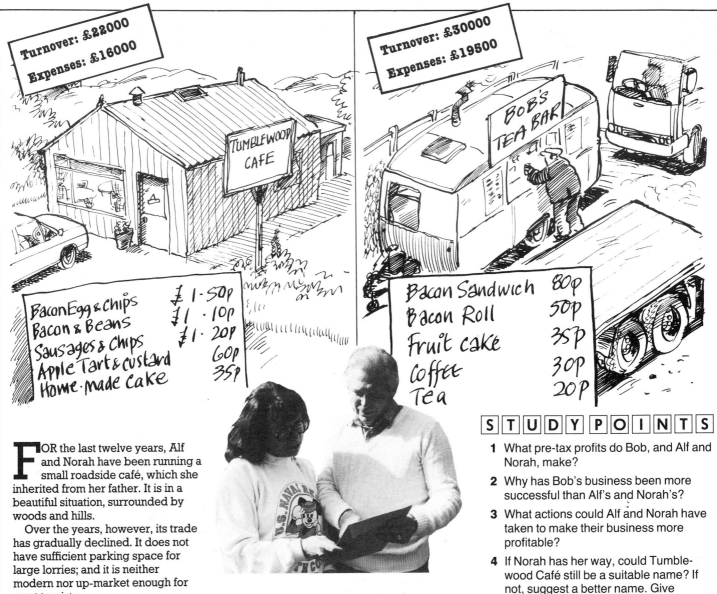

Turnover: £22000
Expenses: £16000

TUMBLEWOOD CAFÉ

Bacon Egg & chips   £1·50p
Bacon & Beans   £1·10p
Sausages & Chips   £1·20p
Apple Tart & custard 60p
Home-made Cake   35p

Turnover: £30000
Expenses: £19500

BOB'S TEA BAR

Bacon Sandwich   80p
Bacon Roll   50p
Fruit cake   35p
Coffee   30p
Tea   20p

FOR the last twelve years, Alf and Norah have been running a small roadside café, which she inherited from her father. It is in a beautiful situation, surrounded by woods and hills.

Over the years, however, its trade has gradually declined. It does not have sufficient parking space for large lorries; and it is neither modern nor up-market enough for most tourists

It is still used by a few lorry drivers who have been coming there for years; but one lorry takes up practically all of the small parking area. They cannot expand the car park as the surrounding land is owned by the National Trust. Their main customers are soldiers from a nearby camp, local van drivers and a few passing motorists.

The café just about provides them with a modest living; but they both wonder if it will do so for much longer. The wooden building now needs extensive woodworm treatment, painting and repairs which will cost at least £2500

Alf has heard that Bob's teabar, which is about three miles away, is up for sale. It is situated in a long lay-by with plenty of parking space for large lorries. Although it opened only four years ago, its turnover has increased every year.

Like Alf and Norah, Bob has always competed on price and quality of food. But when it comes to selling his business, he is not particularly cheap, as he is asking £12000 for the goodwill and the converted caravan, which is now six years old. Alf has told Bob that he would like to buy it. Alf and Norah do not have that kind of money. All they have in their deposit account is £2000. The bank manager has agreed to lend them £10000 with Tumblewood Café as security for the loan.

Alf would like to take a chance and buy the teabar. He says Norah could go on running the café, while he looked after the teabar. Norah says she would like to get the loan from the bank manager and use it to repair the café and to install some modern furniture so that they could attract more of the tourist trade.

STUDY POINTS

1 What pre-tax profits do Bob, and Alf and Norah, make?

2 Why has Bob's business been more successful than Alf's and Norah's?

3 What actions could Alf and Norah have taken to make their business more profitable?

4 If Norah has her way, could Tumblewood Café still be a suitable name? If not, suggest a better name. Give reasons for your choice.

5 What would Alf and Norah expect their total pre-tax profit for the year to be if they bought the teabar? (Refer to Business Techniques box first.)

6 Look at Figure 10.1. If they bought the teabar, what kind of merger would it be?

7 Divide into pairs, with one person taking Alf's role, and the other Norah's. Discuss whether to buy the teabar and come to a decision.

8 When you have done so, write a letter, individually, either to the bank manager or to Bob, explaining your decision and stating what actions you would like them to take. (Make up the names and addresses.)

Risks

Few businesses can afford to stand still for very long. They must constantly change to keep up with the times, and may grow for a variety of reasons.

There is an element of risk in all MERGERS. If Alf and Norah had bought Bob's teabar, they might not have succeeded in running it as well as he did. Perhaps Bob had a more pleasant personality than Alf, or he may have worked harder, been a better manager, or had clearer business objectives. Would Norah have been able to cope with the café single-handed? If she had been forced to employ staff, her operating expenses would have increased. Perhaps it would have been more profitable for them to have sold the café, which had great potential as it was on such an attractive site, and to have run the teabar together. Or they might have considered getting out of business altogether as they have been so unsuccessful. There is never a simple answer to any business problem. All of them involve risks and uncertainties.

Company attitudes towards risk vary greatly. Some firms are content to put most of their efforts into their core business in the hope that this will provide sufficient growth. Others are far more ambitious and dynamic and willing to take greater risks. They are constantly seeking opportunities for expansion and making TAKEOVER BIDS for other companies.

Why expand?

Why do businesses want to expand? There are a number of reasons, which vary with the kind of merger.

Horizontal integration can provide –
● ECONOMIES OF SCALE which reduce unit costs
● Reduced competition when rival firms are taken over.

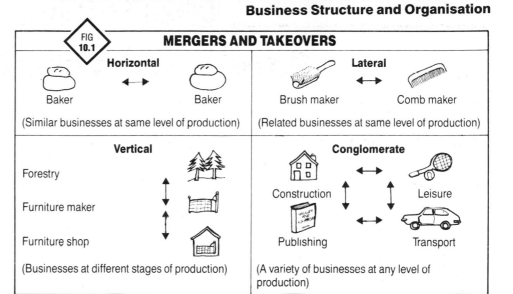

FIG 10.1 — MERGERS AND TAKEOVERS

Horizontal
Baker ↔ Baker
(Similar businesses at same level of production)

Lateral
Brush maker ↔ Comb maker
(Related businesses at same level of production)

Vertical
Forestry
Furniture maker
Furniture shop
(Businesses at different stages of production)

Conglomerate
Construction — Leisure
Publishing — Transport
(A variety of businesses at any level of production)

These kind of mergers have been particularly common among high-street retailers recently.

Lateral integration helps to –
● Give the firm a greater share of the market.
● Extend the product range
● Provide new opportunities when a core product is reaching the end of its lifecycle (See Unit 37)
● Gain technological skills by taking over a smaller, more advanced company
● Use the firm's own skills in another sphere.

For example, a chain of retailers with its own transport fleet might take over a contract-hire car and van firm; or a computer firm might take over a software manufacturer.

Vertical integration may be either backwards or forwards – or both. In the first case, for instance, a big retailer might take over a small manufacturer to ensure continuity of supplies. In the second, a brewery might take over a chain of pubs to give it a secure outlet for the sale of its beers.

There are many other reasons for takeovers. The assets of the company which is taken over may have been undervalued, so the purchasing company can make a quick profit by selling them off. The company may have a tax-loss which the purchaser can offset against his own profits. The purchasing company may believe that its more highly-skilled management will make the other company profitable. Or, it may feel there is a need to diversify from declining industries.

Business Loans

The bank manager has offered Alf and Norah a fixed term loan for a year at 14%. There is also a 1% arrangement fee to cover the cost of setting up the loan, which has to be paid at the outset. Repayments have to be made monthly. How much would they have to pay the first month and in subsequent months?

CHECKPOINTS

1 What are the two main company attitudes towards mergers?
2 Name the two chief advantages of horizontal mergers. Give two examples of this kind of merger.
3 State three advantages of lateral mergers and give actual examples of each.
4 Give two actual examples of vertical mergers. What would be the main advantages for the purchasing firm?

KEY TERMS

MERGERS The joining of two firms to form one new company, which is jointly owned by shareholders of the former companies.

TAKEOVER BID An offer by one company for the shares of another so that it can gain a controlling interest.

ECONOMIES OF SCALE The reduction in unit costs as the scale of production increases.

Friends and Rivals

Tracing UK Companies

What sort of company?	Where to look it up
1 Financial activity: Is the company trading on a stock market or is it publicly listed? If **YES** see **A** ▷▷▷▷▷▷▷▷▷ If **NO** go to **2**	**A** Stock Exchange Official Yearbook or Extel British Companies Services
2 Status: Is the company registered – i.e. does the name end in either Ltd or plc? If **YES** see **B** ▷▷▷▷▷▷▷▷▷ If **NO** go to **3**	**B** Companies Registration Office Directory
3 Products and services: Do you know the company's main activity? If **YES** see **C** ▷▷▷▷▷▷▷▷▷ If **NO** go to **4**	**C** Current British Directories e.g. Yellow Pages or Thompson or UK Kompass Register
4 Relationships with other companies: Could the company be part of a larger company? If **YES** see **D** ▷▷▷▷▷▷▷▷▷ If **NO** go to **5**	**D** 'Who owns Whom' or the Financial Times Index (Company List)
5 Commercial links: Could the company be a member of a Chamber of Commerce or a Trade Association? If **YES** see **E** ▷▷▷▷▷▷▷▷▷ If **NO** go to **6**	**E** Directory of UK Chambers of Commerce or Directory of British Associations
6 Non-registered companies: Could the company be: **6.1** A franchise operation? If **YES** see **F** ▷▷▷▷▷▷▷▷▷ If **NO** go to **6.2**	**F** UK Franchising Directory or British Franchising Association or Small Businesses Guide
6.2 A co-operative? If **YES** see **G** ▷▷▷▷▷▷▷▷▷ If **NO** go to **6.3**	**G** Directory of Industrial & Service Co-operatives
6.3 A partnership? If **YES** see **H** ▷▷▷▷▷▷▷▷▷ If **NO** go to **6.4** **6.4** A sole trader? If **YES** see **H** ▷▷▷▷▷▷▷▷▷ If **NO** go to **7**	**H** National Business Directory or Kelly's Manufacturers and Merchants Directory
7 Still around? Could the company have gone out of business or be dissolved? If **YES** see **I** ▷▷▷▷▷▷▷▷▷ If **NO** try tracing in chart for foreign companies.	**I** Companies Registration Office Dissolution and Changes of Name Index or The London Gazette

Adapted from: *Science Reference Library Aids to Readers No 35* (extracts)

S T U D Y   P O I N T S

1 Where might you find the address of a company whose name ended with plc?

2 How would you find the name and address of a local builder's merchant?

3 Under what sort of headings would you expect to find businesses listed in the UK Kompass Register?

4 You want to find out whether a firm is independent or owned by another company. Where would you look?

5 You cannot get any reply on the telephone to a company which owes you money. How would you find out if it had gone out of business?

6 Your uncle has left you a large sum of money and you are thinking of opening a franchise business (a business which buys the right to make or sell a product belonging to someone else). Where would you look and who would you contact to find out what opportunities are available?

7 All your efforts to find the address of an export agency have failed. Where would you look now?

8 You are working for a charity which wants to send out a standard letter to all manufacturers of hearing aids. Where would you find their names and addresses?

9 You are thinking of setting up a stained glass business. How would you find out the number of rival firms in your area?

10 How would you check that the name you have chosen for your company has not been used by someone else?

Information about other firms

Businesses need to know about other businesses, particularly friendly firms – and rivals. With registered companies, some information is always available. This is because, by law, each company must publish an annual report and accounts every year. This report must include:

● a balance sheet
● profit and loss account,
● details of any companies which have been bought or sold,
● changes in internal organisation. (See Unit 51)

However, a company doesn't have to reveal its trade secrets, or its future plans or even what it is doing at the moment, as the reports are always produced a year later.

Small firms and sole proprietors, or people in business on their own, do not have to reveal information to anyone – except to the Inland Revenue and the Customs and Excise who will want to know about profits and sales in order to know what taxes are owed. If you set up a business of your own you would not expect other firms to tell you what profit they were making, what they charged, how they manufactured a product, who their customers were, or any other trade secrets.

Local co-operation

There is, nevertheless, a considerable amount of co-operation between traders on the local network. They will tell each other about traffic wardens who will always put a penalty ticket on a parked van. They will warn each other about changes in the law which may affect them. They will sometimes tell one another about customers who are well known for being slow at paying their bills. One firm may help another in an emergency by making some urgently-needed parts, or by obtaining supplies quickly or, even, by allowing credit to be extended for a few essential weeks. One firm may contract out to another firm work which it doesn't want to do, or which it cannot cope with itself.

Some firms might help others to solve some technical problem in their own field, knowing that they will be able to go to the other firms for similar help in the future.

Specialist firms

Although not all firms are willing to help others in this way, there are many informal contacts of this kind in the business world. There is also more formal co-operation and **INTER-DEPENDENCE** as work has become more specialised and technological. In becoming more cost-effective, big business has contracted more work out to **SPECIALIST FIRMS**. It is sometimes not worthwhile for a firm to keep its own transport department, its own publicity department or its own research and development department, when the work can be done more cheaply and more efficiently by a small firm. There are, for instance, 45 specialist research and development firms in the United Kingdom employing 10,000 people with a combined turnover of £200 million.

Some small firms exist only to supply bigger firms with products and services: making parts, plumbing, gardening, transport, catering, publicity to name but a few. There are many advantages for these small firms; for example, definite orders which will be repeated if the quality, service and costs are right. That is why it is important for sole proprietors and small firms to know about the wider business world. If they lack this knowledge, they may miss many chances for making a profit.

K E Y T E R M S

INTERDEPENDENCE The reliance of one group upon another for essentials, e.g. consumers rely on farmers, manufacturers on suppliers, retailers on consumers etc.
SPECIALIST FIRMS Businesses which restrict their activities to one area. Their greater knowledge and skills in that area make them more efficient.

International co-operation

In big business, such knowledge is even more essential. Although there is fierce competition, both nationally and internationally, between firms, there is also an increasing amount of co-operation. Electronic goods are made in the Far East for European firms, who then export them world-wide. Parts of cars are made in one country and assembled in another for home sales and exports. There is even co-operation between both foreign firms and governments in such fields as aerospace and the European airbus.

There are opportunities for entrepreneurs in this kind of international co-operation. The *Independent* reported on 5 May 1987 how one small north country health food firm was importing peanuts from the United States and making them into peanut butter, which it sold back to the States – through a London-based marketing firm run by an American!

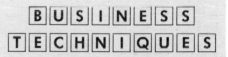

B U S I N E S S
T E C H N I Q U E S

Yellow Pages

The Yellow Pages contain much valuable information for businesses. Firms are listed according to what kinds of goods or services they offer. Businesses can look up other businesses that they might sell to or buy from. For example, a dressmaker might look up material suppliers and shops to sell the finished clothes to. Find three examples of firms which form the chain: *supplier – manufacturer – retailer* in the Yellow Pages.

C H E C K P O I N T S

1 In what ways do small firms help each other?
2 What are the main uses of the Yellow Pages for a small trader?
3 What kinds of goods or services might small firms provide for a) a car manufacturer, b) a solicitor, and c) an estate agent?
4 Why has interdependence increased in recent years?

Social Responsibilities of Business

Air traffic safety fears grow after near miss

There has been another near miss involving two aircraft at Heathrow. There is concern about the amount of work the controllers are doing, and how they are coping with it. The Civil Aviation Authority (CAA), which runs the control service, says it is coping safely with increased air traffic.

The latest near miss was between an Alitalia jet leaving Heathrow and a British Airways Boeing 747 waiting to land. The Alitalia jet was told by the controller to pass under an area of air-space used by aircraft waiting to land at Heathrow, and was told to climb from 6,000 feet to 13,000 feet.

At the same time the Boeing 747 entered the waiting space at 9,000 feet. The captain of the Alitalia jet saw the Boeing 747 just above him as he was climbing. The two aircraft missed each other by a few hundred feet.

It is thought the controller had let the Alitalia jet climb too early, and that he had not realised the Boeing 747 was waiting; he seemed to think it was passing straight on to Heathrow.

The CAA says that although air traffic has increased, near misses are fewer. However, the proportion of near misses in which traffic control has some blame has risen.

Adapted from: *The Independent*, 18 May 1987

Air traffic officers to study low morale

The Guild of Air Traffic Control Officers is carrying out a survey of all its members after near collisions, breakdown of equipment and general discontent at the London Air Traffic Control Centre.

Controllers say management at the Civil Aviation Authority (CAA) are out of touch. The Guild complains of longer hours, fewer breaks, more air traffic and unreliable equipment.

A CAA spokesman said that, 'We can see spirits are low and management are trying their best to sort things out.'

Controllers say the added work pressures will increase the risk to aircraft and passengers this summer.

Adapted from: *The Independent*, 27 May 1987

'The CBI is in business to create a way of thinking in this country in which companies can do business efficiently and profitably for the good of everyone.'

Source: The Confederation of British Industry

Effects of doing business

Businesses do not exist separately from the rest of society. As they are now probably the most powerful group, they have a great number of **SOCIAL RESPONSIBILITIES** to the community as a whole. What are these responsibilities?

The responsibilities of the sole proprietor are decided by the nature of his or her business. The main obligations, or things he or she must do, are to provide high quality goods or services at low prices. If they do not do so, they will soon go out of business as the market is crowded with competitors who are only too eager to take over the trade.

Big businesses have similar responsibilities, but their wealth and power is so great that the things they do can have an enormous effect on the rest of society.

Think what might happen if a company decided to close a big factory and transfer the work to other sites for the sake of greater efficiency and productivity (the number of products being produced over a period of time). If the factory provided most of the work in the town, the effects could be terrible. Not only would many people lose their jobs, but smaller firms which provided the factory with goods and services would also suffer. Shops, pubs, cafés, banks, transport, leisure facilities and much more would also be affected. There would be an effect on the whole of society as social security payments would increase, though these might be balanced by the firm's greater profits and productivity.

Nevertheless, the costs to society could be great: a 'ghost' town of unemployed might result.

STUDY POINTS

1 The captain of the Alitalia jet has been asked by his union to describe the near miss at Heathrow. Write the report, saying what happened from his point of view.

2 What are the main complaints made by the Guild of Air Traffic Controllers?

3 What reply has the Civil Aviation Authority made to these complaints?

4 Who in your view is mainly responsible for the situation at Heathrow? What further action should be taken and how should it be paid for?

Redundancy

Obviously, a firm's first responsibility is to itself – to increase its profits so that it can survive. However, it also has responsibilities to the workers it has made **REDUNDANT**, and to the town which has provided its labour for the past thirty years.

When workers are made redundant, the money they receive from their employer has to equal a certain basic amount by law. (See Unit 76) Some firms feel they have a responsibility to pay more than this, especially if the workers have been there for a long time. Other firms, however, will only pay the basic money that they have to.

Clashes of interests

The shareholders in a company have taken a risk in investing their money in the business. They want to receive the highest dividends, or part shares of the profits, in return for this investment. They might not be too happy if the company pays very high redundancy money and their dividends are lower as a result. So the company also has a responsibility to its shareholders.

The government could help by creating jobs for the unemployed, but this needs money. The government has no money of its own, only what we pay in taxes. The taxpayers might not want more of their money to go to unemployed factory workers.

All too often there is a clash of interests.

● Consumers want low prices.

● Firms want to keep more profit for investment.

● The government wants more taxes to pay for projects that it believes are better for the nation as a whole.

● Taxpayers want lower taxes so that they can spend more money on the things they want.

It is when social costs (See Unit 68) and the environment (see Unit 79) are involved that the arguments become most heated. It may be cost-effective to close down railway lines, but the people who are losing an essential form of transport should also be considered. Firms may produce the chemicals which pollute our air and soil, but money for stopping pollution, or cleaning it up, often comes from our taxes.

The most emotional issues are those concerned with human safety. All forms of transport involve some risk. None can ever be made absolutely safe. However, if there are steps which could be taken, and improvements which could be made, perhaps they ought to be made whatever the cost to the manufacturer.

Transport operators might claim that the risks are so low that it would not make sense economically to spend the money, because their profits would be reduced and fares would have to rise. Most people would say that human life is more important than profit. Different groups in society, however, might give very different answers.

C H E C K P O I N T S

1 Why are the social responsibilities of the sole proprietor limited?

2 What might be the effects on society if a company closed a large factory?

3 What in your view are the social responsibilities of a) a drug company, b) a football club, c) an airline and d) a nuclear power plant. Find out how far they are fulfilled.

4 How far do you think profits should be sacrificed in order to have greater safety in transport? Explain the reasons for your argument.

5 If a firm is deciding how much redundancy money to pay out, which do you think are its most important responsibilities: to its shareholders or to its workers? Give reasons for your decision.

K E Y T E R M S

SOCIAL RESPONSIBILITIES The obligation that one group, e.g. a business, a trade union or the government, has to other groups in society.

REDUNDANT When an employee loses his job because his labour is no longer needed, he is made redundant. This is usually when part of a business is being closed down.

Activities

■ Review points

1 Give one example of horizontal, lateral and vertical integration. Explain the main reasons for each type.

2 Why does a business need to have clear objectives? Give an example of a short-term and a long-term objective. Why do you think it is important to have both?

3 Why do big companies employ specialist firms? Give examples of the work that these specialist firms might do.

4 Describe some of the effects that a big company can have on the rest of society.

5 What are the main social responsibilities of large firms? How well, in your view, do they carry out these responsibilities?

6 What is meant by local co-operation? Give examples of some occasions where this might happen.

■ Essay questions

1 'All businesses must be dedicated to growth'.
   a) What must all businesses do in order to survive?
   b) Give the two main objectives for most businesses.
   c) Do you agree with the above statement? Give reasons for your answer.

2 a) What responsibilities does a business have to society?
   b) Give an example of how a business might cause public argument by its actions.
   c) How might a business create a good public reaction by its actions?

£170 million to cut power station emissions

The Central Electricity Generating Board (CEGB) is to spend £170 million over the next ten years to reduce the amount of nitrogen oxides it releases into the atmosphere.

Nitrogen oxides are an important part of the mixture of chemicals that causes acid rain. They are believed to be especially important in damage to trees. People who want to save the environment believe that a 70% reduction or more in nitrogen oxide pollution is needed quickly if soil damage is to be reversed.

The CEGB has announced its aims to redesign nearly 2,000 burners in 44 boilers in 12 power stations, and to fit burners which do not give off large amounts of nitrogen oxides to all coal-fired stations built from now on. This comes before next week's international meeting on air pollution.

The CEGB's move will lead to a 30% reduction in the amount of nitrogen oxides it gives out by the year 2000, but only 10% overall reduction. This is because vehicles contribute about 40% and industry a further 20% to the total amount given off.

Many countries have made even stronger moves than the UK to reduce nitrogen pollution from cars, but the government believes that the CEGB's move will put it at the front of reductions in power station pollution. Only Germany, it believes, has gone further.

Adapted from: *The Independent*, 11 May 1987

1 What is the main effect on the environment of nitrogen oxides?

2 Who is mainly responsible for this kind of air pollution?

3 By what percentage will the amount of nitrogen oxides given out by the CEGB be reduced by the year 2000?

4 In what way does Britain lag behind some other countries in reducing this kind of pollution?

5 Find out the names of some other kinds of pollution. Who is mainly responsible? What actions should be taken?

Community involvement at Unilever

The Unilever group of companies provides a wide range of products and services in around 75 countries. Its head offices are in London and Rotterdam. Most of Unilever's business is in consumer goods, mainly food and drinks, detergents and personal products. In the UK there are 35 main companies which together account for 20% of total worldwide sales.

Community involvement at Unilever dates back to the days of founder Lord Leverhulme at the end of the last century. Not only did he supply the customer with high-quality products at low prices, he also built Port Sunlight to provide his workers with pleasant living and working conditions. In his will he set up the Leverhulme Trust, a charity which still provides money to pay for research and education.

Over the years Unilever has kept up its tradition of community involvement in various projects. Their first and most important responsibility is to remain profitable, and this is the main contribution they make to the community well-being. However, they have also helped out in other ways, for instance:

● Helping new businesses
● Youth training
● Support for unemployment schemes
● Links with education

● Giving to charity
● Providing money for the arts
● Looking after the environment
● Local neighbourhood schemes

The economic changes which the UK, along with many other countries, has gone through since the 1970s have brought new pressures on society. There has been serious running down of traditional industries in many communities, resulting in high unemployment. There has been a need to help in rebuilding economic life in these communities through new businesses and retraining of unemployed people to help them get jobs. Unilever has been involved in youth training schemes and other ideas, especially in areas of the UK where the company has offices.

In 1980 Unilever set up In Business Limited as one of the first enterprise agencies to provide help and advice to small businesses. This helps the growth and development of a healthy small business sector within the local community.

Source: Unilever Annual Accounts.

1 Why is Unilever's first duty to remain profitable? What would happen if it did not?

2 What are the main economic changes that Britain and many other countries have experienced since the 1970s?

3 What have been the main effects of these changes?

4 In what ways does Unilever provide help for the rest of the community?

■ Coursework

1 Select slogans, or sayings used in advertising, of ten companies which show something about the firm's aims and objectives. For example, 'We are never knowingly undersold'. Discuss the similarities and the differences of these aims. Construct a chart, showing the slogans and objectives, which illustrates your understanding in the clearest possible way.

2 Collect cuttings from a wide range of newspapers about a take over bid from the time it starts until it succeeds or fails. Write a *chronological* report, i.e. one which is in date order, of the whole event, discussing the turning points in the struggle and the reasons for its success or failure. Identify any differences of treatment in the reports of the newspapers you have selected. Draw conclusions about these differences.

3 Send for copies of three annual company reports which you will find advertised in the financial pages of the quality newspapers. Study the chairperson's statements and analyse their objectives. Describe how these aims have been fulfilled in the last year and how they will be achieved in future years. Use the company's accounts to illustrate how these objectives have been achieved, including graphs if you wish.

4 Contact your local Chamber of Commerce, whose address will be found in the Yellow Pages. Find out what support businesses give to the local community. Interview officials of local charities and local councillors to find out their views of business involvement in the community. Write a report discussing and analysing the results.

Sole Proprietors

Personality check

The questions below will help you to assess whether you have the right personal qualities for running your own business. Make a list of the numbers and your answers – a, b or c – then check your scores at the end.

1 If you find your homework difficult, do you
- a) keep trying;
- b) have a rest and then go on with it again;
- c) give it up and do something else?

2 Would you rather have
- a) a job you really liked even if you didn't make much money;
- b) a secure job;
- c) an easy job with lots of money?

3 Do you like taking risks
- a) if you have to;
- b) often;
- c) never?

4 Would you say you are enthusiastic about
- a) everything you do;
- b) things you like doing;
- c) very few things?

5 Do other people come to you for help and advice
- a) almost never;
- b) occasionally;
- c) often?

6 Do you think a business person is someone
- a) who makes use of the workers;
- b) makes a reasonable profit;
- c) provides a useful service for society?

7 Do any members of your own family have their own business
- a) none;
- b) one;
- c) more than one?

8 Do you enjoy working alone
- a) never;
- b) always;
- c) whenever you need to?

9 If you were left a large amount of money, would you
- a) buy a house;
- b) invest it in something you'd always wanted to do;
- c) spend it wildly on all the things you've always wanted?

10 Do your friends ask you to organise events
- a) sometimes;
- b) frequently;
- c) never?

11 Do you write down what you intend to do during the next week
- a) always;
- b) sometimes;
- c) never?

12 If you were doing a complicated task would you
- a) ask other people who knew more about it for advice;
- b) try to do everything yourself;
- c) not bother with the difficult parts?

(Look at the bottom of the page to work out your score.)

STUDY POINTS

When you have found out your score, get into groups to discuss the results and the following points.

1 From the way the marks are given in the quiz, which personal qualities are thought to be important in running your own business?

2 Which in your view is the most important quality?

3 Are there any other personal qualities which you would have included?

4 How far are these qualities reflected in any person you know who runs a small business successfully, either in real life or in a television programme?

5 What else, apart from personal qualities, might be important for starting your own business?

SCORE CHART

	a)	b)	c)
Questions 1–4	5	2	0
Questions 5–8	0	2	5
Questions 9–12	2	5	0

Add up your total number of points. The maximum is 60.

What your score means

40–60 You have excellent personal qualities for setting up your own business.

20–40 You could do well in your own business; but you might be happier working for a firm.

0–20 You need to think seriously about your personal characteristics if you want to get a job at all.

Businesses in the private sector range from those which are owned and run by one person to multinationals which employ thousands of people in many countries. They differ also in ownership and control, how they raise money, and the distribution of profits.

Setting up on your own

The majority of businesses are owned by **SOLE PROPRIETORS**. The owner has complete control of the business, and is totally responsible for its success or failure. Running your own business is extremely hard work. The risks are great, but so are the rewards in job satisfaction, for example, independence and interest.

The main advantages of this form of business are:
- *Small start-up costs* It is simple and inexpensive to set up as a sole proprietor. However, you must tell the income tax authorities and the Department of Health and Social Security, as you will be taxed under **SCHEDULE D** and will pay self-employed National Insurance contributions. You must also keep proper business accounts.
- *Profits are all kept* The owner keeps all the profits, though he must save enough money to pay tax, interest charges on loans and VAT.
- *Offset of losses* Losses made in the first year may be offset, or balanced, against tax paid earlier in the same financial year.
- *Flexibility* The small business is very flexible. If one kind of activity is not profitable, the owner can quickly switch to something else.

Disadvantages

There are also certain disadvantages:
- *Unlimited liability* This means that owners are personally responsible for all the debts of their business.
- *Difficulties in raising money* It is often difficult to raise capital, though government schemes have made this somewhat easier.
- *Slow growth* The firm's growth is often slow as one person can do only a limited amount of work.
- *High risks* The risks of failure are high as there is usually great competition.
- *Lack of continuity* The business stops with the owner's death.

For these, and other reasons, there is a high failure rate among one person businesses.

What is required?

To set up your own business you must be dedicated, hard-working, adaptable and willing to take risks and to overcome problems.

You must have a good basic trading idea and investigate the market thoroughly. A profit and loss budget must be drawn up to make sure that the business will be profitable.

A cash-flow plan will increase your chances of getting a loan from a bank, which will be your main source of finance.

You will need to find a suitable site to work from. You could start at home, but if you don't get planning permission from your local council, you could run into trouble for making too much noise, or having too many visitors. Many businesses, e.g. mobile shops, street traders, mini-cabs, and scrap metal dealers, usually have to be licensed by the local council.

You will need a business plan with both short and long-term objectives.

You will also need to cope with the administration or general organising – financial records, correspondence and filing.

Finally, you will need to have a proper marketing plan, pricing policy and publicity campaign. [See Business Behaviour section]

C H E C K P O I N T S

1 What personal qualities does a sole proprietor need for success?

2 What kinds of businesses usually have to have a licence?

3 What types of business might have trouble with the local council if they were run from a person's home?

4 How could you find out before you started whether or not you would have trouble?

5 If you went to a bank manager for a business loan, what would he like you to bring with you?

6 What are the main advantages and disadvantages of running your own business?

7 State six kinds of businesses which might be run by sole proprietors.

Partnerships

Chi and John had been friends since school. They both became architects and, several years later, decided to set up in partnership together in the North where they lived. As they had been friends for so long, they didn't bother putting anything down in writing. Chi put £1,500 into the partnership and John put in £1,000. The rest of their *start-up costs* came from a bank loan.

They did well from the start. Their *core business* was designing sheltered housing and health service clinics for the *public sector*. They split the profits equally, although Chi thought he should have had a larger share as he had put in more capital.

Shortly after the Conservative government came to power, council housing and National Health Service building were reduced. The partnership lost three quarters of its public sector work. With the *decline of the manufacturing industries* in the North, they could not find much work in the private sector to replace this.

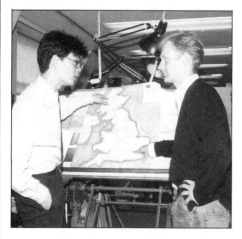

Meanwhile, the economy in the South East was booming. 'That's where we ought to be,' said John. Chi, however, did not want to live in the South East. They had their first big argument and talked of *dissolving the partnership*. Finally they agreed that John would move south and set up a London office for the partnership.

By the end of John's first year in London the partnership was *in the black* again and making more profit than ever before. As the London office was making most of the money, John thought he should have most of the profits. Chi thought this was unfair. The partnership began to go wrong after this. John bought himself a Mercedes as a company car and started drinking heavily.

Not long afterwards, John was driving home late one night after he had been drinking. He crashed his car into a skip and was killed instantly. Later, Chi found that John had run up *partnership debts* which totalled £6,800 in all. As the surviving partner, Chi was *legally responsible* for the debts, and for the income tax which John had failed to pay.

S T U D Y P O I N T S

1 Explain the meaning of the words and phrases in italics.

2 Why do you think it was a mistake for John and Chi not to put anything into writing before they set up their partnership?

3 What agreements could they have come to which might have avoided some of the problems they had later on?

Steps to success in partnership

Before forming a partnership, the persons involved should consider:

1 Name and type of business and starting date.
2 Amount of capital provided by each partner.
3 Dividing up of profits and losses.
4 Voting rights: do the partners have equal or unequal control?
5 Arrangements for retirement, death or change of partners.
6 Choosing whether to have joint or separate bank accounts.
7 The preparation and auditing of annual accounts.
8 Arrangements to cover long absence through sickness or accident.
9 Insurance: both general and against death or illness of partners.

Adapted from: Small Firms Service

Why a partnership?

Partnerships are common among professional people, such as architects, solicitors and accountants. They may also be set up in any kind of business, and are found in the retail trade and among small firms in the services sector, particularly among craft workers, such as potters and weavers.

The main advantage is that they can provide a much greater range of skills than a sole proprietor as each of the partners can specialise. In a firm of solicitors, for instance, one partner might specialise in wills and trusts; another in conveyancing; and a third in criminal law.

There are also other advantages. As more people (usually up to a maximum of 20) are involved, the partnership may have more profitable ideas than a sole proprietor. In addition, it may be easier to raise capital as each partner contributes a share.

Avoiding disagreements

There are also many drawbacks. Although some partnerships have worked successfully for years, there are probably more chances of argument in partnerships than in any other form of business organisation. Many life-long friendships have been ruined by setting up in business together, without drawing up a **DEED OF PARTNERSHIP** first.

This document should cover all possible points of disagreement which could arise. How much capital should each partner provide? How should profits be shared – equally or in proportion to capital provided? Who should control the business? Should it be one partner, one vote, or should one partner be in control? What arrangements should be made for the partnership to be dissolved or for one partner to withdraw? How should the value of the business in terms of its reputation and its clients' loyalty, i.e. the goodwill, be decided if one of the partners withdraws, retires or dies?

If you ever form a partnership, you must remember that all the partners are legally responsible for the partnership's debts. This includes sleeping partners, who invest money or lend their name to the partnership, but take no part in its management.

If you enter into a partnership, make sure that a solicitor or an accountant draws up a proper deed of partnership before, or soon after, the business starts.

K E Y   T E R M

DEED OF PARTNERSHIP A legal document which covers such matters as who provides the capital, control of the business, distribution of profits, settling disputes and so on.

B U S I N E S S   T E C H N I Q U E S

Value added tax (VAT)

VAT is a tax on most consumer spending, although some goods and services are zero-rated, or exempt. The present rate of VAT is 15 per cent.

VAT is paid at every stage of production; but businesses can offset, or balance, the VAT they pay on supplies against VAT received on their sales. For example, a furniture manufacturer pays VAT on the wood he or she buys from the supplier; the input tax. When the manufacturer sells a finished table to a consumer he or she charges VAT on the sales price; the output tax. The manufacturer pays the difference between the output and the input tax to the Customs and Excise. However, if the input tax is larger than the output tax, he or she can claim the difference back from the Customs and Excise.

A manufacturer's input tax in a year was £67,832, and his output tax £139,231. How much VAT did he pay to the Customs and Excise?

C H E C K P O I N T S

1 **What is usually the maximum number of partners?**

2 **What is a sleeping partner?**

3 **Describe the main sources of argument that might arise in a partnership. How could they be avoided?**

4 **Explain the main advantages of partnerships. In what types of business are they usually found?**

5 **Divide into pairs or groups. Draw up a deed of partnership for John and Chi which would cover the main areas of possible disputes.**

Co-operatives

CO-OPERATION

Learning lessons from livestock errors

Last week's two reports on co-operative livestock marketing groups in Wales have placed attention on the other 79 in the UK.

While the collapse of the Welsh Quality Lambs (WQL) co-operative did not kill the Welsh co-operative movement, it certainly did cause some harm. WQL's downfall, with producers owed around £1 million for stock they had supplied, has shattered the confidence of many members in joint marketing schemes.

The report by the Co-operative Development Board (CDB) gives many reasons why WQL closed. Perhaps the most important one – lack of proper control by the farmer directors-shows a basic error in the idea of co-operative marketing.

Co-operatives are run by directors taken from among the members. As membership grows, so does the number of directors. WQL had 16 directors, most of whom were chosen to represent their local stock buying groups, rather than for how well they could manage a business with a turnover of over £30 million a year.

A second report by David Thelwall of Prospect Management Services is even more damning. He was clearly horrified by the lack of proper management and planning at all levels of the co-operative. He also criticized the failure to show clearly the advantages of membership, and the poor leadership compared to that

in industry as a whole. As his report says, if co-operative marketing is to do well, there has to be planning for the consumer market.

Many WQL directors worried about the decision to buy up the Craven Arms plant, which was making a loss. However, no-one asked for a study of whether it was possible to make it more profitable.

WQL's managing director and chairman were deciding both long-term policy and running the day-to-day management. Long-term policy should have been up to the board of directors.

While the CDB report puts much of the blame for the WQL bankruptcy on the directors, it doesn't make it clear that the same sort of thing happens each day in other co-operative boardrooms.

The report's advice applies to all other co-operatives. The directors' responsibilities must be known and understood. They should all receive regular and clear accounts, and should all ask for full investigation of all new projects before these are started. They should also go on the same training courses that directors from non-co-operative companies go on.

Wherever possible, people with non-farming financial experience should be brought onto the co-operative boards. This was advice given frequently to WQL but never acted on.

Adapted from: *Farmers Weekly* 1 May 1987 (Extracts)

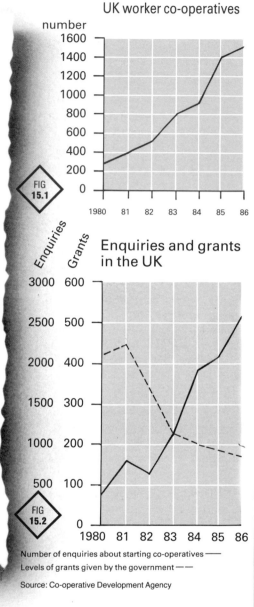

UK worker co-operatives

FIG 15.1

Enquiries Grants

Enquiries and grants in the UK

FIG 15.2

Number of enquiries about starting co-operatives ——
Levels of grants given by the government — —

Source: Co-operative Development Agency

STUDY POINTS

1 How many worker co-operatives existed in 1980 and in 1986?

2 What is the percentage increase?

3 How many enquiries did the Co-operative Development Agency (CDA) receive in 1986?

4 What might be the reasons for the increased interest in co-operatives?

5 What has happened to government grants to the CDA during the six years from 1980 to 1986? How do you explain the change?

6 According to the Co-operative Develop-

ment Board report, what was the most important reason for the closure of the Welsh Quality Lambs co-operative?

7 What were the three main criticisms in Mr Thelwall's report?

8 What actions should the WQL directors have taken at an earlier stage to avoid closure?

9 In the view of the writer of the article, what changes should be made in the management of all farm marketing co-operatives?

Worker co-operatives

A **WORKER CO-OPERATIVE** is different from any other type of business. It is owned and run by the whole workforce. Its members believe in co-operation – working together for a common purpose. It tries to ensure that everyone has a say in how the business is run. In a worker co-operative:

● Membership is open to all workers.

● Each member has one vote.

- Any profit is distributed to members in a fair way.
- Members are in control – not outside shareholders.
- The co-operative educates others in co-operative principles.

Supporters of the co-operative aim believe that it could create a happier and fairer society. They say that:

- The co-operative aim would reduce argument because the worker and the owner is the same person.
- Members would have a greater sense of responsibility and work harder to make the business succeed.
- Work would become more enjoyable and provide greater job satisfaction.
- Increased motivation among the workforce would provide better goods and services.
- As local people are involved in the business, the co-operative would have closer links with the local community.

However, the **CO-OPERATIVE DEVELOPMENT AGENCY (CDA)** warns that a co-operative must make a profit or it will fail.

Problems to be overcome

Poor management, planning and financial controls have closed some co-operatives.

Co-operatives are often formed by the workers of a big company which closes down an unprofitable plant. If the company, with all its resources, cannot make a profit, the chances of the co-operative doing so are small.

A further problem is that as few people have faith in co-operatives, it is often difficult for them to get business.

Consumer co-operatives

Britain had the biggest co-operative movement in Europe in the nineteenth century. The first successful co-operative society,

formed by a group of Rochdale weavers in 1844, was a **CONSUMER CO-OPERATIVE**. It bought food at wholesale prices and sold it to members at the market price.

Shopkeepers were bitterly opposed to the co-operatives. They persuaded some wholesalers not to deal with the co-operatives. As a result, the co-operative movement set up their own Co-operative Wholesale Society in 1863. Eventually, it became a manufacturer too, with its own factories.

There are still about 200 retail co-operatives in the high streets; but they do not have the power which they had in earlier years. Many of them are small and some have joined together to fight the competition from supermarkets.

Marketing co-operatives

There are also the **MARKETING CO-OPERATIVES**. Marketing has always been a problem for co-operatives. One group which has established a marketing co-operative recently is the Independent Designers Society. It consists of 50 designers of interiors, furniture, fabrics and similar goods who have linked together to form a marketing and export organisation.

Although co-operatives have not done so well in Britain in the last 30 years or so, interest has revived in the last few years, because of the closure of many big firms. Although not an easy solution to business problems, they provide a real alternative to the present business world and can be very successful. In Italy, the *consorzi* co-operatives have played a major part in making it easier for small firms to export their products.

The logo in this window is used by many high street retail co-operatives

CHECKPOINTS

1. State three kinds of co-operatives. Give one example of each.
2. What is the role of the Co-operative Development Agency?
3. What are the main differences between a worker co-operative and a limited company?
4. What are the main reasons why co-operatives do not always succeed?

Franchises

Yves Rocher

Picture yourself as a FAST FRAME

expert picture framing

Franchisee!

FAST FRAME is one of the most exciting new retail Franchises to be launched in recent years. It combines an expert picture framing service with an attractive shop layout.

Fastframe provides a total package including site selection, training, launch and ongoing group purchasing and marketing support.

Min. Capital Investment	. . . . . . £15,000
Total Capital Investment	. . . . . . £34,000

Full colour brochure and financial details available from:

Margaret Hewison
Fastframe Franchises Ltd.
28 Blandford St, Sunderland
SR1 3JH. Tel: (091) 565 2233

FRANCHISE SALES DIRECTORY

jet cleen
PROTECTING YOUR IMAGE

Jet Cleen is a mobile steam jet cleaning service run by the specialist division of the Provincial Services Group. The service is mainly aimed at Britain's 1.7 million commercial vehicles. Jet Cleen cleans the bodywork and chassis of vehicles, and customers use the service to help preserve their vehicles, make sure they look smart on the road, and to prepare them for their yearly MOT test. Total investment £6,000 (half can be financed). Contact: Administrative Secretary.

KWIK STRIP

Kwik Strip serves the growing stripping/restoration of furniture market with a well-proven process which is designed especially for the UK market. The process will efficiently strip paint and varnish from all types of wood and metal. Minimum investment: £8,000. Contact: Ivor Chivers, Managing Director.

Kall-Kwik PRINTING

Kall-Kwik Printing is the only licensee for the UK of the US Kwik-Kopy system. Kall-Kwik provides a financial start-up package (with Barclays, Nat-West, Lloyds), choice of site, layout planning and three weeks formal training, plus lots of on-the-job experience. This is backed by after-opening support and instructions for using the machines, and technical, management and marketing assistance. Minimum preferred cash outlay: £20,000. Contact: Anne Wright, Franchise Sales Manager.

Mobiletuning LTD
CRYPTON TUNING AT YOUR HOME

Mobiletuning, set-up in 1977 specializes in tuning vehicles at customers' homes, or places of work. Mobiletuning provides full training, a van (fully equipped with special tools), spare parts, tuning equipment and data. Mobiletuning states that possible earnings are more than £14,000 on an investment of £10,850 (no deposit for suitable candidates). Contact: Anton Rowntree, Director.

Adapted from: Franchise World

WIMPY

McDonald's ™

S T U D Y P O I N T S

1 Look at the franchises shown above. In which kinds of businesses would you expect to find franchises?

2 What is the minimum and maximum investment required for any of the franchises above?

3 What kinds of help are offered by the **FRANCHISORS**?

4 What makes a franchise different from other kinds of businesses? State the names of any firms, apart from those above, which you think might be franchises.

5 If you wanted to become a **FRANCHISEE** and were left £12,000, which of the franchises above would you choose? Explain your reasons.

Franchising is another form of co-operation – between a big firm and a sole proprietor.

The big firm has a well-known product with its own brand name [see Unit 34] such as Wimpy, or a service such as Dyno-Rod, or a special kind of shop such as Holland and Barrett. In return for an initial fee and continuing **ROYALTY PAYMENTS**, the franchisor allows the franchisee to set up his or her own business and to use the firm's brand name.

Many common high street names are franchise operations – Pronta-print, Budget-Rent-a-Car, Foto Inn, Strikes, Spud-U-Like to name just a few. The idea came from the United States where franchises have about 30% of all retail trade. In Britain, it is still less than 2%, but franchising is one of the fastest growing sectors for small businesses.

How does it work?

How does franchising – or **BUSINESS FORMAT FRANCHISING** to use its full name – work? A big firm may decide that it wants to expand without investing large amounts of capital. So it decides to go into franchising instead. First of all, it carries out a pilot operation or trial run to see if the idea is practical. If this trial franchise, which is owned and run by the company, makes a fair profit in the first year, excluding investment costs and overheads, then the company decides to go ahead.

The company sets up a training scheme for franchisees, based on what has been learnt in the pilot operation. When all is ready, it advertises for franchisees. The advertisements bring many replies. The most promising applicants are interviewed; but most of them are unsuitable. The franchisor must be very careful in selecting franchisees. If they do not succeed, they could ruin the company's reputation.

A few people are finally chosen who have the necessary capital and the right qualities. After training, they are given exclusive trading rights in their own areas and set up successful businesses. A few more people are granted franchises in the second year. Later, say in the third year, the franchisor starts to make a profit which increases greatly in later years, as the number of franchises grows.

Advantages for the franchisee

There are great advantages for the franchisees, too. They have a much greater chance of success than most small businesses as the product has been tried and tested and has a secure place in the market. Franchisees also benefit from being able to use a brand name which is advertised nationally. The franchisor provides continuous support. If there are any snags or

Two well known franchise operations

problems, the franchisee can get good advice quickly. There is a better chance of solving problems as they may already have been met and overcome in other franchises.

The franchisee will probably find it easier to raise money from the banks as they are taking less of a risk with a franchise operation than with an untried small business. Some banks will provide medium-term loans of five to ten years for up to two-thirds of the start-up costs and an overdraft for working capital or money to run the business with.

Disadvantages for the franchisee

On the other hand, there are some disadvantages. The franchisee:

- has less independence than other sole proprietors.
- will not be able to sell the business without the franchisor's agreement.
- does not always have the right to renew the franchise automatically.
- has to make continuing royalty payments to the franchisor.

- sometimes has to pay a mark-up, or percentage of the price, on supplies from the franchisor.

There are now nearly 20,000 franchise businesses in Britain. If we follow the American pattern, as we often do, the number could increase considerably.

B U S I N E S S T E C H N I Q U E S

Royalty payments

A franchisee has a turnover of £135,000 in her third year and total operating expenses of £110,575. In addition, she has to pay the franchisor a 5.5% royalty on her turnover. She calculates that if she had set up her own business instead, her turnover in the same year would have been £98,500 and her operating expenses, £87,000. Which course would have been more profitable and by how much?

C H E C K P O I N T S

1 How many small businesses in Britain are franchises?
2 What percentage share of the retail trade do they have in the United States and in Britain? Suggest reasons for the difference.
3 What is the main advantage for the franchisor?
4 Make two lists showing the main advantages and disadvantages for the franchisee.
5 Who takes the bigger risk – a sole proprietor or a franchisee? Explain your answer.

K E Y T E R M S

FRANCHISOR A firm which allows another person to use its tried and tested product, and to trade under its name, for a fee.

FRANCHISEE A person who pays an initial fee and royalty payments for the privilege of trading under another firm's name.

ROYALTY PAYMENTS A percentage payment made for the use of another person's or firm's invention or property.

BUSINESS FORMAT FRANCHISING Trading under the brand name of another firm.

Limited Companies

Companies registered in Great Britain in 1986

FIG 17.1	1986	
	Number	Nominal capital £'000
Jan	10 595	159 799
Feb	9 505	288 855
Mar	11 091	194 531
Apr	11 135	252 618
May	8 859	155 948
Jun	8 625	197 952
Jul	10 290	201 889
Aug	8 341	168 944
Sep	9 141	212 319
Oct	9 912	146 259
Nov	9 247	485 039
Dec	8 090	276 370
Total	114 831	2 740 523

Source: *British Business*, 1 May 1987

Length of time on VAT register (Comparison between industries)

FIG 17.2	Months until one quarter deregistered	Percentage still registered after 10 years
	24	30
All industries of which:		62
Agriculture	88	33
Production	24	30
Construction	25	26
Transport	19	31
Wholesale	21	24
Retail	21	34
Property, finance and prof. services	29	
Catering	23	26
Motor trades	20	30

Source: *British Business*, 3 April 1987
NB All businesses with a turnover exceeding a certain figure have to register for VAT. A business which leaves the register might not have closed, as there are other reasons for deregistration. Its turnover may have fallen below the current limit for registration.

Company liquidations

England and Wales

FIG 17.3 INDUSTRY	Numbers 1986
Agriculture and horticulture	128
Manufacturing:	
Food, drink and tobacco	133
Chemicals	112
Metals and engineering	1,371
Textiles and clothing	1,502
Timber and furniture	427
Paper, printing and publishing	497
Other manufacturing	734
Total manufacturing	4,776
Construction	1,914
Transport and communication	765
Wholesaling:	
Food, drink and tobacco	261
Motor vehicles	165
Other	624
Retailing:	
Food	262
Motor vehicles and filling stations	325
Other	1,383
Financial institutions	251
Business services	935
Hotels and catering	374
Other industries/businesses	2,242
Total	14,405

Source: *British Business*, 1 May 1987

STUDY POINTS

1 How many new companies were registered in Britain in 1986?

2 What was the total amount of **NOMINAL CAPITAL** of these companies?

3 Which industry had the highest number of **LIQUIDATIONS** in 1986? What percentage was this of the total number of liquidations?

4 Which industry had the lowest? What was the percentage of the total?

5 Which kinds of business stay on the VAT register for the longest and shortest periods?

6 Are there any differences between the pattern shown by the number of liquidations in 1986 for various industries, and the figures for length of time on the VAT register? If so, how can these be accounted for?

7 You are thinking of setting up a business. Write a report saying which industry seems to have the highest chance of success. Give reasons for your choice.

Risks

New **LIMITED COMPANIES** are being started all the time. Just look at Figure 17.1. Not all of those set-up in 1986 will survive. Look at the company **LIQUIDATIONS** in 1986 as shown in Figure 17.3. New companies are being formed, and others are closing all the time.

Forming a company seems to be a pretty risky business – and it is. The financial risks, however, are not as great as they might appear to be. A big company may go into liquidation owing hundreds or thousands, even millions, of pounds; but the people who own the company – the shareholders – would not have to pay those massive debts out of their own money. Their responsibility for the debts, or their liability, would be limited to the money they had invested in the company. If they had bought £100 worth of shares, they might lose all of that; but not a penny more. Also, if any money was left, after all the creditors, or people who were owed money, had been paid, the shareholders might even get a little of their money back.

Benefits

Limited liability is a great advantage. A company is legally a separate thing, which means that it has certain rights which are recognised by the courts. It can buy and sell assets; make contracts; sue other companies and individuals; and can itself be sued.

A company's shares can be bought and sold. Unlike a sole proprietor business, which ends with the death of the owner, a company can carry on after the person who started it has sold it or died. The shares can be sold to someone else and the company survives.

The shareholders, who own the company, have control over the company's affairs. Their view is heard at the annual general meeting (AGM), or at any special meetings they call. In practice, few small shareholders attend AGMs, unless there is a crisis in the company's affairs.

Private or public

Shareholders have one vote for each share they hold – very different from a co-operative. As a result, most decisions at AGMs are made by big investors, such as insurance companies or pension funds, who have many shares. The board of directors is chosen at the AGM by the shareholders. It controls the policy of the company [see Unit 22].

A private limited company, (which has Ltd in its name) has a minimum number of two shareholders. Their shares cannot be sold to the general public on the Stock Exchange. Very often, the shareholders are the founders of the firm. They are also the directors. In practice, therefore, they actually own the company and control it, though their liability is limited to the **NOMINAL CAPITAL** they invested. Another great advantage is that they can use some of the profits to set up company pension schemes for themselves.

If a private company is successful and wants to raise money for growth, it can offer shares to the public by making itself into a public limited company or plc. The shares will then be bought and sold on the Stock Exchange.

Disadvantages

There are some disadvantages in forming a limited company:

● It is more expensive to set up a company than to start a sole proprietor business. The company has to be registered with the Companies Registration Office. You will have to employ a solicitor, or a firm specialising in this work, which will cost anything from £100 to £180.

● The accounts must be audited, which means that you will have to employ an auditor as well as an accountant. (As a sole proprietor, there is no legal obligation to employ an accountant at all.)

● There are other legal formalities: for example, you must hold an AGM and send details of the company's financial affairs to the Companies Registration Office every year.

● A company is less flexible in some ways than a sole proprietor business, as it is governed by two documents which are drawn up when it is registered as a company. The memorandum of association states the name of the company, details of the business to be gone into and the amount of capital. In addition, articles of association also have to be sent to the Companies Registration Office. This set of rules governs the internal working of the company.

● It is often no easier for a small private company to borrow money than a sole proprietor. The bank manager knows that there is no limit to the liability of a sole proprietor. With a private company, liability is limited to its nominal capital. As a result, the bank manager will usually want personal guarantees from the shareholders for any loan.

Going public

A very successful advertising agency decides to go public and issue 6 million £1 shares. The founder of the firm retains 45% of the new shares. The issue is oversubscribed, i.e. there are more buyers than expected, and within a week the shares are being quoted at £1.21. How much is the founder worth through going public?

K E Y T E R M S

LIMITED COMPANIES Firms whose financial liabilities are limited to the amount of money put up by the shareholders. Private limited companies must have two or more shareholders. Their shares cannot be sold to the general public. With public limited companies, there is no upper limit to the number of shareholders. The shares can be bought and sold on the Stock Exchange.

LIQUIDATIONS The closing or 'winding up' of a company, which may be either voluntary or compulsory, and involves selling the assets of the firm to pay off debts.

NOMINAL CAPITAL The amount of money which a company can raise from its shareholders. It is also known as authorised capital.

C H E C K P O I N T S

1 What is limited liability? What is its main advantage for shareholders?

3 What is the main difference between a private and a public limited company?

3 Why do large investors have more control over the affairs of plcs than small private investors?

4 What are the main advantages and disadvantages of companies compared with sole proprietors?

Multinationals

Multinational plc

Multinational plc is an imaginary company with world-wide interests in construction, stores, finance, leisure activities and publishing.

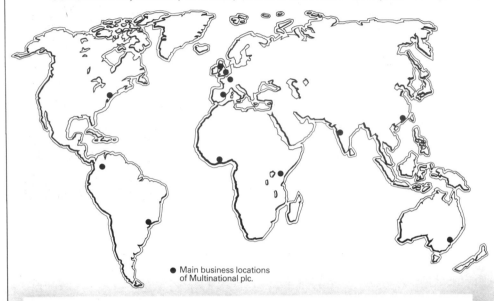

● Main business locations of Multinational plc.

Global turnover and pre-tax profits

	Turnover £million	Pre-tax profit £million
United Kingdom	2,169	228
Continental Europe	1,618	154
USA	987	101
Australasia	564	58
Africa	519	50
South America	256	22
Other	123	11

STUDY POINTS

(See key terms first)

1 Use an atlas to list the countries where Multinational plc has its main businesses.
2 Work out the firm's total global turnover and pre-tax profit.
3 Which area is the most profitable, a) in money terms and b) as a percentage of turnover?
4 Unit costs have risen sharply in a Spanish factory, where Multinational plc has operated successfully for 21 years. The goods could be produced more cheaply in the Far East. What action should be taken?
5 The exchange rate (see Unit 40) of the American dollar against the pound has changed during the past year from 1.40 to 1.81. What effects would this have on the prices of the exports from the company's American SUBSIDIARIES?
6 Would it be a good time for Multinational to buy more subsidiary companies in the States? Give reasons for your decision.

> '*Among the facts of life in international business today are changes in exchange rates and oil prices and a growing mood of* **PROTECTIONISM***'*
>
> Sir John Harvey-Jones

Source: *ICI Annual Report*, 1986

All over the world

Imperial Chemical Industries plc – better known as ICI – is one of the big British **MULTINATIONALS** whose activities cover the globe. It is one of the world's largest chemical groups with interests in oil, gas, agriculture, manufacturing and the consumer market. Some of its non-commercial activities can be seen in the photographs on the opposite page. In 1986:

● Its pre-tax profit was over a billion pounds – £1,016 million.
● The total turnover was £10,136 million.
● The former chairman, Sir John Harvey-Jones, who retired in 1987, received £393,068 a year.
● Two employees had salaries of between £145,001 and £150,000.
● Over 1,000 employees earned more than £30,000 a year.
● The group employed 121,800 people world wide –
  – 56,800 in Britain
  – 15,000 in the rest of Europe
  – 22,800 in the Americas
  – 14,600 in Australasia, Japan and the Far East
  – and 12,600 in other countries, including the Indian sub-continent.

As the firm only started just over 60 years ago, in 1926, that is very big business indeed.

Even though a multinational's main base may be in Britain, it needs to take a global view of business. The parent company's decisions are bound to be affected by changes in foreign countries including changes in:

In India, IEL Limited, an ICI subsidiary, runs a development programme to help local villages. This school is one of ten that are run or helped by IEL.

ICI Europa is a major sponsor of the Chamber Orchestra of Europe, pictured here.

- government help to business
- interest and exchange rates
- political and social stability.

In a similar way, it is also influenced to a lesser extent by similar changes in its own country.

Objectives

The main objectives of a multi-national are to expand its operations in the most profitable areas, to gain as large a share as possible of the world market and to use its skills and expertise for the benefit of all the companies in the group.

To do this, it needs stable exchange rates between currencies, so that it can make firm plans for the future [see Unit 73]. In addition it needs a free flow of international trade, which is not restricted by protectionist policies of high duties on imported goods.

The parent company keeps control over its global operations through its foreign subsidiaries. These are firms which have either been set up by the parent company to produce or market its products, or they are foreign companies which have been taken over. The parent company may own them entirely, or may hold a controlling interest by having 51 per cent or more of the voting shares. In addition, the parent company is often a large shareholder in other companies. Even if it does not have a controlling interest of 51 per cent or more, it can still influence boardroom decisions if it owns a large number of shares.

BUSINESS TECHNIQUES

Report writing

Find out information about a real multinational from a reference book or by writing to the public relations officer of a multinational of your choice asking for the latest annual report and accounts.

Write a short report describing its worldwide operations. Say what its main business is, which countries it operates from and any subsidiary businesses it is involved in.

KEY TERMS

SUBSIDIARIES Smaller companies which are controlled by bigger companies, which own them entirely or have more than 50 per cent of the shares.

PROTECTIONISM This is a policy which favours charges or other restrictions being placed on imports, thus protecting home produced goods and services.

MULTINATIONALS Large conglomerates with a wide range of business interests, which operate in many countries.

CHECKPOINTS

1 **What are the main ways in which a multinational is different from other firms?**
2 **What are the main international problems for multinationals?**
3 **Explain how changes in foreign countries can influence a multi-national's decisions.**
4 **Describe how a multinational controls its operations in foreign countries.**

Insurance

Source: Excess Insurance Group

Avoiding risks

All business persons have to take some risks, but they try to avoid any which are unnecessary. One way of reducing risk is to take out **INSURANCE** to cover any losses. For instance, a successful claim for unfair dismissal [see Unit 76] could cost a firm many thousands of pounds if it had not taken out an insurance policy to cover the possibility of such a claim.

There are many kinds of insurance, but if you had your own business, you wouldn't need all of them. It would be stupid to under-insure, by not taking out cover that you really need, such as fire cover for your office building. It would be equally stupid to insure against unlikely risks, such as bad debts if you don't give much credit.

If you were setting up your own business, you would have to think about the kind of insurance cover you might need. Then you would discuss the matter with the insurance department of your bank or with an insurance broker, whose job is to get the best insurance cover for customers. If you didn't have a broker, you should consult two or three and get advice and a quote from each. Some insurance companies have business packages which cover a large number of risks at a lower total cost than individual policies.

Compulsory insurance

There are only two kinds of insurance a business must have by law:

- *Employers' liability insurance.*
  This provides cover against accidents at work. An employee who has been injured might sue his or her employer. If the court found that the employer had been responsible for the accident, for example by having faulty machinery, damages would be awarded to the employee. The damages would be covered by the insurance.
- *Motor vehicle insurance.* The minimum legal cover is third party, which provides insurance against

S T U D Y P O I N T S

1 Why do you think a firm needs insurance?

2 What kinds of insurance are described in the advertisement?

3 Name three other kinds of insurance, not mentioned in the advertisement, that a firm might also have.

4 Choose three of the following and suggest what kinds of insurance the businesses might take out. Give the reasons for your choice.

- A furniture remover
- An architect who uses computers for design work and word processing
- A window cleaner
- The owner of an inner-city café who employs a lot of casual labour
- A fruit importer
- A big manufacturer of electric lawn mowers
- A pawnbroker
- A builder

the death or injury of people other than the insured. *Comprehensive* insurance provides much wider cover, including damage to the owner's vehicle. It is essential for the business person to tell the insurers the exact use of the vehicle. A vehicle which is insured only for private purposes may not be covered if it is involved in an accident when it is being used for business.

Other kinds of insurance

In addition, there are many types of insurance which a sole proprietor or a firm might take if they seem relevant to the business. These include:

● *Fire* Essential where valuable assets such as machinery, stock or property are involved, especially if fire risk is high. Almost all businesses have fire insurance.
● *Other perils* These include storm, flood, water damage, riot and civil commotion, deliberate damage, aircraft, impact (e.g. of a lorry). This is taken out according to the risks involved.
● *Plate glass* Essential for shop-keepers.
● *Computers* Essential in hi-tech offices where fire or theft could cost thousands of pounds for replacements.
● *Loss of profits* If one of the above events occurs, your insurance would provide only for the replacement of assets. The loss of profits while you were waiting for property to be repaired, or stock or machinery to be replaced, might be enough to put you out of business. This kind of policy can be taken out only by established businesses with proven profit records. It should be carefully considered.
● *Public liability* Provides cover for any injury or damage to third

parties caused by the negligence of the owner or any employees, e.g. if a customer slipped in a shop and a court found the owner was responsible. This insurance is very important.
● *Product liability* Extremely important if defective products are likely to cause injury or damage to a third party.
● *Bad debts* Provides cover against customers not paying their bills. Useful where much credit is given.
● *Theft* Particularly useful where the value of stock is high or attractive to thieves.
● *Money* Provides cover against the theft of money. Useful where large sums of money have to be kept on the premises or are often in transit to or from the business.
● *Fidelity guarantee* Covers dishonesty or fraud by employees.
● *Goods in transit* Provides cover against the loss of goods which are being transported either in the business's own transport or a contractor's.
● *Professional indemnity* Protects professional people, such as solicitors, against errors in their actions or advice. Nowadays, this is compulsory in most professions.
● *Personal accident* Important for sole proprietors, especially when risks are high, e.g. in tree-felling. With a particularly dangerous tree, special cover would be taken out in addition to general cover.
● *Sickness* Adds to the low National Insurance benefits. Recommended for sole proprietors.
● *Permanent health insurance* Protects the self-employed against loss of income if they are unable to work due to long-term illness.
● *Life assurance* Provides a sum of money if a person dies. Useful for dependants of the self-employed. Sometimes this is a condition for getting a bank loan.

BUSINESS TECHNIQUES

Insurance premiums

A sole proprietor receives a quotation from his insurers for insurance of his van for the year. The premium, or amount he must pay, is £95 for third party and £225 for comprehensive insurance. He has a no-claims bonus of 40% of the premium for making no claims against the insurers. What would be the difference in his annual payments for the two kinds of insurance?

CHECKPOINTS

1 What do insurance companies do?
2 What risks must all businesses insure against by law?
3 What is meant by a no-claims bonus?
4 Give examples of businesses for which the following kinds of insurance would be especially important.
   a) Theft insurance
   b) Sickness insurance
   c) Goods in transit insurance
   Give reasons for your choice.

KEY TERM

INSURANCE A contract entered into with an insurance company, where you pay them a fixed amount of money per year, or premium, in return for financial compensation if you or your business suffers a loss of some kind. The item insured is specific and is stated in the contract.

Activities

■ Review points

1 What are the main differences between a worker and a consumer co-operative?

2 How do multinationals differ from all other kinds of firms?

3 What are the main advantages of limited liability to a medium-sized firm?

4 Draw a chart showing the differences in objectives, ownership and control of the kinds of businesses described in Units 13 to 18.

5 State, giving your reasons, what would be the most appropriate business organisation for the following people:
   ● A group of people who wanted to open a Caribbean restaurant in a city.
   ● A young person, whose hobby is restoring old cars, who has always wanted to set up his own business and has just been left £12,000.
   ● A person who has invented a new kind of home-lift for handicapped people.
   ● Three transport and distribution executives who have been given golden handshakes and want to set up their own business in the same field.
   Give full reasons for your choice in each case.

6 Co-operatives and franchises both depend on co-operation. Draw a chart showing the main differences between them.

7 Give one example of when it would be appropriate for a sole proprietor to make his or her business into a) a partnership and b) a private limited company. Give reasons for your choice, supported by financial calculations. Describe how he or she would go about setting up the company.

■ Essay questions

1 Choose examples of a small, a medium-sized and a large business, each showing different types of business organisation.
   a) Describe what each business does, how big it is and how it is organised.
   b) For each business, examine how its size, its growth and the risks it takes all depend on each other. Discuss the relationships between these factors.

2 'Small is beautiful.' For each of the following types of business organisation, discuss the advantages and disadvantages of being small; a) a sole proprietor, b) a small co-operative and c) a small partnership.

New role for co-operatives

CO-OPERATIVES – the teamwork approach to overcoming problems by pooling skills and resources – are being given a boost in Somerset

Efforts to create new co-operative enterprises are being made by co-operative development officer Sue Hackney, who has been actively involved in the setting up of a free advice and information centre, to promote the co-operative way of working in Somerset. Her work is funded by the Manpower Services Commission (MSC) and Somerset County Council.

'My aim is to make people in Somerset aware of the co-operative way of business,' she said. 'In the UK today there are over 1,000 co-operative businesses employing about 10,000 people'.

'We have the famous and successful Minehead Shoe Co-operative, which was formed as a result of workers' redundancies, but we do not have many examples of smaller community-based co-operatives in Somerset.

'I am pleased by the fact that since this service has been made available to the public in Somerset, we have had many enquiries.'

Sue said that working together to achieve a common aim by using individual strengths has always proved to be a good way of solving problems.

She offers a free counselling service, and her office in Bridgewater also has a resource centre containing publications, journals and videos all about the many aspects of co-operatives.

'Co-operatives offer opportunities for people to take the initiative and create their own group enterprises,' she said. 'We are living in a time when new enterprise is encouraged and it is a time when people can take the initiative and create the businesses and services they know are needed.'

Source: *West Somerset Free Press*, March 1988

1 How many co-operative businesses are there in the UK?

2 How many workers are involved in each on average?

3 In what way are workers' co-operatives being encouraged in Somerset?

4 What are the main features of a co-operative in Sue Hackney's view?

5 How is her work funded?

6 What was the reason for one Somerset co-operative being started?

Thatch is a growth industry

The traditional image of thatched property is a pretty little rose covered cottage seen on greetings cards; and most people's idea of a thatcher is a wrinkled old countryman with a ladder and a wheelbarrow full of straw. In fact today's thatching industry is an expanding and varied business dealing not only with repair and rethatch of Britain's 100,000 odd thatched properties, but also becoming involved with the thatching of brand new estate and architect designed homes. Franchise thatchers from Master Thatcher Limited completed a contract in 1985 to thatch four new executive homes for Bovis in Milton Keynes.

Modern thatchers are young, keen business people who see the profession as a skilful, rewarding and profitable area to work in. Today's trainee thatcher with Master Thatcher Limited can be taught the basic skills in a few weeks on the company's practice roof. He or she will then move onto real roofs under the close watch of an expert company thatcher.

The ideal age for someone starting thatching is between 25–35, largely because the work can be physically hard, especially in the winter. A keen and mature outlook is also necessary to ensure success, however, previous experience is not important. When you consider that some Master Thatchers come from backgrounds as different as a commercial diver, a bus driver, a school teacher, a helicopter pilot and a fireman, it is clear how true this is.

Master Thatcher Limited was established by the present managing director, Bob West, in 1974. Over the past 12 years it has become the largest thatching organisation in the UK. From the first franchisee in 1983, who was an ex-company thatcher, the number of Master Thatchers around the country has expanded to 16. These cover the areas of Southern, Eastern and South Western England. One franchisee (one of the most recent to start) operates from Manchester and covers anywhere from Wales to Scotland. If an example of success were needed to show the Master Thatcher idea, he would be it. He now employs three people and has established a successful, rewarding and profitable business.

Source: British Franchise Association

(See Coursework part 1 for questions on this article.)

■ Coursework

1 Look at the article on the thatching industry and answer the following questions:
   ● How long does it take to train as a thatcher?
   ● What is the ideal age to start and what are the right qualifications?
   ● What kinds of job did the trainees do previously?
   ● Who are the customers?
   ● What makes thatching particularly suitable for job franchising?
   Find out the possibilities for setting up as a franchisor in your own area. Use the questions above as a basis for making your choice of a suitable business.
   Write a letter to a bank manager setting out your proposals and asking for a loan to start the business. Use appropriate graphs if they will strengthen your case.
   Assuming that you have obtained the necessary finance, design a newspaper advertisement to attract franchisees.

2 a) Think of a one-person business you would like to set up. Go to three insurance brokers and get brochures, and information if possible about the premiums, for the various kinds of insurance you might need. Make out a list showing what cover you would take out, giving reasons for your choice of policies.
   b) As a result of your experiences in the brokers' offices, write a report analysing the differences in the way in which you were treated by the staff. Say how you would use what you have learned if you started your own business.

3 Over a period of time, collect notices of company liquidations or business insolvencies which are published in local and national newspapers. Write a report analysing the notices and stating how far they are typical of the whole country or whether special local factors were involved.

4 Ask the managers of a co-operative retail store and a supermarket for their permission to interview themselves and their customers. Investigate and describe the main differences between the two stores in terms of evidence for co-operation and competition.

The Public Sector

Enterprises in the **PUBLIC SECTOR** do not exist to make a profit for shareholders, but to provide services for the whole community.

Government control

The **PUBLIC SECTOR** is made up of enterprises which are owned and controlled by the government or local authorities. They range from a municipal swimming bath, with a turnover of just over £100,000, to a huge **PUBLIC CORPORATION** like the Central Electricity Generating Board (CEGB), with a turnover of over £8,000 million.

Some of the services offered by the public sector are provided by the public authorities themselves. For instance, the government controls the armed forces; local councils control fire brigades. Some services are provided jointly by the government and local authorities, as with roads. Other goods and services are provided by industries which have been nationalised, or brought under the control of the government. These industries are run by public corporations.

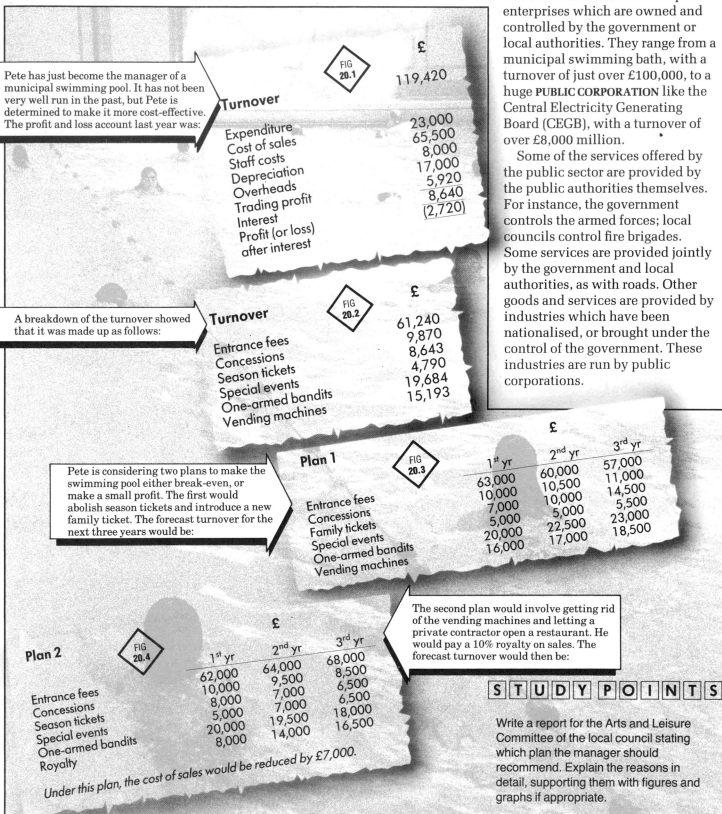

Pete has just become the manager of a municipal swimming pool. It has not been very well run in the past, but Pete is determined to make it more cost-effective. The profit and loss account last year was:

FIG 20.1

Turnover — £ 119,420

	£
Expenditure	
Cost of sales	23,000
Staff costs	65,500
Depreciation	8,000
Overheads	17,000
Trading profit	5,920
Interest	8,640
Profit (or loss) after interest	(2,720)

A breakdown of the turnover showed that it was made up as follows:

FIG 20.2

Turnover — £

	£
Entrance fees	61,240
Concessions	9,870
Season tickets	8,643
Special events	4,790
One-armed bandits	19,684
Vending machines	15,193

Pete is considering two plans to make the swimming pool either break-even, or make a small profit. The first would abolish season tickets and introduce a new family ticket. The forecast turnover for the next three years would be:

Plan 1   **FIG 20.3**   £

	1st yr	2nd yr	3rd yr
Entrance fees	63,000	60,000	57,000
Concessions	10,000	10,500	11,000
Family tickets	7,000	10,000	14,500
Special events	5,000	5,000	5,500
One-armed bandits	20,000	22,500	23,000
Vending machines	16,000	17,000	18,500

The second plan would involve getting rid of the vending machines and letting a private contractor open a restaurant. He would pay a 10% royalty on sales. The forecast turnover would then be:

Plan 2   **FIG 20.4**   £

	1st yr	2nd yr	3rd yr
Entrance fees	62,000	64,000	68,000
Concessions	10,000	9,500	8,500
Season tickets	8,000	7,000	6,500
Special events	5,000	7,000	6,500
One-armed bandits	20,000	19,500	18,000
Royalty	8,000	14,000	16,500

Under this plan, the cost of sales would be reduced by £7,000.

Reasons for nationalisation

Look at the chart showing landmarks in nationalisation. When did most nationalisation take place? The Labour government, which came to power after the Second World War, hoped that nationalisation would:

- increase efficiency through ECONOMIES OF SCALE and greater public investment;
- give the government greater control over the economy;
- provide more integrated services for the benefit of everyone.

To a certain extent, these hopes were fulfilled. Some public corporations were just as efficient and enterprising as private firms. In fact, during the Sixties and Seventies, management in both the private and the public sectors was often weak and inefficient. That is why 'lame ducks', like British Leyland, had to be rescued by the government.

Problems to face

Public corporations, or companies, however, had extra problems to face. Many of the nationalised industries:

- had to pay massive compensation to their former owners;
- were in a poor state because of lack of investment by the former owners, and had to borrow large amounts of money for modernisation;
- found it difficult bringing separate businesses under the control of one organisation;
- did not always have very clear objectives. Some governments wanted them to provide social

benefits for the whole nation, almost regardless of the costs; others wanted to make them more profit-conscious.

Local authorities also run some enterprises of their own, such as swimming baths, leisure centres, markets and crematoria. Their main function, however, is to provide services such as education, police, housing and so on.

Landmarks in nationalisation

1946	British Airways	(Formerly BOAC and BEA)
	Bank of England	Greater government influence on City
1947	National Coal Board	Poor industrial relations, low investment
	National Bus Company	Integration of inland transport
	Cable and Wireless	Control of global communications
1948	National Health Service	Equal health care for all
	British Road Services	Integration of inland transport
	British Rail	Integration of inland transport
1949	British Gas	Economies of scale
	Electricity Council	Central Generating Board created in 1926
1951	British Steel	Privatised, 1953; renationalised, 1967
1965	British Airports Authority	Provision of adequate facilities
1971	Rolls-Royce	Bankruptcy of major defence company
1975	British Leyland	Financial difficulties of major employer
1976	British National Oil Corp.	Exploitation of North Sea Oil
1977	British Shipbuilders	Declining industry; great foreign competition

British Airways was nationalised in 1946

BUSINESS TECHNIQUES

Profit and loss accounts

[see Unit 48]

CEGB Annual Accounts, 1985–6 (£ million)

Turnover	9,015
Expenditure	
Fuel and purchases of electricity	4,711
Staff costs	764
Depreciation	958
Materials and services	937
	7,370
Trading profit	645
Monetary working capital adjustment	(6)
Profit before interest	639
Interest	498

Source: *CEGB Annual accounts*, 1985–6

Work out the profit after interest for the Central Electricity Generating Board (CEGB).

KEY TERMS

PUBLIC SECTOR That part of the economy which is owned and controlled by the State or other public authorities.

PUBLIC CORPORATIONS Bodies set up by the government to run nationalised industries and other enterprises such as the London Docklands scheme. The chairperson, who is appointed by the government, and the board of directors have day-to-day control; but the government minister has final responsibility to Parliament. The government sets financial targets for the corporations to reach.

ECONOMIES OF SCALE As levels of production increase, unit costs get smaller. It is more economical, i.e. cheaper, to produce goods or services on a larger scale.

CHECKPOINTS

1 What are the main differences between the public and the private sectors?
2 Why did the post-war Labour government nationalise many industries?
3 What are the main problems of nationalised industries?
4 Find out what local enterprises are run by your local council. How are they run and controlled? How much of their funding comes from government or local authority subsidising, or financial help?

Privatisation

Rolls-Royce drops by 53p

The Stock Market's crash during the past two days has left many small investors in newly privatised companies with big losses.

People who have finished paying for Rolls-Royce shares with the second 85p payment only last month, have seen their investment lose 53p in three days. Their total investment of 170p is now worth only 153p.

PRIVATISATION STOCKS (Where companies have been privatised by more than one share issue the price and date of the most recent offer is shown.)

Company (year of issue shown in brackets)	Share value at time of issue (p)	Highest price reached (p)	Price on 20 October 1987 (p)
Amersham International (1982)	142	647½	535
Associated British Ports (1984)	270	673	550
BAA (1987)	245	151	118
Aerospace (1985)	375	685	445
British Airways (1987)	125	235	160
British Gas (1987)	135	200	138
British Petroleum (1987)	330	410	285
British Telecom (1984)	130	335½	217½
Britoil (1985)	185	357	246
Cable and Wireless (1985)	293½	507	380
Enterprise Oil (1984)	185	348	256
Jaguar (1984)	165	626	405
Rolls-Royce (1987)	170	240	153

FIG 21.1

Source: *Daily Telegraph*, 21 October 1987

A British Petroleum oil rig

Coalminers leaving the pit

STUDY POINTS

1 Which of the industries in these photographs have been privatised?

2 Make a list, including dates, showing the order in which the companies in Figure 21.1 were privatised.

3 Look at Figure 21.1. Which companies' shares were worth less in October, 1987, than when they were first issued?

4 Find out from the financial pages of a newspaper the price of these shares now. Which are higher than they were in October, 1987? Which one has shown the biggest percentage increase?

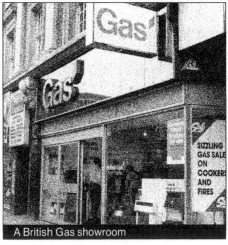
A British Gas showroom

Selling to the private sector

Since the Conservatives came to power in 1979, one nationalised industry after another has been privatised. On 10 February 1986, Mrs Thatcher told Parliament that a total of 12 major companies, making up some 20 per cent of the State commercial sector, had been privatised; and that by the end of that Parliament, another 20 per cent would have been transferred to the private sector.

Parts of other nationalised industries have also been sold off – like Jaguar Cars for £297 million and Sealink for £40 million. In addition, the government has sold its shares in other private companies. At the same time, it has reduced the spending powers of local authorities; and some local Conservative councils have transferred services, such as rubbish collection, to the private sector.

The same sort of thing has been happening in many other countries, including the United States, Japan and France. Some of them have gone much further along the path of **PRIVATISATION** than Britain. In the United States, for instance, some prisons have been privatised. This has led to discussion about whether Britain should do the same.

In theory, there are no limits to what can be privatised. In the past, traders have issued their own coins, and banks their own notes. Even defence was once mainly privatised, with rulers paying mercenary soldiers to do their fighting for them, as a few countries still do to this day.

Reasons for privatisation

Why has there been a return to privatisation? Critics of the nationalised industries claim that:

● Many of them are monopolies, i.e. they are the only enterprise providing a product, and therefore have no competition and no reason to keep costs down, improve choice, or provide better services.

- Even where there was competition, for example, between different fuels, coal could still have been bought at a lower price on the world market.

- Nationalised industries were too concerned with their own growth, rather than national needs. For example, some steel plants, which were no longer efficient, were kept open by British Steel.

- There was too little financial control – a feeling that the taxpayer would pay in the end through increased money from the government.

- Trade union power was too great.

- Control was divided. There were frequent quarrels between government ministers and chairpersons of public corporations.

- Objectives were not clear.

Originally, nationalised industries were only expected to break even, i.e. make enough profit to cover their costs, and concentrate more on social needs and benefits. However, there are few real limits to the amount that can be spent on something like health care. Who is to decide what those limits should be: the Minister of Health, Parliament, National Health Service officials, the hospitals, the doctors, the public, or a pricing mechanism as in the rest of the economy?

Disadvantages

Privatisation has increased the number of individual shareholders to at least 9 million and has provided money for the government; but it is far too early to judge what its final effects will be. Critics of privatisation claim that:

- The government has sold its shares at too low a price, particularly in Amersham International.

- The City businesses which arranged the sales made too much profit.

- Many of the small shareholders made a quick profit by selling their shares. These were bought mainly by big **INSTITUTIONAL INVESTORS**, who now control companies once owned by the State which represented all the people.

- They are one-off sales which will bring no real benefit in the end – like 'selling off the family silver'. The government gains an immediate cash benefit through selling the shares; but it has given up its control over a major part of the economy.

- Monopolies have not been reduced as much as they should have been. For example, British Telecom, although privatised now, still provides most telecommunication services in Britain.

- Attempts to break up large organisations like the National Bus Company have not been very successful; and have produced inefficient public transport.

- The social costs [see Unit 79] may in the end be greater than the short-term financial benefits.

Privatisation has not gone entirely smoothly. There has been great opposition to the proposed

sale of the water authorities; and a proposal to sell parts of British Leyland to the American firm, General Motors, started such great protests that it had to be abandoned. The sale of Government shares in British Petroleum (BP) in 1987 was a failure, as it took place during the Stock Market crash, so that few investors wanted to buy the shares. Other shares in privatised companies also lost value as Figure 21.1 shows.

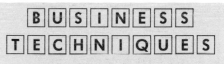

Selling shares

An investor bought 400 £1 shares in Amersham International when it was privatised. Use Figure 21.1 to find out how much profit he or she would have made if the shares had been sold –
a) when they were issued,
b) at their highest level,
c) in October 1987?

CHECKPOINTS

1 How much of the State sector has already been privatised?
2 a) What are the main reasons for privatisation? b) Which, in your view, is the most important reason?
3 Why are some people against privatisation?

KEY TERMS

PRIVATISATION The selling of State-owned companies to the private sector by an issue of shares. It also refers to the sale by the government of its shares in private companies and the sale of other assets such as land, buildings and forests.

INSTITUTIONAL INVESTORS Organisations whose business involves them in investing money which they have received. For example, a bank invests the money its clients keep in their accounts, and pays their interest from its profits.

Activities

■ Review points

1 What is a nationalised industry? Give two examples.

2 What does privatisation mean? State two nationalised industries that have been privatised.

3 Explain how the control of nationalised industries differs from that of firms in the private sector.

4 Who sets the objectives for public corporations?

5 How did nationalised industries get much of their capital in the past? Where do they get it now?

6 What happens to any profits made by nationalised industries?

7 Who has gained most from privatisation? Explain your reasons in full.

■ Essay questions

1 Discuss what effects privatisation can have on:
   a) The objectives of an industry and how it is run;
   b) The quality of the goods and services it provides;
   c) Competition and prices of its products.
   Use examples of recently privatised industries to illustrate your answer.

2 a) Explain what is meant by national-isation.
   b) Discuss the main arguments for and against nationalisation.

About Railfreight

Railfreight is a £650 million a year business – the biggest freight transport business in the country. It carries about 150 million tonnes of freight each year.

Railfreight has been deeply involved with the industry of this country for a long time – in fact British Industry and the railfreight network grew up together. Now, like British Industry itself, the railway freight business presents a completely changed image to the world.

The old marshalling yards have been replaced by just a few main collection/separation centres; computers plan and keep an eye on the movement of every wagon, and the wagons themselves are big, fast and sophisticated.

In order to do this, Railfreight has had to take up a new place in the transport market. It no longer provides a service which transports anything to anywhere, and everything to everybody. It has had to decide which parts of the transport market it can serve well, and which parts are best left to its competitors.

That is why today's Railfreight now concentrates on two main products – Trainload and Railfreight Distribution.

What is Trainload?

Trainload is the product Railfreight has designed for the customer who will need regular shipments of large quantities.

What is Railfreight Distribution?

Railfreight Distribution is the product for customers wishing to transport goods in truckload or containerload quantities.

Railfreight Distribution offers a network of space on container carrying or wagonload ('Speedlink') trains travelling at up to 75 miles per hour, and connecting with every main centre of industry and commerce in this country and on the continent.

Adapted from: *About Railfreight*, British Railways

Railfreight Speedlink

Routes in operation

Source: *Freight*, December 1985

1 Is British Rail privately or publicly owned?

2 What has replaced marshalling yards?

3 What changes have been made to Railfreight's marketing?

4 What goods might be sent by a) Trainload and b) Railfreight Distribution?

5 Study the 'Speedlink' route map. Would you change any of the routes? Give reasons for your answer.

BT refund for angry customers

A telephone engineer's mistake with his soldering iron has left British Telecom with a £68,000 bill.

The money is being paid to 16,000 telephone users who were overcharged for three months.

Telephone bosses, already facing a row over poor service and overcharging, will send each customer a £4 refund and a letter apologising.

They were charged extra because the engineer wrongly connected a wire.

His mistake, discovered during a routine check, will add to the company's embarrassment over billing muddles. Last week BT agreed to pay the Bank of England £250,000 after admitting it had been overcharged.

Source: *Today*, 16 September 1987

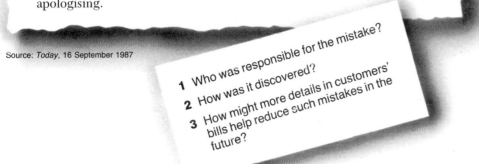

1 Who was responsible for the mistake?

2 How was it discovered?

3 How might more details in customers' bills help reduce such mistakes in the future?

Libraries lend themselves to privatisation

Libraries are the next target of Mrs Thatcher's privatisation plans, it was revealed last night.

Arts Minister, Richard Luce, said he has promised to keep the basic free borrowing service; but he plans for more private sector involvement so that libraries can become more competitive.

This could mean charging for loan of some technical or special kinds of books; letting private enterprise run mobile library services; and charging for the loan or sale of books published by local authorities.

Mr Luce told the Library Association in London that libraries would gain from the new political and economic environment created by the Thatcher government.

Source: *Daily Mail*, 14 October 1987

1 How will the private sector be involved in the library service being planned by Mr Luce?

2 Who runs libraries now?

3 In your view, would libraries benefit from the new political and economic environment? Support your answer with detailed comments.

4 What wider effects might changes in how libraries are run have on the community? Give reasons for your answer.

■ Coursework

1 Collect as many newspaper cuttings as possible of complaints about the services provided by any privatised industry. If you had been chairperson of the board what short-term and long-term actions would you have taken to put these matters right?

2 Make a weekly note over a period of months of the share prices of any firm which has recently been privatised. At the same time choose any other firm in the same sector and make a note of its share prices, too. At the end of the period draw a multiple line graph showing the relative changes in prices. Analyse the reasons for the differences and calculate how much you would have made if you had invested £1,000 in each of the companies.

3 Find out which transport services are run privately and which publicly in the town or city where you live (or one nearby). Write a report describing the main services in the town or city centre. Include charts and diagrams if you wish. Describe the advantages and disadvantages of the present mix. Plan a more efficient service in which services would link up better with each other. Describe how this service would be run.

4 Interview people at bus stops and ask them what they think of the service provided. Write a report analysing their complaints and praises. Send a copy of your report to the authority or company which runs the bus service, asking them to reply to the complaints. State whether you think their answers are satisfactory.

" I – and my colleagues – decide the firm's policies and set the objectives. "

" I see that the firm achieves the objectives that have been set. "

Small businesses

If you were self-employed – as a painter or a gardener – you would have to do everything yourself. Before you started your business, you would have investigated the market and set objectives for yourself [see Unit 13]. It would be your responsibility to see that these objectives were carried out. You would have to look after the production – painting rooms or mowing lawns. In addition, you

STUDY POINTS

1 Who is the most important person in the firm? Explain the reasons for your choice.

2 Which persons are of equal importance to each other?

3 Suggest job titles which might fit the six people in the photographs.

4 Explain in your own words the functions, or jobs, of A and B.

" I make sure that goods of the right quality and quantity are produced on time. "

" My job is to see that consumers know about our goods, like what they see and buy them. "

" My task is dealing with the financial side of the business and making sure that the firm makes a profit. "

" I look after everything involving people such as rates of pay, training and settling disputes or disagreements. "

would have to do all your own buying – tins of paint or garden plants.

It would be your job, too, to market your services by advertising in the local newspaper or by putting leaflets through letterboxes. If you needed finance – to buy a new van, a set of ladders or a lawnmower – you would have to arrange a loan from a bank. There are many other things you would also have to do, such as sending out bills, writing letters, keeping business accounts. You could get help with some of these matters from an accountant or a typist – for a fee. Or you could do everything yourself.

Larger businesses

If your business expanded later, so that you had to employ other people, you would have even more responsibility. You would have to give orders and see that they were carried out. You would have to take income tax and national insurance contributions from your employees' wages. You would also need to know far more about the law and employees' rights [see Unit 76].

The more people you employed, the more complicated it would be to run the firm. Big firms cope with these problems by **ORGANISATION**. In all businesses above the self-employed level, there must be people in **AUTHORITY** who give the orders and see that they are carried out. There is a **CHAIN OF COMMAND** which runs right the way down an organisation from the top – the chairperson – through the managing director and the heads of departments – to the bottom – the shopfloor and office workers who carry out the final orders.

Organisation charts

The way in which a firm is organised can be shown in the form of a chart. The firm in the Study Points is organised by **FUNCTION** – the jobs that people do. This is the most common form of organisation. The top part of the chart looks like this:

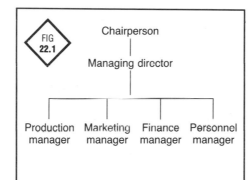

FIG 22.1

Chairperson

Managing director

Production manager | Marketing manager | Finance manager | Personnel manager

The vertical lines of authority represent the chain of command, with orders going down from one level to the one below. The horizontal lines show that people are of equal rank, or importance.

At the top is the chairperson of the board of directors. The board is responsible to the shareholders who have invested money in the firm. The chairperson is the most important person in the company as he or she decides what the policy and the objectives of the firm should be [see Unit 9].

At the next level is the managing director, who is in day-to-day control of the firm and who is also a member of the board of directors. He or she has to decide and plan how the firm will achieve its objectives and also has the responsibility, or duty, of reporting back to the board. Sometimes, the chairperson of the board is also the managing director.

The four people at the next level of the chart in Figure 22.1 are heads of the main departments or divisions. Their job titles describe their functions. If they were also members of the board of directors that would be shown in their title e.g. finance director. With the managing director, they make up the top management team.

Although many firms have an organisation similar to this, it is not a rigid structure. The organisation of a firm develops to suit its own needs. For example, in some firms, there might also be other main departments, such as purchasing or distribution. In other firms providing services, there would be no production department.

Organisation charts can only show what it is hoped will happen in a firm – not what actually does. Some powerful chairpersons often by-pass the formal structure and make deals of their own without the top management's knowledge or go-ahead. On the other hand, there are some managing directors who are so powerful that the chairperson is no real match for them and has relatively little power.

In all organisations, there are also informal groups, cutting right across the formal structure, which can have a great effect on the way in which a firm is run [see Unit 67]. These groups do not appear on the organisation chart.

Organisation charts

Draw suitable organisation charts for a) a firm manufacturing women's clothes and b) a car rental firm.

KEY TERMS

ORGANISATION The way in which a business is structured, or arranged, so that it can achieve its objectives.

AUTHORITY The right to give orders to people at a lower level in the organisation.

CHAIN OF COMMAND The levels through which an order has to pass before it can be carried out.

FUNCTION The jobs that people do which form the basis of an organisation's structure.

CHECKPOINTS

1 What is a chain of command?
2 What does 'organisation by function' mean?
3 Why is authority needed in a business?
4 What are the main weaknesses of organisation charts?

Organisation (2)

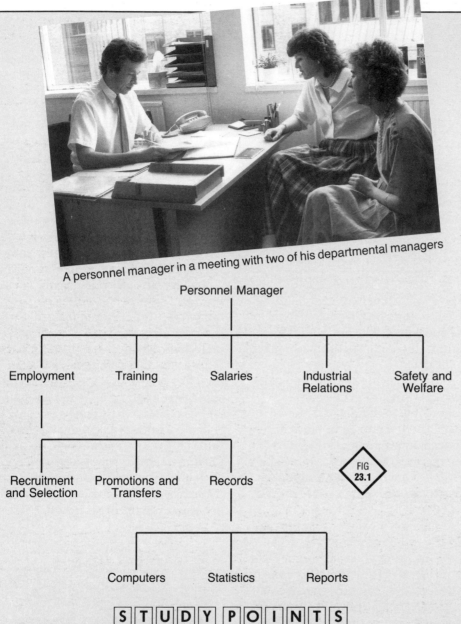

A personnel manager in a meeting with two of his departmental managers

Personnel Manager

Employment — Training — Salaries — Industrial Relations — Safety and Welfare

Recruitment and Selection — Promotions and Transfers — Records

FIG 23.1

Computers — Statistics — Reports

S T U D Y   P O I N T S

The organisation chart above shows the structure of the personnel department in a large company. Say which person or section in the department, and/or in other departments, would make decisions about the following matters:

1 Whether a member of staff should be sent on a training course.
2 Whether a member of staff should be promoted.
3 Whether a service engineer should be called in to repair a computer.
4 Whether an applicant, or person applying for a job, should be chosen for that job.
5 Whether a pay rise should be given to employees.
6 Whether employees who are on strike should be given what they want so that they go back to work.
7 Whether someone should be transferred from the computers section to the reports section.
8 A complaint from an employee that the temperature in one part of the factory is below the legal level.
9 A request from another department for the names of all the people in the company over the age of 58.

Dividing up the work

Every person in an organisation has his or her own job to do; but each of them is also a member of a **FORMAL GROUP** – such as a division or a department. The chairperson and the managing director are members of the board of directors [see Unit 22]. Below that level of the **HIERARCHY**, everyone is a member of a division or a department, each of which is controlled by a working director or a manager.

As you can see in Figure 23.1, the work of a firm can be split horizontally into sections, e.g. Employment or Salaries; and vertically into smaller units, e.g. Records, and even smaller departments, e.g. Computers.

Why formal groups?

Why should firms be split up into formal groups? There are advantages for both employees and the firm itself. For employees, the main benefits are that:

● It gives them a greater sense of unity and purpose as they can see themselves as members of a team.

● It is easier to get help, as they can ask experienced colleagues or take the more difficult problems to their boss.

● It makes it easier to carry out joint projects as everyone involved is working together.

There are even bigger benefits for the company:

● There are economies of scale as specialist staff can do work more efficiently.

● Communications from top to bottom are better, as there are definite channels through which orders can flow.

● Each person has only one immediate superior so that there is unity of command. An employee gets orders only from his or her own boss.

- It is much easier to check that work has been carried out as there are managers or supervisors at all levels.

- Co-ordination between departments is easier since the manager of each can speak for all the employees he or she controls.

Span of control

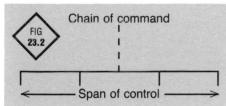

If the organisation is to work effectively, there must be a suitable **SPAN OF CONTROL**. This is the number of subordinates, or persons lower in the hierarchy, that a manager can directly control. This number varies depending on certain factors:

- How good at their jobs the manager and his or her subordinates are.

- The type of work – simple work needs less supervision, or watching over.

- The ease of communication. People who are not in the same building are more difficult to control.

- The kind of decisions that have to be made. If they are difficult, the span of control will be narrower, because more time will have to be spent in making them.

Another important factor affecting the span of control is **DELEGATION**. This means giving people lower in the hierarchy the authority to carry out tasks and make decisions themselves.

If a manager is willing to delegate a lot of work, he or she can have a wider span of control, as his or her subordinates are doing much of the work instead. If, on the other hand, the manager does not give his or her subordinates much authority, they may be working less effectively than they could, and the manager will be snowed under with too much work.

The amount of delegation depends on the structure of the organisation and the type of leader. In a bureaucratic organisation, i.e. one that is run by a central management, everything has to be approved and checked by all levels according to fixed rules and procedures. There will, therefore, be little delegation. So little, in fact, that in some parts of the Civil Service, which is a bureaucratic organisation, it can take up to a year just to recruit a new member of staff!

In a commercial organisation the amount of delegation will depend on what the leader or manager is like. An autocratic leader, i.e. one who likes to

have total control, will want to make all the decisions him or herself. There will be little delegation. A democratic leader, i.e. one who likes everyone to have a say, will be far more likely to delegate. He or she will listen to other people's views. The charismatic leader is one who depends on the appeal of his or her personality; this type of leader will delegate according to their mood at the time.

'Excuse me Sir, can I have 15p for a new pencil?!'

C H E C K P O I N T S

1. **What is a formal group?**
2. **What is the meaning of a hierarchy in business?**
3. **What are the main advantages for employees and firms of working in groups?**
4. **Draw part of an organisation chart showing span of control.**
5. **In what kinds of organisation would you expect to find a) the most delegation and b) the least. Explain the reasons.**

K E Y   T E R M S

FORMAL GROUP A group in an organisation which is set up to carry out clear, set-out tasks.

HIERARCHY The different levels of authority in an organisation, each one above another.

SPAN OF CONTROL The number of subordinates controlled by a manager.

DELEGATION Giving a subordinate authority to do a job without being supervised or watched over, or authority to make decisions in a particular area of work.

Centralisation

Re-organisation of the Central Electricity Generating Board's (CEGB's) production activities

In February 1986 the Central Electricity Generating Board (CEGB) agreed to plans for major changes in the organisation of its production activities. This will benefit the CEGB, the electricity supply industry and electricity consumers.

The aim of the changes is to improve the organisation and make it more able to make best use of resources of all kinds and to take full advantage of modern communications and computing technology.

Background to the changes

Since the start of the CEGB the management of its power stations and electricity supply has been organised into five regions — Midlands, North Eastern, North Western, South Eastern and South Western. Each region was allowed to run most of its own affairs and was given its own senior officers in charge of production, resource planning, engineering, personnel, finance, and other functions. A single region managed as many as 80 power stations and 22,000 employees.

With the changes over the years, however, today's organisational needs are very different from those of the past. In particular, national teams of experts, rather than regional management, are now responsible for keeping all plants running efficiently.

The new production organisation

When the re-organisation of production is started, the CEGB's five regions will no longer be general management centres. Responsibility for production – the generation and transmission (i.e. actually getting it to the consumers) of electricity – will then be with four new divisions and a specialist unit to control nuclear power matters.

```
                    Production
                     Director
    ┌──────────┬──────────┬──────────┬──────────┐
Operations  Engineering  Generation  Transmission
Division    Division     Division    Division
                                              Nuclear
                                              Power
                                              Control
                                              Group
```

STUDY POINTS

1 What is the Central Electricity Generating Board?

2 How was the CEGB organised in the past?

3 What does the CEGB hope to gain by the re-organisation?

4 What might be the effects of privatisation of the CEGB?

A 660 MW generating unit – one of the largest – at Drax power station.

Source: *CEGB Annual Reports and Accounts*, 1985/6 (Extracts)

It is often difficult for even a small firm to find the right kind of organisation to achieve its objectives. These problems are obviously much greater with bigger firms, especially multinationals, operating in a number of continents. Deciding how power should be divided between the parent company and the operating companies in foreign countries, or how communications should be organised, is not easy.

Functional organisation

Whatever kind of organisation is chosen, it will usually be based, at least in part, on function, because the advantages are so great [see Unit 22]. There are economies of scale, division of responsibility is easy and the chain of command is clear. On the other hand, it may produce a narrow outlook. Each department could become more concerned with its own affairs than with the objectives of the whole company. They could become too remote from the market.

Geographical organisation

As a firm expands and its activities spread throughout a country, or over whole continents, it has to give local managers more responsibility. They are more in touch with local markets – for their products, labour and supplies. Production can be organised on a regional basis so that transport and distribution costs are reduced.

It would be useful, for instance, for firms making farm equipment to be organised geographically, as farmers' needs vary greatly from one part of the country to another.

Usually, expanding organisations change from a functional to a geographical structure. The CEGB is an exception. It has changed from geographical to functional, mainly due to a decline in the number of power stations and increased technology, such as more powerful

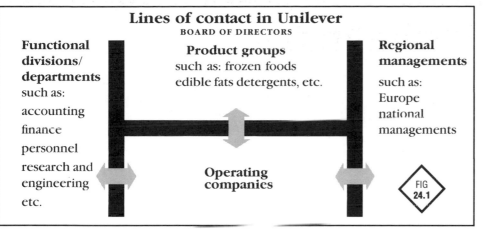

Lines of contact in Unilever
BOARD OF DIRECTORS

Functional divisions/ departments
such as:
accounting
finance
personnel
research and
engineering
etc.

Product groups
such as: frozen foods
edible fats detergents, etc.

Regional managements
such as:
Europe
national
managements

Operating companies

FIG 24.1

Source: *Management and Organisation*, Unilever

computers. This has made it more sensible to have an organisation based on function. Specialists are now controlled by national divisions instead of regional managers. This is called functional specialisation.

Market-based organisation

With a market-based organisation, the business is divided up according to the various groups of consumers or clients – the market segments [see Unit 30]. Some examples are:

- insurance companies with separate departments for car, life, etc.
- publishing firms with separate divisions for educational or general books
- record companies with divisions for classical or pop; cassette or compact disc
- BBC radio with its separate stations for four different kinds of listener.

Product-based organisation

Very large firms which make a wide range of products, for example ICI, usually have separate groups or divisions for each product, e.g. one for paint, another for fertilisers etc. One

advantage is great economies of scale by each department concentrating on just one product. Another is that each product group can have its own profit targets so that it is easy for the parent company to judge if that group is doing well.

In practice most multinationals use a mixture of organisations and try to combine them into a whole. Look at Figure 24.1. How successful has Unilever been in setting up clear lines of authority and communication?

One major problem is always how much CENTRALISATION or DECENTRALISATION there should be in a firm. Both have advantages and disadvantages.

- Centralisation produces economies of scale – in the use of skills, in buying supplies etc. However, long lines of communication can result in slow decision making.
- Decentralisation helps a firm to respond quickly to market changes and speeds decision making. However, it can also cause doubling up of effort and might weaken the power of the parent company.

In practice, most multinationals give a large amount of autonomy, or power to run their own affairs, to their operating companies. However,

general policy, finance, appointment of top managers and relations with other businesses are usually centrally controlled.

Organisation charts

Some organisation charts are drawn as a series of rings, each larger than the one inside it, with the managing director shown in the central, smallest ring. For example:

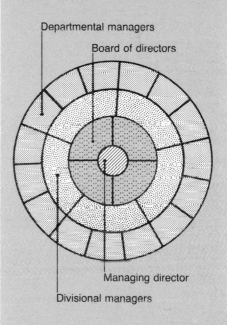

Departmental managers
Board of directors
Managing director
Divisional managers

Draw a chart of this kind to show organisation in a firm with one managing director; a board of eight other directors; three division managers; and four department managers in each division.

KEY TERMS

CENTRALISATION When a firm is organised in such a way that policies and decisions for all branches or offices are made by a central body.

DECENTRALISATION When the policies and decisions of a firm are made regionally. Each office or branch makes its own decisions about how it will be run. Most firms make some decisions regionally and others centrally.

CHECKPOINTS

1. **What is a geographical organisation? Which kinds of firms would use it?**
2. **Why would a firm normally change from a functional to a geographical organisation?**
3. **State two other kinds of organisation and give examples of firms that would use them.**
4. **What are the main organisational problems for multinationals? How do they attempt to solve them?**

Activities

■ Review points

1 List the main advantages and disadvantages of a) centralisation and b) decentralisation.

2 What is meant by a functional organisation? Why is this type of organisation usually included in the structures of all business?

3 What kind of company would be likely to have a product-based organisation?

4 What is meant by span of control? Which factors decide how wide it should be?

5 In a bureaucratic organisation, how likely are the managers to delegate authority? Explain why this is the case.

6 Explain the purpose of a chain of command.

7 List the benefits of formal groups to an organisation.

8 Draw an organisation chart for a market-based company. Explain why you have chosen this form of organisation.

9 If you were the managing director of a firm producing farm dairy equipment what kind of organisation would you have? Explain your reasons?

Competing for business all over the world – ICI

'There are nine major operating units in the UK – the eight manufacturing divisions plus Nobel's Explosives Company Ltd, which operates as a separate company. The chief executives of these units, and of the major overseas companies through which ICI carries out its worldwide business, have to report to the main board of ICI to make sure they have met the performance targets agreed by the board.

Each unit is responsible for the production and marketing of its own products and for the research and development plan to keep ICI ahead of other companies in these areas.

Policies (decisions taken about how things should be done) for personnel, finance, safety, health and the environment are made centrally.

Outside the UK, ICI works through a network of smaller companies which both manufacture and sell most – but not all – of the products coming from the UK set-up.'

1 Find out the full name of ICI and what it produces?

2 How many operating units are there in the UK?

3 Who decides the units' performance targets?

4 What powers do each of the operating units have?

5 a) Which policies are decided centrally?
   b) What do you think might be the reasons for this?

Source: *ICI The Right Chemistry: Worldwide*

■ Case study

Narendra Nanji's small business

Narendra Nanji, a qualified electrician, didn't get on well with his employer, so he decided to leave his job and set up on his own. At first, he had to work twice as hard for half the wages. His wife helped him with the correspondence and accounts every week-end. It went on like that for two years. Then he had a lucky break. He got a big contract to rewire a large house which was being converted into a health centre. He couldn't cope with all the work himself, so he decided to take on a cousin, Harish, as a full-time employee, hoping that he could get enough work to make his decision to expand worthwhile.

Narendra never looked back after that. Within four years, he was employing 9 electricians. He was working 65 hours a week; getting contracts; ordering supplies; organising all the work; and even helping out with jobs which weren't going fast enough. He still did all the paper work with the help of full-time secretary.

The stress of his job, however, took its toll and he had a heart attack. When he recovered, he decided that he would have to re-organise his business so that he delegated more authority.

Show how organisation could reduce Narendra's problems and draw a chart to illustrate your answer.

How the housewife's homely skills can be used to manage the men

Skills developed at home by housewives can be used in jobs as managers, says psychologist Karen Howard.

Ms Howard, head of management consultants Howard Affiliates, says that women need to realise that the skills they use for organising and doing the housework are of use in the world of paid work.

In a study she has made of this subject, Ms Howard points out that male managers often do not believe that this is true. 'It is important that housewives returning to jobs as managers do not feel that they are not good enough at their jobs because of the views of the male managers.'

In the study, Ms Howard looked at different managers' jobs and found that,

for most of them, women returning to work would only need training in order to be able to do the job. 'Where there are differences these are usually in areas where training for special skills is given by the organisation. This means that women returning to work can be given these jobs.' she says.

Ms Howard's advice to women wanting to return to work is that they should start, with a friend, by listing all the different jobs they do in the home. They will be surprised at how much they do, and at the skills they have picked up.

They should find out about the possibility of studying management, perhaps by going on a local course. They should not be afraid to apply for jobs as managers, she says.

Source. *Independent*
19 January 1987

Read the extract from the *Independent* first. Divide into small groups and discuss the following points:
● The kinds of skills in managing that are developed in the home.
● How these skills might be used in the running of a company.
● What kinds of training, which are not around now, should be offered to women.

1 'Skills in dealing with people are more important for a manager than organising ability.'
   a) What sort of skills are needed when dealing with people? How might a manager use these skills to do his/her job better?
   b) What is meant by 'organising ability'? Explain why this is important in managing a department or division of a company.
   c) Do you think the above statement is true? Give reasons for your answer.

2 a) What factors in business organisation are not shown on an organisation chart?
   b) How important are these factors in what actually happens in the business?

■ Coursework

1 Find out from your local council what kind of organisation it has and draw an organisation chart to represent this. Explain why it is divided into different departments and what their functions are. If a new government came to power and decided to build far more council homes to rent and more homes for the aged, what differences would it make to the council's organisation?

2 Imagine you have set up a small business importing clothes from the Far East. Within two years, the business has expanded so much that you have to take on a sales manager and a buying officer. Draw an organisation chart to illustrate this new set-up. Ten years later, the company has gone public. You are the chairperson of the board of directors. Draw an organisation chart which shows the likely structure of the business now.

Business Structure and Organisation

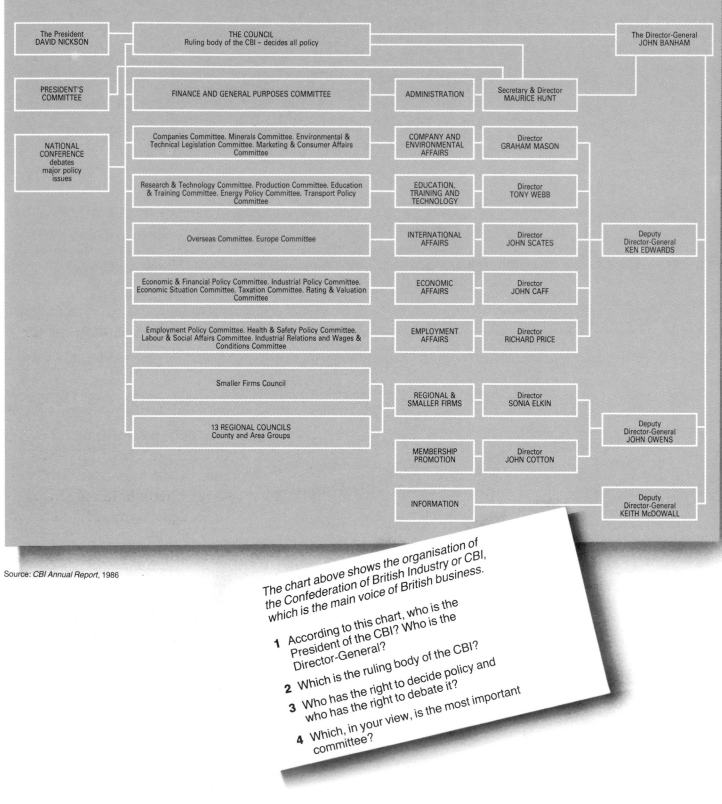

CBI ORGANISATION

| The President DAVID NICKSON | | THE COUNCIL Ruling body of the CBI – decides all policy | | The Director-General JOHN BANHAM |

PRESIDENT'S COMMITTEE

FINANCE AND GENERAL PURPOSES COMMITTEE — ADMINISTRATION — Secretary & Director MAURICE HUNT

NATIONAL CONFERENCE debates major policy issues

Companies Committee. Minerals Committee. Environmental & Technical Legislation Committee. Marketing & Consumer Affairs Committee — COMPANY AND ENVIRONMENTAL AFFAIRS — Director GRAHAM MASON

Research & Technology Committee. Production Committee. Education & Training Committee. Energy Policy Committee. Transport Policy Committee — EDUCATION, TRAINING AND TECHNOLOGY — Director TONY WEBB

Overseas Committee. Europe Committee — INTERNATIONAL AFFAIRS — Director JOHN SCATES

Economic & Financial Policy Committee. Industrial Policy Committee. Economic Situation Committee. Taxation Committee. Rating & Valuation Committee — ECONOMIC AFFAIRS — Director JOHN CAFF

Deputy Director-General KEN EDWARDS

Employment Policy Committee. Health & Safety Policy Committee. Labour & Social Affairs Committee. Industrial Relations and Wages & Conditions Committee — EMPLOYMENT AFFAIRS — Director RICHARD PRICE

Smaller Firms Council

REGIONAL & SMALLER FIRMS — Director SONIA ELKIN

13 REGIONAL COUNCILS County and Area Groups

Deputy Director-General JOHN OWENS

MEMBERSHIP PROMOTION — Director JOHN COTTON

INFORMATION — Deputy Director-General KEITH McDOWALL

Source: *CBI Annual Report*, 1986

The chart above shows the organisation of the Confederation of British Industry or CBI, which is the main voice of British business.

1 According to this chart, who is the President of the CBI? Who is the Director-General?

2 Which is the ruling body of the CBI?

3 Who has the right to decide policy and who has the right to debate it?

4 Which, in your view, is the most important committee?

Business Behaviour

Production Strategies

A A sports car
B A parachute
C A supermarket wine
D A jacket for a party
E A reference book
F A holiday abroad

Deciding what to produce

How do manufacturing companies decide what goods to produce? In the past, firms were more product-orientated than they are today [see Unit 30]. The manufacturer chose a product and then tried to sell it at a price which covered the cost of production and gave a profit.

Now nearly all firms are market-orientated [see Unit 32]. They will study the market to find out whether consumers would prefer cheapness, reliability, quality, design or appearance, and what they would be prepared to pay. Production costs are estimated and profits calculated. Top management then decide whether or not to go ahead with production.

The production manager decides how the goods should be produced. The main tasks are:

- To see that production flows smoothly – through efficient planning and control.

- To maintain, or improve, the quality of the products.

- To ensure that goods are produced on time by working out a production schedule.

- To keep costs within the **PRODUCTION BUDGET**.

To ensure that production flows smoothly, the production manager has to make the best use of physical and material resources. Production must be planned so that materials and components have to be moved for the shortest possible distances; this means finding the best layout of machinery. In this way work will be speeded up and costs reduced. **WORK STUDY** may help the production manager to use the labour more efficiently. Obviously, good relations with workers on the shop floor, i.e. the general employees, is also extremely important, though that is mainly the responsibility of the personnel department [see Unit 59].

STUDY POINTS

1 If you were buying the items above, which would you regard as the most important factor in each case – cheapness, reliability, or appearance and design?

2 Give the reasons for your choice.

3 Get into groups. Discuss the reasons for any differences in your views.

4 In your group, analyse what effects your views might have on a) the firm's production strategies and b) the firm's marketing strategies.

5 Individually, choose one of the items above and write a magazine advertisement for it. Describe the features of the product which would most appeal to the consumer, drawing attention to the most important factor (use your answer to Question 1).

Maintaining standards

All goods have to fulfil a particular purpose, so their quality is important. A pair of shoes must last a reasonable length of time; a chair must not collapse if you sit on it. Some products need to be more reliable than others, for example if a parachute fails to open it can be fatal!

Deciding whether, for example, quality is more important than design, can be more difficult with some products. For example, a woman's dress must not split when worn, but the design and appearance are what will make it sell. The Study Points show that consumer choice is variable.

Whether price or quality is chosen as the most important factor, the production manager has to ensure that all the goods produced are of the same standard.

Efficient QUALITY CONTROL is essential if these objectives are to be achieved. The Japanese are particularly skilled at this. Their little car sticker (shown below) has become a badge of reliability. This is because they have a highly efficient system of quality control. In the past, samples of products were checked for quality as they came off the assembly lines, i.e.

at the end of production. The Japanese were the first to use statistical process control. In this system, the machine operator checks that the machine is working correctly two or three times every shift. This method was introduced at Ford's Dagenham factory in 1982 with excellent results.

Getting the timing right

It doesn't matter how good the price or the quality, if the goods are not produced at the right time to meet the demands that the sales department expect. The production schedule must be worked out to ensure that raw materials, components and labour are all available when needed, and that equipment is all working at the right time. Efficient progress control, making sure work flows smoothly through all stages, helps avoid delays in production.

Keeping costs down

The production manager must keep costs down so that the production budget is not exceeded. To help do this, he or she might use several methods: work study, improved machinery layout, new working methods, simplification of parts, reduction in power costs, or even buying in components from other manufacturers instead of making them themselves [see Unit 11].

Other departments in the firm may also help the production manager to keep costs down. The research and development section [see Unit 28] may suggest improvements in production methods; while the PURCHASING MANAGER can help by buying cheaper raw materials.

Work study

Special symbols are used in work study to identify particular actions. They include:

○ An operation which achieves something, e.g. picking up clothes.

◙ A joint operation and inspection which cannot be done separately, e.g. shaving and looking in a mirror.

D A delay.

⇨ Movement from one place to another or of an object to another place.

Work study charts are usually set out in the following form:

Activity	Symbol	Time (min)	Distance (metres)
Getting out of bed	○	0.02	

Make a work study chart, like the example above, of all your actions, from the time you got out of bed in the morning until you go down-stairs. Time yourself or, if possible, get someone else to time you.

Study the chart and decide how you could speed up the process. Decide on a new target time.

Make out another chart of all your actions the following day. How close did you come to your target time? How could you still improve on your performance?

CHECKPOINTS

1 Name three firms which, in your opinion, produce high quality goods. Give reasons for your choice.
2 How can research and development help the production manager?
3 Describe the two main methods of quality control.
4 What are the main functions of a production manager?
5 Which in your view is more important – the market or production? Explain your reasons.

KEY TERMS

PRODUCTION BUDGET The total costs of production, including raw materials, labour and overheads.

WORK STUDY A method of measuring how long a job should take and how it should be performed.

QUALITY CONTROL Inspecting samples of goods to see that they are up to the firm's usual standard.

PURCHASING MANAGER The manager who is responsible for buying all the raw materials and finished goods that a firm needs.

Location of Business

Burroughs & Jackson, imaginary magazine printers, have had an excellent year with profits increasing 35 per cent to a record £1.45 million. Since the beginning of the financial year, they have won 12 new magazine contracts. As there is no room to expand on their present site in Crouch End in North London, they have decided to open an additional factory.

They are considering two sites at Luton, Bedfordshire; and Cowes on the Isle of Wight. Both sites can provide suitable factories to house the work force of 30 printers. Both sites are easy to get to; this is an important factor as even small shipments may be delivered in articulated lorries as parts of larger loads. The firm plans to do some work at night, but as both the factories are on industrial sites, there will be no problem with nearby residents complaining about noise.

Business is plain sailing on the Isle of Wight

The Isle of Wight is not just a yachting centre, it is also a great place to do business.

Operating costs are generally 10–15% lower than the rest of Britain and the lowest in the South East. Land is available for development at prices lower than regional averages and premises are ready.

Our workforce is a very stable and loyal group. Industrial problems are almost unknown.

The Isle of Wight welcomes investment and financial and promotional support may be offered to companies with great potential.

Europe is only a short ferry ride away and many local companies export to world markets by air and sea.

Why not take a look at the Isle of Wight for your next business location.

Contact: Martin Lloyd, Managing Director, Isle of Wight Development Board, Samuel White's Boardroom, 40 Medina Road, Cowes, Isle of Wight, PO31 7LP, Telephone: (0983) 200222

Source: Isle of Wight Development Board

Luton is open for business

Luton is just 30 miles from London and 80 miles from the Midlands. It has fast road and rail links and an International Airport. For commerce, it provides the fastest delivery service in the UK.

We have business suites from £54 per week; Nursery Industrial Units from £66 per week; Prestigious new office accommodation from £7 per sq ft and new factories from £2.65 per sq ft.

All types of housing are available within the immediate town and the delightful surrounding countryside.

Move in the right direction. Talk to a council that understands business needs. Luton Borough Council works with industry at a pace industry needs.

For more information contact: David Turvey ARICS or John Pearson ARICS, Borough Valuer and Industrial Development Officer, Town Hall, Luton, Beds. Tel: (0582) 31291

Source: Luton Town Council

FIG 26.1

Average floor area (m^2) per worker (by industry)

Industry	m^2
Clothing	11
Research and development	13
Electrical components and assembly	17.5
Surgical instruments/appliances, scientific instruments	19.25
Miscellaneous manufacture	23.50
Leatherwork	24.00
Metal goods, cutlery, jewellery forging, small tools	24.25
Made-up textiles (e.g. bags)	28.75
Packaging, stationery, printing	32.50
Pottery and glass blowing	36.75
Motor repairs, Reprographic services	45.50
Joinery, furnishing upholstery, shopfitting, timber goods	46.75

Source: Jolyon Drury, *Acquiring Industrial and Distribution Premises*

S T U D Y   P O I N T S

1 Look at Figure 26.1. What would be the minimum size of the new factory in square metres for the employees of Burroughs and Jackson?

2 Use an atlas to calculate the distance from each site to the company's present factory.

3 The typical cost of transporting goods one kilometre by a 40-foot truck is 1.14 pence per cubic metre of cargo. Calculate the costs per cubic metre for shipments from each site to London.

4 Using the promotional material above, make two lists showing the advantages and disadvantages of each of the proposed sites.

5 Mr James Gridley, a director of the firm, has asked you to suggest the most suitable site. Write a memorandum giving your opinion [see Business Techniques].

How much rent?

There is no perfect site for a factory. The rent per square foot is obviously important, but the firm also has to consider whether the building is of the right type – single- or multi-storey, for example – and big enough for the kind of goods it produces. A car manufacturer will obviously need a bigger factory than a firm making computer software.

A small manufacturer will need about 60 to 70 per cent of the floor space for production; 20 per cent for storage; and 10 to 15 per cent for offices. Outside, there must be enough room for lorries to turn easily and for staff and visitors to park their cars. Services such as power supplies and drainage are provided on INDUSTRIAL ESTATES; but the firm may have to pay for them to be connected on GREENFIELD SITES, which is an added expense.

Is there labour available?

The supply of labour is another important factor. The business person will need to consider whether the right kind of skilled or semi-skilled labour is available, or grants for retraining if not; what the local wage rates are like; whether the housing, school and leisure facilities will attract and keep labour in the area.

Another important factor is how much government, local authority and EC aid is available [see Units 68, 69 and 72].

How near are the raw materials?

Nearness to sources of raw materials is still important, but much less so than it used to be. The old smokestack industries, such as steel and textiles, which relied on coal and supplies of raw materials from overseas, had to be near coal-mines and big ports. New technology and improved communications by road, rail, air and sea have changed the pattern of modern industry. Chemical pipelines allow aluminium smelters to be situated miles away from ports. Modern manufacturers, apart from those who need heavy, bulky raw materials, have a much greater freedom of choice. To save on transport costs, they may set up near a major supplier of raw materials; but there is less need to do so if there are good motorway and railway connections.

Where is the market?

Nearness to markets is more important. Britain's increased trade with the EC has been one of the main reasons for the shift of industry and commerce from the North to the South East. Nearness to a market is usually more important in the services sector than in manufacturing. Even this factor is less important than it used to be. The increase in car ownership has given big retailers a greater choice, so that, increasingly, they build hypermarkets on edge-of-town sites, where rents are lower.

It is never easy to find the right site. In practice it is often a case of follow the leader; one big firm will pick an area and other large firms will follow. Smaller firms then move in to supply the bigger ones. That is what has happened along the M4 motorway, which is now Britain's 'silicon valley' with its many computer firms.

Most of these factors – rent, labour supply, nearness to markets, financial aid – apply in a similar way to shops, offices and warehouses.

CHECKPOINTS

1 Why does a car manufacturer need a bigger factory than a software manufacturer?
2 What are the main advantages of industrial estates?
3 Why are schools important in deciding where a business should be located?
4 Where would you site a) a flower stall, b) a fruit and vegetable import firm, c) a nuclear power plant? Give your reasons.

KEY TERMS

INDUSTRIAL ESTATES Special factory sites in selected areas of towns and cities which provide new industrial buildings and all necessary services, such as roads, electricity, gas, water, telephone etc, at reasonable rents. They were started in the thirties to provide jobs in areas of high unemployment.

GREENFIELD SITES Industrial developments in areas of the countryside which have previously been used for agriculture or some other purpose.

Methods of Production

A small bakery

Plastics plant

Aircraft plant

Car factory

S T U D Y   P O I N T S

1 Why is there only one worker in the plastics plant?

2 Why can't an aircraft be made in the same way as a car?

3 Use the definitions in the Key Terms to suggest which method of production is being used in each of the pictures above.

4 State one other product which might be produced in each of the four different ways.

5 Draw plans showing how a factory might be laid out for two of the methods of production.

6 In your view, how might each of these four methods affect workers' attitudes towards their jobs?

The way in which goods are produced depends to a large extent on what they are. An aeroplane, for example, has to be made in a very different way from a motor car.

For a start, the aeroplane is much bigger and has many more parts. It is made by craftsmen working together as a team. They start with materials, tools and the bare assembly department, which must be big enough to contain the finished product. Gradually, after months of work, they create an aircraft by their individual skills and the aid of outside firms such as those who make the engines.

Job production

Many goods made in this way by **JOB PRODUCTION** are one-off orders, which may, or may not, be repeated. As each job is different from the last, it presents a great challenge to the workers and provides them with greater satisfaction. Some items, such as ships and railway locomotives are still produced in this way; but new technologies are gradually taking over [see Unit 29].

Job production is now far more common in the service industries than in manufacturing. A copywriter, who writes advertisements, a film director, a personnel officer all have to face new problems in their work every day. For that reason, their job satisfaction is often higher.

Most manufactured goods are now produced by either **BATCH PRODUCTION** or **FLOW PRODUCTION**.

Batch production

A small bakery is a good example of batch production. The baker mixes the dough – usually in a machine, not by hand – and lets it rise. He puts the dough in tins and bakes a batch of loaves in the oven. Chefs in high-class restaurants are another example. Each specialises in one item – meat, sauces, puddings. Their combined efforts produce the complete meal.

Batch production of manufactured

goods involves workers who specialise in one job – welding, drilling or painting. The factory is divided into sections so that all the workers of one skill work together. The product passes through each section until it is finished. This is known as layout by process.

The method is most suitable for short to medium production runs, i.e. when the number of goods being produced is not very many, and for smaller firms making a variety of parts for bigger manufacturers. It is a flexible system as work can be easily switched from one machine to another. Production is not greatly affected if one machine breaks down. On the other hand, it is costly as materials, parts and sub-assemblies, or partly finished goods, have to be moved frequently from one section to another.

Flow production

This problem is avoided in flow production. Products move continuously by conveyor belt from one worker to another, each doing one job. This is called layout by product. Parts or whole units are made on sub-assembly lines or bought in from other firms. Standardised parts, or ones which fit a number of different makes of product, are used, though there can be some variation in finished goods – different car engines or car body colours. The assembly lines – and the speed at which they move – play an important part in the working lives of all employees.

Mass consumption goods, or goods bought by many consumers, such as cameras, television sets, cars – are all made by flow production. The main advantage is low costs per unit through economies of scale [see Unit 10]. Goods are produced more quickly and cheaply because specialised equipment can be used and there are no delays or large material handling costs in moving from one stage of production to the next. The line workers need little training as their work is only semi-skilled.

On the other hand, the capital cost of setting up the lines of production is enormous; and a breakdown of one machine can stop the whole line. Many operatives become bored with the repetitive work, which can lead to a high labour turnover or industrial action [see Unit 65].

Process production

PROCESS PRODUCTION, which is used in the oil, chemical and other industries, is carried out invisibly in tanks and retorts and only a few workers are needed to control the process. This is a more advanced form of flow production, which is usually controlled by computers [see Unit 29].

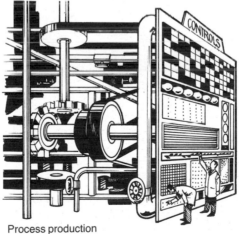
Process production

BUSINESS TECHNIQUES

Production schedules

Production schedules, or timetables, are based on firm orders or forecast sales. They show the number of units which have to be produced each week or month so that the supply of labour and materials can be planned. In making out the schedule an allowance must be made for lead time, the time between ordering a product and receiving it.

Forecast sales of an imaginary brand of sun cream in thousands		
January	8	FIG 27.1
February	7	
March	8	
April	9	
May	10	
June	12	
July	13	
August	17	
September	11	
October	7	
November	6	
December	5	

Use Figure 27.1, showing forecast sales of sun cream, to draw a line graph showing the number of units which will have to be produced in each of the 12 months. Allow for a lead time of one month.

CHECKPOINTS

1 Which method of production would be used for making: paint, tractors, turbines, hand-made shoes, cigarettes, greenhouses?

2 Construct a chart showing the main advantages and disadvantages of each of the four methods of production.

3 Look at Figure 27.1 in Business Techniques. What would be the most suitable method of production in your view? Give your reasons.

KEY TERMS

JOB PRODUCTION Making a single item, usually according to the customer's specification or detailed description of measurements, design etc.

BATCH PRODUCTION Producing a large or small quantity of the same item. The process will be repeated when there is another order.

FLOW PRODUCTION The continuous production of a large quantity of items on a production line, where each worker does the same job time after time as the goods flow past on a conveyor belt or moving platform.

PROCESS PRODUCTION The continuous production of large quantities of materials, such as plastics, which undergo a change in physical or chemical form.

Research and Development

Expensive

RESEARCH AND DEVELOPMENT – or R & D – is carried out by teams of scientists, technologists and engineers. Their two main tasks are:

- to improve a company's products; and
- to consider what products might be profitably produced in the future.

R & D can be very expensive. To develop a new aircraft costs about £1,000 million, plus another billion pounds for the engine. In 1987, the British drug industry planned to spend over £500 million on R & D, which amounted to about 15 per cent of its total sales.

In the fifties, R & D was often so remote from the market that it was not cost-effective. Too much time was spent on doing pure scientific research, regardless of whether the findings would result in new products being developed. R & D is now much more market orientated; it is always planning for the market. In the last few years, some bigger firms have started to divide their R & D departments into specialist sections, which cover a whole range of the firm's products. This is even more cost-effective.

Risky

R & D, however, remains a risky business. Years of research may lead nowhere and the costs of development are high as well. It is estimated that about 30 per cent of new products fail in the laboratory and another 60 per cent during development. Some may even fail later as consumers may not like them, or the market may have changed.

If R & D is so chancy, why do firms bother to do it at all? Some of them don't. In industries such as footwear or furniture, where the products do not change much from year to year, most firms rely on their trade associations or outside bodies for

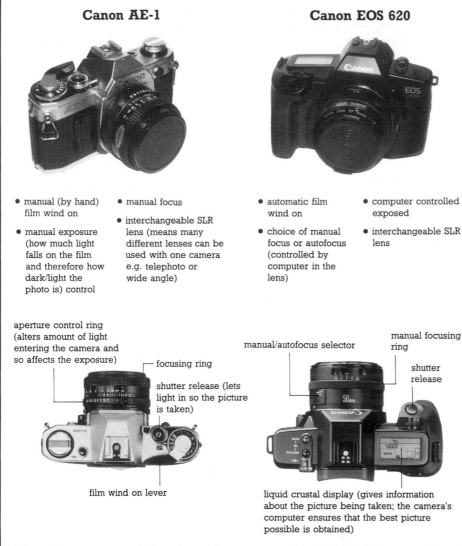

Canon AE-1

- manual (by hand) film wind on
- manual exposure (how much light falls on the film and therefore how dark/light the photo is) control
- manual focus
- interchangeable SLR lens (means many different lenses can be used with one camera e.g. telephoto or wide angle)

Canon EOS 620

- automatic film wind on
- choice of manual focus or autofocus (controlled by computer in the lens)
- computer controlled exposed
- interchangeable SLR lens

aperture control ring (alters amount of light entering the camera and so affects the exposure)

focusing ring

shutter release (lets light in so the picture is taken)

film wind on lever

manual/autofocus selector

manual focusing ring

shutter release

liquid crustal display (gives information about the picture being taken; the camera's computer ensures that the best picture possible is obtained)

The plain outer case of Canon's autofocus camera, the EOS 620, hides a wealth of technology. The autofocus is extremely fast because the focusing motor is in the lens itself.

Gold-plated electronic connections send information between the camera's central computer and the computer in the lens, which then gives out electronic commands controlling autofocus and how much light is let in when a picture is taken.

New technology has made it possible to keep the round, cylinder-shaped lens of SLR lenses. As a result, 13 kinds of lenses can be used.

STUDY POINTS

1 What are some of the main features of the EOS 620? How is the EOS 620 different from the older AE-1?

2 Describe in your own words how the autofocus works.

3 Make a sketch of the kind of camera people may be using in the year 2000, labelling the main features.

4 What kinds of consumers or market segment do you think it would appeal to? Give your reasons.

5 Design a suitable advertisement for the camera, highlighting the features which will appeal to the consumers.

R & D [see Unit 71]. However, in hi-tech industries such as computers, the pace of change is more rapid. Samples of new products are quickly taken apart and copied by rivals, who produce their own, even better product. Hi-tech industries, especially the drug, car, electronics, aerospace and chemicals industries, are forced to spend more on R & D to keep up with the competition.

The R & D department has a big part to play in –

● Improving and finding new uses for products
● Finding uses for by-products or secondary items produced as a result of a manufacturing process
● Cutting costs by creating new processes.

In the food industry, biotechnologists can provide more flavours in foods by developing potato crisps with different tastes, e.g. prawn cocktail. Scientists can develop a car battery that lasts longer than its rivals, or they may invent a new way of making a product which saves thousands of pounds.

Developing new products

The development of new products involves the biggest risks. Before work starts, the idea will go through some form of **PRODUCT EVALUATION**, usually in a team including marketing, financial and forecasting experts. Work will start if funds are available and approval is given. The basic idea is developed by making a prototype, or model, and possibly samples, before starting full-scale production. Much of this work is now done by computers [see Unit 29].

While the new product is being developed, decisions are constantly being made about its future. With some products, such as robots or aircraft engines, it may take as long as ten years to develop them. A manufacturer of an aircraft engine, therefore, has to forecast what the world will be like then. What will the general economic situation be? How much will fuel cost? How much competition will there be between airlines? These trends are far more difficult to predict. That is what makes R & D so risky, particularly as huge investments may be involved.

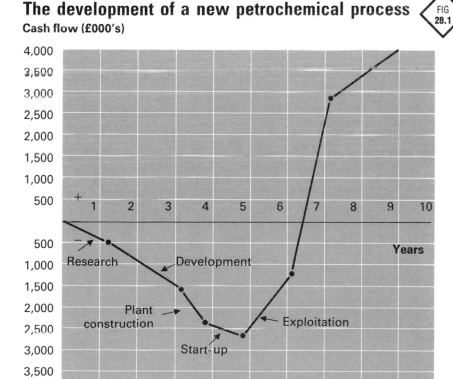

The development of a new petrochemical process FIG 28.1

Cash flow (£000's)

Interpreting graphs

Look at Figure 28.1, which shows the flow of money that a firm paid out and received in developing a new petrochemical process, and then answer the following questions.
1 Which is more expensive – research or development?
2 How many years did it take for the firm to receive a return on its investment?
3 Why do you think the cash flow was still negative during the start-up period?
4 Does it appear that the project will be financially successful?

CHECKPOINTS

1 Explain the difference between research and development.

2 What are the two chief purposes of R & D?

3 What are the main risks in R & D?

4 Why is there more R & D in the drug industry than in the furniture industry?

KEY TERMS

RESEARCH AND DEVELOPMENT (R & D) Scientific research into present and future products, materials and production processes, which is then followed by their practical application and development. Development usually takes longer, and costs more, than the research.

PRODUCT EVALUATION Judging whether a new product or process will be practical, marketable and within the company's budget.

New Technologies

An engineering firm is considering whether to install eight industrial robots to do spot welding in a line. The robots will not have to perform very difficult tasks, so only a small conveyor-belt and simple control systems will be needed. The robots will work two shifts of eight hours for 235 days a year.

Robots last, on average, eight years. It is estimated that the total overhaul and maintenance costs during that time will be £49,200. The firm has received the following quotation:

Spot welding robots

INDUSTRIAL MACHINERY LIMITED
Unit 6, Fountain Industrial Estate, Nottchester, N6 5NY

20th October 1987

To: Mr A. Scott
Engineering Parts plc
27 Millfield Lane
Ludbury
LB3 6FU

Dear Mr Scott,

RE: QUOTATION FOR SUPPLY AND INSTALLATION OF INDUSTRIAL ROBOTS

	£
Robot costs including equipment	720,000
Eight industrial robots	40,000
Site preparation	20,000
System control	20,000
Conveyors	56,000
Welding guns/transformers and controls	856,000
Total	
Installation costs	146,000
Start-up costs, including system design, assembly and shipping costs	

We look forward to hearing from you in the near future, if you are interested in discussing this matter further.

Yours faithfully,

J.A Wyndell

John A Wyndell
Manager

S T U D Y P O I N T S

1 What is the cost of each robot, including equipment?

2 What is the average combined cost of installation and start-up for each robot?

3 How much, on average, will maintenance and overhaul cost for each robot over its life span?

4 What is the total cost over 8-years for each robot, including purchase, installation, start-up and maintenance?

5 How many hours does each robot work over its 8-year life span?

6 What is the cost per hour for each robot, including purchase, installation, start-up and maintenance?

7 If the weekly wage of a welder on a 40-hour week, including employer's national insurance contribution, was £192.38, how much would be saved per hour by using robots instead?

> ‘ Next week, GKN's showpiece £12 million armoured vehicles factory in Telford will be opened formally. GKN claims that the new plant's computer controlled design and machining facilities make it one of the world's most advanced defence vehicles factories. ’

Source: *The Guardian*, 15 May 1987

AUTOMATION is not new. As long ago as 1875, an American, Oliver Evans, built a fully-automatic flour mill, powered by water. Modern automated production methods, however, were only made possible by computers.

Computer-aided manufacturing

Computer-aided manufacturing (CAM) is now widely used in many factories. In the process industries, such as paint manufacturing, computers control the temperature, mixture and rate of flow. In engineering, computers program machines to drill holes in metal to the exact depth required.

The development of much smaller and much cheaper micro-processors has made automation more widespread. A micro-processor, costing around a few hundred pounds, can do the same work as a £200,000 mainframe computer did 25 years ago. One result of this has been an increase in the number of industrial robots, which can be programmed by micro-processors to perform a series of tasks.

Robots

Industrial robots are useful for work that is:
● boring
● requires great strength
● has to be carried out in dangerous conditions.

Robots were first used in the fifties for welding and spray-painting car bodies. They are ideal for moving loads from one conveyor to another; dangerous work in nuclear plants; or diving work underwater. Walking robots have already been produced and experiments are being done with others which will see, hear, speak and even have artificial intelligence, i.e. will think for themselves.

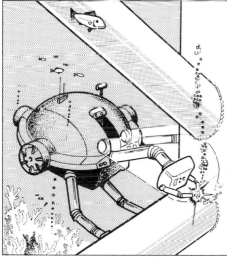

An artist's impression of an underwater robot of the future, repairing an oil rig

Robots became popular because of rising wage costs. They can work 24 hours a day, in any conditions, and are usually faster and more efficient than human labour. One factory making electric motors has recently

increased output by 70 per cent through using robots.

Computer-aided design

Computer-aided design (CAD) makes it possible to design products on the screen of a visual display unit (VDU). This avoids having to build expensive models of bridges or aircraft and makes the design process much quicker and cheaper.

A further use of computers is in production management. Their ability to make complex calculations at great speed is of great value in the planning of:
● material requirements, so that the right quantities are ordered at the right time;
● production schedules, so that work flows smoothly through the factory;
● quality control, so that goods of the right standards are produced.

Computer integrated manufacturing

COMPUTER INTEGRATED MANUFACTURING (CIM) is the combination of all these developments. Some CIM factories already exist, where everything is controlled by computers. The labour force can often be cut by 90 per cent with output remaining the same. Machinery can also be cut back and quality control improved. CIM needs a very large capital investment and careful planning, but some firms have already proved it can be very profitable.

Another great advantage of CIM is its flexibility. It is possible that the mass production of a single product on assembly lines may disappear in some industries. Instead, there will be a return to batch production with these flexible manufacturing systems making a variety of parts and products with much less waiting time between processes than there was in the past.

Despite reduced enthusiasm for robots recently, experts forecast that by the year 2000, only ten per cent of the working population will be employed in manufacturing. There will be far fewer jobs for the semi-skilled and the unskilled. As the remaining work will be done by highly skilled people, this will produce a change in organisation. The programming team will replace the old-fashioned manager who told other people what to do.

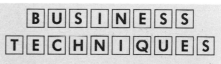
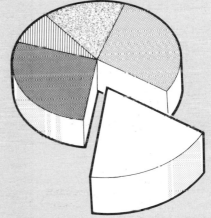
CHECKPOINTS

1 Describe the main use of computers in process industries.
2 What are the main advantages of industrial robots?
3 How can computers aid design?
4 What are the advantages of computer integrated manufacturing?
5 How will batch production in the future differ from that used today?
6 What might be the social and economic effects of automation?

KEY TERMS

AUTOMATION A general term used to describe the automatic production of goods by machines using a minimal labour force to supervise production.

COMPUTER INTEGRATED MANUFACTURING The latest method of automated production in which design, manufacturing and management are all linked electronically and aided, or controlled, by computers.

Activities

■ Review points

1 What are the main tasks of a production manager?

2 Describe two methods of quality control.

3 What are the main factors a business should consider in its choice of location?

4 What is meant by a greenfield site?

5 a) Explain what is meant by process production.
   b) Give two examples of goods which might be produced in this way.

6 Describe the main purposes of research and development.

7 a) What type of jobs might be done by an industrial robot?
   b) Give examples in each case.

■ Essay questions

1 a) Describe what is meant by research and development.
   b) Explain why firms need to spend money on research and development.
   c) Why has research and development become increasingly important in the manufacturing industry?

2 Show, using examples, how the choice of location for a business might depend on:
   a) road communications
   b) government aid
   c) opportunity costs.

3 Mr Kiyoshi Sakashita, corporate director of the Japanese electronics firm, Sharp, has recently said: 'We should not let technology become a barrier between humans and their human nature.'
   a) What do you think is meant by this statement?
   b) How do you think that technology comes between humans and their human nature? Give examples.
   c) How might research and development have an effect on this?

Science parks and the small firm

The environment that the typical science park provides is particularly suited to the formation and growth of high-technology, or 'leading-edge' firms. This is partly because of the links that exist between the science parks and the universities and colleges to which they are connected. In fact, the science parks were specially designed to encourage the growth of 'knowledge-based' businesses.

Science park firms interviewed by the United Kingdom Science Park Association say access to universities and colleges is one of the main reasons for their decision to locate in that type of environment. Most firms say they often use university facilities, with smaller firms using them more than others. Over 70 per cent of firms said they had informal contacts with teachers and lecturers, and 36 per cent used university staff for advice.

One advantage of this close connection with the academic world is the availability of highly-qualified staff. Michael Gardener, who runs Owl Micro-Communication Systems on the Cambridge Science Park, now employs seven staff, all of whom have some connection with the university.

Adapted from: *In Business Now*, April/May 1987

1 What is a science park?

2 In what areas are they likely to be located?

3 What is a 'leading-edge' firm?

4 What are the advantages of being linked to a university?

5 What are the main differences between a science park and an industrial estate?

6 What effects are science parks likely to have in areas of high unemployment?

The car in the 21st century

Cars of the future will be lighter, slicker and smaller. In fact, in the early 21st century, cars may be light enough to fly.

Cars will be aerodynamically sleek, very small, and will not use much fuel, thanks to technological advances in parts and engine design. For example, air conditioning systems that at present would take up a great deal of under-bonnet space will become tiny, efficient devices. Suspension systems may be built into the tyres themselves. Engines will be the size of motor cycle engines – possibly smaller.

Even more significantly, cars of the year 2000 will be modular. This means you will be able to snap parts, or modules, on or off to make anything you want. Let's start with the basic, two-seat runabout car. Add the snap-on engine-suspension module and it becomes a high performance sports car. Attach an extra seating module and you have a car for the family. With even more seating and engine modules you could make it a bus.

Around the year 2025, cars should be able to fly. They'll be so light that it will be more efficient to make cars float on a cushion of air – up to a foot above the ground – than to roll along on tyres. Radar will come into its own as a safety device. Laser beams will guide cars to their destinations.

Adapted from: *Ford Facts*, Ford Motor Company

1 What will be the main difference between the car of the future and today's models?

2 Make a sketch of the car of the year 2025, labelling the features mentioned in the article.

3 Describe what production methods might be used to manufacture the car of 2025.

Drugs industry research budget to top £500m

The drugs industry plans to spend more than £500m this year on research and development, or R and D. This would be 11 per cent of the national total for industrial R and D, although drugs are less than 2 per cent of Britain's industrial output.

The Association of the British Pharmaceutical Industry says the industry is ahead of any other in its research spending.

The £500m figure is about 15 per cent of the industry's UK sales. This is claimed to beat other industries who do a lot of research, such as aerospace, where R and D spending is about 12 per cent of sales.

The Association is unhappy about the return on this outlay. It blames the length of time drugs are protected by patent, a law which prevents other people making or selling someone else's invention.

'Most products in other industries have a patent protection of 20 years, but the average time allowed for a new drug is only eight years,' the Association says.

'This is because it can take 12 years from the date a drug is patented to pass it through the necessary tests and put it on the market. By this time only eight years of the patent are left,' says the Association.

'Medicines entering the Japanese and American markets in the 1990s will have more than twice the protection period that drugs have on the British market. This could have disastrous effects on drug R and D in this country by the year 2000,' says the Association.

While the industry continues to press Parliament for increased patent protection, it is also pressing for faster approval of drugs.

Adapted from: *Financial Times*, 11 May 1987

1 Why does the drugs industry spend more on research and development than other industries?

2 What is the complaint of the drugs industry?

3 How does the industry suggest this problem might be overcome?

4 Can you see any dangers in their suggestions?

■ Groupwork

You are working in a research team in the Royal Mint which has been asked to help design a new British currency. You have been asked to investigate what people think of the present coinage and to obtain suggestions for improving it.

Divide into groups. Each of you should interview individually one of the following:
- an old person
- a blind person
- a shopkeeper
- a bank worker
- a foreigner
- a very young person.

When you have found out their views, come together as a group again to discuss your findings. Write a short report between you, giving your suggestions for changing the coinage, and giving reasons for your decisions. Each member of the group should then either draw, or make a model of, one of the new coins.

■ Coursework

1 Make a study of the changes in design and development over the last ten years of either telephones, hi-fi equipment, sewing machines or radios. Information can be obtained from a local library, old catalogues and magazines, or local retailers and manufacturers. Write a report saying what changes have been made and explaining why the research and development departments chose to alter the products in this way.

2 Interview a sole proprietor – for example, a garage owner, a farmer, a dentist, an odd-job person – and find out how their work has been affected by new technology, such as new tools and machines, materials and processes. Write a report explaining what differences it has made to their working methods, labour costs, productivity and profits.

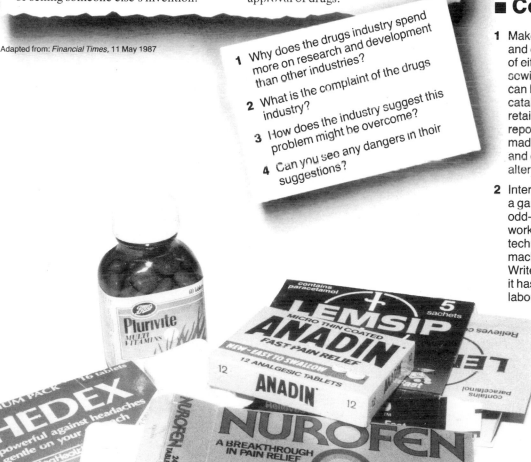

Finding the Market

	Household spending on goods and services 1983–84									
FIG 30.1	Average weekly household spending (£)									
Region	Total	Housing	Fuel, light and power	Food	Alcoholic drink	Tobacco	Clothing and footwear	Durable household goods	Other goods	Transport, vehicles, services, and other spending
North	124.20	17.10	8.60	28.00	7.60	5.00	9.60	9.80	9.00	29.40
Yorkshire & Humberside	132.90	19.40	8.70	28.60	7.20	4.40	9.50	10.10	10.20	34.80
East Midlands	146.30	25.40	8.90	30.30	6.80	4.20	10.00	11.10	11.80	37.80
East Anglia	134.10	21.70	9.80	28.70	5.20	3.20	8.40	10.10	10.70	36.30
South East	169.60	30.00	9.30	32.90	7.50	3.80	12.00	13.00	13.80	47.30
South West	142.60	22.80	9.60	28.80	6.00	3.50	9.60	10.10	11.20	40.90
West Midlands	143.10	23.70	9.10	30.30	7.00	4.00	10.10	9.90	10.10	38.80
North West	137.40	21.20	9.20	29.30	7.70	4.70	9.60	9.90	9.90	35.80
Wales	134.20	17.00	10.00	30.60	7.00	4.90	10.50	10.30	10.30	33.40
Scotland	136.60	16.40	9.50	30.10	7.20	5.60	11.40	10.20	10.40	35.90
Northern Ireland	129.50	15.90	13.40	32.30	4.20	4.50	10.80	7.10	9.50	31.70
United Kingdom overall	146.50	23.20	9.30	30.50	7.10	4.30	10.60	10.90	11.40	39.20

Source: Family Expenditure Surveys

S T U D Y P O I N T S

In Britain, there are great differences in income and spending patterns between the regions. Firms have to take these differences into account in finding a market for their goods or services.

1 Which region has a) the lowest and b) the highest average income per household per week? Suggest reasons for this.

2 Give five examples of durable household goods. Which region spends least on these items?

3 What percentage of households' total spending goes on food in a) the North, b) the South East and c) Northern Ireland?

4 If you sold:
a) alcoholic drinks,
b) luxury cars, or
c) cigarettes and tobacco,
which region of the United Kingdom seems to provide the best market? State the reasons for your choice.

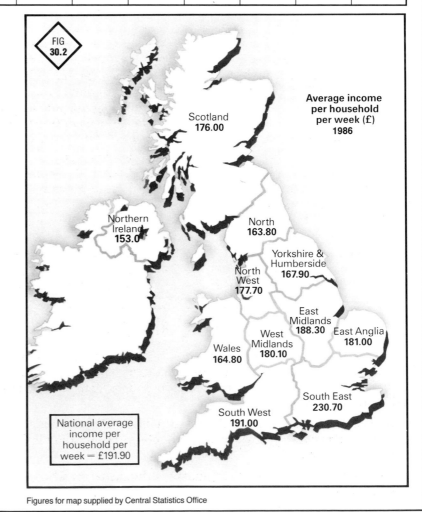

FIG 30.2

Average income per household per week (£) 1986

Scotland **176.00**

Northern Ireland **153.0**

North **163.80**

North West **177.70**

Yorkshire & Humberside **167.90**

East Midlands **188.30**

East Anglia **181.00**

West Midlands **180.10**

Wales **164.80**

South East **230.70**

South West **191.00**

National average income per household per week = £191.90

Figures for map supplied by Central Statistics Office

In today's highly competitive markets, very few firms can afford to be entirely **PRODUCT-ORIENTATED**. A century ago, markets were more local and more limited as most people had only enough money to buy the basic necessities of life. The manufacturer's or retailer's main concern was the quality and the price of the product.

Today, markets are international. The range of goods and services on the market is enormous and most, though not all, British consumers have enough money to satisfy their needs and still spend on their wants or desires [see Unit 1].

Marketing

As a result, most firms are now **MARKET-ORIENTATED**. They have to identify the wants and desires of the consumer, both now and in the future, and provide the right goods or services to satisfy the customer and make a profit for the firm. That, in brief, is what marketing is all about.

Marketing is based on the theory that people of the same age, income, education etc. will spend their money on similar products. For example, most pop records are bought by teenagers, most university graduates don't read the Sun.

Market segments

Marketing people divide the whole population into different groups and categories, called **MARKET SEGMENTS**, and examine each one in great detail. Their main aim is to find out what kinds of goods and services consumers buy.

Geographical and regional differences affect the ways in which people spend their money. You would be able to sell more Wellington boots in the country than you would in the centre of London, for example.

There are other factors which are even more important. Age is one of the most significant [see Unit 7]. As the proportion of old people in the population increases, there will be a rise in demand for medicine, old people's homes and hospital services (both State and private).

There is also a desire among many old people to look young and keep fit. There are also a growing number of old people with large company pensions and more leisure time for spending money. How might the marketing person make use of these business opportunities?

Similar investigations are made into what young people spend their money on, what they are likely to spend more on in the future or what goods are likely to become less popular.

Gender is also important. Women still spend more on clothes, cosmetics and jewellery than men. However, there have been changes in the market; sex-roles have weakened. Look at jeans, or unisex hairdressers!

Income is another important factor. Marketing people put everybody into social grades according to the income of the head of the household [see Unit 31]. Different responsibilities and lifestyles also need to be taken into account. A single woman on the same income as a married man with three children will spend her money very differently.

Education also has a great influence, but less, perhaps, than it once did, mainly because more students now receive the same kind of education. The influence of marketing has also helped to create a more uniform taste for foreign travel, luxury homes or expensive cars.

People's jobs, and whether they are members of religious groups, are other factors which have to be taken into account.

The marketing person puts all this information together and tries to find the market segment in which the largest number of people share a want for a product or service. If the segment has not been catered for by other firms, so much the better.

BUSINESS TECHNIQUES

Attracting the impulse buyer

Most people do not plan all their purchases, but buy some goods on impulse, or on the spur of the moment. Give three examples of goods that you have bought on impulse. State how the marketing of the product – advertising, price, packaging, design etc – may have influenced your decision to buy.

CHECKPOINTS

1 **What does product-orientated mean? Why would a firm which was entirely product-orientated probably go bankrupt?**
2 **Why do firms need to be market-orientated?**
3 **Give one example each of market segments for watches, cars, furniture.**
4 **How do different levels of education affect spending patterns? Why has the influence of education weakened?**
5 **What might be a profitable market segment for a museum, a florist, a computer-dating agency?**

KEY TERMS

PRODUCT-ORIENTATED Where the product and its price are the most important concerns. A manufacturer decides on a product, makes it, prices it, and tries to sell it without first investigating to see if a market exists for the product.

MARKET-ORIENTATED Where market research is carried out to find out what the consumers want before starting production. The product is then made to suit the market.

MARKET SEGMENTS Groups of consumers within a market who have similar wants or desires.

Market Research

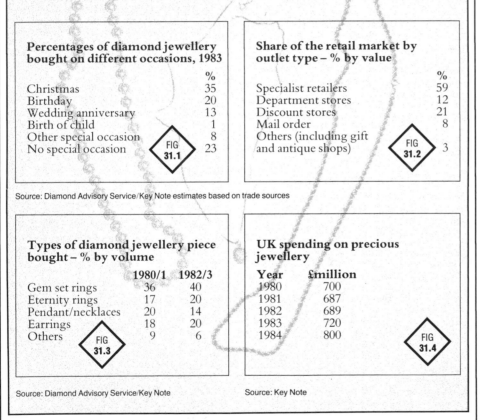

A chain of retailers is considering whether to branch out into the jewellery trade. Their marketing department has come up with an idea for a new type of shop, with an up-to-date image. The windows would have attractive displays for special occasions. Inside, the shops would be far more open. To protect the goods, they plan to use video cameras and other secret electronic devices.

They plan to sell only precious jewellery, which accounts for only about half of the total market by volume, but about 90 per cent by value. As it costs about £200,000 to set up a high street jeweller's shop, they are carrying out a big market research project. They have already collected the data shown below.

Percentages of diamond jewellery bought on different occasions, 1983

	%
Christmas	35
Birthday	20
Wedding anniversary	13
Birth of child	1
Other special occasion	8
No special occasion	23

FIG 31.1

Source: Diamond Advisory Service/Key Note estimates based on trade sources

Share of the retail market by outlet type – % by value

	%
Specialist retailers	59
Department stores	12
Discount stores	21
Mail order	8
Others (including gift and antique shops)	3

FIG 31.2

Types of diamond jewellery piece bought – % by volume

	1980/1	1982/3
Gem set rings	36	40
Eternity rings	17	20
Pendant/necklaces	20	14
Earrings	18	20
Others	9	6

FIG 31.3

Source: Diamond Advisory Service/Key Note

UK spending on precious jewellery

Year	£million
1980	700
1981	687
1982	689
1983	720
1984	800

FIG 31.4

Source: Key Note

S T U D Y   P O I N T S

1 At what time of the year does a jeweller sell most goods?

2 Who is the biggest competitor for the specialist jeweller? Suggest reasons for this type of competition.

3 What would be the best kinds of jewellery for the new shops to stock?

4 What occasions might the shops use for special promotions? Make a sketch of a modern attractive Christmas display for a jeweller's shop window.

5 Look at Figure 31.4. How was the jewellery trade affected by the sudden increase in the price of gold in 1981–82?

6 What other international economic or political events might affect the jewellery trade in this country?

Kinds of data

MARKET RESEARCH is used to look at a market segment in much greater detail. Two kinds of data are used: primary and secondary. Information which has already been collected – like Figures 31.1 to 31.4 – is known as **SECONDARY DATA**. The three main sources of secondary data are:

● Government departments, such as the Central Statistical Office and the Department of Trade and Industry [see Unit 70].
● Trade associations, such as the Diamond Advisory Service.
● The firm's own financial accounts and previous marketing reports (if it is in the trade already).

Detailed examination of this secondary data will help a firm to estimate the size of the market segment. It will also show whether the market is growing, declining or staying the same, which kinds of retailers are increasing their share of the market, etc.

Original, first-hand information about consumers – which is even more valuable – is known as **PRIMARY DATA**. A number of techniques are used to gain this information, but most is collected by market research surveys.

Surveys

The main purpose of surveys is to find out what consumers want, why they prefer one thing to another, and what makes them buy. Surveys may be carried out in four main ways:

● by post (but the response is often poor)
● by telephone (becoming more common)
● by personal interview (the most common method) – based on either a random or quota sample
● in groups (often used for testing samples of the product).

In a **RANDOM SAMPLE SURVEY**, the people to be interviewed (interviewees) are selected from a printed list, such as the telephone directory or the

See Units ▶ 34, 35, 70

FIG 31.5

SOCIAL GRADES

Social grade is based on the job of the head of the household and gives an idea of the household's spending power. The table shows the approximate proportion of each grade in the total UK population in percentages.

Grade	Job description	% of UK population
A	Higher managerial, administrative and professional	3.1
B	Intermediate managerial, administrative and professional	13.4
C^1	Supervisory or clerical and junior managerial, administrative and professional	22.3
C^2	Skilled manual	31.2
D	Semi-skilled and unskilled manual	19.1
E	Casual labourers, state pensioners + the unemployed	10.9

Source: Advertising Association

---

electoral register, at fixed gaps of every fifty or a hundred names.

The **QUOTA SAMPLE SURVEY** is more common. The interviewees are chosen – by social grade, by sex, by age – in proportion to the total number in the whole population. For instance, out of 100 people, you would choose three from social grade A, because the proportion of grade A people in the total population is 3.1 per cent (see Figure 31.5). Out of 100 people, how many would you choose from social grades B to E?

It is not easy to make up a good questionnaire. Before you start, you must have a clear idea of exactly what it is you want to find out (your objectives). The questions must be clear, precise and easily understood. Care must be taken not to ask more than one question at a time. Always test the questions on someone else before you start, and rewrite any that are unclear.

Personal interviews can also be used to test people's reactions to a brand name, packaging, an advertisement or the product itself [see Units 34, 35].

Using the information

When all the interviews have been completed, the information has to be put together (or collated), and then analysed according to the sampling method chosen.

Some interviews, which are not usually conducted in the street, look much more deeply into people's attitudes and behaviour. For example: how they spend their leisure time,

their interests and preferences, and their attitudes to themselves, other people and the social issues of the day.

From this information, market researchers hope to find out what can appeal to people's deepest wants and desires. For instance, it was discovered that some anti-drug posters and advertisements have been counter-productive – that is, produced the opposite effect to what was planned – in some parts of the country. The lifestyles they showed appealed to young people so much that more of them started using drugs.

BUSINESS TECHNIQUES

Questionnaires

Questions in surveys may require:
- a direct 'Yes' or 'No' (or 'Don't know') answer
  e.g. Have you ever bought Brand X?
- a scale of answers
  e.g. How would you rate the cleaning power of Brand X?
  Very good ☐   Good ☐
  Fairly good ☐   Poor ☐
  Bad ☐   Very bad ☐
- a range of answers
  e.g. Which of the following have you used in the last seven days?
  Brand X ☐   Brand Y ☐
  Brand Z ☐

Make up a questionnaire on a breakfast cereal using questions of each type.

KEY TERMS

MARKET RESEARCH Getting information about consumers by studying statistics and reports and gathering new data by surveys of individuals or groups.

SECONDARY DATA Information which already exists due to other people's research.

PRIMARY DATA First-hand information from market research surveys of the consumers.

RANDOM SAMPLE SURVEY Surveys where those being interviewed are picked by taking names from a printed list, such as a telephone directory, at fixed gaps of say 50 or 100 names.

QUOTA SAMPLE SURVEY Interviewees are chosen by group, for example, age, sex or social grade, in the same proportion as the number found in the total population.

CHECKPOINTS

1. What kinds of data are used in market research?
2. What are the three main sources of secondary data?
3. State three kinds of information which might be obtained from secondary data.
4. What are the three main aims of surveys?
5. How would you plan a random sample survey?
6. You have been asked to carry out a survey about pet ownership among young people between the ages of 11 and 16. Draw up a suitable questionnaire.

The Marketing Mix

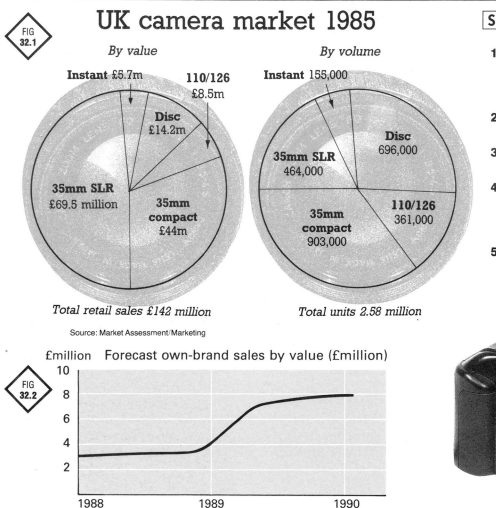

FIG 32.1

UK camera market 1985

By value

Instant £5.7m

110/126 £8.5m

Disc £14.2m

35mm SLR £69.5 million

35mm compact £44m

Total retail sales £142 million

By volume

Instant 155,000

Disc 696,000

35mm SLR 464,000

110/126 361,000

35mm compact 903,000

Total units 2.58 million

Source: Market Assessment/Marketing

FIG 32.2

£million Forecast own-brand sales by value (£million)

10
8
6
4
2

1988   1989   1990

STUDY POINTS

1 Which kind of camera had the biggest sales in 1985 a) by value and b) by volume? How would you explain the difference?

2 Why has the firm chosen to market a 35mm compact camera?

3 What sort of people make up the market segment which the firm has chosen?

4 If sales of compact cameras totalled £56 million in 1990, use Figure 32.2 to work out what the firm's share of that market segment would be.

5 Which, in your view, would be the best time to launch the camera? Give reasons for your choice.

A national chain of fashion shops has decided to market its own-brand 35mm compact camera, which it will buy from the Far East. It will sell at £39.99.

The cameras will be launched with a £300,000 advertising campaign. The firm is studying some of the comments from the market research surveys which will help it to plan its campaign.

'I only ever use mine at Christmas and on holiday.' *Woman, aged 40, social grade B*

'Those black cameras are so dull.' *Woman, aged 38, social grade A*

'I'd never learn how to use one, dear.' *Woman, aged 48, social grade C*

'I wish they'd make one with a really nice case.' *Woman, aged 39, social grade B*

'I'd just rush in and buy one.' *Woman, aged 45, social grade B*

'How much? £39.99. Yes, I might buy one.' *Woman, aged 42, social grade C*

'I used to have an SLR camera. By the time, I'd set the focus and the aperture, the picture had gone.' *Woman, aged 45, social grade A*

When a market segment has been identified, a **MARKETING PLAN** has to be worked out. The main aim is to make sure that the greatest number of people in the segment become aware of the product and are attracted by it.

Pricing and packaging

There are many ways of achieving this. Let's consider the product – in this case, a camera. Pricing is obviously an important factor; but the lowest price is not always the best [see Unit 33]. The brand name could be nothing more than the firm's name; but that might sound rather dull. So the camera might be given a name of its own which has more appeal [see Unit 34].

Packaging can also have a great effect on sales. Should the camera be packaged in a cheap, but colourful, box? Or put in a plastic, blister pack, which would increase its shelf life? Or should it be sold complete with a case? However it is packaged, it is essential that it appeals to the chosen segment [see Unit 34].

Promotion

Advertising is extremely important, but it is expensive. Why can some newspapers – like the *Daily Mail* – charge more than the *Observer* for advertisements? How do advertisers know that they are reaching the right market [see Unit 35]? Then there is publicity. Should there be a special launch for the camera? Where should it be held? Would it be possible to get a well-known photographer to attend the launch? If not, what kind of famous person would appeal to the chosen segment?

How should the camera be sold? Should there be special sales promotions from the start? Or should they be held back just in case the camera doesn't do as well as expected [see Unit 36]?

All these questions are very important and so is the **MARKETING MIX**. This includes not only those elements mentioned above, but many others such as marketing, market research, design, production, and research and development (see Figure 32.3).

Changing the mix

The mixing process does not happen only once, but continues throughout the life of the product. If sales start to fall, a new promotion might revive

The marketing mix

them. When the product starts to age, the Research and Development department might come up with a good idea to keep it selling longer. Marketing and market research will need to estimate how well the camera will sell. The price may need to be looked at again.

During the product's life cycle, the market segment may change. In fact, it almost certainly will, as tastes and fashions are changing all the time. The marketing mix and plan will have to be changed to allow for new demands.

The marketing plan allows for different interests by stressing the various qualities of a product in different media. For example, a TV ad may stress a camera's ease of use; an advertisement in a women's magazine may emphasise the fashionable colour of the case; while an advertisement in a photographic magazine would stress the camera's technical features.

A firm can also take advantage of changes in taste by extending its

PRODUCT MIX. The basic product can be changed to suit a variety of needs. Changes in the colour of the camera case may widen its appeal. The introduction of attachments or optional extras, such as a carrying case, may help to put up sales. The changes that can be made are limited only by the imagination of the marketing staff.

B U S I N E S S T E C H N I Q U E S

Single column centimetre (scc)

Newspapers usually charge a higher rate for a front page advertisement because it is displayed in an easily seen position, alone on the first page of the newspaper. There is a standard charge for each single column centimetre (scc) in depth for display advertisements on other pages. The 1987 scc charge for the *Observer* was £40, and for the *Daily Mail*, £75. Using these values, and your own investigation, work out the cost of a two column display advertisement, four centimetres deep in a) the *Observer*, b) the *Daily Mail* and c) your local newspaper.

C H E C K P O I N T S

1. **What are the main elements in the marketing mix?**
2. **Give three examples of how they interact with one another.**
3. **Why is there never a final marketing plan?**
4. **How can changes in the product mix help to maximise sales?**
5. **State three kinds of market segments for a) watches, b) furniture, and c) computers. What would be the main features of the marketing mix for each?**

K E Y T E R M S

MARKETING PLAN The plan by which a firm hopes to sell its product or service to the chosen market segment.

MARKETING MIX The factors, such as product design, price, packaging, promotion etc, through which a firm hopes to sell its product to the market segment.

PRODUCT MIX The different qualities of a product which can be changed to suit the tastes of the market.

Activities

■ Review points

1 What is a market segment?

2 Describe the main methods of market research.

3 Explain how a market research questionnaire should be drawn up.

4 What is a marketing mix? Explain the main jobs of the various departments of a firm which play a part in the marketing mix.

■ Groupwork

A supermarket chain has decided to open a new store in your area. You have been asked to carry out a market research survey about people's views of other supermarkets in the area. You have also been asked to conduct some in-depth interviews about their attitudes to shopping – their dislikes, their hopes, their needs, their reasons for shopping. The six groups of people you have chosen to interview are:

Men, aged 18–25, social grades A, B, and C^1

Women, aged 18–25, social grades C^2 and D

Men, aged 26–45, social grades C^2 and D
Women, aged 26–45, social grades A, B, and C^1

Men, aged 46–65, social grades A, B and C^1

Women, aged 46–65, social grades C^2 and D

1 Make up a questionnaire as a group. Decide which of you will interview which category, or type, of people.

2 Interview, by yourself, one or more persons in the category you have chosen. Bring the results back to your group.

3 Discuss the results as a group. Write a report by yourself, giving the results of your group's survey. In the report say what sort of store the supermarket chain should open if it wants to meet the needs and wants of the people you interviewed.

Orangina goes national in the UK

Orangina – claimed to be the only soft drink brand to have outsold Coca-Cola and Pepsi Cola in any developed country in the world – is finally going national in the UK.

Owned by Pernod Ricard and distributed in the UK by HP Bulmer, the slightly fizzy real orange drink has been available in this country, in one form or another, since 1982.

Now the companies hope to repeat Orangina's French success in the UK market (it is second best seller in France), by investing £2.5 million on a marketing support programme. This includes a £1.5 million national TV campaign which starts this June.

Since Bulmer's took on the brand, which is targeted at young adults, the company has been testing it in the Central region. While the company described the test as 'highly successful', it is thought that Orangina's penetration of the market could be higher if it came in large bottles.

However, the unusual bulb-shaped individual-serve bottle is an important aspect of the brand's presentation.

The test-market plan – 'Shake the bottle. Wake the drink.' – is being carried through nationally with a new 40-second commercial filmed on the Cote d'Azur.

Bulmer's marketing manager, Heidi MacDougall, says: 'Orangina has the potential to become one of the really big, successful soft drinks brands in the UK.'

'It has all the features sought by the modern, young, image-conscious drinker – Orangina is natural, lightly sparkling and stylishly packaged – that's a perfect profile for success in today's market.'

Orangina: Perfect profile?

Source: *Marketing Week*,
8 May 1987

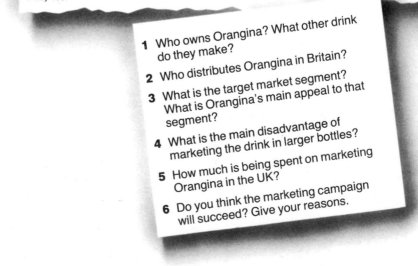

1 Who owns Orangina? What other drink do they make?

2 Who distributes Orangina in Britain?

3 What is the target market segment? What is Orangina's main appeal to that segment?

4 What is the main disadvantage of marketing the drink in larger bottles?

5 How much is being spent on marketing Orangina in the UK?

6 Do you think the marketing campaign will succeed? Give your reasons.

Philips aims for younger buyers

Philips: Backing a range of audio products targeted at teenagers.

Philips consumer electronics division is following last year's launch of the Roller Portable cassette machine with a push into the market for audio equipment as a fashion extra.

The company is introducing a range of audio products with bright colours and 'fun' designs, all aimed at teenagers and carrying the 'Moving Sound' label.

In a further development it is to sell a stereo radio for children, complete with a set of transfers that allows the owner to decorate their own set, under the name 'Fashion Sound'.

The moves are part of Philips' continuing efforts to shed its old-fashioned image and get into the youth market where there is much money to be made.

'Moving Sound' is seen as a sub-brand by Philips, and apart from the Roller, it includes new designs like the Wedge, a wedge-shaped personal stereo, and the Boom Box.

Aart Timmer, marketing manager for portable audio at Philips, says: 'The introduction of Fashion Sound and Moving Sound shows our determination to liven up the audio market, to make it more attractive to young people and to offer products which are youthful and stylish.

Philips is supporting Moving Sound with a £1.5 million advertising and promotional budget through Ogilvy & Mather featuring a road show.

Source: *Marketing Week*, 8 May 1987

1 How much is Philips spending on its advertising and promotional campaign for its new products?

2 What are the main features of Moving Sound and Fashion Sound?

3 What market segment has Philips targeted? Why has it decided to target this new segment?

4 How will Philips promote its new products?

5 Imagine you carried out the market research for Philips before the new products were launched. Make up comments from three people you might have interviewed in your survey which would have made you decide to go ahead with the new projects. State the sex, age and social grade of each person.

■ Essay questions

1 a) Why does a firm need to market its products?
   b) What changes in the business environment have led to marketing becoming more important in the modern world?

2 You are setting up a market research firm. State:
   a) What kinds of people you would employ as interviewers.
   b) Why you think the things you looked for are important.
   c) What sort of training you would provide for your new employees.

■ Coursework

Observation is another form of market research. Its main disadvantage is that it doesn't reveal the reasons for people's choice; but it does provide useful additional data.

1 Find an eye-catching poster and observe the age, sex and likely social grade of people who look at it during a ten-minute period. Note if they glance at it, look at it, or stop and study it. Note the number of people who ignore it.

[For the next two pieces of work, you must first obtain permission from the store manager.]

2 Choose a counter in a high street store. Over a ten-minute period, note the age, sex and likely social grade of customers who look at it and buy from it.

3 Position yourself by the entrance door of a high street store. Note where customers go first and whether they move quickly, stroll or change their direction. Note their age, sex and likely social grade.

Write a report in each case, presenting your data clearly with graphs and flow charts if necessary. State how effective the poster, counter display or store layout is and suggest changes for their improvement.

Pricing Decisions

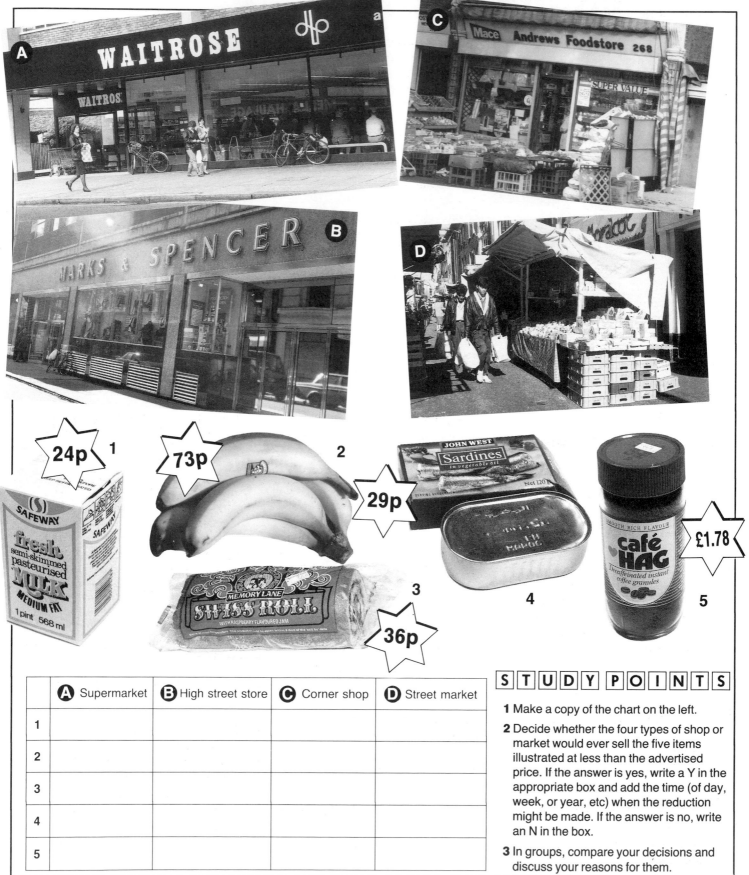

	Ⓐ Supermarket	Ⓑ High street store	Ⓒ Corner shop	Ⓓ Street market
1				
2				
3				
4				
5				

STUDY POINTS

1 Make a copy of the chart on the left.

2 Decide whether the four types of shop or market would ever sell the five items illustrated at less than the advertised price. If the answer is yes, write a Y in the appropriate box and add the time (of day, week, or year, etc) when the reduction might be made. If the answer is no, write an N in the box.

3 In groups, compare your decisions and discuss your reasons for them.

Supply and demand

Pricing is an important factor in the marketing mix. Price is decided, to a certain extent, by supply and demand [see Unit 2]. In summer, when there are plenty of home-grown and imported vegetables, prices will tend to fall. In the late spring, when vegetables are often scarce, prices will rise.

The economic law of supply and demand works most strongly in primary production [see Unit 3]. If there is an excess supply of oil, the price of petrol should fall – all other things remaining unchanged. Where there are few buyers, prices will be low. But where there are many buyers and wealthy buyers, the prices will rise.

In the secondary and tertiary sectors of production – such as manufacturing, retailing, service industries – this law still operates but with much less force. Other factors, such as what competing firms charge for similar products; whether the product is a new one; or whether it is for a special occasion, also affect the price and give more freedom to price fixing.

Price fixing methods

How do firms decide upon the price of their products? The simplest method is the cost-plus approach, that is:

> unit cost + overheads + profit margin
> = selling price

Some firms still set their prices in this way. In theory, they can never go bankrupt. However, what happens if the labour force goes on strike for higher wages; or if sales decline; or if their price is undercut by cheap foreign imports?

Some of these problems can be avoided by using a **MARKET-ORIENTATED PRICE** instead. With this method, the firm finds out (by market research) what customers are prepared to pay before the price is set.

There is a **PRICE PLATEAU**, which represents the level of price that a market segment expects to pay for a particular product. If a firm's price is too much below the plateau, consumers will think the product is inferior, so they won't buy. If it is too far above the plateau, they won't buy either.

Professional 'tricks'

There are many professional 'tricks' which can be used in pricing.

● A firm entering a new market may use a **PENETRATION PRICE**, which is low enough to allow it to get a share of the market. Once the product has been established, however, the price may rise.

● A firm may try to capture its customers by selling a ballpoint pen at a low price, but making the refills fairly expensive.

● Supermarkets may have wire baskets full of **LOSS LEADERS** just inside the entrance to attract customers.

● The same product may cost more in wealthier areas of the country (regional price variation).

● A multiple firm may charge more for the same products in a small country town than it does in a city only a few miles away where competition is much greater (local price variation).

The same product may have a different price at a different time and in a different place (as the Study Points have shown).

In fact, in the full marketing mix, there is no single product anyway. A firm making or selling watches may offer as many as ten different models to cater for different parts of the market segment. And all of them will have different prices. Optional extras are often the key to success in pricing . . . until another manufacturer comes along and offers the extras as standard features, when the whole business of pricing will have to start again.

Loss leaders in a supermarket

Product pricing

The unit cost of making a cheap ballpoint pen is 3.5p. If the overhead costs were 1.3p per pen and the manufacturer wanted to make a profit of 25 per cent, what would be the selling price per pen to the wholesaler?

CHECKPOINTS

1 What kind of price might a firm use if it was trying to enter a new market?

2 Why do supermarkets have loss leaders?

3 What is cost-plus pricing?

4 What is the importance of the price plateau in fixing prices?

5 In which areas of production does the law of supply and demand have the greatest influence on prices? How do you account for this?

KEY TERMS

MARKET-ORIENTATED PRICE A price which is decided by the whole range of factors in the marketing mix instead of by the cost-plus price of the product.

PRICE PLATEAU The level of price that consumers expect to pay for a particular product.

PENETRATION PRICE A price which is set low enough to allow a firm to enter a new market.

LOSS LEADER A product which is sold at, or below, cost price to attract customers.

Branding and Packaging

Three sixth-formers at a comprehensive school in East Anglia have decided to go into business, selling their own brand of honey to local shops. Teresa's retired uncle has agreed to sell them all the honey he produces and they hope to buy more from other local bee-keepers. Jamie's father is willing to take their product to local towns in his van once a week; while Sam's mother has agreed to let them use a spare room at home.

East Anglia is a relatively prosperous region with many rich farmers, a growing number of entrepreneurs in the sunrise industries, and a large number of professional people from London who have a second home there. Teresa, Jamie and Sam have identified these groups as their target consumers. They realise that their product will be no better in itself than other honey, and will face stiff competition from the supermarkets, so that the **BRAND NAME** and **PACKAGING** will be vitally important in persuading consumers to buy. They have chosen Honeywell as their brand name and are now working on the packaging of their product, by considering the variety of shapes and sizes which could be used for the jar.

Teresa has made a few rough sketches. They all think that the rounded glass jar as shown here (in the middle), has a comforting appearance and would be an elegant addition to the dining-room tables of their target consumers.

  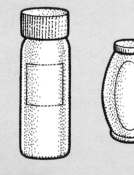 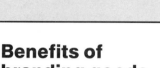

Benefits of branding goods

A brand name is sometimes the name of a firm, such as Black and Decker, but it is usually an invented name, such as Kit-Kat or Weetabix.

More and more goods are now being sold under brand names. Big manufacturers have found that a brand name helps to sell their products. Instead of asking for detergent, shoppers will ask for Persil; instead of asking for tonic water, they will ask for 'you know who', as the television advertisements say. This **DIFFERENTIATION** helps manufacturers to keep or increase their share of the market, or to break into a new one.

There are many other advantages for manufacturers.

● They can advertise their goods nationally, knowing that they are promoting only their own products; Heinz beans, for instance, and not some other make.

● They receive larger orders from retailers, as a big advertising campaign increases consumer demand for the product.

● The name helps to create brand loyalty among consumers, who will go on buying the same brand of goods year after year.

S T U D Y P O I N T S

1 Which of the jars above do you think would appeal most to the target consumers? State your reasons.

2 Think of another shape for the jar. Draw it.

3 What colour do you think the cap should be?

4 Suggest a suitable slogan to go on the jar's label.

5 Can you think why they would be unable to use Honeywell as a brand name? Suggest another name instead.

6 Design a label, including both the brand name and the slogan.

7 Could the container be made of some other material than glass? What would be the advantages and disadvantages of using the other material?

8 In your view, what kind of jar would be most suitable for a mass market? Give your reasons.

9 Why do you think an increasing number of goods are sold under brand names?

Retailers also benefit because national advertising creates a big demand for the goods. Goods which are all of the same size and packed in the same way are easy to handle and to display. On the other hand, a retailer may have to stock a large range of brands if he is to please all his customers – that is, other makes of baked beans, not just Heinz.

Goods sold under a brand name are usually of the same quality, which is an advantage for consumers, who then know what they are getting.

Branding is also used increasingly for consumer durables, i.e. goods which last longer than a few days, such as electrical power tools, furniture and cars. It is less easy to introduce branding in some fields, such as fresh vegetables or meat and poultry, because here it is more difficult to keep the same quality and packaging – though there are some examples, like Matthews turkeys, with the slogan, 'They're bootiful'.

Own-brand products

Branding has been so successful that many of the big high street stores, like Sainsbury, Boots and Marks and Spencer, have got into the act by selling their own-brand products. These goods are usually made by outside manufacturers but sold under the firm's own name. There has been an enormous growth in own-brand goods. They now account for about 20 per cent of the total retail sales of £90 billion and about a third of all sales in supermarkets.

It is never easy to find a suitable brand name. Marketing men and women often spend weeks discussing before deciding on their choice. The name should be short, descriptive, easy to pronounce, and appeal to the target consumers. Legally, a name

must not be the same as one which is already registered in the country or countries where a product is to be sold. In view of this, would you make any change to the name you chose for the honey?

Purposes of packaging

The right packaging is just as difficult to design. It must provide:

- effective protection for the goods
- ease of use
- consumer appeal
- promotional possibilities
- ease of transport and display.

As we have seen in the Study Points, packaging involves three main elements: the choice of material; size and shape; and surface design, including the label. In addition, the label must provide space for any notices legally required under the Trade Descriptions Acts [see Unit 77] and other regulations, such as EC rules on food additives.

Costs and competition

Although branding and packaging produce benefits, some economists argue that they also have harmful effects. The enormous costs of advertising branded goods may prevent a small firm from entering the market, even though its product may

be better.

No brand name can provide a manufacturer with complete protection against market forces. If the quality of a manufacturer's goods declines, or fashions change so that they lose their popularity, sales will fall. Consumers always have the final word. If they don't like a product, they won't buy it, whether it is branded or not. This can be clearly seen in the food trade, where the failure rate among new branded products is around 40 per cent in the first five years.

BUSINESS TECHNIQUES

Brand names

A thesaurus can be useful for inventing brand names. Look up a word which describes a product, and suitable brand names can be chosen from the list of words with the same meaning. Find a suitable name for a lipstick, a pop group, a furniture polish.

CHECKPOINTS

1. Give six examples of brand names.
2. Why are brand names used?
3. What are the main purposes of packaging?
4. Why do you think some supermarkets have introduced unbranded goods?
5. What would be the main effects on businesses and the economy if brand names were abolished?

KEY TERMS

BRAND NAME A registered name for a product, which can be used only by the manufacturer, wholesaler or retailer.

PACKAGING The physical container or wrapping of a product which is also used for promotion and selling appeal.

DIFFERENTIATION The way a producer makes his or her goods different from similar products, e.g. by using a brand name.

Advertising and Publicity

UK market size guide, 1984 FIG 35.1

Product group	Number of manufacturers	£ million spent
1 Homogenised baby foods	3	43
2 Detergent powders for domestic use	10	312
3 Toothpastes and powders	13	72
4 Potato crisps and snack products	11	351
5 Tablet soaps for domestic use	16	120
6 First-aid dressings	5	40
7 Tights and pantihose	34	131

Adapted from: IMAC Research

Advertising expenditure as a % of sales, 1984 FIG 35.2

Product group	%
1 Homogenised baby foods	8.7
2 Detergent powders for domestic use	7.3
3 Toothpastes and powders	18.9
4 Potato crisps and snack products	5.5
5 Tablet soaps for domestic use	11.8
6 First-aid dressings	9.3
7 Tights and pantihose	1.8

Adapted from: Advertising Association

Advertising expenditure by medium, 1986

Medium	£ million
Press	3136
TV	1675
Poster and transport	196
Cinema	19
Radio	91
Total	5117

Source: Advertising Association

FIG 35.3

‘Advertisements are messages, paid for by those who send them, intended to inform or influence people who receive them.’

Source: The Advertising Association

Cost of advertising

Advertising is big business. The total amount spent on advertising in 1986 was £5,117 million, an all-time record. That represents 1.35 per cent of the gross national product.

Advertisements are not just used for selling goods or services. The purpose may be to give information or influence opinion. Suggest ways in which the DSS, a political party and a charity organisation might use a non-sales advertisement.

With a few exceptions, anyone can advertise what they have to sell. If you wanted to sell your bike you could put a card in a newsagent's shop window for about 30p or, for a few pounds, a **CLASSIFIED ADVERTISEMENT** in the local

S T U D Y P O I N T S

1 How much, on average, would each manufacturer in the seven product groups in Figures 35.1 and 35.2 spend on advertising?

2 Which product group spends a) the most and b) the least on advertising as a percentage of sales? Suggest reasons for the difference.

3 Look at Figure 35.3. What percentage of the total is spent in the five branches of the media?

4 Why is the name 'Golden Wonder' given such an important position in the prize-winning advertisement on the right?

5 If you had a £1 million advertising budget for the Golden Wonder advertisement, what percentage would you spend in each of the five branches of the media? Explain your reasons.

6 Why do you think this advertisement was awarded a first prize?

Potted for you by Golden Wonder

Source: J Walter Thompson

The Institute of Practitioners in Advertising awarded first prize in the consumer goods class 1986 to this advertisement. It was created by the advertising agency J. Walter Thompson to increase sales again in what had been a declining market. The new campaign was designed to 're-excite remaining buyers', and to place the range of snacks with 'pots of taste, pots of warmth, pots of satisfaction – even pots of fun'.

newspaper. A campaign to advertise a newly opened shop, using **DISPLAY ADVERTISEMENTS** in the local press and a few short 'spot' advertisements on regional TV, need cost no more than £3,000.

Most advertising campaigns, however, cost much more than that. A national advertising campaign with TV 'spots' in peak viewing time and big display advertisements in the daily newspapers would cost at least £1 million. In 1986, the top advertiser was Unilever and its various subsidiary companies. They spent over £100 million.

Skills

Advertising is highly skilled and involves the work of so many different specialists that it would be uneconomic for even the biggest firm to have its own staff. So the firm decides how much it can spend – its advertising budget – and then chooses an independent **ADVERTISING AGENCY** to advertise the product. The chosen agency appoints an account executive to be in charge of the campaign.

After discussing the campaign with the client the agency does its own market research (see Unit 31). Then it puts forward its ideas and rough sketches for the whole campaign, listing which media it will use – TV, newspaper, radio, etc. Once the client-firm has approved the plan, the agency instructs its various departments to go ahead with the detailed work.

● The media department buys TV and radio time, and space in newspapers and magazines.

● The creative department takes care of the advertisements themselves. A copy writer writes the text. The artwork is done by a visualiser (who does the general present-ation), an artist (who does the drawing), and a layout person (who does the detailed design).

● The art buying department gets a photographer and film production company to make the TV commer-cials.

Throughout the campaign, market research will be used to check on its effectiveness. The final test is to compare the sales figures before and after the campaign.

Public relations

Bob Geldof's campaign for the starving people of Ethiopia was so effective because it used all the resources of modern pubicity and promotion. As well as the pop concerts, sponsored runs, t-shirts and TV satellite links, the campaign had plenty of free publicity because Geldof's visits to Ethiopia and his views were widely covered in the media. It was a most successful **PUBLIC RELATIONS (PR)** exercise for a worth-while cause.

The main difference between advertising and public relations is cost. Advertising has to be paid for but PR gets free publicity. Most firms and organisations – unless they are tiny – have their own PR department or employ an outside consultant. One of the main tasks is sending out press releases to the media – information about a new product, an appeal for funds, or just a story about something

a famous person is doing – in the hope that it will be printed or broadcast free of charge.

Although PR methods are different, it shares the same aim as advertising: to persuade people to look and think about what they see.

BUSINESS TECHNIQUES

Advertising media

Type	Number
National daily paper	11
National Sunday papers	9
Regional morning papers	18
Regional evening papers	73
Regional Sunday papers	6
Local weekly papers	860
Free newspapers	1,000s
Magazines	2,300
Trade, technical magazines	5,500
Independent television	17
Independent radio	46
Cinema (screens)	1,250
Street poster sites	170,000

There are many other outdoor advertising sites (including advertisements on buses and taxis, at railway and bus stations, at sporting events).

Source: Advertising Association

Business persons have to know where products can be advertised. Look at the table above. What is the total number of: a) regional newspapers, b) magazines, c) poster sites, d) independent radio and TV stations?

KEY TERMS

CLASSIFIED ADVERTISEMENT An advertisement in small type which is charged according to the number of lines.

DISPLAY ADVERTISEMENT A larger advertisement, which is ruled off from others, and charged according to the number of single column centimetres or by the proportion of a page it takes up.

ADVERTISING AGENCY A firm which produces advertisements for other firms or organisations. There are 300 advertising agencies with annual turnovers of more than £1 million.

PUBLIC RELATIONS (PR) Distributing information about a firm or organisation with the aim of improving its public image.

CHECKPOINTS

1 How much was spent on advertising in 1986?
2 What is the final test of an advertisement?
3 Name three kinds of people who work in advertising agencies and state the work each one does.
4 What are the three main aims of advertisements? Give one example of each kind.
5 How does advertising differ from public relations?

Selling

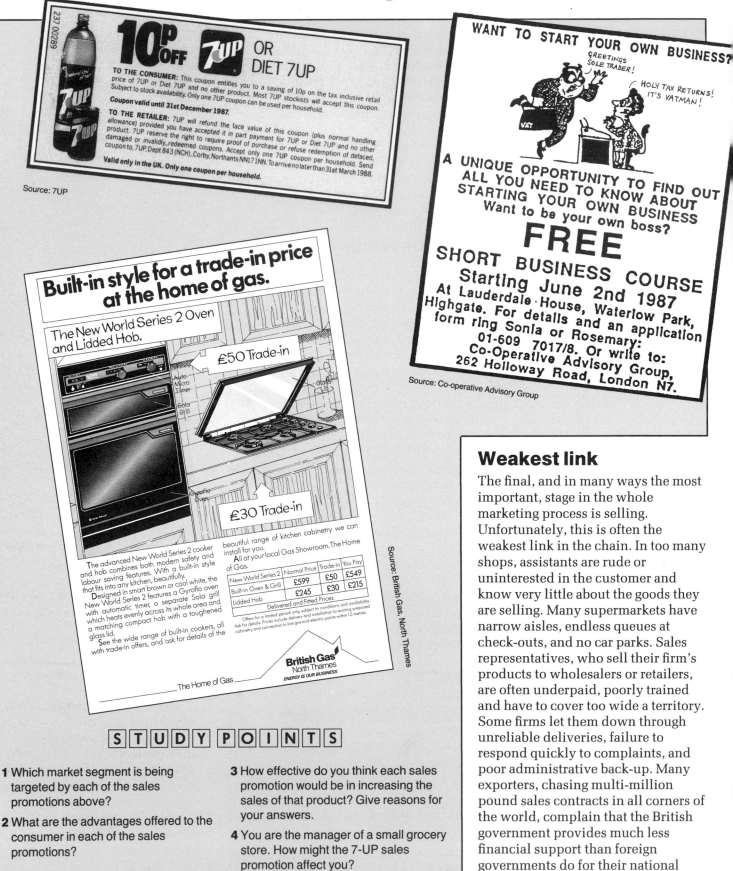

TO THE CONSUMER: This coupon entitles you to a saving of 10p on the tax inclusive retail price of 7UP or Diet 7UP and no other product. Most 7UP stockists will accept this coupon. Subject to stock availability. Only one 7UP coupon can be used per household.

Coupon valid until 31st December 1987.

TO THE RETAILER: 7UP will refund the face value of this coupon (plus normal handling allowance) provided you have accepted it in part payment for 7UP or Diet 7UP and no other product. 7UP reserve the right to require proof of purchase or refuse redemption of defaced, damaged or invalidly redeemed coupons. Accept only one 7UP coupon per household. Send coupon to, 7UP, Dept 843 (NCH), Corby, Northants NN17 1NN. To arrive no later than 31st March 1988.

Valid only in the UK. Only one coupon per household.

237 00289

Source: 7UP

10P OFF 7UP OR DIET 7UP

WANT TO START YOUR OWN BUSINESS?

GREETINGS SOLE TRADER!

HOLY TAX RETURNS! IT'S VATMAN!

A UNIQUE OPPORTUNITY TO FIND OUT ALL YOU NEED TO KNOW ABOUT STARTING YOUR OWN BUSINESS

Want to be your own boss?

FREE

SHORT BUSINESS COURSE Starting June 2nd 1987

At Lauderdale House, Waterlow Park, Highgate. For details and an application form ring Sonia or Rosemary: 01-609 7017/8. Or write to: Co-Operative Advisory Group, 262 Holloway Road, London N7.

Source: Co-operative Advisory Group

Built-in style for a trade-in price at the home of gas.

The New World Series 2 Oven and Lidded Hob.

Auto Micro Timer

£50 Trade-in

Sola Grill

Glass Lid.

Gyroflo Oven

£30 Trade-in

The advanced New World Series 2 cooker and hob combines both modern safety and labour saving features. With a built-in style that fits into any kitchen, beautifully.

Designed in smart brown or cool white, the New World Series 2 features a Gyroflo oven with automatic timer, a separate Sola grill which heats evenly across its whole area and a matching compact hob with a toughened glass lid.

See the wide range of built-in cookers, all with trade-in offers, and ask for details of the beautiful range of kitchen cabinetry we can install for you.

All at your local Gas Showroom. The Home of Gas.

New World Series 2	Normal Price	Trade-in	You Pay
Built-in Oven & Grill	£599	£50	£549
Lidded Hob	£245	£30	£215
Delivered and Fitted Prices			

Offers for a limited period only, subject to conditions and availability. Ask for details. Prices include delivery and installation to existing prepared cabinetry and connection to live gas and electric points within 1.5 metres.

British Gas North Thames ENERGY IS OUR BUSINESS

The Home of Gas

Source: British Gas, North Thames

STUDY POINTS

1 Which market segment is being targeted by each of the sales promotions above?

2 What are the advantages offered to the consumer in each of the sales promotions?

3 How effective do you think each sales promotion would be in increasing the sales of that product? Give reasons for your answers.

4 You are the manager of a small grocery store. How might the 7-UP sales promotion affect you?

Weakest link

The final, and in many ways the most important, stage in the whole marketing process is selling. Unfortunately, this is often the weakest link in the chain. In too many shops, assistants are rude or uninterested in the customer and know very little about the goods they are selling. Many supermarkets have narrow aisles, endless queues at check-outs, and no car parks. Sales representatives, who sell their firm's products to wholesalers or retailers, are often underpaid, poorly trained and have to cover too wide a territory. Some firms let them down through unreliable deliveries, failure to respond quickly to complaints, and poor administrative back-up. Many exporters, chasing multi-million pound sales contracts in all corners of the world, complain that the British government provides much less financial support than foreign governments do for their national firms [see Units 68 and 70].

Short-term boost

In the long term, sales can be increased only by efficient marketing, management and sales planning. In the short term, however, sales can often be boosted by **SALES PROMOTIONS**. Some of the most common are:

- *Free gifts*. Favourites of garages and chemists. Customers collect enough tokens and get a gardening tool, a wine glass, etc; or buy two bars of soap and get another one free.

- *Competitions*. Often used by newspapers, which offer cash or other prizes. They range from *Bingo* in the *Mirror* to *Portfolio* in *The Times*.

- *Special offers*. Used by many manufacturers. They range from 3p off a bar of chocolate to £50 trade-in on your old cooker.

- *Discount vouchers*. Popular for foods and cleaning materials. Vouchers give a few pence off your next jar of instant coffee or packet of detergent.

- *Better value offers*. Widely used. Manufacturers produce bigger bars of chocolate for the same price, or improved quality detergent.

- *Special purchase offers*. Widely used. The customer buys six packets of an item and can send for a cookery book at a reduced price.

- *PR promotions*. Occasionally used. For each product the customer buys the firm will donate money to a charity.

Some sales promotions can produce an enormous increase in sales. Persil ran one of the most successful in the eighties – a tie-in scheme with British Rail for cheap rail tickets. In fact, some promotions have been so popular that the supplier of the free gifts cannot keep up with demand. Many promotions, however, produce only a brief increase in sales, as afterwards consumers switch to any other brand which introduces an attractive offer.

POINT-OF-SALE MATERIAL may also help to increase sales. Examples of this include posters; showcards; display stands and cases; dump bins (wire or plastic containers filled with one brand of goods); wire racks (like those at checkouts full of chocolate for impulse buyers); illuminated displays; pavement models (such as a fisherman outside a fish shop); and many more. Anything, in other words, which will attract consumers' attention to the goods or the firm.

Direct marketing

Both sales promotions and point-of-sale material are designed to set-up direct links with the consumer. **DIRECT MARKETING** goes one step further. It cuts out the shop altogether and tries to build a personal, long-term link with targeted consumers through:

- direct mail (personalised letters to chosen consumers)

- mail-order catalogues

- press advertisements or magazine inserts with reply coupons

- telephone calls

- electronic shopping.

It is estimated that over £10 billion of sales are now made through direct marketing. Many people believe that direct marketing will increase its share enormously in the next ten years. One of its greatest advantages is that money spent on selling can be related directly to individual sales.

If a firm sends out a new direct mail letter it can see almost immediately the effect it has on sales.

Value added tax (VAT)

VAT is tax which is charged on most goods and services. Any discounts are taken off before VAT is added, for example:

	£
List price	100.00
Less: trade discount 10%	10.00
	90.00
Plus VAT at 15%	13.50
Total price	103.50

What is the total selling price, after trade discount at 10% and VAT at 15%, when the list price is a) £3,126, b) £34.76?

C H E C K P O I N T S

1 What is a) the main advantage and b) the main disadvantage of sales promotions?

2 What is direct marketing? Suggest why many people believe this is a growth area.

3 Give six examples from your own observation of point-of-sale material.

4 Give one example, which you have seen yourself, of each of the seven kinds of sales promotions mentioned in the text.

5 State whether the following are sales promotions or point-of-sale material:
   a) a supermarket plastic shopping bag with the firm's name on it
   b) a booklet of discount offers given out free at a checkout
   c) a drip mat in a hamburger bar, with details of a competition on it
   d) a free ballpoint pen sent to customers through the post.

K E Y   T E R M S

SALES PROMOTIONS Schemes which offer customers a special bargain in the hope of increasing sales.

POINT-OF-SALE MATERIAL Physical objects designed to draw consumer's attention to a product or a firm.

DIRECT MARKETING Selling direct to consumers on an individual level either through the post or some other means.

Life Cycles

STUDY POINTS

Look up the history of each of the four items above in an encyclopaedia or a reference book. Find out from retailers or from manufacturers (by using the Yellow Pages) what is happening to the sales of each item now – are they falling, rising or more or less stable? Then go on to the following questions.

1 Which of the items above has the longest history? What might be the reasons for this?

2 Have there been any peaks of popularity with any of the items? If so, give dates.

3 What do you think will happen to sales of each in the future? State your reasons. Will any of them disappear from the market altogether? If so, when, in your view, will that happen?

4 For each of the items draw a line graph, like those on the opposite page, for the **PRODUCT LIFE CYCLE**, using your own data and predictions. Do not put any figures on the vertical sales axis, but include dates in the horizontal time axis.

Risks

All good things come to an end, but some products reach that point much more quickly than others. However brilliant the advertising may be, however efficient the marketing, a product that consumers don't want, or don't like, will never sell.

Sinclair C5 electric vehicle

Look at Sir Clive Sinclair's battery driven three-wheeled vehicle, which was introduced in 1985. It had many new and interesting features. The body was built from two of the largest plastic mouldings ever made. It was cleverly designed. Although it looked cramped, it was comfortable and easy to drive. There were other points in its favour. New traffic regulations, introduced two years before, meant that it could be driven by anyone over 14, without road tax, insurance or a driving licence. It was also cheap – only £399, including VAT.

Yet it was a flop. Looking back, it is easy to see the reason. People just didn't want to drive at 15 mph in such an exposed vehicle with other traffic blowing exhaust fumes in their face. It was not only Sir Clive who thought it would be a success: some people said it would reshape the market for personal transport.

In business, there are many similar failures. Even with the best market research, it is not always possible to predict whether people will like a new product.

Changing tastes

It is difficult to forecast how long the public will go on liking a product. Public tastes change very quickly. Even if a product is successful at first, this may not last for very long, as rival products may begin flooding the market or another manufacturer may produce a more advanced product.

Each product has its own life cycle. Some, like packaged foods, may last only a few months; others, like some games and toys, may last a year or so. Some branded goods go on year after year; while a few primary products, such as salt, go on for centuries.

Sales patterns

The traditional **PRODUCT LIFE CYCLE** has five main phases: introduction, growth, maturity, saturation and decline. Economists usually show a rounded curve like that in Figure 37.1 for the life cycle; but in the real world there are very few example of this kind. What actually happens is shown in the other three graphs.

Product life cycle

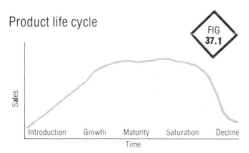

The traditional economic view of a product's rise and fall which is rarely found in the real world.

In Figure 37.2, the product follows the traditional pattern of increasing sales until maturity is reached. When sales begin to fall at saturation, the marketing department starts to fight

back. Sales promotions, special offers, changes in design may all be used to prolong the product's life. Various models of motor cars often have a life cycle of this kind.

Marketing life cycle

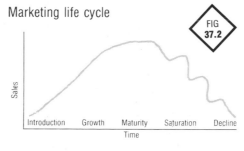

Marketing techniques such as sales promotions or advertising can often delay a product's decline after saturation point has been reached, e.g. certain kinds of car.

Some branded goods defy all the laws and continue to show an upwards sales trend long after maturity, saturation and decline would normally have been reached. For example Rolls-Royce cars, which have such a reputation for excellence that new customers are coming forward all the time. Their life cycle is illustrated in Figure 37.3. Although the brand name remains the same, the product itself may be continuously changing to take advantage of all the latest improvements and developments in technology.

Brand life cycle

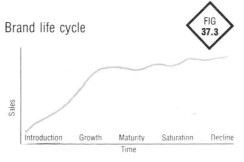

Some branded products have a continuous rise in sales through brand loyalty and clever marketing, e.g. Rolls-Royce cars.

Very often the product life cycle looks like that in Figure 37.4. The product may have been an instant failure. It may have been quickly outshone by rival products which were rushed on to the market. Or it may simply have been ahead of its time, the public not being ready for it – just yet.

Aborted life cycle

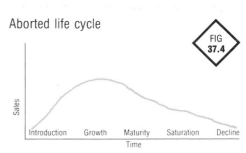

The fate of products which do not appeal to consumers, e.g. the Sinclair vehicle.

The firm will have to go back to the beginning again. A new product must be developed and marketed and before that reaches its decline yet another product must be underway. In business, this chain of events is repeated endlessly.

Learning from the past

Fashions often repeat themselves. Look at some old clothes, toys, books or other goods and decide which might be revived in the future.

CHECKPOINTS

1 What are the five phases in a traditional product life cycle?
2 Why is the sales pattern shown in Figure 37.1 rarely found in the real business world?
3 What kinds of marketing might be used to reverse the decline in sales seen in Figure 37.2?
4 Why do you think that Figure 37.3 shows a continuous upwards trend?
5 Find two examples of products which might have had a life cycle like the one shown in Figure 37.4. What could have been done to reverse the pattern?
6 If you had been the Sinclair marketing manager, suggest what other market segment you could have found for the car. Write a report outlining your proposals for capturing this market segment.

Activities

■ Review points

1 What is differentiation? Why is it important?

2 What are the five main stages in a product life cycle? Give two ways in which marketing might be able to halt decline.

3 What is the difference between a classified and a display advertisement?

4 Give three examples of a) point-of-sale material and b) sales promotions schemes.

5 How does public relations differ from advertising?

6 What is the meaning of a price plateau? Who would be likely to use a penetration price?

■ Essay questions

1 Describe the various methods by which the life cycle of a product might be extended.

2 Jill is opening a boutique in a small country town. She has asked you to give her some advice – for a fee – about:
   a) publicity in local newspapers
   b) promotional events on the opening day
   c) advertising on local radio and TV stations.
   Write a report giving your advice.

■ Coursework

(Before you start this task, you should ask to speak to the store managers. Tell them what you want to do and ask for their permission.)

You are employed by a supermarket. The manager has asked you to carry out a check on the prices charged for some manufacturer-branded goods in other stores. Go to a supermarket and find out the prices of two loss-leaders, two cleaning materials, and two luxury branded food items. Note the brand names, weights and prices. Go to one or more other stores and check their prices for the same, or similar goods. Compare the prices and analyse what these figures tell you about the pricing policies of the stores. Repeat the price check on the same goods at 3-monthly intervals over a year. Write a report, analysing the prices over the whole period, indicating what changes there have been in pricing and policy.

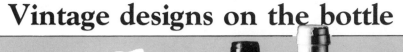

Vintage designs on the bottle

Asda wines carry the Asda name discreetly at the bottom of the label

MARY LEWIS, director at Lewis Moberly, has done much of the wines and spirits packaging design for Tesco and is now working her way through the Asda list. She has come up with a range of labels that combine modern illustrations with classic lettering. The result is sophisticated labels good enough to steam off the bottle and frame on the wall.

And the branding is deliberately not too obvious—Asda appears in tiny letters at the base of the label. Director Robert Moberly says: "It's not the name that's being promoted, but the image. Asda sees its wine and spirits as a way of making a good name for the store."

The supermarkets may have gone for an up-market look, but the price is usually low. What the brand-name products need to do now is put the value back into the market.

This is a view shared by Dennis Rudkin, marketing director of Peter Dominic: "If we try to compete with the supermarkets on price, we'll lose." He believes that the local off-licence offers the consumer a service with which the supermarkets cannot compete: "We're open much longer hours, we carry a wider range, train our staff to know about the products, and offer a pleasant environment in which to shop."

Adpated from: *Marketing*, 14 May 1987

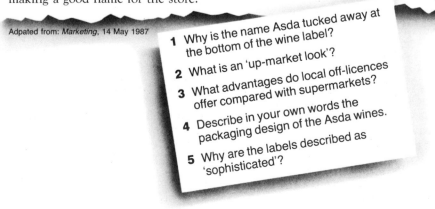

1 Why is the name Asda tucked away at the bottom of the wine label?

2 What is an 'up-market look'?

3 What advantages do local off-licences offer compared with supermarkets?

4 Describe in your own words the packaging design of the Asda wines.

5 Why are the labels described as 'sophisticated'?

Source: J Sainsbury plc

Source: Asda

1 Which pre-Christmas advertisement gives more information?

2 Which advertisement, in your opinion, is most likely to attract the attention of the reader? Give your reasons.

3 What is your opinion of the main heading, the design and the lay-out of each advertisement? Are there any changes you would make?

4 Write and design a pre-Christmas advertisement for the food section of an up-market store.

■ Groupwork

A record company has asked your advertising agency to promote a pop singer who has not yet gained the fame he or she deserves.

- Divide into groups of five and appoint one person as the account executive, who will be in charge of the whole campaign. Choose a pop singer. Your first objectives will be to find out as many facts about the singer as possible and to discover what people think of him or her.
- Start by getting some basic factual information about the singer. Obtain this information individually, bring it back to your group and make up a basic factual sheet as a group.
- Now you will need to do some market research to find out what consumers think. Decide as a group on the quota sample of people you are going to interview. Draw up a suitable questionnaire as a group.

You will need to know whether they have heard of the singer; where and how they first heard of him or her; if they buy the records; where they buy them; how often they listen to them, etc. You will also need to discover what they particularly like about the records; whether they would go to a concert and how much they would pay for a seat; and, if they used to buy the records but no longer do so, why they have stopped.

- Interview individually as many people in the quota as possible and bring back your reports to the group. Study all the results and analyse them. From this, you will be able to decide on your market segment and how you are going to appeal to it.
- Draw up a plan for the advertising campaign, indicating your target segment, giving as much detail as possible. The plan should also show the ways in which you will appeal to that segment and which

branches of the media, including a teenage magazine, you will use.

- The account executive should now discuss the plan with the client-firm (your teacher). The firm will almost certainly want some changes to be made. It always has the last word, as it is paying for the campaign.
- The account executive should now report back to the group. Make any necessary changes and write out a new plan.
- Decide which members of the group are to be the copywriter, the artist, the visualiser, the layout person, and arrange how the work is to be shared out between them.
- Produce a rough version of a full-page advertisement for the teenage magazine.

When it is complete, the account executive should present the group's advertisement to the client-firm for approval.

Distribution

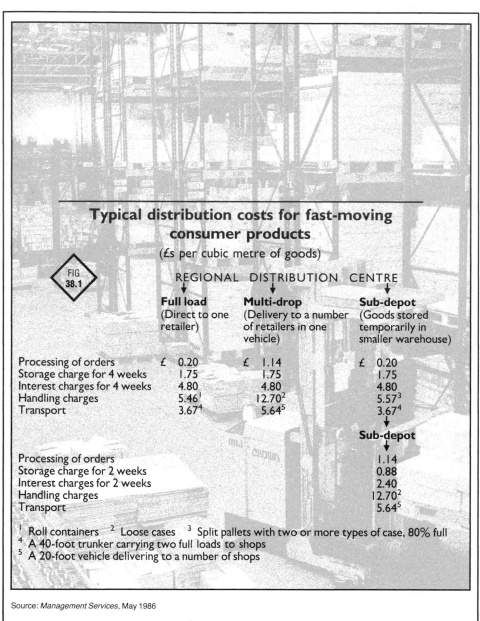

Typical distribution costs for fast-moving consumer products
(£s per cubic metre of goods)

FIG 38.1

	REGIONAL DISTRIBUTION CENTRE		
	Full load (Direct to one retailer)	**Multi-drop** (Delivery to a number of retailers in one vehicle)	**Sub-depot** (Goods stored temporarily in smaller warehouse)
Processing of orders	£ 0.20	£ 1.14	£ 0.20
Storage charge for 4 weeks	1.75	1.75	1.75
Interest charges for 4 weeks	4.80	4.80	4.80
Handling charges	5.46[1]	12.70[2]	5.57[3]
Transport	3.67[4]	5.64[5]	3.67[4]

			Sub-depot
Processing of orders			1.14
Storage charge for 2 weeks			0.88
Interest charges for 2 weeks			2.40
Handling charges			12.70[2]
Transport			5.64[5]

[1] Roll containers   [2] Loose cases   [3] Split pallets with two or more types of case, 80% full
[4] A 40-foot trunker carrying two full loads to shops
[5] A 20-foot vehicle delivering to a number of shops

Source: *Management Services*, May 1986

STUDY POINTS

(Study the Key Terms before you answer these questions)

1 What is a **MULTI-DROP**?

2 Why does a multi-drop cost more than a full load?

3 What would be the total distribution cost per cubic metre of goods from a **REGIONAL DISTRIBUTION CENTRE (RDC)**,
a) for a full lorry load to one retailer
b) for a mixture of goods to a number of shops
c) for a mixture of goods which had previously been stored in a smaller warehouse or sub-depot?

4 What is a **HANDLING CHARGE**? What percentage does it form of the total costs for each of the four journeys? Why, in your view, is it the most expensive item?

5 In what kind of area might a regional distribution centre set up a **SUB-DEPOT**? What would be the effect on prices in the shops? Where could a retailer obtain his goods instead?

Warehousing employs at least one and a quarter million people — and employment has been rising in recent years.

Source: *British Business*, 16 January 1987

Major industry

In the last few years there has been a major change in the way goods are distributed. Distribution has become such a highly-skilled and expensive business that it is now a major industry in its own right. Huge warehouses of a quarter of a million square feet are equipped with the latest computers and automated handling devices.

Only twenty years ago, about three-quarters of goods were delivered to wholesalers or retailers in the manufacturers' own transport. Dozens of lorries would deliver different kinds of goods to a big high-street store in a single day. From the retailer's point of view it would have been far more convenient and cost-effective if all the manufacturers' goods could have been delivered at the same time.

The big high-street retailers have now become so powerful that they can make the rules. Some of them decided to set up their own regional distribution centres to serve all their stores in the area. Each store could then be supplied with all it needed for that particular day.

It made more sense for retailers to keep their own capital for improving and developing their stores, or mainstream business, and to let a specialist firm do this new kind of distribution work for them.

Distribution specialists

These specialist firms provide a range of distribution services for an increasing number of high-street stores and manufacturers of consumer goods. They run the warehouse, employ the drivers and provide vans and lorries with the retailer's or manufacturer's own distinctive colours, or liveries.

The National Freight Consortium's Distribution Group handles goods for many of the best-known brand names, including Sainsbury's, Mars, Black and Decker, Shell, Esso and many more. One of its divisions has 600 vehicles specialising in high street distribution. It also provides a **BREAK BULK**, stockholding and conventional warehousing service. There are other divisions specialising in the distribution of confectionery; frozen food and ice-cream; and fragile and high value goods, such as china, glass and photographic equipment.

Retailers need these more efficient methods of distribution if they are to keep prices down; distribution accounts for between 8 per cent and 25 per cent of the shelf price of consumer goods. Bulk deliveries cost less as handling charges are reduced. Quicker distribution also helps to reduce costs in another way. Manufacturers and retailers borrow money to finance their operations. They have to pay interest on these loans. The longer their stock, or **INVENTORY**, remains unsold in the factory, warehouse or shop, the more interest they are paying.

Channels of distribution

This new **CHANNEL OF DISTRIBUTION** is shown as type 3 in Figure 38.2. Many of the older methods of distribution still survive. Look at Figure 38.2

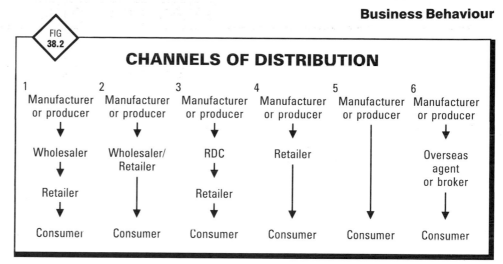

FIG 38.2

CHANNELS OF DISTRIBUTION

1	2	3	4	5	6
Manufacturer or producer	Manufacturer or producer	Manufacturer or producer	Manufacturer or producer	Manufacturer or producer	Manufacturer or producer
↓	↓	↓	↓	↓	↓
Wholesaler	Wholesaler/ Retailer	RDC	Retailer		Overseas agent or broker
↓	↓	↓	↓	↓	↓
Retailer		Retailer			
↓		↓			
Consumer	Consumer	Consumer	Consumer	Consumer	Consumer

again. Examples of the other channels are:

- Type 1 – a screw manufacturer sells his products to a wholesaler, who breaks bulk and sells them in smaller quantities to retailers.

- Type 2 – a car manufacturer sells to a main distributor, who acts both as a wholesaler, by selling to smaller garages, and as a retailer, by selling direct to individual customers.

- Type 4 – manufacturers of consumer durables, such as furniture, distribute direct to retailers.

- Type 5 – corner-shop bakers make their bread on the premises and sell it to consumers. Some farmers sell produce direct to 'pick-your-own' customers.

- Type 6 – publishers employ agents to handle their books in foreign

countries where sales are not high enough to make setting up their own company worthwhile.

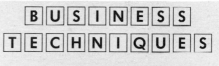

BUSINESS TECHNIQUES

Stock control

Firms keep information about each item of stock on a stock card or a computer. It is necessary to decide:

a) the *maximum* quantity of stock which can be held (based on the total storage space, likely sales etc); and

b) the *minimum* amount to which stock should be allowed to fall, so that the firm does not run out of goods.

Stock must be re-ordered before the minimum level is reached to allow time for delivery.

If a garden centre can hold a maximum stock of 200 Christmas roses and the minimum stock is 40, how many would they order if the current stock was 55?

KEY TERMS

MULTI-DROP Delivering goods to a number of shops by one vehicle.

REGIONAL DISTRIBUTION CENTRE (RDC) A large warehouse, with the latest computers and handling equipment, which distributes goods to all the branches of a retail chain in one region.

HANDLING CHARGE The cost of loading and unloading goods on vehicles.

SUB-DEPOT A small warehouse used to store goods for local delivery in country areas.

BREAK BULK The repacking of goods which have been bought in bulk, or very large quantities, into smaller packages for re-sale to small retailers. Cash-and-carry warehouses often do this.

INVENTORY The stock of either raw materials or finished goods held by a firm.

CHANNEL OF DISTRIBUTION The method by which products are distributed from the producer to the consumer.

CHECKPOINTS

1 Give an example of one of the six main channels of distribution.
2 What is breaking bulk? Give two examples of when it might be used.
3 What is a regional distribution centre? Why were they set up?
4 Why do some high street retailers use specialist distribution firms?

Transport

These heavy-duty six-wheeled tippers were matched against each other on a Northern road circuit. The route crossed Manchester and the area around it from Whaley Bridge to Worsley; crossed the Peak District from Ashbourne to Whaley Bridge, including the climb up the twisty Ashbourne Hill with its one in seven gradient; and followed the motorway from Haydock to Cannock.

Iveco Ford Cargo 24.24

Standard chassis price	£36,405	
Body price	£ 4,783	
Vehicle weight as tested	9.52 tons	
Payload carried on test	14.34 tons	

	miles per gallon (mpg)	miles per hour (mph)
Motorway	9.88	54.00
Hills	7.76	30.29
Main road	12.77	43.35
Route overall	9.03	38.87

Leyland Daf Constructor 6 24.23

Standard chassis price	£36,550	
Body price	£ 5,460	
Vehicle weight as tested	8.02 tons	
Payload carried on test	15.93 tons	

	miles per gallon (mpg)	miles per hour (mph)
Motorway	8.18	54.10
Hills	7.87	32.29
Main road	10.47	41.90
Route overall	8.35	39.91

Source: *Truck*, May 1987 (Extracts)

STUDY POINTS

1 What are the main uses of vehicles of this type?

2 What is the difference in the total price of each vehicle?

3 Which vehicle is more economical in fuel overall?

4 If each vehicle travelled 750 miles per week on routes like the test route, and fuel cost £1.60 a gallon, which would have the lower fuel costs? What would be the annual amount saved compared to the other vehicle?

5 If you were starting your own haulage or transport business, which vehicle would you buy? What elements in the above data would have most influence on your decision? Explain the reasons for your choice.

6 Imagine you are starting your own business as
a) a florist
b) a dress manufacturer
c) a haulier of coal from mines to power stations
d) an exporter of heavy machinery to the Continent.
Which of the vehicles shown in this Unit would you choose?

Road transport

The great advantage of road transport is its flexibility. Different shapes and sizes of vans and lorries (up to 38 tonnes) are available to meet all kinds of needs. Door-to-door deliveries can be made in all areas of the country, so that expensive **DOUBLE HANDLING** is avoided. Roll-on roll-off (known as 'ro-ro') ferries now make it possible for lorries to transport goods to all parts of the Continent without unloading and reloading goods at Channel ports.

Containers have made it much quicker and cheaper to transport goods to all parts of the world. Manufacturers pack their goods in huge metal boxes. These containers are then taken by lorry to a port, where they are loaded on to ships mechanically, with a great saving in time and handling costs.

Modern technology has increased the flexibility of road transport. Computers can be used to map out round-trip and multi-drop routes which will prevent lorries returning to base without a load. Cellular phones [see Unit 55] keep drivers in touch with base so that they can easily be diverted or directed to other jobs.

Lease, hire or buy?

Firms also have a greater choice in the way they can acquire vehicles.

● They can buy their own vehicles for cash or by hire-purchase. A disadvantage is that this ties up capital which could be more profitably spent on the firm's mainstream activities.

● They can lease vehicles – including fleets of company cars – for a fixed term. The hirer pays a regular charge over the period of the lease, which covers the total cost of the vehicle, plus interest. At the end of the period, he receives a percentage of the sale price as a rebate. The disadvantage of the **FIXED TERM LEASE** is that the hirer still has to maintain the vehicle.

This scene shows some of the many different shapes and sizes of vans and lorries available to businesses

- That disadvantage is avoided with **CONTRACT HIRE**. The hirer pays a fixed monthly rental for the use of the vehicle, which is maintained by the contract hire company.

- Vehicles of all kinds can also be rented. This is useful for one-off operations or emergencies – for example, when there is a rush of orders; but it is expensive for longer periods.

Importance of road transport

For all these reasons, road transport has become the undisputed leader in inland transport. In 1985, for example, 1,707 million tonnes of goods were carried in Britain by road, rail, pipeline, coastal shipping and inland waterways. No less than 84 per cent travelled by road. The network of motorways, totalling nearly 1,800 miles, has also been one of the main factors in making transport by road the leading form. In the past, industry huddled around railway stations. Nowadays, nearness to motorways has become one of the most important factors in locating businesses. [See Unit 26]

Other forms of transport

In deciding which method of transport to use, the cost, the type of goods, the urgency, and the distance to be travelled, all have to be taken into account.

Although railways are much less important than they once were, they are still useful for moving bulk freight over long distances. As their fixed costs are high, they are less economic on shorter runs. This is a serious drawback since some 70 per cent of goods transported in Britain are moved less than 30 miles. However, rail still carries 150 million tonnes of freight a year.

Pipelines are used for transporting oil, gas, petro-chemicals and even some solids; but capital costs are high. Inland waterways – canals and rivers – and coastal shipping play only a limited role in British transport, though they are more widely used on the Continent.

Air freight is particularly suitable for long hauls and goods which either don't keep very long, or are needed in a hurry, such as flowers, newspapers, machinery and parts which are wanted urgently, and livestock including day-old chicks, which can survive for up to 36 hours without food.

KEY TERMS

DOUBLE HANDLING Moving goods from one form of transport to another, which greatly increases total costs.

FIXED TERM LEASE A long-term contract which gives a firm full use, but not ownership, of a vehicle (or other property) for a fixed period.

CONTRACT HIRE Long-term leasing of vehicles from a specialist firm, which provides all services, including drivers if required.

BUSINESS TECHNIQUES

Hire or lease?

Choose the vehicle you would need for any business that you would like to set up. Find out from a local garage what it would cost to acquire
a) on hire purchase, and
b) on a fixed term lease.
Calculate which would be better for your business.

CHECKPOINTS

1 What are the main advantages of road transport?
2 What is double handling? What is its main disadvantage?
3 What is a fixed term lease?
4 How does a fixed term lease differ from contract hire? What is the main advantage of contract hire compared to leasing?
5 Name two kinds of goods which would be best suited for transport by rail.
6 What kinds of goods might be transported by plane. What are the main advantages of air freight?

Activities

■ Review points

1 What are the main advantages of air transport?

2 State two drawbacks of using railways for transporting goods. For which kinds of goods is rail most suitable? Give one example.

3 Why is rail freight more economic on longer hauls?

4 What would be the most suitable form of inland transport for long distance haulage of a) supermarket foods, b) ice cream, c) delicate porcelain, d) very large turbines and e) flowers? Give your reasons.

5 How do business persons gain greater freedom by using road transport? If they do gain more freedom, why do so many still use trains or planes for personal travel?

6 What are the main channels of distribution? Why are they important for business?

■ Essay questions

1 What has been the most important change in distribution in recent times? Explain the reasons fully.

2 You are thinking of setting up a courier service for overnight deliveries of urgent packets and parcels from your own area to other parts of the country. Explain, giving reasons for your answers:
   a) What kind of vehicles you would need.
   b) What kind of equipment would be useful.
   c) How you would set about marketing your firm's services in your local area.

Road haulage hit by inefficiency

THE ROAD haulage industry is operating inefficiently and is being affected by high costs which are eating profit margins.

This is the major finding of an ICC Business Ratio Report, 'Road Hauliers' reflecting the industry's bad fortunes.

It comments that: 'Any regular motorway traveller will have noticed the number of empty or part-filled lorries crossing the country – showing how the system used by most haulage firms is not good enough'.

'Running costs are extremely high in this business, and have increased in the three years covered by the Report.'

'Fleet replacement is expensive and, with high rates of interest, borrowing money has become a risky business.'

'Also, poor organisation of routes, and many lorries travelling back to base empty, means the problem is only increasing.'

Average profit margins, says the Report, stood at 3.5 per cent in 1985/86. This was a decline from the better figures of 1984/85 when average profit margins were 4 per cent.

ICC stress that improved profit margins will 'only result from more efficiently controlled fleets'.

'General economic growth in the UK should benefit road hauliers by strengthening the market and helping cash flow.

Source: *Roadway*, June 1987

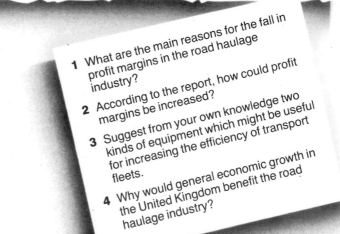

1 What are the main reasons for the fall in profit margins in the road haulage industry?

2 According to the report, how could profit margins be increased?

3 Suggest from your own knowledge two kinds of equipment which might be useful for increasing the efficiency of transport fleets.

4 Why would general economic growth in the United Kingdom benefit the road haulage industry?

Give the driver his due regard

Dear Sir,

What I have to say may be of interest to your Association and to fellow drivers.

I have been employed in the industry since 1953 in various driving jobs and, being a sensible person, approach everyone in a correct manner and appreciate other people's views.

The first point I would like to bring to your notice is the lack of understanding by some individuals and some authorities to the driver, who is just trying to do his job – in particular, shop deliveries.

Years ago most shops had numbers, but very few have them today. So as you can appreciate it is a hazard driving along, trying to find the shop for delivery while watching traffic movements. If I know of a particularly busy street I make a point of phoning the shop to ask for their location or a landmark.

It is fully appreciated that police and traffic wardens have a job to do, yet if it wasn't for the delivery driver the shops would be empty.

My second point relates to overnight vehicles. You will know that it can be difficult to make sure loads are evenly distributed, especially if the

lorry is fully laden (depending on the load carried). An over-loaded vehicle is a serious offence, but not many vehicles have the necessary equipment to make sure a load is easily spread between the wheel axles.

My third and final point relates to multi drop runs and the serious situation with regard to roadside tea-bars.

Some local authorities and some MPs are trying to get rid of all roadside snack bars in the interests of the environment and road safety.

Roadside tea bars provide a necessary service and most I have come across are kept clean and welcome health inspectors any time. As you are aware the commercial driver must by law have a set amount of breaks each day, yet transport cafés have been closed or been taken over.

So what does the genuine lorry driver do? He cannot pull up in a town area where there is a café unless there is enough parking space for his vehicle. I now carry a flask and biscuits, but it's not the same as stopping at a good old warm and friendly teashop.

Source: Letter to the Roadhaulage Association Ltd, *Roadway*, June 1987

1 How long has the writer been employed in road haulage?

2 What would he like shopkeepers to do?

3 How in his view could big lorries with full loads be made safer?

4 Why is it difficult for a lorry driver to have a snack in a town?

5 Why in his view are roadside tea bars being closed? Does he make out a good case for keeping them?

6 Draw a picture or make a plan of the perfect roadside tea bar showing all the facilities you think necessary; or write a report outlining your ideas.

7 If you were an MP representing the Transport and General Workers' Union what would you say to the House of Commons about the tea bar issue. Write a speech stating your point of view.

■ Coursework

1 Find, in the Yellow Pages, a manufacturer of any kind of goods and twelve wholesalers and retailers in different parts of your area to whom he or she might deliver. Work out the best route for a driver who can cover 160 miles on multi-drop deliveries in a day. Draw a map of the proposed route and write a list of the wholesalers and retailers in the order they should be visited. Include their names and addresses; add any other information which might be of use to the driver, using your own local knowledge.

2 Two partners have a transport problem in their expanding florist's business. They own a small shop, but make most of their money by supplying garage forecourts with pre-wrapped bunches of flowers on a sale-or-return basis. For transport, they use two four-year-old Ford Transit vans, but these are now becoming much more expensive to run because of their age. One partner would like to replace the vans with two new vans on a fixed-term lease. The other would like to get two new vans on contract hire.
   ● Divide into pairs, with each person taking the role of one partner.
   ● Find out, individually, the best trade-in price for the two vans and what it would cost per month to lease or to hire new ones.
   ● When you have gathered all the information, discuss the question with your partner. Decide which course of action you will take.
   ● Write a letter to the firm which provided the information, informing it of your decision.

3 The transport manager of a national firm of public hauliers is worried about the rising fuel bill for his fleet of a hundred 32-ton articulated lorries. He has obtained all the daily *tachograph* charts for the last week; these automatically record the vehicles' speed, distance travelled, hours of driving, and rest times. An analysis of the charts has shown that there is too much high-speed driving. Tests with a 32-ton articulated vehicle revealed that fuel consumption at 40 mph is 10.5 mpg; at 50 mph, 7.9 mpg; and at 60 mph, 6.4 mpg.
   a) Each of the vehicles in the fleet does 40,000 miles a year on main roads and motorways. Calculate the total saving on fuel per year at £1.60 per gallon if the vehicles travelled at 50 instead of 60 mph.
   b) Gather any relevant information about road safety or reports of accidents involving lorries in your area.
   c) As the transport manager, compose a letter to your drivers, urging fuel saving and trying to persuade them to drive at lower speeds.

Management Accounting

BA glides to £162 million

British Airways easily beat its forecast privatisation profits of £145 million yesterday with pre-tax profits of £162 million for the year up to March 31.

Even so, the result represented a drop of 17 per cent on the previous year.

The improvement on the forecast results was due to lower-than-expected fuel prices and better sales in the last two months of the year. Fuel costs were £371 million, £199 million less than the year before. Of this, £32 million was due to the weaker dollar and the rest to falling oil prices.

Total staff costs last year rose by 13 per cent due to wage increases, wage drift (increases given as a result of long service) and overtime.

Lord King, the chairman, explained that the company had increased staff, expecting a good summer. This did not happen due to the Chernobyl disaster and fears of international terrorism. By the autumn, costs were under control.

However, varying from the normal seasonal pattern, BA enjoyed higher traffic and a better level of business in the second half of the year, resulting in more overtime in what is usually the quieter part of the year.

Costs also arose from the move to Terminal 4 at Heathrow, which opened during the year.

The effect of currency on last year's results was not worked out, although it was agreed that profits would have been higher without exchange rate changes.

BA calls for help to stay on top

The chairman of British Airways, Lord King, made it clear in London yesterday that he believed the Conservative Government had failed to understand the airline's continuing fight against foreign competition. He asked the next aviation minister to stop trying to protect other British rivals at the expense of British Airways.

Lord King said: 'I would like the government to understand the real nature of competition. They must understand that we are in competition with the rest of the world and not with one another.'

Adapted from: *The Times*, 20 May 1987

Terminal 4 at Heathrow Airport

STUDY POINTS

1 By how much did British Airways exceed its forecast profit?

2 What did it save on fuel costs compared with the previous year? Explain the two reasons for the fall.

3 Make lists of a) the external and b) the internal factors which affected British Airways during the year. Show how each factor affected profits.

4 Could the directors of the company have foreseen any of these events? If so, explain the reasons.

Exercising financial control

No business of any size can succeed unless it keeps a close watch on its financial affairs to see that the firm's resources are being used in the most profitable way. This is the main task of **MANAGEMENT ACCOUNTING**. It uses a wide range of financial information to control the firm's activities and to provide a sound financial basis on which management decisions can be made. Some of its main functions are:

● To make sure that there is enough capital

● To analyse costs and keep them as low as possible

● To plan for the future by making forecasts and exercising budgetary controls

● To analyse the firm's financial performance

● To make comparisons with similar firms.

In addition, management accounting also has to cope with day-to-day changes and risks, or uncertainties about success or failure, by using such techniques as **RISK ANALYSIS**. As the Study Points have shown, business is greatly affected by external events over which it has no control and which are often very difficult or impossible to foretell. The speed of change is now so rapid and the interdependence of countries so great, that no business, even the smallest, can avoid these risks.

Effects of exchange rates

Look at changes in exchange rates. [See Business Techniques]. These were identified by Sir John Harvey-Jones, the former chairman of ICI, as one of the three main problems in the business world today [see Unit 18]. They affect not only big firms like ICI or British Airways, but many other kinds of firms too. For example:

- A small publisher who had been doing rather well with her books in the United States, would find it much more difficult to export if the price of the pound suddenly rose, for her books would then cost more in America.

- A small importer of quality French wines might face disaster if the franc rose in value, as he would then have to pay more pounds to buy the same amount of wine. If he put his prices up he might find that fewer of his British customers were willing to buy.

There is very little that such firms can do about these contingencies, or chance events. The wine importer could buy French francs in advance, so that he knows exactly what he will have to pay for francs at a fixed date in the future. Even this is still something of a gamble as, meanwhile, the franc might fall, and then the firm would be

---

BUSINESS TECHNIQUES

Exchange rates

(see also Unit 73)

Changes in exchange rates can have a great effect on a firm's profit over a longer period of time.
This summary outlines the change in exchange rates for the period 1 March to market closing on Friday 4 March. What would be the effects of these changes on:

a) an American firm which was owed £1,000,000 by a British firm;

b) a British firm which was owed 2,400,000 Deutchmarks (DM) by a German firm?

BUSINESS & CITY

SUMMARY

	Fri. Close	1 March
£/$ (London)	$1.7745	$1.7740
£/DM (London)	DM2.9975	DM2.9930

Source: *The Independent*, 7 March 1988

---

paying more for its francs than if it had not bought them in advance.

Businesses have to learn to live with such risks. This has made contingency planning (planning for these chance events) or **MANAGEMENT OF CHANGE** even more important for firms. In making decisions, allowance is made for external events over which the firm has no control. Mathematical models are used to determine the probability of certain events and the best and the worst effects that they could have on a business. These help a firm to make decisions which appear to produce the highest profit and the least risk.

CHECKPOINTS

1 Explain in your own words the main functions of management accounting.

2 What is risk? Name three other kinds of external risk, apart from those in the Study Points, which might affect a business.

3 Explain, using an example other than those mentioned in the text, how changes in exchange rates can affect a business.

4 Why has management of change become more important in business?

5 Rule a line down the centre of a page. Head the columns
a) Development, and b) Effects.
List the developments given below in column a). Then write down in column b) all the ways in which they might affect a business, including the risks involved and the opportunities available. For example:

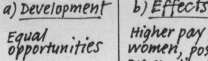

a) Development	b) Effects
Equal opportunities	Higher pay for women, possible prosecutions, male resistance etc.

The developments are: equal opportunities; immigrants; new technology; lower fuel prices; arms reductions; a fall in cigarette smoking.

KEY TERMS

MANAGEMENT ACCOUNTING Using financial information to control a firm's operations and to make management decisions.

RISK ANALYSIS A way of including variations when estimating sales, costs etc, so that possible effects on profits, and therefore the risk attached to each situation, can be looked at.

MANAGEMENT OF CHANGE Making allowances for uncertainty and for events which, because there are no known facts or statistics, can only be anticipated by creating possible situations and feeding in variable data.

Sources of Finance

A firm of estate agents with a total of six branches has decided to equip each office with a fax machine, which can transmit documents, plans and photographs over the normal telephone lines [see Unit 55]. The firm could a) buy the machines out of **RETAINED PROFIT**, b) get a bank loan for a year to pay for them, or c) rent them first for a trial period of six months. The partners in the firm are finding it difficult to come to a decision.

Two of the firm's partners try to reach a decision.

Cost of each fax machine	£3,895
Monthly rental charge for each machine	£ 265
Annual interest charge for bank loan	13 per cent

STUDY POINTS

1 How much would it cost to buy the machines?

2 What would be the total rental charges for six months?

3 If the firm got a loan, how much would it have to pay in interest?

4 What might be the opportunity cost of buying the machines for cash?

5 If you were one of the partners, which method would you choose? Give your reasons.

If you wanted to buy a radio, you could either pay for it out of your savings or you could try to borrow the money from someone, for example your parents. Firms have a similar kind of choice if they want to acquire an asset, such as equipment, vehicles, buildings. They can use their own **INTERNAL SOURCES** of finance, such as money they have saved for future investment; or they can borrow money from an **EXTERNAL SOURCE**, such as a bank.

Internal sources

The main internal source of finance for a firm is retained profit – the money that it saves each year out of its net profit [see Unit 48]. Retained profit can be used for buying further assets or for expanding the business. It is the most important internal source of finance because the money is immediately available without interest charges.

Other internal sources include:

● *Selling investments.* Money which is not immediately required, such as retained profits, can be invested so that it makes a profit. When working capital or money for expansion is needed, these investments can be sold.

● *Selling assets.* This method needs careful consideration. An asset should not be sold just because the firm is desperate for ready cash; but only if it is not making a high enough contribution to the firm's profits. The sale of an asset provides only a 'once-off' source of cash.

● *Sale and lease-back.* Instead of selling an asset, such as a building, outright, it is possible to sell it and then lease it back from the new owner. Firms then have the cash they need from the sale, and still keep the use of the asset.

External sources

There are many external sources of finance for businesses: high-street banks, merchant banks, finance houses, etc. The most important ways of obtaining money are:

- *Overdrafts.* This is the most common method of obtaining money for a short period of time. High-street banks allow credit-worthy firms to draw more money than they actually have in their account, up to an agreed limit. Interest is payable on the amount overdrawn.

- *Discounting bills.* This is another way of obtaining short-term finance. Bills of exchange, which are similar to cheques, demand that a fixed sum of money is paid to a particular business or individual on a certain date. Merchant banks, which deal mainly with the business world, will discount bills of exchange by advancing ready cash before the actual date of settlement. In a similar way, factors are firms which will buy the debts owed to other businesses for cash, including a service charge, and then collect the debts themselves (see Unit 42).

- *Hire purchase.* Finance houses provide money for a medium period of time for firms which wish to buy assets such as machinery or vehicles on hire purchase. The finance house buys the asset and the firm pays it money in monthly instalments (fixed sum, plus interest). The asset does not belong to the firm until the last instalment is paid. The advantage is that the firm doesn't have to use its capital (apart from the deposit). Tax relief is given only on the interest charges.

Letter headed paper of some of the larger merchant banks

- *Leasing.* Assets can also be leased. Equal payments are made at regular intervals, as with hire purchase. The advantages are that tax relief is given on the whole of the payment (not just the interest) and there is no deposit, so that the firm does not have to use any of its capital.

- *Loans.* Merchant banks, highstreet banks and finance houses will give loans for a short, medium or long period of time at a fixed rate of interest [see Unit 42]. Merchant banks are often more willing than the high street banks to provide long-term loans.

- *Government loans.* The government now offers many kinds of short- to long-term financial aid to business [see Unit 68].

- *Debentures.* This is another method of long-term borrowing. Members of the public (debenture holders) lend money to a firm for a fixed period of time at a fixed rate of interest. The terms of the loan are set out in a document called a debenture. The interest has to be paid even if the firm does not make a profit.

Another way of raising additional capital is by changing the structure of the business. For example, a sole proprietor may decide to take on a partner who will invest capital in the business [see Unit 14]. Or a bigger firm may decide to go public, selling shares to provide new capital; in return, some of the net profit of the firm is paid to the shareholders as interest (dividends).

BUSINESS TECHNIQUES

Compound interest

Savings which are left invested without the interest being withdrawn will increase at a faster rate. For instance if the interest rate were 10% per year, a saved £1 would be worth £1.10p in a year's time (£1 + 10p interest). In two years' time, it would be worth £1.21p (£1.10 + 11p interest). This is known as compound interest. What would be the value of £2,000 in three years' time if the rate of interest was 5% per year?

CHECKPOINTS

1 What are the two main sources of finance for business?
2 Describe two kinds of internal sources of finance.
3 Describe three external sources of finance.
4 Which kind of external source might be used by a) a small builder; b) a large firm with many debts; c) an exporter? Give reasons for your answers.

KEY TERMS

RETAINED PROFIT Money which is kept by a business for its future use.

INTERNAL SOURCES Finance which comes from retained profit and selling off assets.

EXTERNAL SOURCES Money obtained from financial institutions such as banks and from shareholders willing to lend money to obtain interest.

Short and Long-Term Borrowing

Victor Forman and his wife Jo, who are both in their early thirties, have been in the hotel business ever since they left school. Victor worked his way up to becoming manager of a big hotel with 300 bedrooms and Jo, who is a qualified cook, has also been a hotel receptionist. Three years ago they left their jobs and bought a small guest house, which they have just sold at a great profit.

The Formans have now bought a bigger, 15-bedroom hotel in the country. It is in need of some urgent work on the building and in the garden. They plan to expand the business by providing conducted tours of the nearby moors and stately homes in a hotel minibus, and by building a small health and fitness centre.

They are hoping to borrow all the money they need from their bank. They will ask for SECURED LOANS, with the hotel property being used as security. This will be cheaper than an UNSECURED LOAN.

STUDY POINTS

1 Study the sketch above. What seem to be the two most urgent jobs the Formans have to do?

2 Draw a plan or make a sketch of the hotel's new fitness centre.

3 Find out how much it would cost, or make estimates of your own, to:
  a) buy a new minibus
  b) build a new fitness centre
  c) restore the front garden
  d) repair the roof.

Costs of borrowing

Most businesses are run on borrowed money. A new business may need to borrow for a long period of time; an older firm may need cash to expand or for a large unexpected expense. The cost of all borrowing is based mainly upon the amount of money borrowed and the length of time for which it is required.

Short-term finance

Short-term finance is normally for a period of up to three years. It is suitable for firms which need money for working capital and for day-to-day expenses. Ways of obtaining short-term finance are:

- *Overdrafts* These allow the business to spend more than it has in its current bank account, up to an agreed limit. Interest is charged on a daily basis only on the amount overdrawn on that day, so overdrafts are a relatively cheap method of borrowing. Businesses with an uneven cash flow [see Unit 46] – such as farmers, who have to spend large sums on fertilising the land and sowing seed but get no financial return for months – make use of overdrafts.

- *Short-term loans* These are loans given at a fixed rate of interest for a fixed period of time. Loan and interest are usually repaid in monthly instalments. Usually this costs more than overdrafts.

- *Factoring* This alternative to borrowing suits firms which do a great deal of business on credit. The firm can 'sell' its debts (money owed to it by its customers) to a FACTOR, who collects all the payments due and pays the firm the amount owed, less the charges for the factoring service. Although these factoring charges can be high, the firm saves money by not having to employ its own staff for debt collection.

Medium-term finance

Medium-term finance is for a period of three to ten years and is intended for the purchase of more expensive equipment, machinery or premises and for the expansion of the business. Examples of this type of finance are hire purchase agreements and loans from banks [see Unit 41].

The government tries to help small firms which do not have enough security to satisfy the bank through its Small Firms Loan Guarantee Scheme. This provides loans of up to £75,000 for two to seven years.

Long-term finance

This is for periods of over ten years or permanent. The most common method of obtaining permanent finance is to form a company and give investors a chance to buy shares, or become shareholders. Established companies may raise new capital by a rights issue, which gives existing shareholders the opportunity to buy more shares at a special price, in proportion to their existing shares. For example, they may be allowed to buy three new shares for every two they own.

Other ways of obtaining long-term finance are through debentures – loans with a fixed rate of interest for a fixed period of time. The money for this comes from members of the public – debenture holders.

Interest rates on secured loans

FIG 42.1

Length of loan	Nominal interest rate (%)	Annual percentage rate (%)
3 years	Flat rate of 7.5	14.5
5 years		14.1
7 years		13.7
10 years		13.1

Rates for unsecured loans will be higher; these will be quoted on request.

Source: Midland Bank plc

Interest rates

If you borrowed £100 at a NOMINAL INTEREST RATE of 8 per cent for a year, the total amount you would have to repay would be £108. This would be divided into 12 equal monthly repayments of £9 each.

However, the nominal interest rate does not give a true picture of the interest rate you are paying. Each time a monthly repayment is made, some of the original loan is paid off. Since the repayments are the same each month while the amount of loan still left to be paid off is decreasing, the true interest being paid each month is increasing. This rate, expressed as the average percentage interest paid over the whole period of the loan, is the ANNUAL PERCENTAGE RATE (APR). It is usually about twice as much as the nominal rate. By law, lenders must also quote the APR so that borrowers are aware of the real amount of interest they have to pay.

BUSINESS TECHNIQUES

Nominal interest rate

If you borrowed £2,500 for two years at a nominal interest rate of 20 per cent, a) How much would you have to pay back in total? b) How much would your monthly instalments be? and c) How much of the original loan would there be left to pay at the end of the first year?

CHECKPOINTS

1 Why might a firm prefer to have an overdraft rather than a short-term loan?
2 Which kind of firm might use a factor? What would be the main advantage and disadvantage for the firm?
3 What is APR? Why is it important for borrowers to know this rate?
4 What is security? Why does it keep the interest rate on a loan lower if you can offer some security?
5 Look at the table in Figure 42.1.
   a) What length of loan would you advise the Formans to get for each of the developments described in Study Points Question 3?
   b) Using your own estimates from Study Points Question 3 for the amounts of the loans needed for these developments, work out the total interest the Formans would have to pay on each loan over the periods you suggested above.

KEY TERMS

SECURED LOAN The borrower offers some security in the form of an asset (such as a building) which could be quickly converted into cash to repay the loan if this became necessary.

UNSECURED LOAN The borrower offers no security, so the risk of the lender losing his or her money is increased. This is why interest rates on unsecured loans are usually higher.

FACTOR A specialist firm or bank which takes over the collecting of all the debts of another firm for a fee.

NOMINAL INTEREST RATE The rate of interest stated by the lender, applied to the whole loan at the start of the loan period.

ANNUAL PERCENTAGE RATE (APR) The true annual rate of interest paid when money is borrowed or goods are obtained on credit. The APR is higher than the nominal interest rate.

Activities

■ Review points

1 What is meant by management of change?

2 What are the two most important tasks of management accounting?

3 Explain the differences between internal and external sources of finance and give two examples of each.

4 For how many years does a) short-term, b) medium-term and c) long-term finance usually last?

5 What is a rights issue? When is it used?

6 Explain how profit can be a source of finance for investment. Why is it such an important source?

7 What is APR?

■ Essay questions

1 Explain why businesses try to keep risk as small as possible. Give examples of how management accounting can help to achieve this.

2 Omar is starting a mobile TV repair service in an enterprise area. You have been asked to advise him.
   a) State where he might obtain finance for his capital expenditure.
   b) What kind of government aid might be available?
   c) How should he advertise his business?

■ Coursework

1 Find out from three different sources of finance what the interest rate would be for a short-term personal loan. Work out the interest you would have to pay on £1,500 for nine months. Explain which source you would use and why the interest rates vary.

2 You are going to open a sports equipment shop. Go to an estate agent and get the details of an empty shop in your area. Visit the shop to see what work would need to be done before it could be opened. Use the Yellow Pages to get real estimates of what each job would cost. Write a report showing the total cost and explaining where you would get the necessary finance, either for the whole cost or for separate items.

Short on cash? You can still start your own business

How many times have you, or a friend, thought about starting your own business and ended up saying, "It's a lovely idea but I haven't got the money."?

The obvious solution is to borrow somebody else's money, but that's not always easy, as Kate Desmond discovered when she decided to go into business for herself. A freelance journalist, she had her typewriter and her story ideas, but she had no commissions.

Kate wanted to get on the Government's Enterprise Allowance Scheme which pays recipients £40 a week in the first year of their new business. The snag is, people on the EAS must have £1,000 to qualify.

Kate's request for an overdraft was turned down by nearly a dozen bank managers before she eventually found a bank that would help.

Borrowing money for start-ups is not the only course. The successful businesses described here made clever use of five key business points:
- Obtaining credit or weekly billing facilities from suppliers.
- Obtaining immediate cash payment from customers.
- Offering a service which larger competitors are too big or too lazy to offer.
- Keeping costs within profit margins and expanding slowly and steadily.
- Making use of a skill requiring low start-up costs.

THE TOYMAKERS BRANCH OUT ....

Finding the future in a garden shed

Gill and John Honeychurch had always made toys for their children and their friends. In 1968 they heard that a newly opened toyshop called Tridias was looking for original toys, so they went calling.

The visit was successful; Tridias gave them a contract and agreed to pay them a monthly fee. Honeychurch Toys was born. John and Gill both gave up their jobs.

"Our factory was a shed at the bottom of the garden," said Gill, "and our machinery was an ordinary set of household tools and some paint brushes."

They had to work long hours but the monthly fee from Tridias meant there was a steady cash flow.

Gill Honeychurch and partner Robin Brooke: Original toys

"Our bank didn't want to help because the business wasn't about things they could understand," said Gill. "We survived because we thoroughly enjoyed doing it."

Sadly, John died in 1979 but with new partner Robin Brooke expansion has continued.

Adapted from: *Daily Mail*, 23 September 1987

Stitching up the rag trade for tots

Anne and Finn Kennedy: Colourful clothes for children

Anne Kennedy, a textile designer, and her husband Finn, an industrial design engineer, went into business together in 1969, designing clothes for children.

"We both felt there had to be an alternative to the boring children's clothes in the shops," said Finn. We had absolutely no money. We were so full of enthusiasm for what we were doing that we just never thought about the financial side.

"We knew there was a market for colourful clothes. The first thing we did was design a dress and pants set for two or three-year-olds. It was put on display at the Design Centre and caught the eye of the Press, which gave us some publicity."

In the sixties, customer credit of 30 and 60 days was easier to obtain than today. The Kennedys ordered 100 metres of fabric and got to work in their living room. Orders (all accompanied by cheques) for 400 sets followed from their first Press publicity.

"Because we had low overheads," said Finn, "we never even needed an overdraft for the first two years. Because we were mail order we were paid before the goods were sent out, and our suppliers were paid after we were paid. The business just took off."

...... A MOTHER MAKES A MEAL INTO MONEY

Taking a tasty bite at lunch

Five years ago, Sally Greenwood found herself divorced, aged 36, with two young children, a £3,000 overdraft, and no job. She had not worked for the past ten years of her married life.

"I couldn't even get a job as a temporary junior clerk, she said. "Finally a firm took me on at no salary to sell security locks for commission only. After a week I'd sold nothing and I was desperate.

"One day when a local caterer delivered the lunch sandwiches they looked so dreadful a colleague said: 'You'd have to try hard to do worse than this lot. Why don't you run a sandwich service?' So I gave in my notice and set up the Lunch Bunch.

Sally Greenwood: Providing a sandwich service

"In my spare time, I called on other firms, and the business picked up. I got the shock of my life at the end of the first year when my accountant rang and said I'd made over £17,500. This year's turnover is £80,000."

Study these stories of business enterprise carefully, and then answer the following questions.

1 What is the Enterprise Allowance Scheme? How much capital do you have to raise yourself?

2 Why is it not always easy to borrow money to set up a small business? What are the alternatives? Explain the advantages of each.

3 Which external and internal sources of finance did each of these businesses use?

4 For what reasons did these people set up a business of their own? How did they get the idea for their business?

5 What in your view are the personal qualities which made these people successful in business?

6 Think of a business you would like to start. What have you learnt from these real-life stories which would help you in your own venture?

Costs

SONIA'S FRESH FLOWE
WREATHS & BOUQUETS TO ORDER

TIME AND COSTS FOR ITEMS SOLD

FIG 43.1

	Time taken	Selling price	Cost of materials
Displays	2 hours	£20	£12
Wreaths	2 hours	£15	£10
Bouquets	1 hour	£10	£7

SONIA got a part-time Saturday job in a florist's shop while she was still at school. The owner thought she had promise and trained her to make displays, wreaths and bouquets.

When Sonia left school, she decided that she could make a living by having a flower stall of her own. She knew that flowers bought wholesale for, say, 75p a bunch were sold in the shop at £1.50. Wreaths sold for £10 to £20 each and displays were anything from £5 to £30.

Sonia hired a stall in the local covered market for £10 a day. That was her main cost. She also needed moss, wrapping paper, tools, tape, a cover for the stall, accounts books and many other items.

STUDY POINTS

1 Make a list of all the things that Sonia will need to buy for her business, including any that you can think of yourself.

2 Study the Key Terms. Make a list with the headings Capital Expenditure and Revenue Expenditure and put each item you listed in Question 1 in the correct column.

3 Sonia planned to make displays, wreaths and bouquets when she wasn't serving customers with bunches of flowers. Not only would she be using her time profitably, but she thought that more people might be attracted to the stall to watch her working. She timed herself and costed the materials to see which item was the most profitable. Look at Figure 43.1. What was Sonia's profit per hour on each item?

4 Sonia decided to concentrate her main effort on making displays. What sales promotions could she have used to increase sales of these items?

Different categories of cost

In general terms, all the money that a business spends on producing its goods or services are its costs. In management accounting, these costs have to be put into separate categories or groups and analysed before a true picture of the business can be seen.

CAPITAL EXPENDITURE is money spent on permanent acquisitions – such as buildings, land, vehicles, equipment – which are necessary for the running of the business. In accounting terms, this normally includes anything that lasts for more than a year. Capital expenditure appears as assets in the firm's balance sheet [see Unit 49].

REVENUE EXPENDITURE is all the money that is paid out to run the business. This will include the cost of buying stock, expenses like rent and heating bills, and any losses (such as discounts or unsaleable stock). Revenue expenditure appears in the profit and loss account, which sums up exactly how much profit or loss a business has made during the year [see Unit 48].

It is important to distinguish between capital and revenue expenditure, because only revenue expenditure affects profit. Sometimes the line between what is capital expenditure and what is revenue expenditure may vary a little, depending on the kind of business being carried on. For example, a furniture shop buys furniture as part of its stock for re-sale. Is this capital or revenue expenditure? A builder buys furniture to furnish his new office extension. Is this capital or revenue expenditure?

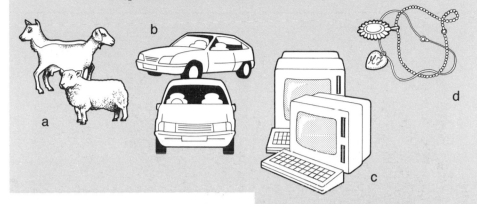

BUSINESS TECHNIQUES
Capital and revenue expenses

Each of the items a to d would be a capital expense for one type of business but a revenue expense for another. State which of the businesses below might buy these items: electronics equipment manufacturer; farmer; taxi-driver; museum; secretarial agency; children's zoo; car sales show-room? Say in each case what type of expense each item would be.

Further cost break-downs

To get a more detailed financial picture of the business, the revenue expenditure is broken down again into two more categories.

Some of the costs under revenue expenditure have to be paid for whether the firm is making a profit or not, and they are not affected by the amount of sales or production. These are called **FIXED COSTS**. Examples of fixed costs are rent or mortgage repayments, rates and salaries. There will be changes in these from time to time due to outside factors: rates may rise or salaries increase.

Other costs relate to how many goods are produced or how much is being sold. For example, to produce more goods, more materials will be needed, more electricity may be used and more overtime may have to be worked. These costs are higher at some periods than at others, and are not known for certain in advance. They are called **VARIABLE COSTS**. Other examples are petrol and repairs.

CHECKPOINTS

1. A building firm pays out money on the following items. Which of them are items of capital expenditure: Ladders, cement, scaffolding, lorries, repainting the premises (the cost will be spread over 3 years), stationery and printed invoices, small hammers, wages for permanent staff, an extension to the offices?
2. List some of the items of capital expenditure a hairdresser might have.
3. What would be the revenue expenditure of a high street shop selling electrical goods?
4. A firm decides to expand and move to larger premises. It also decides to give the executive staff smarter offices and to employ more office staff. Which of the firm's fixed costs will change?
5. Say which of the following costs are fixed and which are variable: Electricity, transport of goods, rent, materials, rates, maintenance of equipment, interest on loans, salaries, insurance.

KEY TERMS

CAPITAL EXPENDITURE Money spent on acquiring assets for a business which will normally last for more than a year.

REVENUE EXPENDITURE Money paid out for the running of the business.

FIXED COSTS Expenditure which is not affected by the amount of trade done by a firm or by the number of goods produced. A business cost which must be paid whether the firm is making money or not.

VARIABLE COSTS Any costs which change according to the amount of business done or the number of goods produced.

The Concept of Break-even

Valerie Ashford lives on a large housing estate in the Midlands. She is a fully-qualified hairdresser and works in a Unisex salon in the town. For some time, she has been thinking of opening her own salon on the estate as many of the young mothers find it difficult to get into town. She has discussed her plan with many friends and acquaintances, and they all think that it would be a good idea.

This has encouraged her to go ahead. She plans to rent a small shop unit and employ a cleaning lady for an hour a day. The shop-fitting will be done by a friend and paid for out of her savings. She will hire all the necessary equipment such as driers, chairs, towels etc.

Valerie is now trying to work out when her business would become profitable by jotting down some figures about her fixed and variable costs and the prices she will charge. Her variable costs for each client (including extra electricity) are £1 on average, but she also has the cost of the materials.

Fixed costs per year

Rent	£1,000
Rates	£ 300
Hire of equipment	£ 750
Wages	£ 500
Heat & light	£ 450

Variable costs of materials

Cut & style	50p
Shampoo & set	£1.50
Tinting	£4.00
Perm	

plus £1 per client for extra electricity.

Valerie's Salon
PRICE LIST

Cut and style	£7
Shampoo and set	£4
Tinting	£6
Perm	£11

*

S T U D Y   P O I N T S

1 What would the total fixed costs be per year?

2 Calculate the average variable costs per appointment including materials and extra electricity.

3 What would the average price per appointment be?

4 Describe some of the likely effects if Valerie increased her prices by 10 per cent.

BREAK-EVEN is the point reached in a business after which its activities begin to become profitable. It is, of course, essential for any business to pass this point because it could not continue for very long if it just managed to cover its costs.

Finding the break-even point

By adding together fixed and variable costs and comparing these with sales revenue we can see at which point average costs equal average revenue – the **BREAK-EVEN POINT**.

This can be shown graphically by a **BREAK-EVEN CHART**. Look at Figure 44.1, which shows the break-even point for Valerie Ashford's business.

● Valerie's fixed costs per year were £3,000. She had to pay these no matter how many appointments she had, so they are shown as a straight line across the graph.

● Valerie's variable costs have to be added to the fixed costs, so they start on the costs/revenue axis at the same point. The average variable cost for each appointment was £2.50 so points are plotted on the graph to show the average variable cost of 100 appointments, 500 appointments, and so on. These points are then joined to make a diagonal line showing total costs.

● Valerie's revenue is based on the average charge for each appointment, which was £7. This will begin at 0. Plot the points for 100 appointments at £7 each, 500 appointments at £7 each etc, and join them to make the revenue line. The break-even point is where the revenue line and the total costs line intersect or cross each other. Below that point there is a loss. Above that point, there is a profit.

Look carefully at Figure 44.1. How many appointments will Valerie need to reach her break-even point? What will be her revenue at that stage?

The number of appointments she has above the break-even point is known as the **MARGIN OF SAFETY**.

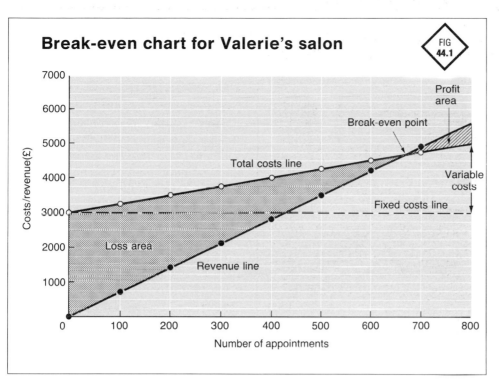

Break-even chart for Valerie's salon

FIG 44.1

Only a guide

Break-even charts do not give an exact picture of when a business will start to make a profit. In a business like Valerie's, as in most service industries, it is difficult to know exactly what the revenue will be. If most of her customers chose to have only a cut and style, the revenue figure would be different. That is why the average price was used in the forecast.

The break-even chart, however, does provide a very useful guide. If you were thinking of forming your own group to play in clubs, you could estimate what the fixed and variable costs would be and find out what managers would be likely to pay you for each session. Then you could make out a break-even chart to give you a good idea of when you would reach break-even point and go on to make a profit.

Limitations

It is easier to draw a chart for a manufacturing firm where the unit price of each product is known precisely than for a firm providing a service. Even then, however, the chart can never be entirely accurate. Fixed costs are shown as a straight line; but if production goes beyond a certain point, new machinery or a new plant may have to be bought, which will increase fixed costs. A line with steps in it for each increase in fixed costs usually gives a more accurate picture. Variable costs may rise steeply too if overtime has to be increased to keep up production.

Also, the chart makes no allowance for stock. Some of the goods may be sold long after they were produced, so that the chart does not always show a true relation between costs and revenue over a fixed period of time.

CHECKPOINTS

1 What is the break-even point?
2 Why is it more difficult to draw an accurate break-even chart for a services than a manufacturing firm?
3 Explain the limitations of break-even charts.
4 A firm is planning to produce small toy cars for the Christmas market. It thinks it could market these at £2 each. The firm's annual fixed costs are £20,000 and it has estimated that the cost of producing each car will be 40p.
a) Draw a break-even chart for the toy manufacturing firm.
b) How many items must the firm sell to break even?

KEY TERMS

BREAK-EVEN The relation of income and costs to the amount produced.

BREAK-EVEN POINT The point at which costs and expenses are exactly equal to sales, so that no profit or loss has been made.

BREAK-EVEN CHART A graph showing the point at which sales and costs are equal.

MARGIN OF SAFETY The amount produced after the break-even point has been reached.

Forecasting and Budgetary Control

A young and inexperienced couple have taken over a small unlicensed café in a Devon village from two old ladies who are retiring. The café has been well maintained and all the delicate china crockery is supplied. There are 20 tables, oak polished chairs and linen tablecloths. The floor space is 40′ × 20′. The village is dependent on tourist trade and there are two large holiday caravan sites on the outskirts.

The couple move in during October when most of the tourists have gone. During the autumn and winter they find that most of the customers are retired ladies having morning coffee and afternoon tea. The café has always opened from 10 to 4.30 for 6 days a week, closing on Sundays. The previous owners served a standard lunch menu of steak and kidney pie and a choice of sweets for £3.95.

STUDY POINTS

1 To what kind of customer is the café appealing?

2 What can the couple expect to happen to the business during the winter months?

3 How many old ladies would they need to serve each day with a coffee and piece of cake to cover the rates of £30 a week?

4 What other overhead costs will they have? List as many as you can.

5 The young couple realise that there is very little winter trade. They have to decide how to build up the business. Make a list of short-term objectives for dealing with this problem.

6 What changes would you suggest for the future? Divide your plan into sections on:
a) Physical environment, furniture and equipment
b) Food offered
c) Drinks
d) Opening times and days.

Forecasting

FORECASTING is one of a business person's most difficult activities. All forecasts attempt to estimate what is likely to happen in the future based on what happened in the past. They range from what the weather will be on Christmas Day to whether a new pop group will reach the top of the record charts.

Business persons cannot afford to make hopeful guesses. They use various methods to make forecasts which are as accurate as possible and then they use these to plan ahead. As circumstances change, they make adjustments to their plans.

SHORT-TERM PLANNING is easier than **LONG-TERM PLANNING** because fewer changes are likely. It is not possible, for example, to forecast correctly how much new equipment will cost in 10 years' time, what new products will be required, or where the markets for those products will be.

Short-term planning

It is vital for any business to know what its turnover, or sales, is likely to be in the following year. Otherwise, it would not know whether it was likely to make a profit or not, whether it was wise to make capital expenditure, or even how to plan its production schedules [see Unit 25].

Short-term forecasts are based on both internal and external sources. Firms use their own records of what has happened in the past to make predictions about the future.

The example shows the sales figures for the past three years for Brand X, a non-biological detergent.

BRAND X SALES – £m		
1986	1987	1988
10	11	11.5

The figures show that sales have gone up over the last three years, but not at a steady rate. There was an increase of 10 per cent in 1987, but only 4.5 per cent in 1988. Was this a temporary drop, or does it mark the beginning of a downward trend? External sources will be used to check what is happening in the whole market [see Unit 31]. Are people buying less non-biological detergent? Has competition increased? These questions – and many more – must be answered before a reasonable forecast can be made about the following year's sales of Brand X.

Budgets

Similar forecasts are made about the firm's capital expenditure, demand for manpower, materials, etc. These forecasts are used to make the firm's BUDGET for the following year.

Forecasts are only a prediction about what is likely to happen in the future. Budgets are a detailed statement of the financial objectives – or targets – month by month, or quarter by quarter, for the coming year. Each department has to prepare its own budget. These are then put together to make a master budget for the whole firm.

Departmental budgets provide a valuable check on performance, as the forecasts in the budgets can be compared with actual results. If there is a large gap between them, reasons can be found and action taken. This is known as BUDGETARY CONTROL.

Long-term planning

Long-term planning needs great skill. Many projects may take years to develop or to show any return on the investment – which can be millions of pounds – so it is vital to make some plans for the future. However, there is no way of knowing how high interest rates may be in 10 years' time or what the unemployment rate might be. Long-term planning, therefore, is more about applying principles than definite amounts of money. It shows intentions rather than decisions.

CHECKPOINTS

1 What is the importance of a budget?
2 How does budgetary control make it easier to manage a firm?
3 Which of the following forecasts could the directors of a company reasonably make for a 10-year period based on present situations?
   a) The price of oil will increase.
   b) There will be increasing opportunities to trade with the USSR.
   c) Further privatisation of public industries will give possible opportunities for expansion.
4 Look at Figure 45.1 showing fictional bookshop sales. What trends can be seen from these figures? Explain your answer.
5 Make your own forecasts for the sales of each category of book for 1987.
6 Now look at the actual figures for 1987 at the side of Figure 45.1. If your forecasts do not match these, try to think of reasons for the difference.

FIG 45.1 — Bookshop sales
£million

	1984	1985	1986
Hardback			
1) School textbooks	12.74	12.76	10.32
2) Technical and scientific	26.10	26.88	26.70
3) Fiction and literature	24.00	22.80	20.30
4) Children's	12.00	11.00	10.50
5) Women's	8.50	12.70	13.90
6) Thrillers and horror	20.70	18.83	15.60
7) Biographies and other	16.20	11.70	9.35
8) Bibles	4.00	3.75	3.25
Paperback			
1) School textbooks	20.10	19.50	15.00
2) Technical and scientific	12.80	15.90	16.10
3) Fiction and literature	23.50	24.50	24.70
4) Children's	5.00	4.80	3.90
5) Women's	6.30	7.40	8.80
6) Thrillers and horror	4.60	6.30	7.50
7) Biographies and other	3.20	3.40	3.30
8) Bibles	2.50	2.70	1.80

(These figures are all fictional)

1987 figures
Hardback: 1) 11.38; 2) 30.50; 3) 17.05; 4) 10.75; 5) 15.20; 6) 20.85; 7) 14.62; 8) 3.50. Paperback: 1) 13.40; 2) 20.20; 3) 25.30; 4) 5.30; 5) 10.30; 6) 6.80; 7) 3.50; 8) 1.00.

KEY TERMS

FORECASTING An attempt to estimate future expenses and profits based on past experience. Also, an attempt to plan future action based on current trends.

SHORT-TERM PLANNING Usually any plan which will come into effect within the next three years.

LONG-TERM PLANNING Plans for any period up to 10 years or more ahead.

BUDGET A summary of all planned expenditure and expected returns or income.

BUDGETARY CONTROL Comparing actual figures with budgeted estimates so that plans can quickly be adjusted to new circumstances.

Cash Flow

Bill and his wife Pat run a small organic farm which uses no chemicals or fertilisers. They grow most of their own vegetables and fruit and keep a pig, a few ducks and geese, and a couple of nanny goats to milk. They also grow some grain to feed their large flock of free-range chickens, which is their main business activity.

During the last five or six years, their business has improved greatly as the demand for free-range eggs has grown. Three times a week, Bill drives to nearby towns to sell the eggs to health stores.

Bill and Pat bought their farm cheaply in the sixties. They don't make very much money, but they like their way of life. The only time they have any big financial problem is in March when they buy a new flock of day-old chicks. They are trying to find out whether they will have enough money by working out a **CASH-FLOW FORECAST**. This shows their estimated receipts (money coming into the business) and payments out, and their bank balance at the beginning and end of each month. The surplus (or deficit) on the receipts and payments is added to (or taken away from) the balance in the bank.

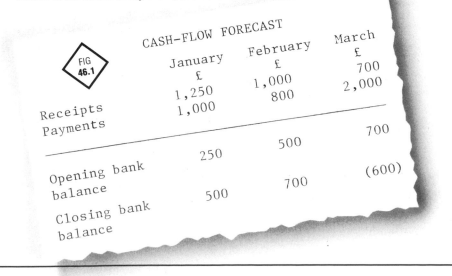

FIG 46.1 CASH–FLOW FORECAST	January £	February £	March £
Receipts	1,250	1,000	700
Payments	1,000	800	2,000
	250	500	700
Opening bank balance		500	(600)
Closing bank balance	500	700	

CASH FLOW refers to money coming into and being paid out of a business over a period of time. Unit 45 showed that it is possible to make forecasts which accurately predict how profitable a business will be in the future. Detailed budgets may show that sales can be maintained and increased; that there is a definite market; that the business is being run efficiently; and that, at the end of the year, a healthy profit will be made. This is very encouraging – but is it enough?

What about the day-to-day financial situation? Will the firm be able to meet its commitments as they become due? Will it have the cash to pay the staff every week or month? Many promising companies have been forced to close simply because they did not have that ready cash when it was needed. In other words they had a **LIQUIDITY PROBLEM**: they did not have enough ready money that they could lay their hands on immediately to pay their bills.

Controlling the cash flow

It is very important indeed for a business to know exactly what cash will be available month by month and even week by week.

Large firms will get this information from their various departments,

42, 45 ◄ See Units

Cash Flow Forecast

for _____

(name of firm)

FIG 46.2

ENTER PERIOD (e.g. monthly or quarterly)		
RECEIPTS	BUDGET	ACTUAL
REVENUE ITEMS		
Collections from debtors		
Cash sales		
Other income		
Commissions		
Rent		
Investment income		
Repayment of VAT		
Repayment of Corporation Tax		
Other – specify 1		
2		
CAPITAL ITEMS		
Net proceeds on disposal of assets		
Loans received		
Capital grants		
Capital introduced		
TOTAL RECEIPTS A		

PAYMENTS		
REVENUE ITEMS		
Trading expenses		
Payments to trade creditors		
Cash purchases		
Gross wages (including NHI)		
Administration expenses		
Gross salaries (including NHI)		
Directors' remuneration		
Rent		
Rates		
Insurance		
Repairs and renewals		
Heat, light and power		
Hire and leasing charges		
Printing and stationery		
Legal and professional		
Postage and telephone		
Vehicle running costs		
Entertaining and travelling		
Selling and distribution expenses		
Advertising		
Carriage and packing		
Finance costs		
Overdraft/loan interest		
Bank charges		
CAPITAL ITEMS		
Capital purchases		
HP instalments (including interest)		
Loan payments		
OTHER PAYMENTS		
VAT		
Corporation Tax		
Dividends		
Sundry – specify 1		
2		
3		
TOTAL PAYMENTS B		

If A greater than B – surplus If B greater than A – deficit – show thus ( )		
OPENING BANK BALANCE C		
CLOSING BANK BALANCE		

Source: Barclays Bank

In reality, banks demand an enormous amount of detailed information about cash flow before they lend money.

which each make out individual budgets of income and expenditure. The firm can then plan in advance with a bank what can be done during the difficult periods.

Some businesses have a seasonal trade, some will be influenced by weather; but all businesses can work out at which times of the year it is best to be more careful about spending – just as individuals may plan to spend larger amounts at Christmas and on summer holidays, while keeping spending down to the minimum at other times of the year. Another way of trying to avoid a liquidity problem is for a firm to alter its credit policy, asking debtors to pay their bills more promptly. The firm can also try to delay the payment of its own bills.

Help with cash flow

There is a limit to these strategies and a business may find that it is still short of cash at times. A bank will normally give an overdraft or loan to such firms, but will ask the firm for a detailed cash-flow forecast. This will show what cash receipts and payments are expected over a future period.

A cash flow forecast, like the one in Figure 46.2, can be prepared after a firm has prepared a budget. The budget shows the sales that a firm expects to make, what it will cost to buy the stock, and any other capital expenditure to be made. It uses these figures to estimate the pre-tax profit. However, the budget shows only the overall plan of what a firm hopes to achieve. The cash-flow forecast shows the week by week flow of cash in and out of the business.

KEY TERMS

CASH-FLOW FORECAST A statement of estimates of cash receipts and payments over a future period.

CASH FLOW The relationship between money coming into a business (receipts) and money going out of a business (payments).

LIQUIDITY PROBLEM A lack of cash at the time it is needed because a firm's receipts cannot keep pace with its payments.

BUSINESS TECHNIQUES

Factoring

One way of solving a cash-flow problem is by using a factor [see Unit 42].

A firm has a forecast cash-flow deficit of £8,750 and outstanding invoices of £12,000. If a factor offered an immediate cash advance of 80 per cent on the invoices, would it solve the cash-flow problem? If so, what would be the total of surplus cash?

CHECKPOINTS

1 What are cash-flow forecasts?
2 Why are they important for all types of businesses?
3 Study Figure 46.3 which shows a holiday tour firm's forecast and actual receipts and expenditure up to July, and the forecasts for August. Then answer the following questions.

Cash-flow forecast

FIG 46.3

	June £	July £	August £
Receipts			
Forecast	70,000	60,000	55,000
Actual	68,000	45,000	
Expenditure			
Forecast	65,000	55,000	50,000
Actual	62,000	59,000	

a) If the firm had an opening bank balance of £4,000 at the beginning of June, what would be the balance at the end of July?
b) If there is a cash-flow problem, would the forecast figures for August solve it?
c) If you were the firm's bank manager, what questions would you ask if the firm applied for an overdraft?

Activities

■ Review points

1 Why is a satisfactory cash flow important for a business?

2 When might a cash flow forecast be prepared? What use might be made of it?

3 What are the main differences between short-term and long-term planning?

4 Why are both short-term and long-term planning necessary for the good management of a business?

5 What is the difference between fixed and variable costs?

6 List the costs a mini-cab driver might have and group them into fixed and variable.

7 Explain the concept of break-even and draw a chart to illustrate it.

■ Coursework

1 You have decided to become a self-employed gardener. Describe what market research you would do before you set up the business. Make out a short-term plan for six months showing your estimated income and expenditure, and draw a graph showing when break-even point would be reached. Explain how you would obtain any capital you need.

2 Take any commodity, such as a raw material like copper or tin, or a foodstuff like tea or coffee. Collect information from the financial pages of a trade magazine about the changes in price over a three-month period. In addition, collect any information about developments which might affect the market price in the future. Write a report, illustrated with graphs, showing what has happened to the price in the past three months and your predictions for the future. State what actions you would take now to turn possible future changes in price to your profit and advantage.

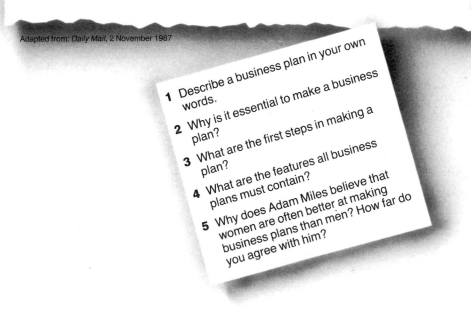

How the best laid plans can protect you from disaster . . .

There's probably nothing more important to the success of the small business than the business plan. Without it, it will be almost impossible to raise start-up money or working capital.

'A lot of people starting up a business simply don't understand what's involved in a business plan,' says Adam Miles, principal lecturer at the Department of Management and Organisation Studies at Sheffield City Polytechnic. 'It's not just a money-raising necessity – it's a vital part of turning a business idea into a practical reality.

'A business plan takes time – you can't just knock one up in a weekend. It means detailed market research, perhaps going out on to the streets and handing out a questionnaire or any other down-to-earth method that may suggest itself.'

One of the dangers that has to be avoided is the plan based on hope.

'A businessman made redundant is desperate to find new employment to keep his self respect,' explains Adam Miles. 'He'll convince himself his idea will work and he'll skip the hard realistic slog of really testing the validity of his idea. At Sheffield City Polytechnic we also get a lot of women taking our seminars and I'm bound to say they're often more businesslike and methodical in their attitude than the men.

'A business plan is a full statement of what you need to achieve,' says Mr Miles. 'You have to put down why you think you can achieve your goals, how you will do it, and with what financial resources.

'It's true that the first purpose of a business plan is to back up any loan applications. But second, and more important, it's necessary for making everything clear in the mind of the person starting up the business.'

Adapted from: *Daily Mail*, 2 November 1987

1 Describe a business plan in your own words.

2 Why is it essential to make a business plan?

3 What are the first steps in making a plan?

4 What are the features all business plans must contain?

5 Why does Adam Miles believe that women are often better at making business plans than men? How far do you agree with him?

Forward with factoring

For Diskxpress, a small company in the computer industry, the route to factoring started with the search for a higher overdraft limit than the company's bank could give. Rejecting the other option of additional outside shareholders, because it would weaken control, Diskxpress discussed their requirements with a number of leading factoring companies, eventually deciding on NatWest Bank's Credit Factoring International (CFI).

Among the immediate effects of factoring for Diskxpress was the solution to its cash-flow problem. The factor at once made available 65 per cent of the value of outstanding invoices – around £120,000 – with the remaining 35 per cent, or £80,000, guaranteed after 60 days.

Other benefits of factoring for Diskxpress include 100 per cent protection against bad debts on sales approved by the factor.

The factor also took over complete responsibility for the running of the Diskxpress sales ledger and for collection, including issuing statements, reminder letters and any necessary telephoning to chase payments or sort out payment queries.

Factoring has enabled Diskxpress to expand its sales without the need to employ two or three full time credit control staff.

Adapted from: *In Business Now*, April/May 1987

■ Essay question

You are running a disco which has a liquidity problem. You have decided to take urgent action on three fronts. Explain how you would:

a) prepare a cash-flow forecast for a bank;
b) make immediate cuts in costs;
c) plan to increase revenue.

Accountants add up to a saving

What are the advantages of going to an accountant? Mary Reilly, senior manager of leading accountants Binder Hamlyn, answers some basic questions . . .

When do I need an accountant?
The basic rule is to seek the advice of an accountant whenever you are making, or planning to make, a change which will affect your financial arrangements.

Will an accountant save me tax?
He frequently will. His job is to ensure that you pay only the legal minimum amount of tax according to your circumstances.

How do I decide what is a reasonable fee?
For a senior manager's time in London, think of £50+ an hour, £25–£33 outside. Always discuss with the accountant at the outset exactly what the basis of his charge will be and how much time he thinks he will have to spend on your affairs. Reckon on at least five hours.

How do I find an accountant?
The Institute of Chartered Accountants, Moorgate Place, London EC2 (tel. 01-628 7060) will list local societies. Or try the Yellow Pages.

Adapted from: *Daily Mail*, 17 June 1987

1 Why did Diskxpress seek the help of a factoring firm?

2 What other action could it have taken? Why did it reject that course?

3 Explain in your own words how factoring helps to solve a cash-flow problem.

4 Why is factoring helpful to a firm with bad debts?

5 What is the other main advantage of factoring?

6 What other kinds of firms might find factoring useful? Give three examples.

1 How would you find an accountant?

2 What other matters do accountants deal with in addition to tax?

3 If you were going to set up your own business and decided to use the services of an accountant, what would be the likely cost?

4 You are going to set up your own business. Think of three things you would like to discuss with an accountant. Write down the questions you would ask, and your reasons for asking them.

5 Where could you go for financial advice instead of an accountant?

Trading Accounts

Every year, a business person prepares final accounts which provide a financial summary of all the trading activities during the year. They are the **TRADING ACCOUNT**, the profit and loss account [see Unit 48] and the balance sheet [see Unit 49].

The trading account shows what has been spent on buying **STOCK**, how much money was made when it was sold, and the **GROSS PROFIT** (or loss). The trading account of a manufacturing firm will also show the costs of producing the goods.

Gross and net profit

Sarah has a gift shop in a cathedral city. Look at Figure 47.1 which shows her trading account for the last financial year.

- The first item in the debit column (left hand side of table) shows the value of Sarah's stock at the beginning of the financial year.

- The second item – **PURCHASES** – is the value of goods for re-sale which Sarah bought during the year. The figure of £160,000 is reduced to £158,000 as some faulty goods were returned to the manufacturer. This reduces the total stock figure to £198,000.

- The cost of the goods sold during the year is found by subtracting the amount of stock held at the end of the year (still unsold) from the total value of stock. This produces a figure of £108,000.

- Now look at the credit column (right hand side of table). **SALES (TURNOVER)** during the year totalled £150,000. If the cost of sales figure is taken away from the sales figure (£150,000 – £108,000) it shows that Sarah's gross profit was £42,000.

This doesn't mean that Sarah actually made £42,000 during the year. All the expenses of running the business and the overhead costs have now to be subtracted to find

Supplement to THE GROCER

50

OSEM FOODS

Snacks:	Trade per case	Retail each
Mini Pretzels 100g × 48	£12.15	32
Salt rings 100g × 48	£12.15	32
Salt sticks 100g × 48	£12.15	32
Bissli Falafel 2½oz × 48	£15.39	40
Bissli Bar-B-Q 2½oz × 48	£15.39	40
Bissli Onion 2½oz × 48	£15.39	40
Bissli Smokey 2½ × 48	£15.39	40
Bissli Pizza 2½oz × 48	£8.50	22
Bissli Bamba 25g × 100	£15.19	19
Bissli Bar-B-Q 25g × 100	£15.19	19
Bissli Onion 25g × 100	£15.19	19
Snack Sticks 3½oz × 48	£17.81	46
Soup Tidbits 3½oz × 48	£17.81	46
Snack Tidbits 3½oz × 48	£17.81	46
Croutons Snack Sticks × 24	£11.14	58
Croutons Mini Mandels × 24	£11.14	58
Croutons Maxi Mandels × 24	£11.14	58

LAUREATE

Balkan 'Extra' Jams:	Trade per case	Retail each
Apricot 1lb. × 12	£6.50	66
Blackberry 1lb. × 12	£6.87	71
Black Cherry 1lb. × 12	£6.87	71
Blackcurrant 1lb. × 12	£6.87	71
Morello Cherry 1lb. × 12	£6.87	71
Peach 1lb. × 12	£6.50	66
Plum 1lb. × 12	£6.50	66
Raspberry 1lb. × 12	£6.50	66
Strawberry 1lb. × 12	£6.50	66
Sweet Orange 1lb. × 12	£6.50	66
Balaton Pure Fruit Jams:		
Apricot 1lb. × 12	£5.87	60
Gooseberry 1lb. × 12	£6.32	65
Redcurrant 1lb. × 12	£6.32	65

PARRISH & FENN

Grand Italia Range:	Trade per case	Retail each
Long Blue Spaghetti 500g × 24	£11.88	60
Short Spaghetti 500g × 24	£11.88	60
Farfalle (Bow Ties) 500g × 24	£9.90	60
Fusilli (Spirals) 500g × 20	£9.90	60
Pipe Rigate (Snail Shells) 500g × 20	£9.90	60
Penne Rigate (Quills) 500g × 20	£9.90	60
Sedanini (Tubes) 500g × 20	£9.90	60
Conchiglie Rigate (Cockle Shells) 500g × 20	£9.80	99
Lasagne 500g × 12	£10.40	£1.05
Lasagne Verdi 500g × 12	£5.84	59
Cannelloni 250g × 12	£11.78	£1.19
Egg Tagliatelle 500g × 12	£13.37	£1.35
Egg Tagliatelle Verdi 500g × 12	£22.77	£1.15
Tortellini with meat filling 250g × 24	£22.77	£1.15
Tortellini with cheese filling 250g × 24	£7.72	39
Grissini Breadsticks 125g × 24		
Make your own Fresh Pizza Napoletana Kit 450g × 30	£22.03	89

SCOTFRESH LABEL

Vegetables	Trade per case	Retail each
Petit Pois Peas 2lb. × 12	£10.20	£1.02
Garden Peas 1lb. × 12	£4.39	44
Garden Peas 2lb. × 12	£8.18	82
Choice Peas 2lb. × 12	£7.80	78
Choice Peas 4lb. × 6	£7.50	£1.50
Value Peas 2lb. × 12	£7.35	74
Button Brussels Sprouts 1lb. × 12	£5.40	54
Button Brussels Sprouts 2lb. × 12	£9.83	98
Medium Brussels Sprouts 2lb. × 12	£9.23	92
Medium Brussels Sprouts 4lb. × 6	£9.08	£1.82
Baby Broad Beans 1lb. × 12	£5.40	54
Broad Beans 2lb. × 12	£8.93	89
Fine Whole Beans 1lb. × 12	£6.68	67
Whole Beans 2lb. × 12	£10.52	£1.05
Sliced Beans 2lb. × 12	£9.54	95
Sliced Beans 4lb. × 6	£9.38	£1.88

Source: *The Grocer*, 2 May 1987

STUDY POINTS

Salim Patel has a grocery store in the suburbs of Birmingham. Like many small shop owners, he is restricted for space and has to order stock regulary. His weekly stockcheck shows that he needs further supplies of: Balkan 'Extra' Jams, strawberry (1 case); Scotfresh Label 1 lb garden peas (2 cases); Grand Italia short spaghetti (1 case); and Bissli Bamba (2 cases).

1 Work out from the price lists above what the cost per case for each item would be.

2 How much profit will Mr. Patel make on each case?

3 What will his total profit be when he has sold all the stock he ordered?

4 Which item should he try to sell more of? Suggest how he might increase the sales of that item.

See Units ▶ 48, 49

> **FIG 47.1**
>
> ## Sarah's gift shop
>
> ### Trading account for the year ending 31 May 1988
>
> | | £ | £ | | £ |
> |---|---|---|---|---|
> | Stock at 1/6/87 | | 40,000 | Sales | 150,000 |
> | Purchases | 160,000 | | | |
> | *less* returns | 2,000 | 158,000 | | |
> | Total stock available for sale | | 198,000 | | |
> | *less* stock on hand at 31/5/88 | | 90,000 | | |
> | Cost of sales | | 108,000 | | |
> | Gross profit | | 42,000 | | |
> | | | | | |
> | | | 150,000 | | 150,000 |

the **NET PROFIT** [see Unit 48]. Even then the figures have to be compared with past results, forecasts, or with those of similar firms, before you can see if the business is doing well.

Comparing trading figures

Various ratios or percentages are used to make comparisons easier. Two important comparisons we need to make when looking at trading accounts are gross profit expressed as a percentage of sales and rate of stock turnover.

The gross profit margin shows how much of the money from sales is actual gross profit and the formula for calculating this is:

$$\frac{\text{gross profit}}{\text{sales}} \times 100 = \begin{array}{l}\text{percentage}\\\text{gross profit}\end{array}$$

In the case of Sarah's gift shop the answer would be:

$$\frac{£42,000}{£150,000} \times 100 = 28\%$$

Sarah's gross profit ratio of 28 per cent is not a particularly high margin – many similar businesses would have a margin of 50 per cent or more.

Another good indication of how well a business is doing is the rate of stock turnover, which shows how quickly or slowly the business is selling its stock of goods. To work this out we first have to find the average stock held. This is given by the formula:

$$\frac{\text{stock at start} + \text{stock at end}}{2} = \begin{array}{l}\text{average}\\\text{stock}\\\text{held}\end{array}$$

In Sarah's case, the figures would be:

$$\frac{£40,000 + £90,000}{2} = £65,000$$

The rate of stock turnover is worked out by another simple formula:

$$\frac{\text{cost of sales}}{\text{average stock held}} = \begin{array}{l}\text{rate of stock}\\\text{turnover}\end{array}$$

The gift shop's rate of stock turnover for the year was:

$$\frac{108,000}{65,000} = 1.7 \text{ times}$$

This calculation shows that Sarah has sold her average stock 1.7 times in the year. This is not particularly good for this type of business and it means that either trade is slow or she is holding too much stock at one time.

Cost of goods to sales ratio

To find out what percentage of the sales value went on buying the goods, use the following formula:

$$\frac{\text{cost of sales}}{\text{sales}} \times 100 = \begin{array}{l}\text{cost of goods}\\\text{to sales ratio}\end{array}$$

In the case of Sarah's gift shop, this would be:

$$\frac{£108,000}{£150,000} \times 100 = 72\%$$

The rest (28%) is gross profit.

CHECKPOINTS

1 What is the main information provided by a trading account?
2 What is the difference between gross profit and net profit?
3 Why is the rate of stock turnover important for a business? What is the formula for finding it?
4 What is the formula for finding percentage gross profit? If the gross profit was £120,000 and the sales were £200,000 what would be the percentage gross profit? Do you consider this to be a good figure?

KEY TERMS

TRADING ACCOUNT The trading account shows the gross profit for the year.

STOCK Goods which have been bought for re-sale by the business.

GROSS PROFIT Total profit made, before considering running and overhead expenses.

PURCHASES Further goods bought for re-sale during the trading period.

SALES (TURNOVER) Total goods sold both for cash and on credit.

NET PROFIT The true profit made over a trading period, after all the expenses have been subtracted.

Profit and Loss Accounts

Car facts

FIG 48.1	price	engine power	number of doors	fuel grade	overall fuel consumption	fuel consumption at steady 70mph	fuel consumption in a city	time to reach 60mph	top speed
	£	bhp		star	mpg	mpg	mpg	sec	mph
Citroen BX	5,750	62	5	4	34.7	37	15.9	15.2	94
Ford Escort 1.4L	6,833	75	5	4	36.7	36	17.0	14.0	100
Mazda 323 1.3LX	6,449	67	5	2	32.5	34	16.0	14.0	92
Peugeot 309 1.3GL	6,835	65	5	4	34.8	34	18.2	15.6	93
Renault 11 GTL	6,660	68	5	4	35.9	36	16.9	13.6	97
Seat Malaga 1.5GL	5,420	85	5	4	32.6	34	14.3	11.2	101
Vauxhall Belmont 1.3L	6,989	75	4	4	37.1	41	18.2	13.0	108
VW Golf C	6,843	55	5	2	35.0	37	17.8	17.6	94
Volvo 340 1.7GL	7,110	80	3	4	32.1	32	15.9	13.2	100

Source: *Which?*, April 1987 (Extracts)

Car ratings – at a glance

FIG 48.2	brakes	steering	road-holding	space	comfort of ride	security	wear/tear	safety
Citroen BX	○	○	○	○	★	●	★	3
Ford Escort 1.4L	★	○	○	○	○	●	○	4
Mazda 323 1.3LX	○	○	○	○	○	●	★	3
Peugeot 309 1.3GL	★	○	○	○	○	●	[1]	4
Renault 11 GTL	★	○	●	★	○	●	○	4
Seat Malaga 1.5GL	★	○	○	●	●	●	[1]	4
Vauxhall Belmont 1.3L	○	○	★	●	○	●	○	4
VW Golf C	★	○	★	○	●	●	○	4
Volvo 340 1.7GL	★	○	●	○	●	●	○	5

Key ★ = very good ○ = OK ● = poor [1] = not enough data Safety ratings: The higher the number the higher the chances of surviving an accident without serious injury.

Volvo 340
1.7GL

Seat Malaga
1.5GL

VW Golf C

Mazda 323
1.3LX

Renault 11
GTL

Peugeot 309
1.3GL

Citroen BX

Vauxhall Belmont
1.3L

Ford Escort
1.4L

The **PROFIT AND LOSS ACCOUNT** is a continuation of the trading account [see Unit 47]. It shows how much net profit a business has actually made during the previous year. All the expenses are taken away from the gross profit to show the true or net profit.

gross profit − expenses = net profit

Credits

Look at Figure 48.3 which shows the profit and loss account for Sarah's gift shop. Her gross profit for the previous financial year was £42,000 [see Unit 47]. This is entered on the credit (right hand) side of the account. Any additional income such as discounts, commissions, rent or interest received would also be entered on that side.

Debits

All expenses, losses and costs are entered on the debit (left hand) side of the account. In Sarah's case, these are

S T U D Y P O I N T S

The directors of a growing firm selling office furniture and equipment have decided to replace the present fleet of cars used by their sales representatives. They wish to buy cars for 10 reps who each travel about 1,000 miles a week. Reliability and economical running are as important as price and the 'image' created. The cars are expected to have a useful life of two years. The firm could easily afford to buy the cars out of its large cash resources.

1 Which car would in your opinion be most suitable? Give your reasons.

2 Study the Business Techniques. What would be the total depreciation on the fleet of cars after two years using the diminishing balance method?

3 In your view, should the cars be bought for cash or should some other method be used? [See Unit 41]

4 Write a full report for the directors of the firm, giving all your suggestions about replacing the cars.

wages; rent, rates and insurance; heating and lighting. The fourth item is a **PROVISION** for **BAD DEBTS**. Any business is likely to have some bills which will never be paid, and these are included as an expense (written off). The final item is another provision for **DEPRECIATION**.

Comparing profits

When all these expenses are taken away, the gross profit of £42,000 is reduced to a net profit of only £9,100. This is certainly a very low figure, but it doesn't tell us much by itself. How do we compare it with the profits of similar shops which have lower or higher total sales? As before, it is easier to compare figures when they are expressed as a percentage.

Another ratio – the percentage net profit to sales – provides the answer. This ratio shows how much of the income from sales is net profit. The formula is:

$$\frac{\text{net profit}}{\text{sales}} \times 100 = \text{percentage net profit to sales ratio}$$

In Sarah's case the percentage would be:

$$\frac{£9,100}{£150,000} \times 100 = 6\%$$

In comparison with other gift shops 6 per cent is a low percentage. Sarah might be better off putting her money into a savings account which earns a nominal rate of interest of 8 per cent.

KEY TERMS

PROFIT AND LOSS ACCOUNT A summary of the expenses, losses and overheads of a firm which is used to calculate the net profit over a period.

PROVISIONS Allowances for general or specific losses which may occur. A provision does not involve any actual expenditure.

BAD DEBTS Bills which will never be paid and which are written off (and therefore treated as an expense of the business).

DEPRECIATION Reduction in the value of an asset over a period of time.

FIG 48.3

Sarah's gift shop

Profit and loss account for the year ending 31 May 1988

	£		£
Wages	15,000	Gross profit	42,000
Rent, rates, insurance	16,000		
Heat and lighting	1,000		
Bad debts	500		
Depreciation			
Equipment and fittings	400		
Net profit	9,100		
	42,000		42,000

BUSINESS TECHNIQUES

Depreciation

A car will be worth much less than its original value after a period of time. The difference is called **DEPRECIATION**. One way of calculating depreciation is by the *diminishing balance method*. A percentage, say 25 per cent, of the car's value would be written off the value of the car each year. In the first year the original cost of the car, £10,000, would be used. The depreciation would be 25 per cent of this value, i.e. £2,500. In the second year, the depreciated value of the car, £7,500 (£10,000 − £2,500), would be used to calculate depreciation, i.e. 25 per cent of £7,500 (£1,875) and so on each year. The full depreciation over four years is shown in Figure 48.4. What would be the depreciation in the fifth year?

Another way of calculating depreciation is by the *straight line method*. This produces an equal reduction in value each year. It is often used with leasehold property, or large machinery. An estimate is made of how long the machinery will last, and what its value as scrap metal will be at the end of its useful life. The formula for finding the depreciation is:

Car depreciation over 4 years

FIG 48.4

	Value of car	Depreciation
	(To nearest pound)	
	£	£
1st yr	10,000	2,500
2nd yr	7,500	1,875
3rd yr	5,625	1,406
4th yr	4,219	1,055

$$\frac{\text{initial cost} - \text{scrap value}}{\text{useful life in years}} = \text{annual depreciation}$$

Use this method to find the annual depreciation on a machine which cost £12,000, if its scrap value at the end of 10 years was estimated at £2,000.

CHECKPOINTS

1 What is the main information provided by a profit and loss account?

2 What is meant by bad debts?

3 In the town where Sarah has her shop there are two other gift shops for sale. One is in a smart shopping centre and has high overheads; its sales are £300,000 with a net profit of £20,500. The other is much smaller with a turnover of £170,000 and net profit of £16,500. Compare Sarah's shop with both of these. Which is a) the most and b) the least profitable?

Balance Sheets

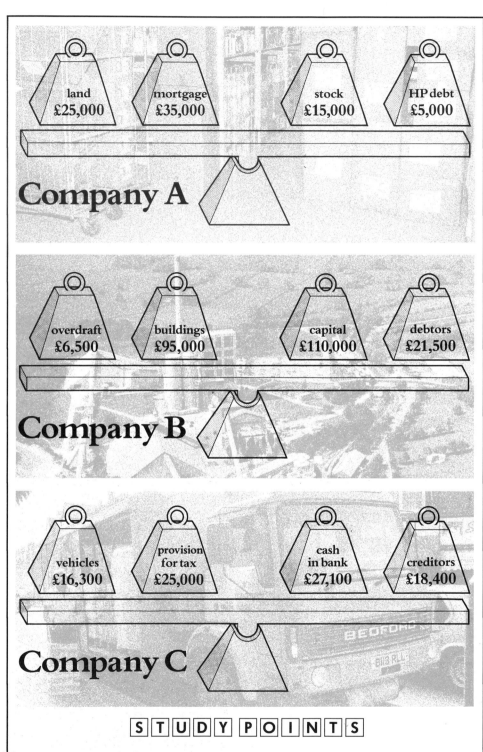

Company A

| land £25,000 | mortgage £35,000 | stock £15,000 | HP debt £5,000 |

Company B

| overdraft £6,500 | buildings £95,000 | capital £110,000 | debtors £21,500 |

Company C

| vehicles £16,300 | provision for tax £25,000 | cash in bank £27,100 | creditors £18,400 |

STUDY POINTS

(Study the Key Terms before you attempt the tasks below)

In a balance sheet the two sides must balance. The liabilities (all that is owed) on the left hand side must equal the assets (all that is owned) on the right.

1 Put the items above from the balance sheets of three companies on the correct side of the scales so that they balance.

2 Make a list of your results under the headings Liabilities and Assets.

3 Suggest any other liabilities or assets a company might have.

What is a **BALANCE SHEET**? It is a statement of the financial position of a business at one moment in time, showing all that it owes (its liabilities) and owns (its assets).

Liabilities

Let's go back to Sarah's gift shop again and look at her balance sheet for the previous year. The first item – **CAPITAL** – shows the amount that was invested in the business at the beginning of the year.

You may be wondering why the capital is a liability; but just think a minute! We are not considering Sarah's *own* financial affairs, but those of her shop. The capital is the amount of money that the shop owes to Sarah, the amount she might receive if the shop were sold.

The capital of £100,000 has increased by £9,100 during the year, thanks to the net profit which was calculated in the profit and loss account [see Unit 48]. During the year Sarah drew £8,000 out of the business to live on, which reduces the total to £101,100.

The final item on the liabilities side is the creditors – the firms or people to whom the shop owes money. These are **CURRENT LIABILITIES**. The shop has no **LONG-TERM LIABILITIES** – debts such as mortgages or loans which do not have to be paid within a year. Normally, these are listed before the current liabilities.

Assets

Now let's look at the other side of the account – the assets. The equipment and fittings, which are **FIXED ASSETS**, were worth £4,000 at the beginning of the year; but depreciation of £400 has reduced the figure to £3,600 [see Unit 48]. Stock at the end of the year was valued at £90,000.

Debtors owed the shop £3,500; but a provision has been made for bad debts of £500, which reduces the figure to £3,000. There was £9,100 in the bank and another £400 in cash. These are CURRENT (OR CIRCULATING) ASSETS.

If you study the balance sheet, you will see that most of the assets consist of stock. As we saw in the trading account [see Unit 47], the value of stock had risen by £50,000 during the year. A shop with a large amount of stock that it has been unable to sell is definitely not the sort of business you would want to buy unless you could see some big hidden potential. Even then, it would depend on the valuation of the stock when you bought it.

FIG 49.1 — Sarah's gift shop

Balance sheet

Liabilities	£	£	Assets	£	£
Capital	100,000		Equipment & fittings	4,000	
Net profit	9,100		Depreciation	400	3,600
	109,100				
less Drawings	8,000		Stock		90,000
	101,100		Debtors	3,500	
Creditors	5,000		*less* Bad debts	500	3,000
			Bank		9,100
			Cash		400
		106,100			106,100

BUSINESS TECHNIQUES

Goodwill

When a small business is sold, an extra amount is sometimes charged for goodwill. This usually represents the benefit of profitable contacts with customers which have been built up by the owner.

There are many complicated formulas for calculating goodwill. One way is to take the difference between actual profit and what is considered to be a reasonable profit for a business of that size, over an agreed period of time.

If the reasonable profits of a business had been £110,000 and the actual profits £140,000 over a three-year period, what would the goodwill be worth?

CHECKPOINTS

A year ago, Mr Ronald Jackson opened a small bicycle shop called Spinning Wheels. He now has £10,000 in the bank.

This year he has made a net profit of £11,000 but he has withdrawn £9,000 for living expenses.

He has £8,000 worth of stock but owes £5,300 to his suppliers. The small amount of equipment he has on the premises is valued at £800. His credit customers owe him £3,500. Mr Jackson's shop premises are valued at £45,000. He had already paid £27,000 as a deposit from his building society account, but this will not appear in his business accounts. The balance was financed by an £18,000 mortgage.

1   Make out a balance sheet for Spinning Wheels, setting out the items under the headings: fixed assets; current assets; capital; long-term liabilities; current liabilities. (The capital is calculated by deducting total liabilities from total assets.) Your balance sheet should total £67,300.

2   What is the total value of Mr Jackson's fixed assets?

3   If Mr Jackson had not started his business, how much interest would he have gained during that year from leaving the money in his Building Society, if it had been in a long-term account paying 9 per cent interest?

4   What was the opportunity cost to Mr Jackson of investing £27,000 in his business premises?

5   If Mr Jackson had taken a job paying £12,000 a year instead, do you think he would have been better off?

6   Make a list of the benefits of running your own business, apart from purely financial considerations.

KEY TERMS

BALANCE SHEET A statement of the financial situation of a business at a specified moment in time.

CAPITAL Money invested in a business representing a claim on the assets.

CURRENT LIABILITIES Debts demanding short-term payment, such as tax, money owed to creditors, and overdrafts.

LONG-TERM LIABILITIES Debts not due for payment within one year, such as mortgages and bank loans.

FIXED ASSETS Permanent possessions which enable the business to function, such as buildings, machinery, vehicles and land.

CURRENT (OR CIRCULATING) ASSETS Asset items which constantly change and are easily converted into cash, such as stock, debts owed to the business (debtors) and cash in the bank or in hand.

Company Balance Sheets

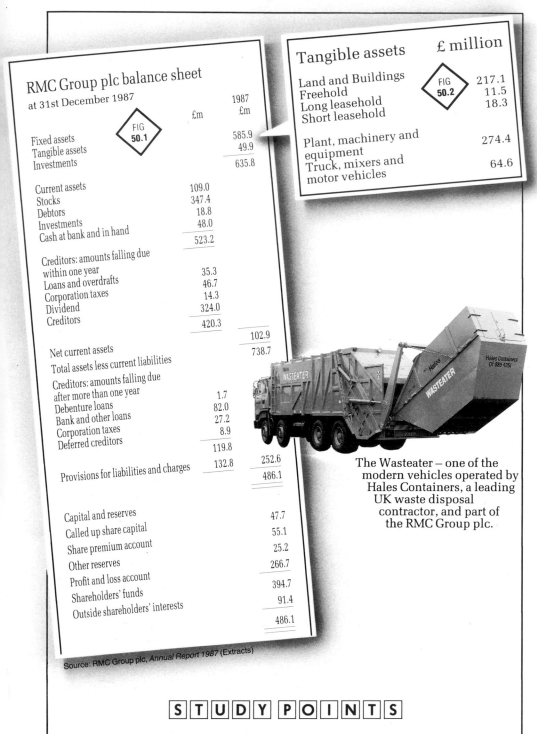

RMC Group plc balance sheet
at 31st December 1987

FIG 50.1

	1987 £m	1987 £m
Fixed assets		
Tangible assets		585.9
Investments		49.9
		635.8
Current assets		
Stocks	109.0	
Debtors	347.4	
Investments	18.8	
Cash at bank and in hand	48.0	
	523.2	
Creditors: amounts falling due within one year		
Loans and overdrafts	35.3	
Corporation taxes	46.7	
Dividend	14.3	
Creditors	324.0	
	420.3	
		102.9
Net current assets		738.7
Total assets less current liabilities		
Creditors: amounts falling due after more than one year		
Debenture loans	1.7	
Bank and other loans	82.0	
Corporation taxes	27.2	
Deferred creditors	8.9	
	119.8	
Provisions for liabilities and charges	132.8	252.6
		486.1
Capital and reserves		
Called up share capital		47.7
Share premium account		55.1
Other reserves		25.2
Profit and loss account		266.7
Shareholders' funds		394.7
Outside shareholders' interests		91.4
		486.1

Source: RMC Group plc, *Annual Report 1987* (Extracts)

Tangible assets £ million

FIG 50.2

	£ million
Land and Buildings	
Freehold	217.1
Long leasehold	11.5
Short leasehold	18.3
Plant, machinery and equipment	274.4
Truck, mixers and motor vehicles	64.6

The Wasteater – one of the modern vehicles operated by Hales Containers, a leading UK waste disposal contractor, and part of the RMC Group plc.

Annual report and accounts

A sole proprietor does not have to show his accounts to anyone except the Inland Revenue and the Customs and Excise, which administers VAT. A limited company, however, is bound by law to publish an annual report and final accounts giving information about its operations during the previous 12 months. This document usually contains:

● a profit and loss account, with notes of explanation giving further details

● a balance sheet, with similar kinds of notes

● the directors' reports about what has happened during the previous year. This must legally contain details of the main activities during the past year, any acquisitions and disposals of other companies, important changes in the organisation of the company, and certain other information.

A true and fair view

The accounts must also be audited. This means that they have been checked by an independent person, an **AUDITOR**, for truth and fairness.

Even so, the report and accounts do not give a complete picture of the company's financial state at that time. The auditor doesn't have to check every small detail in the accounts for accuracy. He or she simply has to make sure that they present a true and fair view of what has happened in the business during the previous year. Furthermore, the company does not have to reveal information which would be of value to its competitors or harmful to itself, unless it is required by law. Nevertheless, the published accounts do provide a large amount of valuable information about the company.

STUDY POINTS

1 What is the total value of the RMC Group's fixed assets? Give three examples.

2 Which is the most valuable type of fixed asset?

3 State the current assets and the current liabilities of the Group.

4 The stocks held at 31 December 1986 were valued at £93.4 million. What was the average stock held during 1987?

5 The cost of sales was £1,304 million. What was the rate of stock turnover during the year?

Shares

The main difference between a limited company and a sole proprietor is that the company has a separate identity which is recognised by law [see Unit 17]. The company is owned by its shareholders. Their liability, or responsibility for the company's debts, is limited to the amount of money they have invested in **ORDINARY SHARES** or **PREFERENCE SHARES**.

The **AUTHORISED CAPITAL** of the RMC Group is 280 million shares of 25p each. The nominal value of the called up share capital or **ISSUED CAPITAL** is £47.7 million, as the balance sheet shows. How many shares have been issued?

Not all of these shares were issued at the nominal value; some were issued at a higher price. The next item on the balance sheet – the share premium account – shows the reserve which has been created by issuing shares at this higher price.

Solvency

One of the most important figures in a balance sheet is the working capital, which shows whether the company is solvent – able to pay its debts. It is vital for any business to have enough money to pay its debts as they arise, otherwise it would have a cash flow or liquidity problem [see Unit 46]. Working capital, or net current assets, is calculated by the following formula:

$$\text{current assets} - \text{current liabilities} = \text{working capital}$$

RMC's working capital was £102.9 million, i.e.

$$£523.2 \text{ million} - £420.3 \text{ million}$$

The current ratio shows how many times a company could afford to pay its current liabilities out of its current assets. It is worked out by the following formula:

$$\frac{\text{current assets}}{\text{current liabilities}} = \text{current ratio}$$

The RMC current ratio was:

$$\frac{523.2}{420.3} = 1.24{:}1$$

The acid test ratio provides an even more realistic picture of a company's financial affairs [see Unit 51]. In calculating this ratio, stocks, which cannot necessarily be sold immediately, are deducted from the current assets. The acid test ratio shows whether a company would be able to meet its liabilities immediately.

In this case, however, there would be little point in using the acid test ratio. The RMC Group's core activities are producing ready mixed concrete and the extraction and sale of sand and gravel – which are mixed with cement to make concrete. These activities do not involve holding large volumes of stock.

The stocks shown in the balance sheet, totalling £109 million, consist largely of finished goods and goods for resale in the group's DIY and builders' merchants stores. As the Study Points have shown, there is a rapid turnover of this stock.

In interpreting company accounts, it is essential to take account of all the relevant information that is available.

CHECKPOINTS

1 What is the current ratio? What information does it provide?
2 What kind of people would be interested in the current ratio?
3 When does the acid test ratio provide a more realistic picture of a company's solvency than the current ratio?
4 Draw a pie chart to show the fixed and current assets of the RMC group.

KEY TERMS

AUDITOR A qualified, independent person who examines a company's accounts to make sure that they have been properly kept and that they give a true and fair picture of the financial situation.

ORDINARY SHARES Shares (also known as equity) in a company, which are bought on the Stock Exchange. Shareholders can vote at annual general meetings.

PREFERENCE SHARES Shares which have priority over ordinary shares when dividends are paid.

AUTHORISED CAPITAL The total amount of money that a company is allowed to raise through issuing shares.

ISSUED CAPITAL The actual amount of capital which has been raised and paid for at a particular time.

Comparisons of Final Accounts

Profit and loss account

FIG 51.1

	1989		1988	
	£m	£m	£m	£m
Sales		34		18
Cost of sales (−)		17		9
Gross profit		17		9
Administration (−)	6		4	
Distribution (−)	2		1	
Pre-tax profit		9		4
Tax (−)		3.5		1.5
Net profit		5.5		2.5
Dividends paid (−)		2.5		2
Retained profit		3		0.5

Balance sheet

FIG 51.2

	1989		1988	
	£m	£m	£m	£m
Fixed assets		1		1
Current assets				
Stocks	8		4	
Debtors	6		4	
Cash	1		0.5	
TOTAL		15		8.5
Current liabilities				
Creditors (−)	12		6.5	
Net current assets		3		2
TOTAL assets less current liabilities		4		3

⬛ S T U D Y P O I N T S ⬛

(Study the simplified profit and loss account and balance sheet of an imaginary firm, Bartons Babyfoods plc, in Figures 51.1 and 51.2 and then answer the following questions.)

1 What has been the percentage rise in Bartons' sales over the year?

2 How do you find the gross profit?

3 What makes up current assets? By how much have they increased in 1989 compared with the previous year?

4 For what reasons might the level of stocks have increased?

Who reads accounts?

Company reports and accounts are eagerly awaited and read by a wide range of people. These include:
● shareholders who want to see what dividends they will get and how their company is doing,
● unions looking for information to support their case for better wages and conditions for their members,
● other firms who might want to make a take-over bid,
● stock exchange speculators like **BEARS**, who want to sell shares, and **BULLS**, who want to buy them in the hope of making a profit,
● creditors, who want to make sure the company can pay its bills,
● financial journalists and City analysts, so that they can keep up-to-date with business trends.

Interpreting accounts

Skilled analysts will sift carefully through the accounts looking for clues to the company's performance. But how can that be judged?
● One way is to compare the current year's result with previous years', using ratios where possible [see Units 48 and 50].
● Another way is to compare the company's performance with those of similar companies.
● A third way is to compare the performance with a budget [see Unit 45]. Only managers who work in the firm can do this, however, as a company's budgets are not published.

First, let us compare one year against another, using some of the ratios used in previous units.

Is the company profitable?

The Study Points showed that Bartons Babyfoods plc had an 88.8 per cent rise in sales during the year, which looks good. However, we need to know how much it cost the company to sell its products. The following

Bulls and bears are stock exchange speculators who buy and sell shares.

45, 48, 50 ◄ See Unit

formula [see Unit 48] gives the net profit on each pound of sales:

$$\frac{\text{net profit}}{\text{sales}} \times 100 = \text{net profit per pound of sales}$$

Using this formula and comparing the ratios, a respectable rise in net profit ratio of 2.3 per cent is shown:

1989
$$\frac{5.5}{34} \times 100$$
$$= 16.1\%$$

1988
$$\frac{2.5}{18} \times 100$$
$$= 13.8\%$$

Is the company solvent?

Now let's look at the balance sheet. In 1989 the current assets increased by £6.5 million, which looks good. During that period, however, Bartons' liabilities increased from £6.5 million to £12 million. What do these figures really mean?

To find out, we have to calculate the current ratio which was discussed in Unit 50. The formula is:

$$\frac{\text{current assets}}{\text{current liabilities}} = \text{current ratio}$$

The ratios for the two years show that there has been a decline:

1989
$$\frac{15}{12} = 1.25{:}1$$

1988
$$\frac{8.5}{6.5} = 1.3{:}1$$

The ratio, however, is satisfactory as the current assets will still cover current liabilities, but a downward trend needs to be watched. Bartons is solvent. Or is it? To find out for sure we must apply the acid test ratio [see Unit 50].

If we deduct the value of the stock from the current assets for each year we obtain the following figures:

1989
$$15 - 8 = 7$$

1988
$$8.5 - 4 = 4.5$$

Divide these figures by the current liabilities to find the ratios:

1989
$$\frac{7}{12} = 0.6{:}1$$

1988
$$\frac{4.5}{6.5} = 0.7{:}1$$

The ratios give quite a different picture of Bartons' solvency. These figures also show there has been a decline during the year and Bartons are risking insolvency should any of their creditors call in their debts quickly.

Is the company efficiently run?

Finally, let's see how often the current assets were turned over in each year. The formula is:

$$\frac{\text{sales}}{\text{current assets}}$$

The figures for the two years are:

1989
$$\frac{34}{15} = 2.3{:}1$$

1988
$$\frac{18}{8.5} = 2.1{:}1$$

In this respect, Bartons Babyfoods plc is operating more efficiently, as more sales are resulting from the same value of current assets.

BUSINESS TECHNIQUES

Measuring administration

The efficiency of administration is measured by the formula:

$$\frac{\text{administration}}{\text{sales}} \times 100$$

This percentage shows whether the cost of managing the company has increased or decreased in relation to sales. Calculate the percentages for 1989 and 1988 using the profit and loss account in Figure 51.1.

CHECKPOINTS

1. **What are the three main ways of comparing final accounts?**
2. **Who are the people mainly interested in company accounts and for what reasons?**
3. **Explain the general importance of ratios.**

KEY TERMS

BEARS Speculators on the Stock Exchange who sell shares in anticipation of a fall in their price, when the bears will buy back the original shares.

BULLS Speculators who buy shares in the hope that they will rise in price, when the bulls will sell the shares for gain.

Profitability

At the age of 19, you decide to set up your own business, even though you have only a small amount of money in your bank account. You believe there is a gap in the local market for light removals. To find out the current market prices, you find the names and addresses of four firms in the Yellow Pages and ring to ask what they would charge to move a desk, a double bed and six packing cases from your home to another house two miles away. You write down the details given to you by each firm on the telephone.

LIFT AND LOAD:

Charge for service,
 - £14 per hour

 - payment is from their depot (8 miles away) and includes the journey back.
 - 2 men to do the job.
(say they are fast workers!)

MARIO FURNITURE DEALERS:

 - also do local removals

Payment by distance at £1 per mile, including distance to and from premises. (2 miles)

plus   £4 per item moved.

MOVING ON:

Desk, bed + 6 boxes = £25

 - large transit van
 - 2 men will make sure all goods are safely strapped down.
 - includes total insurance of goods removed - up to a value of £1,500
(sounded helpful)

NATIONAL MOVES:

Packing, insurance all included.
 - £50 a part load

plus
£10
£15
£25
£50

removal dist.
up to 10 miles
up to 20 miles
up to 30 miles
up to 100 miles

£1 each refund on packing cases when collected.

FIG 52.1

BANK LOAN APPLICATION

Customer's name ....
Address ....
....
If customer has a bank account, for how
long has the account been held ....
Income per month/projected income ....
Expenditure : per month
                        Living expenses ....
                        Loans and HP ....
Purpose of loan ....
Total amount required ....
Customer contribution ....
Length of time of loan ....
Does customer have any security? ....

STUDY POINTS

(You will have to use both desk and outside research to do some of these tasks.)

1 Using the information here and your own research, estimate the minimum capital needed to start the business.

2 List the fixed and variable costs. Estimate a) the fixed costs per month, and b) the variable costs per mile.

3 Make out a schedule of prices. Compare it with those of rival firms. If your prices are higher, see if you can cut your costs.

4 Forecast your revenue per month for the first three months. Make out a cash-flow forecast for the period.

5 Construct a break even chart showing when you expect your business to break even.

6 Estimate the amount of money you will need to live on until you break even and add this to the amount of capital required.

7 You have obtained a loan application form from your bank. Copy out the form shown in Figure 52.1 and fill in the details.

8 Write a covering letter to your bank manager to send with your completed form, cashflow forecast and break even chart.

9 If the loan was granted and the nominal interest rate was 8%, what would be the monthly repayments over the period you have chosen?

Increasing profitability

The purpose of management accounting is to see that a business is profitable and to find ways of increasing profitability. It does this by analysing company performance, exercising financial controls and analysing costs. The principles can be applied to both large and small firms. The four main ways of increasing profitability are:
● to take over other firms
● to use assets more efficiently
● to increase revenue
● to reduce costs.

Taking over other firms

Management accountants decide whether a firm is worth taking over by answering such questions as:

- Could the assets be sold off at a profit?
- Are there opportunities to increase the firm's current market share?
- Could the firm be profitably reorganised?
- Can the present growth rate be maintained or increased?
- What is the **RETURN ON CAPITAL EMPLOYED (ROCE)**? [See Unit 50]
- How would changes in exchange rates, increased foreign competition, etc affect the firm?

Judging performance

The simplest way of judging a firm's general performance is to find out the ROCE by using the formula:

$$\frac{\text{net profit} \times 100}{\text{capital employed}} = \text{ROCE}$$

So a net profit of £2.9 million and total assets, or capital employed, of £15 million would give ROCE of:

$$\frac{£2,900,000}{£15,000,000} \times 100 = 19.3\%$$

Now the management accountant has to ask:

- How does it compare with similar firms?
- How does it compare with past performance?

If the answer to both questions is 'better', the company is doing well in general terms.

If the firm's ROCE percentage has decreased, the reason could be declining sales, increasing costs, or inefficient use of assets. Or it may be only a temporary decline. If a firm bought new machinery to meet an expected increase in sales (bringing higher net profits in a few months' time) what would happen to the ROCE percentage during that period?

Analysing costs

One of the main methods of analysing costs is by using the **MARGINAL COST** – the extra cost it takes to produce one more unit. For example:

Total cost for 50 units	£100
Total cost for 51 units	£101
Marginal cost = £1	

As the fixed costs have stayed the same, the marginal cost must be the extra costs of wages and materials – in other words, the variable costs [see Unit 43]. The difference between variable (marginal) costs and the sales revenue they bring is the **CONTRIBUTION**. This is calculated by the formula:

$$\text{sales revenue} - \text{variable costs} = \text{contribution}$$

The contribution is not profit as fixed costs have not been included. The profit is calculated by the formula:

$$\text{contribution} - \text{fixed costs} = \text{profit}$$

For example:

Calculating profit

	£	£
Sales revenue	30,000	40,000
less Variable costs	17,000	22,000
Contributions	13,000	18,000
less Fixed costs	10,000	10,000
Profit	3,000	8,000

Costs can be analysed in another way by relating them to **COST CENTRES** – a department, a section, or even an individual manager. Costs are divided into various categories:

- direct costs which relate only to that centre (cost of labour, materials, etc)
- indirect costs which are shared with other centres (like heating the whole factory)
- general costs, or overheads in administration, distribution etc.

When the firm's total costs have been allocated to each cost centre, the total costs of each centre can be analysed.

Cost analysis

The annual costs of labour in a department are £1,213,498 and of materials £577,641. The indirect costs are £28,998 and its share of the firm's overheads is 5 per cent of £347,303. What are its total weekly costs?

CHECKPOINTS

1 What are the four chief ways of increasing profitability?
2 What is meant by return on capital employed?
3 What is marginal cost?
4 Explain the meaning of contribution in your own words.
5 What is a cost centre?
6 Give two examples each of direct costs, indirect costs and overheads.
7 Give three reasons why a firm's ROCE percentage may have declined.

KEY TERMS

RETURN ON CAPITAL EMPLOYED (ROCE) A ratio which gives a general indication of a firm's performance.

MARGINAL COST The marginal cost is the extra cost it takes to produce one more unit of output.

CONTRIBUTION The difference between variable (marginal) costs and sales revenue.

COST CENTRES Part of an organisation whose costs are analysed in great detail so that they can be more strictly controlled.

Activities

■ Review points

1 What is a trading account?

2 What are ratios and why are they important in interpreting accounts?

3 In comparison with a trading account, what additional information is provided by a profit and loss account?

4 What information does a balance sheet provide?

5 What are the three main purposes of a balance sheet?

6 Name three kinds of assets and say which ones are fixed and which are current.

7 What is depreciation?

8 What is the main difference between current and long-term liabilities?

9 What information is *not* provided in a balance sheet?

10 What is the work of an auditor?

11 Explain the difference between a bull market and a bear market.

■ Essay questions

1 What is the importance of balance sheets for:
   a) investors
   b) takeover bidders
   c) the labour force?

2 A friend has asked you to help her get a bank loan to start her own business. What advice would you give her in relation to:
   a) filling in a loan application form
   b) other documents she might send
   c) the interest she might have to pay on the loan?

Auditors are your watchdog

THE AUDITOR'S job is to declare that a set of accounts is honest; to state that, in his opinion, the figures 'give a true and fair view of the state of the company's affairs'.

Signed and dated, the auditor's rather dull report will be addressed to the company's shareholders. It is perhaps the most important part of the whole set of accounts. Profits, turnovers, assets – none can be trusted without the auditor's stamp of approval.

Paid by the company, the auditor acts as a policeman, patrolling the company in the interests of its shareholders – those who own the business, but don't necessarily run it. His job is, quite simply, to give his opinion on the accounts. He doesn't actually prepare the company's figures. He tests their accuracy. So he'll check that the company cash book agrees with the bank statement, or scout around the building matching typewriters and desks to invoices received.

He'll judge whether anyone is walking off with the petty cash and he'll be on the look out for fraud. But he is under no legal obligation to detect it.

Nor does he have to say that the figures are deadly accurate. What is 'true and fair' allows fairly wide limits. Many of the mistakes he discovers while going through the company's books are simply ignored, passed as 'unimportant'.

Often, in small companies in particular, the profit figure is a fairly rough calculation agreed between auditors and management. A difference between profit estimates of £20,000 on turnover of £5m might mean all the world to interested parties but in the company it is no more than a dash of double entry. In a big multinational plc, 'errors' of millions of pounds are seen as unimportant.

It's not always a danger sign when companies and their auditors part company. For example, Dixons have just moved from a small, North London accountancy firm to a big international one which is more in keeping with the size of the group now. But investors were worried when last February Spicer & Pegler gave up auditing the sugar and commodity group SW Berisford, after 50 years. The reason given: differences over 'management style'.

1 What is the main job of an auditor?

2 Who pays for the work?

3 Who benefits most from the auditor's report?

4 How is the work done?

5 Why are some mistakes and errors ignored?

6 Why might investors be worried if a firm changed its auditor?

Woolworth rides storm to success

Since Geoff Mulcahy's management team took over Woolworth five years ago, it has expanded greatly. The group's profits rose £32 million to £141 million in 1987–88

THERE are now five distinct, and profitable, businesses: B&Q; Superdrug; Comet – which has now been strengthened with the £8m purchase of Harris's rival Ultimate chain; Woolworth stores, which is the original business; and Charlie Brown's APOS autopart operations.

One of Woolies' key bear market qualities is its property portfolio valued at between £800m and £900m.

Not many of Woolworth's shoppers are major stock market investors, so there is no sign of any fall-off in sales since the stock market crash.

Superdrug is Woolworth's newest addition. Bought in the spring for £300m, the original 260 outlets will be up to 310 by the year end. Superdrug makes a return of over 50% on its capital, even though the average amount each customer spends is only £2.

Last week's acquisition from Harris Queensway of 94 Ulti- mate electrical goods outlets, 48 of them in Debenham's stores, got a warm reception in the City. Mulcahy expects to push an additional £90m of sales through the outlets, which will all take the Comet name.

Woolworth Holdings makes a third of its profits in the six week run-up to Christmas. If all goes well, the group could top £150m before tax against £110m last year which puts in a prospective p/e ratio of 12.5.

RATINGS OF THE BIG STORES

	Share price, p	P/E ratio	Gross dividend yield %
Boots	230	13.5	4.76
Burton	219	11.1	3.92
Dixons	244	13.6	2.24
Harris Queensway	116	13.3	6.77
Laura Ashley	114	16.1	2.82
Marks & Spencer	195	18.5	3.27
Next	282	18.3	2.67
Ratners	241	10.8	2.74
Sears	128	13.5	4.63
WH Smith 'A'	306	15.0	3.50
Storehouse	263	13.2	4.47
Ward White	306	11.7	3.53
Woolworth	289	14.1	4.03

Source: *Datastream*

Adapted from: *Sunday Times*, 15 November 1987

Notes on table, 'Ratings of the big stores'

● The price/earnings ratio (p/e) represents the market price of the share divided by the earnings per share. It shows how long it would take for shareholders to get their investment back. For instance, if the ratio is 12, investors would get their capital outlay back in 12 years if earnings remain unchanged.

● The gross dividend yield is calculated by the following formula:

$$\frac{\text{gross dividend} \times 100}{\text{current market price of share}} = \text{gross dividend yield}$$

Investors who bought the shares in the past at a lower price are still getting a good return on their money even when yield appears to be small. For example, if shares were bought at £1, the current price was £2 and the yield was 4%, the real return to an investor would be 8%. The yield makes comparisons between returns on investments easier.

1 What factors make Woolworth a good investment?

2 Draw an organisation chart showing a possible structure for Woolworth Holdings.

3 When does Woolworth make most of its profits?

4 Study the table of big store ratings, and the notes below the article. On the basis of p/e, which would be the best stores' shares to buy?

5 Where does Woolworth come in the stores p/e league table? Would this affect your decision to buy these shares?

6 If the article's prediction about the future p/e ratio came true, where would Woolworth have stood in the stores p/e league table after Christmas, assuming that the others had not changed?

7 Where does Woolworth stand in the stores league table for gross dividend yield?

8 Which kind of investor would go for a high yield?

9 Which kind of investor would favour a low p/e?

■ Coursework

1 Write to a big plc for a copy of its latest annual report and accounts. Look at the profit and loss account and explain in your own words
   a) how the net profit (or loss) is arrived at
   b) what proportion of the profit is paid to shareholders and what proportion is retained
   c) what indications you can find in the report to explain these proportions.

2 Choose any share in a section of the Stock Exchange listing which you think likely to rise. Record its daily price over a period of weeks. At the end of that period, write a report stating your reasons for choosing the share and saying whether the price has risen or fallen. Analyse the factors which resulted in the change in price and evaluate whether they could have been predicted or not. Illustrate the report with a line graph showing the daily change in price.

Internal Communications

The Stock Exchange

- 23-storey high-rise tower.
- Built about 15 years ago.
- Tower and Stock Exchange trading floor occupy 341,000 square feet of space.
- High proportion of space (approx. $\frac{1}{3}$) is taken up by office services.
- If they were moved, it would take about 3 years to relocate them and their complex computer systems.
- Site alone could be worth £100m.
- Situated in heart of City next to Bank of England very valuable site.
- Could be redeveloped as low-rise office block for letting.
- Trading floor no longer used by Stock Exchange because of Big Bang.
- Trading in stocks and shares now goes on worldwide on computers 24 hours a day.
- Trading floor closed March 87.
- About $\frac{2}{3}$ trading floor space now used by traded options market.
- Dealings in stocks and shares are now done on computers instead of face to face, as a result of Big Bang in October 1986.
- Redeveloping the site could bring in a great deal of money for the Stock Exchange.
- Annual office rents in such sites are about £60 per square foot.
- The back-up and administrative staff still occupy part of the building, but they could easily be moved away from the City to a cheaper site.
- Would it be better to redevelop site or to sell it?
- Cost of redevelopment would be high.
- Even in outer London, air-conditioned low-rise office blocks cost about £800 per square metre to build, and would cost even more in the City.

Source (in part): *The Guardian*, 4 June 1987 (adapted)

STUDY POINTS

Brian Wood, who works in the Stock Exchange, has been asked by a senior manager to write a report on the possibility of redeveloping the Stock Exchange building. He has jotted down the notes shown here about the future of the building.

1 Study the information about the Stock Exchange building and put the points in a logical order.

2 Write the report for the senior manager using the format given below.

Title

1 History
2 Recent changes
3 Present situation
4 Redevelopment
5 Conclusions
6 Recommendations

The importance of good communications

Good communications are the life-blood of any organisation. The trouble is that we can all speak and write, so we tend to think we know all about communication.

Thousands of pieces of paper containing views, information, commands and requests are being circulated around large organisations every minute of the day. The International Data Corporation has estimated that the average office worker in the United States – and there are 30 million of them – uses 48 sheets of paper each day. In addition, millions of words are spoken at meetings, conferences, presentations and on the telephone – often to little real effect. Communication is one of the great waste areas of business, with too many words chasing too few ideas.

Even in small firms with just one or two employees, communications are vitally important. Fewer words may be used, and they are more likely to be spoken face-to-face than written, but the words may have to be even more carefully chosen if they are not to cause bad feeling. What would happen if you were working part-time in a shop and you spoke sharply to your employer? Or what would you do if the supermarket manager was always criticising you? Even if you weren't sacked or didn't leave your job, relations might not be very good afterwards.

Some professional people, like teachers, are trained to communicate their knowledge and their skills; but many business persons have not received that kind of training. Yet to write and speak effectively is a priceless business asset.

What are communications?

Communications are simply the passing of messages from one person, or group of persons, to another. The channels along which they flow may be:

- *Spoken* Face-to-face conversations, telephone calls, meetings, conferences, presentations, public address systems etc, or
- *Written* Reports, notices, memoranda, letters, invoices etc.

The main advantage of written communications is that there is a permanent record on paper or on disc.

The main advantage of verbal communications is that the **FEEDBACK** is quicker. If you are negotiating with someone by letter, you have to wait

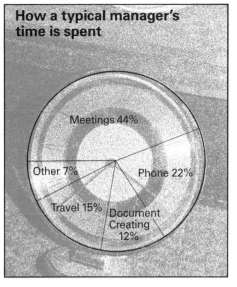

How a typical manager's time is spent

Meetings 44%

Other 7%

Phone 22%

Travel 15%

Document Creating 12%

for a reply before you can make a new offer. If you are negotiating on the phone, you can make a new offer straight away and, perhaps, finalise the deal. You might decide to tape-record your conversation if it is very important, so that there is a permanent record.

How do communications work?

In communications, there is always a two-way interaction:

Sender ....▸ Receiver

The message goes out from the sender to the receiver along some chosen channel of communication, such as a **MEMORANDUM**, and the feedback comes back to the sender through the same channel – a memo – or another channel, such as a telephone call.

The relative strengths of the message and the feedback will depend on the organisational structure [see Unit 24] and the direction in which the message is going.

- If the message is going downwards, as in a staff-board **NOTICE**, it will usually be strong, clear and decisive. The main feedback will be if the orders are carried out.
- If it is going upwards, as in a **REPORT** to higher management, the message will tend to be more persuasive. The main feedback will be approval or disapproval.
- If it is going sideways, as in a **PRESENTATION**, the message will tend to be more open-ended and the main feedback will be interest and reactions.

These factors will depend on the organisation's management policy. If management is dictatorial, there will be fewer internal communications going upwards than there would be if management were more democratic.

Vital questions

You can check if a message has provided all the main information by seeing if it answers the five W's – Who? What? When? Where? Why? – and How?

Find a report of a court case in a newspaper and mark the places where it answers these questions. If some questions are not answered, explain the reason.

KEY TERMS

FEEDBACK The response to a message which is transmitted back to the sender. It indicates whether the message has been received and understood and gives the sender the opportunity to modify the original message if necessary.

MEMORANDUM A written message between members of the same firm, usually on a standard form.

NOTICE A public message which gives instructions or an invitation or issues an appeal.

REPORT A written account in a standard format of what has been investigated, discussed or done.

PRESENTATION A talk, often illustrated with visual aids, describing what has been done or what should be done in the future.

CHECKPOINTS

1 How much time does the average manager spend at meetings each day?

2 What percentage of a manager's time is spent on less productive work?

3 Name some kinds of a) written documents, and b) verbal communications a manager might use.

4 Why are good communications just as important in a small firm as in a large organisation?

5 What is the importance of feedback for the sender and for the receiver?

External Communications

Nursing home is a landmark for high standards

NORTHGATE House, a nursing home development in Highgate, North London, has recently been completed and is now open.

The building has been renovated and refurbished to a very high standard and will provide varied and attractive accommodation, including several lounges, dining rooms and a conservatory. Each bedroom has been furnished to give a warm atmosphere and most have en suite bathrooms.

The aim is to provide each resident with a comfortable, safe and happy home, in which dignity can be maintained and independence encouraged. The very best of professional care for 24 hours a day is under the personal supervision of the Matron, David Gaskell. Director of nursing is Jean Walker and the managing director is Mike Newman.

The staff will achieve the aims by careful consideration of each resident's needs and wishes, and the encouragement of their hobbies and interests.

One of the outstanding attractions of medical care at Northgate House is the magnificent therapeutic wing containing both hydrotherapy and physiotherapy.

Source: *Hampstead Advertiser*, 10 December 1987

One of the residents of Northgate House talking to members of staff.

STUDY POINTS

1 Study the feature above. State where it answers the vital questions – the five W's and How? (See Business Techniques, page 137).

2 Write a similar feature for a local paper about any business you would like to start yourself.

> ' Remember that you have two ears and one mouth. Try to use them in roughly that proportion. '

Source: *Sunday Times*, Lifeplan, 7 June 1987

Good **EXTERNAL COMMUNICATIONS** are just as important for a business as its internal communications. What are good communications? Why are communications sometimes ineffective? How can they be improved?

Basic communication skills

In today's competitive world, speed is essential in all communications [see Unit 55]. In addition, whether you are writing a business letter, telephoning, or using the latest electronic device, there are certain skills which help effective communication.

- *Accuracy* is vital. In both face-to-face and telephone conversations it is essential to listen carefully to what other people are saying, to gain an accurate idea of their views. Accuracy is just as important in writing. Check everything that you write to make sure it is accurate. If you don't know how to spell a word, use a dictionary. If you are not sure where a place is, look it up in an atlas. Don't make guesses.
- *Clarity* is also necessary. People must understand immediately what you are saying or what you have written. Before you write a word or open your mouth, make sure that you know the exact message you want to get across. Then make the message as clear and as simple as possible.
- *Simplicity* in speech or writing is also desirable. Short words are usually more effective than long ones, and being brief saves time and money. Communications can often be made simpler by using well-designed forms. Firms use many kinds of forms for routine external communications: invoices, delivery notes, orders, etc. These save time and make sure the message is accurate and complete.

LOVELY MOVES
12 Wilton Way
Worrall
Southshire

FIG 54.1

Telephone: 0234 667459

Letterhead including writer's address

Reference → WP/WH

Date → 3 November 1989

Inside address → Mrs J Brown
11 High Road
Worrall
Southshire

Salutation → Dear Mrs Brown

Text of letter →

Close → Yours sincerely
Winston Powell

● *Completeness* is another important factor. Did your newspaper feature in the Study Points answer the vital questions – the five W's and How? A communication which misses out a vital piece of information will fail.

Achieving the main objective

These are the basics of communication. The main objective of every communication is to influence the receiver.

It is not only what you say – which should be accurate, clear, simple and complete – but how you say or write it which is important. Not only do you want to get your message across but you want a particular response – you want the receiver to do something, or not to do something, as a result of it. Remember the advertiser designing his advertisement for the chosen market segment? [See Unit 35] In the same way, your message should be designed for the person or organisation it is being sent to. The person who is receiving the message is just as important as the message itself.

To communicate well, you need to use your knowledge of other people.

When you are talking to someone, study their reactions. Watch what makes them annoyed, pleased, interested. Use these facts to shape your message so that it will appeal to these qualities.

Timing is important. If you want to interview a shopkeeper about his or her business, it is not a good idea to visit when the shop is full of customers or when he or she is busy ordering goods from a salesperson. Always try to pick the right time and place for the communication.

Finally, the way in which the message is presented – or packaged – will also have an effect on the receiver. If you speak clearly, correctly and politely, people will be more inclined to listen. A letter which is neatly written or – better still – typed on good-quality paper will be much more effective than one scrawled on a torn-out page from an exercise book.

KEY TERM

EXTERNAL COMMUNICATIONS The spoken, written or printed messages that a firm sends to other firms or people.

BUSINESS TECHNIQUES

'It's the way that you say it'

A florist imported some rare houseplants from Australia which proved so popular that the initial batch sold out on the first day. Using this information, write:
(a) a notice for the shop window
(b) a press release for the local newspaper
(c) a press release for a trade magazine
(d) a letter to the Australian supplier.

CHECKPOINTS

1 Why do businesses use forms? Name two kinds of forms they use.
2 Why is listening even more important than speaking?
3 Name three qualities you would expect to find in good communications.
4 Explain in your own words why it is important to think of the receiver when you are communicating.
5 Give two examples of how speed and timing could be important in communications.
6 Give three examples of when communications might go wrong.
7 Mrs Brown has written to your firm, Lovely Moves, to complain that an antique chair valued at £150 was scratched by one of the firm's workmen. She didn't notice it until after the move which was why she didn't mention it at the time. You have spoken to the man concerned and he denies it. He said that, as the chair was obviously valuable, he took particular care with it. Write a letter of reply explaining why your firm is not willing to accept responsibility. Use the business letter format in Figure 54.1.

Information Technology

Confravision

Cellular phone

Panafax UF-600AD

Fax

Telex

Personal computer

STUDY POINTS

1 How would you send an urgently wanted diagram to New York?

2 What is the main advantage of Teletex compared with Telex?

3 Which of the services described here would you use to find the latest foreign exchange rates?

4 How would you send a message to a business person who was on holiday in a remote Welsh cottage without a telephone?

5 What service would you need if you wanted to have video-conferences between your head office and a branch office?

6 Name three kinds of information provided by Prestel.

7 What equipment would you need if you wanted to send messages from your computer along the public telephone lines to another computer?

The computer has brought about great changes in today's office. Thirty years or so ago a **MAINFRAME COMPUTER** took up a whole room. Now, a small personal computer, taking up only a few square feet of desk space, can store **MEGABYTES** of data.

Variety of tasks

The personal computer, with the right software, can perform a great variety of tasks. Word processing, one of the most common, allows text to be altered on the screen of a **VISUAL DISPLAY UNIT (VDU)** before it is printed. This saves hours of retyping. Standard documents can be stored on **DISCS** and printed out when needed. Standard letters can even be printed each with different names and addresses, or changes in paragraphs, by means of mail merge, which also prints individual labels for envelopes.

Mail merge can be used together with a **DATABASE** to send personalised letters to a selection of targeted customers as direct marketing [see Unit 36]. The database, built up from sales records and customer enquiries, is the direct marketer's main tool.

Databases provide a quick and

Telex Sends messages by teleprinter over the ordinary telephone lines to other Telex subscribers in this country and abroad. The message is printed out on their teleprinter. It is one of the oldest forms of electronic communications, but still one of the most widely used.

Fax A fax, or facsimile machine, transmits an image of a document along the telephone lines to another fax machine. Letters, invoices, plans, diagrams etc can all be sent. It takes only 20 seconds to send a document anywhere in the world.

Confravision A British Telecom service, linking eight major British cities, which allows business persons to hold face-to-face conferences with their distant colleagues. Videostream provides a similar service between the firm's own offices.

Telemessage A British Telecom service which delivers a message – in its bright yellow envelope – to any destination in the United Kingdom by the next working day.

Teletex A new service, faster than Telex, which allows business letters to be sent from one computer terminal to another in any part of the world over the public telephone network. While the message is being sent or received, the terminal can be used for some other function, such as word processing.

Personal computer The basis of the revolution in information technology, which processes data at enormous speed. With suitable **SOFTWARE**, it can process various kinds of data, such as words, graphs, numbers; and with a **MODEM**, it can send data through the public telephone network.

Cellular phone A portable radio telephone which allows the user to have phone conversations in cars or other locations. The messages are transmitted by radio beacons.

Prestel A British Telecom service which links adapted television screens to computers through the ordinary telephone lines so that information can be sent directly to offices and homes. As it is a two-way system, customers can send messages, make bookings or ask for information. It has more than 300,000 pages of information, including train timetables, the latest news, stock market and commodity prices, foreign exchange and interest rates etc. Prestel opened the way to electronic shopping from home.

efficient way of searching electronically through large amounts of information for particular data. They can be used in stock control, for searching through insurance records and in many other ways.

SPREADSHEETS allow a computer to make calculations at great speed and are widely used, for example, in financial forecasting. Graphics software allows charts and graphs to be drawn quickly and accurately.

All these new developments mean that a company can now present sales figures or forecasts for the future either in columns, using a spreadsheet, or as graphs or pic charts, using graphics software. A brochure containing these charts can then be produced by a **DESK-TOP PUBLISHING** system, which uses a laser printer to give high-quality printed material.

Computers can also be connected with each other in a local area network (LAN) as shown in Figure 55.1. This involves a number of computers which share the same facilities. A modem connects them all

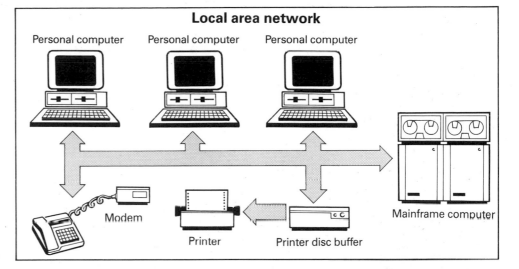

Local area network

Personal computer   Personal computer   Personal computer

Modem

Printer

Printer disc buffer

Mainframe computer

with the outside world. A printer prints all their work, once it has passed through a buffer, which checks if the printer is free, and stores the data if it is not.

The mainframe computer stores a master copy of, say, a complex contract, and amends it as each personal computer operator adds data. A LAN can save much time and money in business.

KEY TERMS

SOFTWARE A program fed into a computer which enables it to carry out a particular task, such as word processing.

MODEM A piece of equipment which turns the signals from a computer into different signals suitable for sending through the public telephone network.

MAINFRAME COMPUTER A powerful computer which can store more data and work more quickly than almost all personal computers.

MEGABYTE (MB) Megabytes are used to indicate the capacity of a computer – the amount of information it is able to store. One Megabyte is a million bytes, equivalent to 1,024,000 characters. (A character is one letter, symbol, or space. One word, on average, is six characters.) A smaller measure, a **KILOBYTE (K)**, with 1,024 characters, may be used to describe the length of an item stored or sent.

VISUAL DISPLAY UNIT (VDU) The computer's television-type screen.

DISCS Flat, circular plates used for storing computer data. There are floppy discs and hard discs, which store more data.

DATABASE A collection of information needed for a particular task. It is stored in such a way that required data from all the records are easily found.

SPREADSHEET A software package which allows the operator to make financial calculations with a very large number of figures, and with great speed.

DESK-TOP PUBLISHING A system which enables a leaflet, magazine or even a book to be written, edited, designed, illustrated and printed within the computer.

BUSINESS TECHNIQUES

Databases

The files in a database contain a large number of separate records. Each record holds information about, say, a firm – its name, address, telephone number, services offered, membership of a trade federation, etc. Each item of information is called a field. The name would be one field; the address, which is divided up into street, town, etc, might be three or four fields; the telephone number, one field, and so on.

Find six display advertisements in the same section of the Yellow Pages. You want to store this information on a database. Create records for each of the firms.

CHECKPOINTS

1 In which department of a firm would you expect to find a spreadsheet being used?
2 Name three departments in a multinational which might use data-bases. For what would they be used?
3 What are the main advantages of a local area network?
4 Describe four pieces of information technology equipment and state their uses.

Activities

■ Review points

1 Give examples of situations when you would use:
- a memo
- a report
- a notice
- a circular letter
- an invoice.

2 Explain why communications are not always effective and how they can be improved.

3 State when you would use:
- fax
- teletex
- Prestel
- a teleprinter
- software.

4 What are the most important factors in verbal communications?

5 Why is it important to be aware of the other person when you are trying to communicate?

■ Coursework

You have been asked to re-equip a surveyor's office with the latest information technology. There are three typists who are currently using electric typewriters. Plans and drawings frequently have to be sent to clients, both in this country and abroad, at the greatest possible speed. When surveyors are on sites, it would be extremely useful if they could be contacted by the office. The firm is trying to build up its business in Europe, so it would like to have some form of electronic mail. Telex would also be useful, but it would not be used very often.
- Write a report to the managing director explaining what information technology equipment you have chosen and the advantages it will bring.
- Include an estimate of the total cost.

The paying proposition

MOST PEOPLE are sympathetic to the idea of insurance; 'Putting a little bit away for a rainy day' is dear to the British heart. The same reasoning can be applied to health insurance. None of us really knows when we may become ill, however strong and fit we may be.

Some health insurance schemes pay for a private room in a hospital and the necessary treatment. Contributions towards this type of scheme are obviously high, increasing yearly and beyond most people's pockets. Also the principle of private medicine is not everyone's cup of tea.

At the Hospital Savings Association (HSA) we pay you a guaranteed *cash* benefit as soon as you let us know you have been in hospital – either NHS or private. And that's not all, one contribution helps you and your family to pay a wide range of NHS charges. You'll see for example that we help out with eye and dental treatment costs, and also maternity.

Open to all

Virtually anyone can join the HSA, but you and your dependants must be in good health at the time of joining and you the contributor must be under the age of 61. Options may be increased at any time before the sixty-sixth birthday provided the good health declaration can be signed. Membership may continue as long as you wish, provided your contributions continue to be paid.

Source: Hospital Savings Association

The impact of new technology

Measurement of productivity

Productivity can be roughly defined as the ratio of the total quantity of output to the quantities of inputs used.

To illustrate this idea, we can use the simple example of the introduction of a wordprocessor. At first the wordprocessor may be used simply as a super-typewriter with the only difference being the speed of operation. Here a simple comparison of productivity before and after the wordprocessor would be possible.

Over time, however, as further new processes and products are developed, the nature of the output may vary as the wordprocessor is capable of producing documents which it couldn't before. Equally the quality of the documents produced may be expected to change.

At the same time there may be changes to the input side of the productivity equation. Wordprocessing requires skills rather different to those of typing and so the nature of the labour will have changed. The new technology may also affect the working conditions and job satisfaction, which might in turn affect the motivation and effort of the employees, which will also influence productivity.

It is because of these more complex effects that we need to study questions other than just whether or not employment will rise or fall after the introduction of new technology. We need further information on the changes in the products or services produced, as well as the changes inside the firm.

Adapted from: *Economic Review*, September 1986

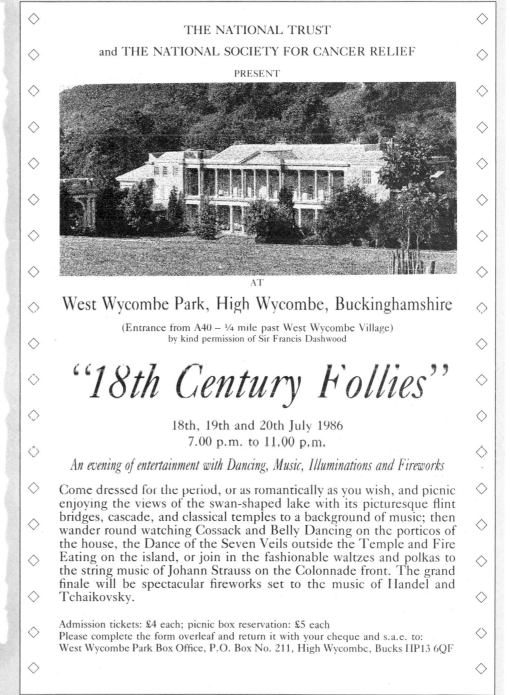

THE NATIONAL TRUST

and THE NATIONAL SOCIETY FOR CANCER RELIEF

PRESENT

AT

West Wycombe Park, High Wycombe, Buckinghamshire

(Entrance from A40 – ¼ mile past West Wycombe Village)
by kind permission of Sir Francis Dashwood

"18th Century Follies"

18th, 19th and 20th July 1986
7.00 p.m. to 11.00 p.m.

An evening of entertainment with Dancing, Music, Illuminations and Fireworks

Come dressed for the period, or as romantically as you wish, and picnic enjoying the views of the swan-shaped lake with its picturesque flint bridges, cascade, and classical temples to a background of music; then wander round watching Cossack and Belly Dancing on the porticos of the house, the Dance of the Seven Veils outside the Temple and Fire Eating on the island, or join in the fashionable waltzes and polkas to the string music of Johann Strauss on the Colonnade front. The grand finale will be spectacular fireworks set to the music of Handel and Tchaikovsky.

Admission tickets: £4 each; picnic box reservation: £5 each
Please complete the form overleaf and return it with your cheque and s.a.e. to:
West Wycombe Park Box Office, P.O. Box No. 211, High Wycombe, Bucks HP13 6QF

Source: The National Trust

1 Study the three extracts on this page and opposite.

2 With which segment of the population are the authors trying to communicate?

3 Explain how the authors have attempted to make their communication effective. How successful do you think each one has been?

4 Take the extract which, in your view, is the least effective and rewrite it.

MicroLink

Electronic mail sends letters direct from one computer to another over the public telephone network. As many computers cannot understand messages from other makes of computers, the messages are often sent through electronic mailboxes, such as British Telecom's Telecom Gold. Microlink is associated with Telecom Gold. The message is sent down the telephone line to Microlink, which then transmits it to the other subscriber. Microlink has links – called gateways – to large databases which contain useful business information. It also offers a Telex service.

Communications not only have to be quick, but they also have to be cost effective. Even a small firm could waste hundreds of pounds a year if it didn't keep a firm check on its communications bill and work out a policy which will provide the most cost-efficient and effective service. In a large firm, the waste could run into many thousands of pounds.

Business people must be aware of the relative costs of communications.

How much it costs to use MicroLink

Initial registration fee: £5.

Standing charge: £3 per calendar month or part.

Connect charge: 3.5p per minute or part – cheap rate; 11p per minute or part – standard rate.
Cheap rate is from 7pm to 8am, Monday to Friday, all day Saturday and Sunday and public holidays; Standard rate is from 8am to 7pm, Monday to Friday, excluding public holidays.

Telex registration: £10.

Outgoing telex: 5.5p per 100 characters (UK); 12p per 100 (Europe); 18p per 100 (N America); £1.25 per 400 (Rest of world); £2.75 per 400 (Ships at sea)

Incoming telex: No charge.

Telemessages: £1.45 for up to 350 words.

International Mail: For the first, 2,048 characters – 20p to Germany and Denmark; 30p to USA, Australia, Canada, Singapore, Hong Kong and Israel. For additional 1,024 characters – 10p; 15p.

Source: MicroLink

International dialled telephone calls

Approximate charges in £s at standard rates, including VAT

Charge Band	1min	2min	3min	4min	5min
A	0.46	0.86	1.32	1.73	2.19
B	0.58	1.15	1.73	2.30	2.82
C	0.69	1.38	2.07	2.76	3.45
E	1.04	2.01	3.05	4.03	5.00
G	1.15	2.30	3.45	4.54	5.69

Source: British Telecom

1 What is the annual standing charge for Microlink?

2 What would be the cost for using Microlink's inland services for three minutes during normal office hours?

3 How much does a telemessage cost?

4 How much would it cost to send a 3k (kilobyte) letter to the United States by Microlink (1k = 1,024 characters)

5 What would a three-minute telephone call to the United States (Charge Band C) cost? How many words could you use for the same price if you used electronic mail?

6 Calculate the cost of a 66-word telex message and a 66-word electronic letter to Australia? What is the relative cost – i.e. the difference in costs, expressed as a percentage? (Assume 6 characters to an average word.)

7 How much would a 4-minute telephone call to Japan (Charge Band G) cost?

People in Business

Why Work?

Naveen, *Age 41, Bank executive*
Salary £15,500 a year
'My job in the bank has given me everything I want. It's as secure as any job can be nowadays. We've got a highly beneficial pension scheme and I've also taken out two big life insurance policies. I've got a detached house in a delightful suburb, a lovely wife and two nice children. You can't ask for much more, can you?'

Jill, *Age 29, Self-employed potter*
Income £3,500–£4,500 a year
'Yes, sometimes it's a real struggle to live, especially in the winter when we don't get many visitors. But I'd always wanted to be a potter ever since I made my first pot at school. Art college followed, where I met Barbara. We set up the pottery together. It's worked out like a dream: We get on very well and we both love what we're doing.'

Derek, *Age 57, Unskilled worker*
Wage £110 a week
'I was lucky to get this job, I can tell you. After two years on the dole I never thought I'd work again, not at my age. It doesn't bring in much; but it's better than sitting at home watching the telly all day. That's what I did when I was on the dole. Now I've got enough to go out with my friends now and again.'

Martin, *Age 33, Occupation unknown*
Income not declared
'Work! What's that? Never heard of it – not since I left school. What do I do? Let's say a bit of this and a bit of that. Like last week, I got all these cheap sweaters to sell, didn't I? Next week, it might be a car to respray. There's always work out there to do if you know the right places. Enterprise! That's what they call it. Know what I mean?'

Sue, *Age 31, Finance director*
Salary £35,000 a year
'I work 16 hours a day and most weekends, too. But I don't mind. There are very few women who have gone as high in the company as I have. Now I've even got a chauffeur-driven car, which I like!'

STUDY POINTS

Study the data above and then form small groups to discuss the following topics.

1 What are each of the five people mainly working for?

2 What else do they get out of their work?

3 Which person gains most satisfaction from the actual work?

4 What other attitudes to work could there be?

Why do people work? Is it just for money? Or because they are genuinely interested in what they do? Or because being a manager makes them feel important? Or because they would be bored if they did nothing? Or because they like working with other people? Or because they take a pride in doing something better than other people?

All these questions are important for business. If people did not work, the business world and the whole economy would collapse overnight. So business must try to understand why people work and provide the right motivation, such as money or interest, to make them work more keenly and efficiently.

Money

One of the main reasons for working is money. How many people would work if they did not get paid? Basically, people work to get enough money to satisfy their basic needs for food, water, shelter, clothes, warmth [see Unit 1]. Even when those needs have been met, money still remains a strong motivation, as it buys the luxuries that most people cannot afford – a country mansion, a Rolls-Royce, a diamond necklace.

Affiliation

Money is rarely the only motivation. People want more out of work than that. Some people, but not all, would prefer to do any kind of job, rather than sit idly at home. Like Derek, they would miss the company of their workmates. The sense of **AFFILIATION**, of having friends, of belonging to a group, is a strong motivation for all kinds of working people. Businesses can use this personal need to motivate the work force by:

- providing company uniforms or overalls
- organising company entertainments and sports events

- running sweepstakes for the whole work force

- providing free company trips for employees – and sometimes their wives or husbands – too

- producing a company newsletter or magazine

- forming working groups in the factory, so that the members feel part of a team.

Security

A sense of **SECURITY** is another basic need which businesses use to motivate and keep their work force. The majority of people probably like to feel secure, to think that they have a job for life and will not be poor when they are too old to work. Businesses can help to increase their workers' sense of security by:

- providing good pension schemes

- giving employees greater job security

- providing sick pay schemes and private health care, such as BUPA, for workers

- giving priority to promoting company employees when job vacancies occur

- making sure that the work force knows of any changes in company policy or working conditions.

However, too much security may make the workforce too relaxed. What could happen if an employee knew for certain that there was no possibility of losing his or her job, and increases in salary were guaranteed?

Self-importance

Another strong motivation for some people is a sense of **SELF-IMPORTANCE**. Everyone likes to feel important; but these people want to feel much more important than others. Money in the form of large salaries or big expense accounts is one way in which this need can be met [see Unit 59], and another is by offering fringe benefits such as company cars ranging up to Rolls-Royces, and other luxury extras. Businesses exploit this need in many other ways by:

- giving people glorified job titles ('Police officer', instead of 'policeman' or 'police woman'; 'rodent operative', instead of 'rat catcher'; Director of Corporate Planning Objectives.)

- providing status symbols such as personal assistants or secretaries, thicker carpets, bigger desks

- arranging first-class travel on planes and trains

- organising week-end events at stately homes or theatre tickets in the company box.

For some people, this motivation is so strong that they can become almost entirely dependent on company approval. To gain more and more approval they become workaholics, unable to stop themselves working and perhaps putting in 16 hours or more a day. Sue is an example of this type, though like many people of this kind, she also gets some **JOB SATISFACTION** from her work.

Job satisfaction

Job satisfaction – a sense that the work is worthwhile, that you are doing something you really want to do and

using all your skills and creativity – is just about the hardest thing to get from work. Of the five people shown here, Jill probably gets the most job satisfaction, even though her income is the lowest. Low income and job satisfaction don't always go together. Many sports people, professional and self-employed persons get a large amount of job satisfaction and a much higher income than Jill. Perhaps she did not research the market for hand-made pottery carefully enough before she went into business!

Finally, there is a group of people – like Martin – who work outside the mainstream economy, on the borders of legality. This black economy is growing fast, encouraged by the high rate of unemployment. Its total turn-over is estimated at billions of pounds, all of it untaxed!

Status symbols

You work for a private bus company which is competing for routes in a big city. The drivers are to be provided with smart new uniforms by a local soft drinks firm. In return for their sponsorship, the drinks firm's name will be prominently displayed on the jackets. Explain how the sponsorship scheme will increase the status of a) the bus drivers, b) the bus company and c) the soft drinks firm.

CHECKPOINTS

1 **What is the main reason for working?**

2 **Explain how a sense of self-importance can motivate people at work.**

3 **Define job satisfaction. Give two examples of people who obtain it.**

4 **What do members of your family and other people you know obtain from work apart from money?**

KEY TERMS

AFFILIATION A sense of belonging to a group or an organisation.

SECURITY Freedom from worry and fear; knowing that your job and salary are safe.

SELF-IMPORTANCE An exaggerated view of one's own worth.

JOB SATISFACTION Obtaining pleasure from doing work which is satisfying for its own sake.

Wages and Salaries (1)

How workers get paid

Most **MANUAL WORKERS** receive **WAGES** calculated on an hourly basis, e.g. £2.75 an hour. Non-manual **WHITE COLLAR WORKERS** receive **SALARIES**, calculated for the whole year, e.g. £10,000 per annum.

Although there are still big differences between wages and salaries and the ways in which they are paid, there have been some major changes in the last few years.

● Although some manual workers are still paid in cash, since the 1986 *Wages Act*, employers have the right to pay all new manual workers by cheque. (This was done to reduce wage robberies.)
● Wages used to be lower than salaries, but many manual workers now earn much more than clerical workers. Some, with bonuses, earn more than their salaried supervisors, and a few earn more than some professional people.
● Unions used to be concerned mainly with negotiating wages. They now negotiate salaries for many white collar workers too, e.g. bank workers or clerical staff.

A few firms have tried to get rid of the distinctions between manual and white collar workers by paying annual salaries to both. However, most manual workers are still paid by the hour.

National basic wage

The national basic wage, or **TIME RATE**, for an industry is usually settled once a year by the employers and unions involved. The basic wage is decided mainly by the supply and demand for that kind of labour. Generally, wages will be low if a job can be done by almost anyone, and high if a job requires qualifications and training. Other factors, such as work conditions or health risks, are also taken into account. The strength of the union involved, the skills of its negotiators and the personality of its leader, will also have a great influence on the agreed basic wage.

Extra payments

Workers can receive many extra payments on top of their basic pay. Some of these are negotiated nationally, and some at the firm where they work. They include:

● *Overtime pay* for work done outside normal working hours, such as at week-ends or on holidays. Payment can vary from time and a quarter to double time. Increased supervision may be needed to prevent workers deliberately slowing down in working hours, so that they can do more of the better-paid overtime.

● *Piece rate* which pays workers a set rate for each article produced. This was popular in the past when more goods were produced individually. Some firms still use it but it is more usual for home-workers. One drawback is that low quality goods may be produced, so careful inspection is required.

● *Bonuses* which are paid for production beyond an agreed amount. A standard rate of production is fixed for each job by measuring the time taken to do it. A bonus is paid to the worker if more goods are produced in the stated time. Individual bonuses may be replaced by group or team bonuses, but this can cause resentment if there are slow-working members of

GROSS PAY		DEDUCTIONS			
SCALE PAY	671.00	INCOME TAX	153.30	TAX CODE	TAX BASIS
LONDON ALLCE	51.25	NAT INS BASC	12.67	178L	0
NON TAX	9.86	NAT INS C/O	39.83	TAX WK/MTH	TAX REFUND HELD
		SUPERANN	43.34	02	

FIG 57.1

CUMULATIVES TO DATE

TAX GRS.	1357.82
TAX	317.70
SUP.	86.68
NAT. INS.	105.00

TOTAL GROSS PAY	732.11	TOTAL DEDUCTIONS	249.14	NET PAY	482.97

'-' after an amount indicates a DEDUCTION   'R' after an amount indicates a REFUND

the team. Company bonus schemes are based on the total output of the whole factory, but the bonus is often too small to motivate individual workers.

● *Profit sharing* schemes set aside a proportion of the firm's profits for distribution among the work-force. A reasonable percentage needs to be set aside to have any motivating effect on the workers.

● *Merit pay* for constant good performance at work. This may cause resentment among other workers who think their work is just as good.

Take-home pay

Employers must make certain deductions under **PAYE** from their employees' **GROSS PAY**. Income tax and national insurance are statutory

deductions, which must be made by law. These are shown in Figure 57.1. Other items, such as union fees, subscriptions or savings are voluntary deductions. What is left, after all deductions, is the **NET PAY** or take-home pay.

BUSINESS TECHNIQUES

Take-home pay

A worker does a 40-hour week at a basic rate of £2.67 an hour plus two hours' overtime at time and a quarter and one hour at time and a half. His income tax that week is £15.18 and his national insurance £11.18. He saves £1.50 a week voluntarily and his union dues are £3.50 a month. What is his take-home pay?

KEY TERMS

MANUAL WORKERS Employees who do mainly physical work.

WAGES Pay for manual workers which is usually based on an hourly rate plus additional payments for high productivity, etc.

WHITE COLLAR WORKERS Non-manual workers.

SALARIES Pay for non-manual workers which is based on an annual rate.

TIME RATE The basic rate for manual workers based on an hour's work.

PAYE (Pay As You Earn) A system under which the employer deducts income tax and National Insurance from employees' pay before they receive it.

GROSS PAY The total amount an employee earns.

NET PAY The amount an employee receives after statutory deductions for income tax and National Insurance, and any voluntary deductions, have been made.

CHECKPOINTS

1 Which kinds of employees are usually paid wages?
2 What is the difference between gross pay and net pay?
3 Who generally settles the time rate for an industry?
4 What is the main drawback of piece rates? Where might they be used as a method of payment?
5 State three kinds of bonus schemes. What are some of the advantages and disadvantages?
6 Why can wages of newly employed manual workers be paid by cheque?

Wages and Salaries (2)

For many years, workers at a chocolate manufacturers in the Midlands had received a low basic wage plus many extra payments. Then the firm was taken over by a big company in the leisure sector. Most of the previous managers were dismissed. Shortly after that, the new management announced that it wanted to introduce a new wage structure. Under the new system, overtime, merit payments and bonuses would be abolished. So would the subsidised canteen, which would be let out to a private contractor. Instead, production workers would be paid an annual salary. The agreement, linked to **PRODUCTIVITY DEALS**, would run for a three-year period. It could then be renegotiated.

Copies of a lengthy document, outlining the plan, were given to union representatives. One of them, Rachel, decided to jot down some figures to see what the new scheme would mean for workers of her grade.

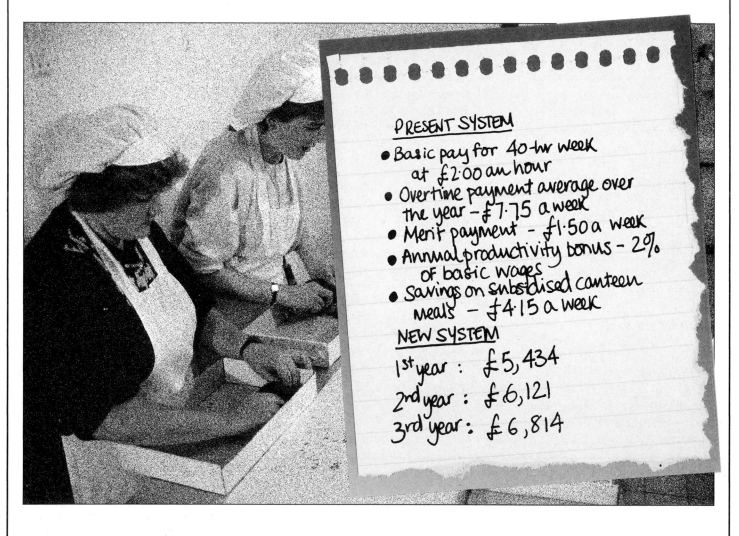

PRESENT SYSTEM
- Basic pay for 40-hr week at £2.00 an hour
- Overtime payment average over the year — £7.75 a week
- Merit payment — £1.50 a week
- Annual productivity bonus — 2% of basic wages
- Savings on subsidised canteen meals — £4.15 a week

NEW SYSTEM

1st year : £5,434

2nd year : £6,121

3rd year : £6,814

STUDY POINTS

1 What is Rachel's total weekly wage at present?

2 How much would she earn per week under the new system in the first year? What would be the percentage increase?

3 What would be the average percentage rise in salary over the three years? What factor might reduce the value of this increase?

4 How would management benefit by introducing the new system?

5 Rachel has to explain the scheme to her fellow workers. Write her speech explaining why the new scheme should be supported or rejected. You may use charts or graphs to support your case.

Some salaries for white collar workers are decided in the same way as wages – by national agreements between union and employers' representatives. The main difference is that the salaries are based on an annual, not an hourly, rate of pay.

In the public sector, there is usually a minimum and maximum rate of pay for each kind of job, with an **INCREMENTAL PAY SCALE**. For example, the salary range for a council typist might be:

$$£4,100(+ £250) → £5,350$$

This means that he or she would get a rise of £250 each year until the maximum salary of £5,350 was reached. Some other salaries in the public sector, such as those of doctors and judges, are fixed by independent review bodies.

Private sector salaries

Some salaries in the private sector are also decided by national agreements between unions and management, as in banking. There are national rates of pay for various grades of jobs, with extra cost-of-living allowances for workers in particularly expensive areas, such as London.

Many large firms use job evaluation to grade jobs throughout the organisation [see Unit 59]. A salary range is then decided on for each grade of job, as in the public sector. In many private firms, however, pay rises depend on some form of **APPRAISAL**, which assesses how well each employee is performing. Merit payments are awarded for good performance.

Many salaried employees do not receive overtime payments; but their pay may be increased in other ways:

- commission is paid to sales people on the goods they sell
- annual bonuses are paid in many service industries
- profit-sharing in some form is becoming increasingly common.

In small firms, pay is often negotiated by the individual. The salary is decided at the interview. Employees may be given pay rises for good work or long service; if not, they have to ask for them.

Fringe benefits

The majority of employees receive some **FRINGE BENEFITS** in addition to their wages or salaries. These goods or services have one great advantage for employees: either they are not taxed at all, or they are taxed at a reduced rate, according to the estimated money value of the benefit. If the employees were given a pay rise instead, they would have to pay more tax.

Many manual workers receive some fringe benefits. Many big firms provide pension and sick pay schemes, and some also provide private health insurance. In addition, employees may receive free uniforms, discounts on shopping, free travel to work, subsidised meals, free sports facilities and day trips abroad. Fringe benefits for managers include:

- company cars
- private health care
- cheap loans and mortgages

- moving expenses
- holidays abroad
- company flats
- big expense accounts
- golden handshakes and hellos (sums of money given on leaving or joining a company)
- preferential share offers
- payment of school fees.

The higher you rise in a firm, the more fringe benefits you are likely to receive.

BUSINESS TECHNIQUES

Fringe benefits

You are employed by an executive employment firm which deals only with top managers. You are trying to persuade a financial director to move from his present company to another firm. He is known to like drinking vintage wine. He has two children who are just leaving private junior school. His wife likes holidays in exotic places. Construct a package of fringe benefits which might attract him and estimate their money value.

CHECKPOINTS

1 What is a fringe benefit? State two which a manual worker might receive and three that a manager might get.
2 What is the main advantage of a fringe benefit for an employee?
3 What is an incremental pay scale? Give three examples of employees who would be paid in that way.
4 Explain how salaries are determined in the private sector. What are the main advantages and disadvantages of each method for the firm.

KEY TERMS

PRODUCTIVITY DEALS Agreements where employers give increases in wages, or other benefits, in return for an increased output from the workforce.

INCREMENTAL PAY SCALE A range of pay with regular increases, or increments, each year. It is used, for example, in the civil service, local authorities and nationalised industries.

APPRAISAL A method of assessing how well an employee is performing his or her job. Performance is often rated against a list of pre-set achievements.

FRINGE BENEFITS Goods or services for employees which are provided in addition to wages and salaries.

Job Evaluation

(You are part of a team carrying out a job evaluation in your organisation.)

1 Decide the number of points which should be awarded to the jobs of a receptionist/ typist and a word processor operator for each of the 13 items in Figure 59.1.

2 What is the total number of points for each job?

3 If a word processor operator is paid £8,500 a year, how much is one point worth per year?

4 Using the points you have awarded to the receptionist/typist, calculate what her annual salary should be.

5 Discuss the points you have awarded to each worker with someone in your class. Try to come to an agreement about any differences.

6 When you have finished, find the new total number of points for each worker. If the word processor operator is still paid £8,500 a year, what would the salary of a receptionist/typist now be?

FIG 59.1

	RECEPTIONIST/ TYPIST	WORD PROCESSOR OPERATOR	Maximum points
Skills required			
1 Education level	GCSE English Grade D	GCSE English Grade B and 2 others	40
2 Training	Pitman's Typing Grade 1	RSA Word Processing (advanced) Stage III	60
3 Previous experience	Work experience	One year in job	80
4 Initiative	Medium	Occasionally great	30
Responsibility			
5 Equipment	Herald terminal	IBM personal computer	25
6 Safety	General security	Computer	20
Effort			
7 Work level	Simple clerical	Complex keyboarding	50
8 Social contact	Continuous	Very small	40
9 Mental effort	Low	High	40
Working conditions			
10 Noise	High	Low, except for printer	20
11 Visual	Good lighting	VDU glare	20
12 General environment	Draughty	Well controlled	15
13 Danger	Uninvited visitors	VDU health hazards	15

Why the opera chorus sings a sad song

MR RICHARD HAZELL sings in the chorus of the Royal Opera House. He can sing in five languages. Yet he is paid 50 times less for a week's work than an opera star commands for a single performance and has about half the income of a stage electrician... New chorus members earn £158.15 a week.

Source: *The Times*, 5 September 1987

Measuring differences

Why should an opera star get paid so much more than a member of the chorus? To a large extent, this is a matter of supply and demand. There are very few opera stars who are so brilliant that opera lovers will pay almost any price to hear them. Why, however, does a member of the chorus earn much less than a stage electrician? Is that a fair assessement of their respective value, or is it more to do with the strength of their unions?

It is never easy to decide how important one job is compared with another quite different job. To measure the differences more fairly, many big firms now use **JOB EVALUATION**. This technique tries to place jobs in order of importance, or rank. A points system is often used, as in the Study Points. Each job is given a certain number of points for such factors as:

- *Skills* Education, training, experience, initiative, competence
- *Responsibility* For equipment, safety, welfare of others, security
- *Effort* Physical, mental, stamina, concentration
- *Working conditions* Boredom, danger, noise, nervous strain, temperature, health hazards.

The number of points for each kind of job is then added up to give the ranking order. The higher the total

IT LOOKS LIKE A NICE, PLEASANT JOB TO ME

YES, I'VE ALWAYS FANCIED AN OUTDOOR LIFE MYSELF!

Two work study experts . . .

JOB DESCRIPTION

Title:	Word Processor Operator
Department:	Secretarial Services Department
Function:	To provide word processing services for all heads of department as required
Responsible to:	Secretarial Services Manager
Responsible for:	No—one

Duties:

1 Programming the machine at the start of the day

2 Word processing letters and other documents for heads of department

3 Maintaining a suitable filing system on disc

4 Ordering all necessary office supplies for the word processor and ensuring that there is a sufficient stock of these supplies at all times

5 General care of the machine

6 Ensuring that the machine is disconnected at the end of the day

FIG 59.2

---

number of points, the higher the rank.

The total scores can then be used as a basis for fixing a pay scale for each kind of job. However, the actual wages or salaries will be affected by many other factors, including union strength and the supply and demand of labour.

Job descriptions

Job evaluations are carried out by the firm's **PERSONNEL DEPARTMENT**. Another of its tasks is writing **JOB DESCRIPTIONS**. These contain much less information and are used mainly for recruiting staff. The description must give people who have applied for the job an accurate picture of what will be required of them. Although job descriptions vary from one firm to another, most of them give the following information in this order:

- *Title* of the job (e.g. secretary, waiter)
- *Department* of the firm in which the person will work (e.g. finance department, restaurant)
- *Function* A summary of the job

- *Responsible to* The person who will be in charge of the new employee
- *Responsible for* Any persons who will be in the charge of the new employee (e.g. an office junior)
- *Duties* A numbered list of duties that the employee is required to perform.

An example of a job description for a word processor operator is shown in Figure 59.2.

C H E C K P O I N T S

1 Why does a member of the chorus earn so much less than an opera star?

2 What is the main purpose of a job description?

3 How does job evaluation help to determine pay? What other factors are involved.

4 What other points might be considered when making job evaluations?

5 Make out a job evaluation form for teachers and award points out of a maximum of 20 for each item.

K E Y   T E R M S

JOB EVALUATION Putting jobs in order of rank, mainly to decide rates of pay.

PERSONNEL DEPARTMENT The department of a firm which deals with people at work and the relationships between them.

JOB DESCRIPTION A brief description of a job and its duties which is given to job applicants.

Recruitment and Selection

Sir Frederick Snow & Partners
Consulting Engineers

INFORMATION and MARKETING ASSISTANT

Our Business Support Group is responsible for, among other things, project information, market sector intelligence, press releases, submissions, presentations, and general research.

An assistant is required in the Business Support Group, to be involved in the above areas. It is envisaged that the person appointed will be a graduate, aged 20 to 30, artistic and thorough, computer literate and creative. Knowledge of marketing or the engineering profession is not required, but some administrative experience would be useful.

If you are interested in being considered for this interesting, but challenging post, please write, giving full details of experience and salary history to: The Personnel Manager, Sir Frederick Snow & Partners, Ross House, 144 Southwark Street, London SE1 0SZ.

ASSISTANT GENERAL SECRETARY

We are a busy trade association serving the amusement and leisure industry in the UK and associated with the world's largest annual exhibition of amusement machines and allied equipment.

Applications are invited from graduates or equivalent with good administration skills who are capable of working with a small team to organise and service committees. An academic qualification or experience of legal work is essential and ability to prepare draft agendas and minutes would be a definite advantage.

The job entails working closely with committees and the members generally and becoming familiar with all aspects of the Association's activities so as to be in a position to offer accurate advice to members.

Salary according to qualifications, ability and experience. Company car and pension in due course.

Applications with a CV should be sent to:

The General Secretary,
British Amusement Catering Trades Association
Bacta House
122 Clapham Common North Side
London SW4 9SP

HELP!

Looking for a career in publishing?

Leading watersports magazine *urgently* requires young intelligent person to take on the role of **ADVERTISING ASSISTANT**. Duties will include selling space, chasing copy and general administration. Typing would be an advantage, as would an interest in watersports. Rapid career growth opportunities for the right person.

Please telephone Andrew Harte, 01-828 4551.
Ocean Publications Ltd
34 Buckingham Palace Rd, London SW1W 0RE

2 ADMINISTRATIVE ASSISTANTS

22–28 years of age

We consist of several large successful companies with offices throughout the UK and Western Europe.

We are seeking bright, vivacious persons with accounting, book-keeping/administrative experience to assist in our various offices. You must be well educated, self-motivated, able to travel and knowledge of foreign languages would be an advantage.

If you are interested in a fulfilling career with good prospects, please write with c.v. to:

Pamela Schofield,
Global Holiday Services Ltd.,
9 Melbourne Street,
Royston, Herts SG8 7BP

As the imaginary story of Kevin and Joe shows, offering a job to a complete stranger is very unwise. If Joe had followed one of the regular procedures (and if they had been properly insured), he and Kevin would still have been in business today.

There are several ways in which staff can be obtained:
- On the recommendation of a reliable employee or trustworthy person.
- From **JOB CENTRES**.
- Through **EMPLOYMENT AGENCIES**.
- Through executive employment agencies, or **HEAD HUNTERS**.
- By advertising.

Advertisements

Advertisements are one of the most common methods of obtaining staff.

To attract suitable people, the advertisement should state clearly what is being offered by the firm and what is required from the applicant. The right branch of the media must be used [see Unit 35].

Classified advertisements often produce just as good results as large display advertisements, and are much cheaper.

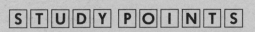

S T U D Y P O I N T S

1 Which of these jobs in your view demands the most qualifications?

2 Which advertisement gives the most information about the job? Suggest the reasons for this.

3 Which advertisement do you think will attract the biggest number of replies? Explain your reasons in full.

4 Take the advertisement which you think is least successful and rewrite and redesign it.

Application forms

People applying for a job may be asked to fill in an **APPLICATION FORM**. Usually this requests the following information:

- title of job applied for
- applicant's name in full
- address and telephone number
- age/date of birth
- nationality
- sex
- if married or single
- if registered as handicapped
- schools attended (with dates)
- further education (with dates)
- qualifications and training
- previous employment (names and addresses of employers, jobs held, wages or salary, reasons for leaving)
- any other information
- references.

Having every applicant's details listed in the same order helps firms to check and compare their abilities more easily. The forms also provide a formal record of each applicant's qualifications and experience, which is useful if there are any later disputes.

When all the application forms have come in, the firm may sort them into three groups of hopeful, doubtful and hopeless. A decision has to be made about the doubtful cases. The most suitable applicants are invited to come for an **INTERVIEW** on a stated date and at a stated time. Other candidates should be informed that they are unsuccessful.

Interviews

The interview is the main means of selecting staff. For minor posts, it is usually conducted by one person. With more important jobs, there is usually a panel of interviewers. Careful planning is needed if the interview is to achieve its objective of finding the most suitable person for the job.

The main purposes of the interview are:

- to gain a first impression of the applicant and some idea of his or her personality
- to assess the applicant's general intelligence, powers of communication and special aptitudes or abilities
- to obtain more detailed information about the facts given in the application form
- to find out whether the applicant's special interests or hobbies might help him or her at work
- to make sure that the applicant does really want the job and knows all that it involves.

Notes should be kept of the interview in case an unsuccessful applicant protests later about unfair treatment because of his or her race or sex [see Unit 76].

When a person has been selected, he or she may be informed at the time or within a few days. A written offer is then sent.

Application forms

Design an application form for the following vacancy, adding any headings which seem appropriate for the firm.

Busy Estate Agents
Intelligent school-leaver wanted to train as junior negotiator. Business skills and knowledge useful salary negotiable.

Then complete the application form yourself. Be sure to sign and date it.

CHECKPOINTS

1 **What is a job application form? Describe its main purposes.**
2 **What is a job centre? How does it differ from an employment agency?**
3 **State three other ways in which staff can be recruited. What are the advantages and disadvantages of each (e.g. costs, time, quality of applicant, etc)?**
4 **What hints would you give to someone writing a job advertisement? Using your own advice, write a classified advertisement for a local newspaper, for a part-time assistant in a café.**
5 **Describe the main purposes of an interview. What do you think are its main drawbacks as a method of selection?**

KEY TERMS

JOB CENTRES Government offices which advertise vacancies for employers and provide other services for the unemployed.

EMPLOYMENT AGENCIES Private agencies which provide employers with staff for a fee. Many of them deal mainly with office and specialist staff.

HEAD HUNTERS (or executive employment agencies) Agencies which provide employers with top management and scarce professionals for large fees.

APPLICATION FORMS Standard forms which have to be completed by applicants for a job.

INTERVIEW Inviting the applicants for a job to come in for individual meetings, so that the employer can assess who is the most suitable.

Training

You go and watch Bill. He's been here 10 years. There's not much he can't tell you about cars.

It's not fair! You're always the interviewer. It's about time I had a go!

In technical drawing, cross-hatching is used to show solid areas...

In gravure printing, the colour balance is obtained by running each colour through the press in turn...

COULD YOU SAY THAT AGAIN, PLEASE?

WHAT DID HE SAY?

STUDY POINTS

(Study the chart in Figure 61.1 before answering the questions.)

1 In the examples above, which are manual workers and which are white collar workers?

2 What knowledge or skills are being taught in each case?

3 What kinds of training methods are being used?

4 In what kinds of firms might you find these four kinds of training?

5 Describe one other form of training which might be used in each case. Explain why it would be more or less effective.

'Call this training? My dad calls it slave labour.' YTS trainee

'If you train youngsters too well, they just go off and get a better job.' Small employer

'Give us more training, equipment and staff, and we could do a more professional job than anyone.' Teacher

Attitudes to training vary. All progressive firms agree that much more business training is needed. The main arguments are about what kind of training is needed, what methods should be used, and who should do the training.

Clear objectives

If training is to be effective, the firm must have clear objectives. It may want to:

- introduce a new process or new equipment
- improve efficiency and performance
- train **UNSKILLED WORKERS**, to avoid a labour shortage
- reduce the supervision needed
- provide greater chances for internal promotions.

Trainees also need clear objectives. These might be:

- to increase their pay
- to obtain promotion
- to reduce the chance of accidents.

Unless trainees see some personal benefit in the training, they will not be highly motivated, and the course will fail.

Selecting the methods

Once the objectives are clear, a suitable programme can be planned. The three main purposes of training are to:

- instil knowledge
- change attitudes
- increase skills.

The importance given to these purposes will help decide what training methods are used.

Look at Figure 61.1. The first two training methods are concerned

Training methods

FIG 61.1

Method	Level	Advantages	Disadvantages
1 **Lecture**	General	Economical in resources	Little audience participation
2 **Visits**	General	Realistic	Difficulties in comprehension
3 **Case study**	Managerial	Stimulating	May be unrealistic
4 **Role-play**	White collar	Increases confidence	May not transfer to work situation
5 **Group therapy**	General	Increases self-awareness	May cause resentment
6 **Personal skill instruction**	General	Immediate	Depends on quality of trainer
7 **Skills analysis**	Manual and white collar workers	Very effective	Expensive
8 **Discovery**	General	High degree of involvement	Time-consuming

mainly with increasing knowledge. Methods 3 to 5 also develop knowledge but they are more concerned with changing attitudes. The last three methods are mainly concerned with increasing skills.

● A lecture is often used for the **INDUCTION** of new employees. However, if the quality of the lecture is poor, the audience's attention will soon wander.

● Visits to other parts of the firm may be part of the induction process, to increase knowledge of other stages in the production process, and to establish good relations between departments.

● Case studies present trainees with a business problem which they have to solve as a group. Attitudes and emotions may be involved here.

● In role play, where trainees act out a real-life business situation to gain confidence and experience, emotional involvement is often fairly high.

● In group therapy, trainees come together to explore their attitudes to one another by speaking their minds freely. Emotional involvement is very high.

● Personal skill instruction – the traditional method of watching an older, experienced worker – is still widely used for training unskilled or **SEMI-SKILLED WORKERS**.

● Skills analysis is used with **SKILLED WORKERS**. The job is broken down into stages and trainees are told, and shown, how to do each stage before doing it themselves under supervision.

● The discovery method – now used for industrial skills training – offers little formal instruction. Trainees find out for themselves how to do a job. The instructor helps only if asked or if there is any danger.

Who will do the training?

Training may be done internally, within the firm itself, or externally at a college or school. Internal training provides constant work experience and can be more easily controlled by the firm itself. External training may be more professional and give a broader view.

Most longer-term training, such as the **YOUTH TRAINING SCHEME (YTS)**, uses both internal and external training. This two-year course for school leavers combines training and work experience in a firm with off-the-job training in social and work-related skills at a college.

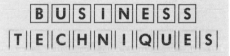

Skills analysis

Take one job that you often do, such as mending a puncture or making a cake, and describe how you do it stage by stage in the minutest detail. Note any snags or difficulties which trainees might encounter at each stage.

CHECKPOINTS

1 Give four reasons why a firm might set up a training programme.
2 Why is it important for trainees to be motivated?
3 Choose four methods of training. Describe when and for whom they might be used and their advantages and disadvantages.
4 Explain, with examples, why it is sometimes important to change the attitudes of employees. What training methods can be used?

KEY TERMS

UNSKILLED WORKERS Manual workers who need scarcely any training to do their jobs, such as a cleaning person.

INDUCTION The process of introducing a new employee to colleagues and to the firm and explaining its activities, purposes, and customs.

SEMI-SKILLED WORKERS Manual workers who require very little training, for example a packer.

SKILLED WORKERS Manual workers who have some specialised skill, such as a carpenter.

YOUTH TRAINING SCHEME (YTS) A government scheme, started in 1983, to provide work training for school-leavers who couldn't get jobs. They are paid a small allowance, currently £27.30 a week in the first year and £35 in the second.

Activities

■ Review points

1 What are the two main kinds of deductions from pay? Give two examples of each.

2 Explain the differences between an unskilled, semi-skilled and skilled worker. Give examples of each.

3 Describe the various methods of payment for a) manual workers, and b) white collar workers.

4 What are fringe benefits? Give three examples.

5 What is job evaluation? What is its main purpose?

6 What is a job description?

7 When is induction used? What forms does it usually take?

8 What is YTS? Why was it introduced? What are the main benefits for a) employers, and b) trainees? Why has it provoked some opposition?

9 Describe how work helps to satisfy basic physical and social needs and the need for self-fulfilment and creativity.

10 List the main points which should be included in a job advertisement and comment on the writing and the design of the advertisement. Where would you advertise for a) skilled workers; b) professional people; c) managers; d) typists?

11 Describe the main ways in which various kinds of staff can be recruited.

12 Describe the main stages in selecting staff from the job application form to the final choice.

13 What are the main advantages and disadvantages of both internal and external training?

14 Describe four of the main forms of training in business. State when they would be used and their advantages and disadvantages.

■ Essay question

A firm is trying to reduce the dividing line between manual and white collar workers. Describe what changes it could make in relation to:
a) hours of work
b) fringe benefits
c) methods of payment
d) employee car parking.
What would be the benefits of the changes in each case?

STRESS

Take a stretcher, Miss Jones

THERE ARE few secretaries who would know what to do if they found their boss on the carpet crying. A new project working with over-stressed executives in the North West suggests that certain factors can make some high flyers more likely to have a nervous breakdown.

Around 40 per cent of executives hospitalised through mental breakdown end by committing suicide. Typical victims will have seemed to be highly successful from an early age. At school, college and university, academic and sporting honours will have been easily won.

From there, the trend of continually striving to prove that they are the best goes on. Their career is short-lived. Eventually they reach the point where their professional role has little more to offer. They are sitting on a peak with nothing left to aim for. Frequently this has happened by the time they are 40.

This is the stage when breakdowns occur, often triggered by events such as the death of a relative or family problems.

One victim describes the feeling: 'When the end comes it really is dramatic. Physically you feel like stone. Your limbs won't move, your head falls in your hands and you cry.'

Some executives may still struggle on, but their behaviour eventually becomes impossible. They are anti-social, aggressive, and start to make bad decisions – entering into strange financial arrangements, cancelling engagements without notice or reason. Total collapse is not far away.

Adapted from: *The Guardian*, 14 May 1987

1 What is a high flyer?

2 What kinds of people are likely to suffer breakdowns through work?

3 Describe the symptoms leading up to the breakdown.

4 What percentage of executives who have been in hospital because of mental breakdown eventually commit suicide? What age might they be?

5 Who would be mainly responsible in a company for noting the problem before it became serious? What actions do you think they should take?

Simply a great organiser

JENIFER ROSENBURG, winner of this year's Veuve Cliquot Business Woman of the Year Award and managing director of J&J Fashions, the company she founded in 1974, scored 18 in the workaholics quiz – a surprisingly low total in view of her action-packed life.

She works a 10-hour day and, although she doesn't take paperwork home, being married to the chairman of her firm, Ian Rosenburg, means they nearly always talk shop after hours.

Despite this, every evening they either go out – at least once a week to the theatre or cinema – or entertain at home, in which case the cooking is done by the Rosenburgs' live-in couple, closely supervised by Jenifer. Each evening the Rosenburgs walk their dog for about 20 minutes and they give him a 'good run' at weekends. Jenifer swims regularly in the summer.

Jenifer and her husband take regular holidays but, unless the factory is closed, Jenifer rings the office every day.

In addition to her work at J&J Fashions, Jenifer lectures at a number of design colleges and is a member of the Government's Committee 2000 (designed to ensure that college courses are equipping students with skills essential to industry).

'The very thought of her life would tire most of us but Jenifer – who gets on average five hours' sleep a night – simply says she is 'a great organiser'. She rarely feels stressed, but when she does she 'just makes a list of what needs to be done and then I feel better'.

Source: *Daily Telegraph*, 6 May 1987 (Extracts)

1 How long does Jenifer Rosenburg work each day?
2 How many hours' sleep does she have a night?
3 What do Jenifer and her husband do in the evenings and at the weekends?
4 What does she do when she feels stressed?
5 Why do you think she does not often feel stressed?
6 Would you like this sort of life? Give your reasons.

Councils pay agency £1,000 a week to fill accountant's post

SOME LOCAL COUNCILS are paying £1,000 a week to specialist employment agencies to fill a single accountant's job.

According to a survey of councils carried out by the Local Authorities Conditions of Service Advisory Board, shortages of staff in accounting and computing have forced councils to pay large sums for temporary staff.

One council, Bath, has been paying £2,000 a week to the Chartered Institute of Public Finance and Accountancy to supply two temporary qualified assistants in its treasurer's department.

The survey found that 41 per cent of local authorities in England and Wales are reporting difficulties with recruiting and keeping staff. It confirmed that recruitment is most difficult in London and the South East.

In London, two-thirds of councils say they have trouble getting the right staff.

The rate at which people leave council employment in London is also higher. Turnover there is 17 per cent a year for white collar staff, compared with 15 per cent nationally.

In parts of London, councils have been paying computer consultants up to £1,000 a week for short-term cover for vacancies.

A spokesman for the board said: 'Local authorities are competing with private firms which offer a variety of perks for workers including cars, mortgage assistance and other fringe benefits.'

Source: *The Times*, 5 September 1987

1 What percentage of local councils have difficulties in recruiting staff?
2 What kinds of staff are mainly involved?
3 Where is the problem worst? What are the main reasons?
4 What is a specialist employment agency?
5 How would you solve this problem?

■ Coursework

1 The Manpower Services Commission (MSC) has asked you to make a report on the value of work experience to trainees in your area by carrying out a series of interviews. Draw up a suitable questionnaire for trainees. Explain how you would make sure that you got an accurate sample of views. Carry out the first three interviews and summarise the results.

2 Write to the public relations officer of a multinational or any large public limited company in your area, asking for a copy of the latest annual accounts and report and any other general information about the company. From this material, prepare a talk which will be used for the induction of new employees. Construct any diagrams or charts which will be used to illustrate the talk. Explain what other kinds of audio or visual aids you would use. Write a minute-by-minute list of what would be happening during each stage of the talk.

3 Ask at your local library for any information in the council minutes or reports about the numbers employed, the rates of pay, conditions of work and employment etc. within the council. Find out from private employment agencies or local newspapers the rates of pay and conditions for similar jobs elsewhere. Contact the personnel department of the council to find out any further information which is needed to make a better comparison. Design two job advertisements for posts with the council, stressing the advantages.

■ Groupwork

1 Divide into groups of six. Decide on a job: fix its rate of pay, conditions of service, any fringe benefits, the kinds of work that would be done, the qualifications and experience needed, etc. Decide where the job should be advertised. Three group members should now write and design the advertisement for the specified publication and the other three should plan the interview. The group members who wrote the advertisement should now be interviewed in turn for the job. Finish by discussing whether any improvements could have been made to the advertisement and the interview plan.

2 Divide into groups. You are setting up a sports coaching school for young people. Decide on the best training methods. Discuss how these training methods might be applied to industry.

3 Divide into pairs. One takes the role of a customer who has come back with a complaint, and the other the role of the shop assistant. Act out the situation. Write, individually, a short report on what took place, analysing its value (or lack of it) for training.

Employers' Associations

Guidelines for government

If Britain is to prosper, British business needs:

1 Greater international co-operation to bring about a healthier world economy and resist protectionism. This is vital to the creation of more jobs.

2 A united European Common Market.

3 Freedom from controls such as exchange control or restrictions on inward or outward investment.

4 A competition policy which allows British companies to reach the scale and the effectiveness needed to compete with success internationally.

5 Government support for exporters matching that provided by foreign governments until real multilateral reductions in state aids can be agreed.

6 Growth in real public expenditure held to below 1% per annum and taxes reduced.

7 A stable framework for decisions and closer talks on major policy issues, including the Budget.

8 A stable fiscal and monetary framework and UK entry into the Exchange Rate Mechanism of the European Monetary System.

9 No extension of public ownership and control and a climate which encourages the start-up and expansion of small businesses and self-employment.

10 A system of business law and regulation which weighs benefits against the costs of compliance.

11 Relief from excessive outside costs, especially rates.

12 Fewer cost burdens imposed on business through European Community 'social engineering'.

13 Greater importance given to helping the unemployed without damaging economic recovery.

14 More effective government measures to tackle the underlying causes of regional problems.

15 A climate encouraging free pay determination and freedom from interference by national minimum wage laws or by controls over increase in wages.

16 No going back on the 'step-by-step' reforms made in industrial relations law, with more time to absorb them.

17 An education and research support system encouraging international competitiveness, particularly in science and technology.

18 More consistency in vocational and educational training and better use of resources, particularly in schools.

19 Methods of judging infrastructure projects that take full account of all their benefits, and more-effective spending on the urban (or town) environment.

20 A system of health, safety and environmental laws based on sound knowledge and what is possible for business.

21 Consistent long-term energy planning, with an increased use of nuclear energy for safe, lower-cost electricity generation.

Source: *CBI Business Manifesto*, 1987

STUDY POINTS

(*The text on the opposite page explains the points in the* Guidelines for government *above. Study the* Guidelines for government *and read the explanatory text, before doing these questions.*)

1 Make a list of the ten points in *Guidelines for government* that you think are the most important.

2 Put them in order of importance.

3 Form small groups. Discuss your 'top ten' and try to come to some general agreement as a group about which points to include and their order of importance.

Most industries have their own **EMPLOYERS' ORGANISATIONS**. Firms which make furniture, for example, can join the British Furniture Manufacturers Federation while farmers can join the National Farmers Union. These associations have three main functions:

- They negotiate national wage settlements with trade unions [see Unit 64].
- They present the views of the whole industry to the government and to the public.
- They provide advice and information, and sometimes carry out industrial research, for member firms.

Most of these associations are affiliated to the **CONFEDERATION OF BRITISH INDUSTRY (CBI)**, which also has more than a quarter of a million individual firms as members.

Although many firms do not belong to the CBI, it has so many members that it is the main voice of British business. If we – or the government – want to know what business people are thinking, it is important to understand what the CBI is saying.

Guidelines for government

In 1987, the CBI published *Guidelines for government* (see Study Points) which listed 21 changes that business needed if Britain was to be prosperous again. Let us look at some of the points in greater detail.

Point 1 Business people believe that **FREE TRADE** helps Britain to export more goods and services, thus providing more prosperity and jobs. They are opposed to **PROTECTIONISM** which puts up barriers against trade. Governments do this officially by putting customs duties on imported goods and limiting the amount of goods that can come into a country (imposing quotas). Some countries also use unofficial ways of discouraging trade by introducing

difficulties. For instance:
- making exporters fill in long questionnaires which can be thousands of pages long
- building testing stations for imports miles away from main markets
- taking many months to do the tests
- rejecting goods containing certain substances, even though these are in common use throughout the rest of the world.

Exporters who feel they have been unfairly treated may persuade their own governments to take similar actions against the other country. This reduces international trade even more. Many British business persons see this trend towards protectionism as one of the biggest problems in the world today.

Point 3 For similar reasons, the CBI wants freedom for British business to invest its money in companies abroad and for foreign firms to invest in Britain. This free flow of money across the world gives business greater opportunities for profitable investment.

Point 4 follows from points 1 and 3. Although consumer interests should be protected, restrictions on international growth should be as few as possible, so that British business can compete effectively in world markets.

Point 5 Foreign governments provide much greater export finance and practical help for their own exporters than the British government does. The CBI would prefer to see all such aid reduced by agreement between countries. Meanwhile, the British government should match what is provided by foreign governments [see Unit 68].

Point 6 The CBI wants the government to keep public expenditure down so that taxes can be reduced [see Unit 5].

Point 7 The CBI would like all political parties to agree on national and business objectives in as many areas as possible, including educational, social, physical and legal fields. This would provide a stable framework in which business could make long-term decisions more easily.

Point 8 The CBI would like more co-operation between members of the European Community (EC) (see also Point 2). It would like Britain to join the European Monetary System (EMS), which tries to keep exchange rates between EC countries stable, thus making it easier for businesses to make long-term plans. Stable exchange rates also help to keep interest rates steady, so firms know what they will have to pay in the future on borrowed money [see Unit 68].

Point 10, 12 and 20 The CBI does not want the government or the EC to pass laws making it more difficult for business to be efficient. For instance, it might be desirable to make a rule that lawn mowers should be less noisy, or to have a minimum wage throughout Europe, but the CBI wants the costs of such changes on business to be considered too.

Points 13 and 15 Help for the unemployed should be designed to make them more adaptable and efficient. There should be no control over wage bargaining [see Unit 64] and less interference by wages councils, which lay down minimum wages in low-paid industries [see Unit 76].

Point 16 The CBI supports the trade union reforms of 1980 to 1984 on secondary picketing and ballots, but wants time allowed to get used to the changes brought about.

Point 19 The government should improve the physical infrastructure, paying particular attention to roads and inner cities, so that business can be more efficient.

Point 21 Low energy prices are needed as they reduce business costs.

The CBI not only speaks out on behalf of its members, but also provides information on a wide range of topics to its members. These include company and employment law, industrial relations, taxation and overseas trade.

Press releases

Public relations tries to present an organisation in the best light [see Unit 35]. Write a press release for the CBI about your top ten points (from the Study Points), explaining why they are so important for Britain's prosperity.

Remember that hundreds of press releases are sent into national newspaper offices every day. Unless the title and the first sentence attract attention, journalists will not bother to read the rest.

K E Y T E R M S

EMPLOYERS' ORGANISATIONS Associations of employers in particular industries which negotiate national wage settlements with trade unions and advise members on problems connected with their industry.

CONFEDERATION OF BRITISH INDUSTRY (CBI) An organisation formed in 1965 to represent British business.

FREE TRADE Trade between countries or areas which is free from customs duties and quotas (or limits on amounts of goods imported).

PROTECTIONISM Restricting imports into a country by open means, such as customs duties and quotas, or by unofficial means, such as needless red tape.

C H E C K P O I N T S

1 How many firms belong to the CBI?
2 What is the full title of the organisation?
3 Explain the main functions of an employers' organisation.
4 What is the European Monetary System? How would it benefit business if Britain were a member?

Trade Unions

FIG 63.1

UNION MEMBERSHIP

TASS	+20%
UCATT	28%
EETPU	16%
USDAW	19%
ASTMS	21%
NUPE	5%
NALGO	0.3%
GMBU	16%
AEU	34%
TGWU	34%

0 0.2m 0.4m 0.6m 0.8m 1.0m 1.2m 1.4m 2.0m

1986 1979 % FALL

UNION ASSETS £m

TASS	300%
UCATT	100%
EETPU	87%
USDAW	83%
ASTMS	150%
NUPE	61%
NALGO	176%
GMBU	71%
AEU	−14%
TGWU	90%

£m 0 10 20 30 40 80

1979 1986 % RISE

Source: *Sunday Times*, 6 September 1987

Key

TASS	(former name Technical, Administrative and Supervisory Staff)
UCATT	Union of Construction Workers, Allied Trades and Technicians
EETPU	Electrical, Electronic, Telecommunications and Plumbing Union
USDAW	Union of Shop, Distributive and Allied Workers
ASTMS	Association of Scientific, Technical and Management Staff
NUPE	National Union of Public Employees
NALGO	National and Local Government Officers Association
GMBU	General Municipal, Boilermakers and Allied Trades Union
AEU	Amalgamated Engineering Union
TGWU	Transport and General Workers Union

Union organisation

FIG 63.2

Title	*How elected*	*Assistance*
National Executive Committee	Ballot of all members or at national conference	General secretary and full-time officials
District or regional commitees	Branches	Paid officers and organisers
Branch officials	Branch members	District officers and headquarters
Shop stewards	Union workmates	District officers

STUDY POINTS

1 What is the full name of the biggest union? How many members does it have?

2 What was the average percentage decline in membership of the top ten unions between 1979 and 1986? What do you think might be the reason?

3 What is one likely reason for the increase in the membership of TASS?

4 Explain in your own words the typical organisation of a trade union.

5 Why might the assets of most unions have increased when membership has fallen?

Union membership

In firms where employees do not belong to a **TRADE UNION** they often know far less about their rights. They may have no one to fight for them over pay and working conditions. In most big firms, managers in the personnel department talk with union representatives about problems in **INDUSTRIAL RELATIONS** all the time.

The main objective of all trade unions is to look after the interests of their members. Unions believe that by speaking for a large number of workers they have more power and can get better deals than individuals. Pay is always a major topic of discussion, but others include: working conditions, maternity rights, holidays, redundancies etc. For a subscription of a few pounds a month, unions also provide members with other benefits, such as strike pay or legal advice during disputes.

Although unions have been responsible for getting better pay and working conditions in most firms, all the employees benefit, whether union members or not. This is why many trade unionists are in favour of **CLOSED SHOPS**, where all employees must belong to a union. (Since 1980, a closed shop can be set up only if 80 per cent of the members vote for it in a secret ballot. Even then, workers with strong objections cannot be forced to join.)

There are about 350 unions in Britain. Over half of them are small craft unions for skilled workers in one trade – such as the Pressed Glassmakers' Society or the Spring Trapmakers' Society – which all have fewer than 100 members.

Industrial unions are the main unions within a single industry. For example, the National Union of Railwaymen or the National Union of Seamen.

Many professions have their own unions or associations; examples include the Royal College of Nursing and the National Union of Teachers. In recent years there has been increased union activity among white collar workers.

About 80 per cent of trade unionists belong to one of the 21 big general unions with over 100,000 members each. These usually represent both skilled and unskilled workers in a variety of industries. (See Figure 63.1). Most of the bigger trade unions are attached to the **TRADES UNION CONGRESS (TUC)**, which represents the union movement as a whole, just as the CBI represents business.

Organisation

Unions vary in organisation but the basic pattern is shown in Figure 63.2. Full-time paid officials represent their union during national disputes. Most negotiations on a local level, however,

National Union of Public Employees (NUPE) members at a 'day of action' against government pay policy, January 1979

will be handled by **SHOP STEWARDS**, elected as spokespersons by their workmates. They are not paid by the union, but their employers allow them time off to do union work without loss of pay. Shop stewards are perhaps the most important union representatives, dealing with all aspects of industrial relations and providing management with useful links with the workforce.

Reduction in power

Since the Conservatives came to power in 1979, unions have less power. One main reason is the increase in unemployment – workers usually leave the union when they lose their job. There are also more part-time workers, who are often less keen to join a union.

Union power has also been reduced by new laws making striking more difficult. Peaceful **PICKETING** is still allowed, but not by workers not involved in the dispute, and secondary picketing of other places of work is illegal. If a strike is held

without a secret ballot, the union and its officials can be sued.

These new laws, and continuing unemployment, have greatly reduced the number of working days lost through strikes. Most unions are richer because they have not had to pay out so much strike money in recent years.

In addition, some union leaders have made no-strike deals with employers; their main features are:

- *Sole recognition of the union*. It is easier for management to make deals with only one union, and easier for the union to recruit new members.
- *Single status employment*. Manual workers and other staff have the same working week, holidays, canteen facilities etc.
- *Labour flexibility*. All workers do any job they are capable of doing.
- *Binding arbitration*. Both sides have to accept this in any disputes.

Some trade unionists see no-strike deals as the way forward into the future. Others believe that it is a sacrifice of their basic rights.

B U S I N E S S T E C H N I Q U E S

Answering complaints

You own a small firm and have received a letter from a union official asking you to explain why you have failed to pay the National Insurance contributions of your employees for the last six weeks. Write a letter in reply, explaining your reasons.

C H E C K P O I N T S

1 What are the advantages for workers of belonging to a trade union?
2 What is a closed shop? What recent changes in the law have affected it?
3 Name three kinds of unions and give two examples of each.
4 What are the main features of no-strike deals? What are the advantages of these deals for manual workers and management?

K E Y T E R M S

TRADE UNIONS Groups of workers who join together to protect their interests.

INDUSTRIAL RELATIONS The relations between employees and employers, or management.

CLOSED SHOPS Places where only union members may be employed.

TRADES UNION CONGRESS (TUC) A voluntary association of unions which decides the policy of the trade union movement and expresses it to business, the government and the media. It also deals with disputes between unions.

SHOP STEWARDS Voluntary trade union representatives in a workplace who are elected by their fellow union members.

PICKETING Trying to persuade people who are still going to work during a dispute to join a strike.

Collective Bargaining

STAFF NOTICE

Proposed changes following the takeover

RECORDS – All records would be transferred to the group's mainframe computer in London. This would be linked to a local area network in the West Country firm, which would also be used for communicating between departments in the firm.

TYPEWRITERS – All typewriters would be replaced by word processors.

MESSENGERS – Messengers would be replaced by a smaller number of Youth Training Scheme (YTS) trainees. All messengers would be offered places on training courses.

GRADING – After job evaluation, a simpler system would be introduced with 9 grades instead of 15. It would apply to all departments.

PAY – The annual bonus and automatic pay rises would be phased out. Pay would be decided individually by an appraisal system, based on how each person performs in his or her job. All present employees would be guaranteed a 30 per cent pay rise on their present salaries over the three-year period. Some would get much more.

REDUNDANCIES – There would be no redundancies. Reductions in the labour force would be achieved by natural wastage, i.e. by people leaving or retiring.

TRAINING – A full training scheme would be started for all grades of workers. Promotion would depend on performance on the training courses.

NEW STAFF – Some computer staff would be brought in from the London office.

A big London insurance group has taken over a small insurance firm in the West Country. The small firm was very old-fashioned; all records were kept on cards which were filled in by hand. Some of the clerks had been working for the firm for years. A large team of young messengers was employed to carry files and records from one department to another. Manual typewriters were used in all the offices. Different job grading systems were used in various departments.

The London management team knew there would have to be big changes. After initial talks with union representatives, the team produced a staff-notice outlining the changes they wanted to make over a three-year period.

The management team calculated that these changes would reduce the labour force by the following amounts: messengers, 27 heads; clerks, 53 heads; typists, 12 heads; supervisors, 5 heads.

They predicted that by the end of the three years, there would be no net increase in labour costs. After that, there would be a dramatic rise in annual profits and great opportunities for expansion.

STUDY POINTS

1 What would be the total loss of heads over three years?

2 Which group of employees would lose most heads and for what reasons?

3 Why would there be no net increase in labour costs at the end of the three-year period?

4 What would you expect the main union objections to the plan to be?

5 If you were the firm's management, how would you answer these objections?

Discussing conditions of employment

Firms cannot treat their employees any way they like. Employers must obey certain laws protecting employees [see Unit 76]. Most larger firms have to get union agreement to changes in rates of pay or other terms of employment. These talks between employers and unions are known as **COLLECTIVE BARGAINING**. They take place at two levels – national and local.

The national talks usually involve the employers' organisations [see Unit 62] and top officials of the trade unions involved. Both sides try to reach agreements for the whole industry covering:

● pay levels for various grades of workers
● overtime rates
● the length of the working week
● the minimum length of holiday.

The needs of firms vary so much within each industry that national agreements can only lay down minimum standards. The really detailed – and hard – bargaining takes place at company, or more usually, local levels between management and the shop stewards of each union involved.

Although pay is always one of the main topics, many other subjects may be discussed, including:

● hours of work
● pensions
● sick pay
● maternity leave
● fringe benefits
● holidays
● recruitment
● redundancies
● changes in working practices
● training
● promotion
● health and safety.

Different objectives

Management and unions have different objectives. The shop stewards are trying to get the best deal for their members, whilst management is trying to get the most profitable deal for the firm. The main aim of management is to see that each benefit the workers receive is matched by improved efficiency or productivity. So, for example, if a big pay rise is granted, **DEMARCATION** lines might be got rid of, allowing a production worker to replace a light bulb without calling an electrician. **PRODUCTIVITY DEALS** of this kind mean that the workers have to give something in return for pay rises and other benefits.

Government interference

Both business and unions want free collective bargaining without interference by the government. (Apart from some unions, which would like to see a national minimum wage set to protect the lowest paid.) Governments have interfered in the past by introducing a **WAGE FREEZE** in times of economic crisis to keep inflation down. Wage freezes are unpopular with unions as their members cannot get big pay rises. Employers dislike them too, as workers put in high pay claims when the freeze ends.

The government is directly involved in collective bargaining in cases where it is the employer, as with the Civil Service. Since 1979, the Conservative government has tried to keep pay rises down in the public sector. This has pleased the CBI [see Unit 62] but not the unions.

Bargaining

To bargain successfully, you must always know in advance the price you are willing to pay for what you want. Imagine that you wanted to do a deal with a friend for his or her camera. Write out a list of six items you could offer in exchange, starting with the least valuable. It could be a ticket for a concert, a tennis racket, a radio, a stamp collection, a bicycle, or cash. Decide how far down your list you are willing to go.

Divide into pairs. Try to persuade your partner to swap his or her camera for the first item on your list. If you are unsuccessful, make your second bid and go on until you have reached your stopping point.

Then change roles. If you both succeeded in making a deal, discuss who got the best bargain. If only one person – or none – made a deal, discuss what might have been offered instead.

CHECKPOINTS

1 What is collective bargaining?
2 What is usually decided in national collective bargaining?
3 Why is it necessary to have local collective bargaining? What subjects could be discussed at this level?
4 Describe a productivity deal and give two examples. Why are they important for business?
5 When might a wage freeze be introduced? What could be the disadvantages?

Industrial Action

Stoppages of work: cause

FIG 65.1

United Kingdom

Cause	12 months to June 1987	
	Stoppages	Workers directly involved
Pay – wage-rates and earnings levels	361	622,900
– extra-wage and fringe benefits	27	37,700
Duration and pattern of hours worked	43	9,200
Redundancy questions	80	76,000
Trade union matters	26	18,100
Working conditions and supervision	151	27,400
Manning and work allocation	232	64,100
Dismissal and other disciplinary measures	108	40,000
All causes	1,028	895,500

Source: *Employment Gazette*, September 1987

Stoppages of work: industry

FIG 65.2

United Kingdom — 12 months to June 1987

Industry	Stoppages in progress		
	Stoppages	Workers involved	Working days lost
Agriculture, forestry and fishing	—	—	—
Coal extraction	345	102,700	170,000
Coke, mineral oil and natural gas	—	—	—
Electricity, gas, other energy and water	7	1,700	8,000
Metal processing and manufacture	6	1,000	4,000
Mineral processing and manufacture	10	2,200	18,000
Chemicals and man-made fibres	10	1,800	11,000
Metal goods not elsewhere specified	17	4,300	32,000
Engineering	102	49,000	345,000
Motor vehicles	58	54,100	51,000
Other transport equipment	38	57,400	123,000
Food, drink and tobacco	27	7,000	29,000
Textiles	6	1,700	20,000
Footwear and clothing	20	8,100	27,000
Timber and wooden furniture	2	200	1,000
Paper, printing and publishing	14	1,900	30,000
Other manufacturing industries	16	1,900	9,000
Construction	22	3,600	18,000
Distribution, hotels and catering, repairs	14	1,900	10,000
Transport services and communication	137	192,900	1,666,000
Supporting and miscellaneous transport services	26	3,000	12,000
Banking, finance, insurance, business services and leasing	3	200	3,000
Public administration, education and health services	135	423,700	945,000
Other services	20	3,200	39,000
All industries and services	1,028	923,600	3,572,000

Source: *Employment Gazette*, September 1987

STUDY POINTS

1 Which industry lost most working days through strikes in the 12 months up to June 1987?

2 What was the reason most workers went on strike in this time?

3 Which workers did not go on strike during this time? What might be the reasons for this?

4 Construct a bar chart showing the total numbers of working days lost due to strikes in the primary, secondary and tertiary industries for the 12 months to June 1987.

5 A manufacturing firm, which has had a large number of strikes over the years, has been bought by the existing management team. They have given all the workers a chance to buy shares in the firm and about 80 per cent have done so. Suggest what effects this might have on the number of working days lost due to strike in the future. Give your reasons.

There are bound to be conflicts in business. Managers want to make deals with the workers which are most profitable for the firm. Workers want to make deals which give them the best working conditions. Governments may also cause problems. They may decide to privatise a nationalised industry which may lead to protests by the workers.

Talks between management and unions often break down; managers may try to drive too hard a bargain, workers may make impossible demands. If the managers refuse to offer anything more, the workers may take **INDUSTRIAL ACTION**.

Four kinds of action

There are four main kinds of industrial action. They are:

● *Non-co-operation.* The workers may boycott, or refuse to have anything to do with, a new working practice of which they do not approve. For example, a new method of keeping records may have been introduced without prior talks with the unions. The workers may refuse to operate the new system.

Workers may boycott a scab, or a person who has continued to work during a strike. They will refuse to talk to him or her.

Goods from non-union firms or countries, such as South Africa, may be blacked; this means workers will refuse to handle them.

● *Working to rule.* There are many official rules in workplaces about the conditions and terms of employment. For example, they may specify all the parts that should be checked before a machine is used; or all the protective clothing that should be worn for a particular job. In practice, some of these rules are often ignored in the interests of greater speed and efficiency. However, when there is a **WORK TO RULE**, or go slow, all the rules will

TUC demonstration in support of the National Health Service, March 1988

be strictly observed. As a result, the jobs take much longer, and productivity falls.

There may be strict demarcation lines between unions to stop one worker doing another trade unionist's job [see Unit 64]. During a work to rule, these will all be observed and production will fall.

Shop stewards may take every single complaint and grievance to management, which she or he would previously have settled on the spot. As a result, management time is wasted.

It is very difficult for management to do anything about these time-wasting devices, particularly as the workers are not breaking their contract of employment or losing any pay.

● *Overtime ban.* Workers may refuse to work beyond the normal hours. Firms which rely heavily on overtime working to keep to their production schedules will be affected. The workers are also affected as they lose valuable overtime pay.

● *Strikes.* These are the workers' final weapon. The firm loses because it cannot produce its goods or services. The workers lose, because they lose their normal pay. Consumers are often badly affected too.

Strikes

There are two main kinds of strikes; **OFFICIAL STRIKES** and **UNOFFICIAL STRIKES** or wildcat strikes. Official strikes usually follow lengthy talks between employers and unions and, now, a ballot or vote by all members. Strike pay, which is less than normal pay, is paid, so workers are not keen to strike without a good cause.

Official strikes are more likely in industries going through periods of change. In recent years, miners have been faced with pit closures, bus drivers with privatisation and teachers with loss of pay-negotiating or bargaining rights. This has led to strikes in these industries. Isolated workers, as in farming, or well paid workers, as on oil rigs, are less likely to strike.

A union may decide to call a **SELECTIVE STRIKE** of only some of its members. For example a teachers' union may call out some teachers in certain areas. The effects can be almost as great as an all-out strike, but far fewer members lose their pay.

Negotiations

You are working as a manager in the London headquarters of a trade union. The shop stewards have put in a claim for a bigger London allowance. In support of their claim, they have quoted the following figures for other central or inner London allowances:

National Westminster Bank £3,000 a year
Royal Bank of Scotland £2,200 a year
Abbey National Building Society £1,950 a year
Automobile Association £1,785 a year
Civil Service (white collar) £1,527 a year

They also refer to the large union assets, which are currently £26 million.

The current inner London allowance for the union employees is £978 a year.

Write a letter of reply to the shop stewards, including any other information you have been able to find which will support your case for refusing a large increase.

KEY TERMS

INDUSTRIAL ACTION Action taken by union members designed to reduce or to stop production.

WORK TO RULE Obeying every official rule so that work is slowed down.

OFFICIAL STRIKES Withdrawal of labour with full union support.

UNOFFICIAL STRIKES Withdrawal of labour at the orders of shop stewards, without official support of the union. These are also known as wildcat strikes.

SELECTIVE STRIKE Calling out only some members of the union instead of the whole membership.

CHECKPOINTS

1 Describe the four main kinds of industrial action.
2 What is the difference between an official and an unofficial strike?
3 At which time of the year would you expect air traffic controllers to go on strike? What would be the reason?
4 Which would be the most effective time for miners, teachers and nurses to take industrial action?
5 What is a selective strike? What are the main advantages for unions?
6 What is working to rule? Give three examples.

Conciliation and Arbitration

Pendulum arbitration

MOST OF THE NEW no-strike agreements [see Unit 63] allow for pendulum arbitration. This is where the arbitrator has to make a straight choice between the employer's case and the union's, and give a verdict or decision in favour of one side or the other. It is claimed that this kind of arbitration encourages both sides to be moderate, as they know that if their demands are extreme they are likely to be rejected.

In the following case, the union had put in a claim for £160.30 per week pay and the company had offered £151.91.

'In early 1985 the company had moved to a new location with the aim of increasing its production capacity. This involved the introduction of shift working. An agreement was reached with the trade union which covered most aspects of the shift arrangements but a difference over rates of pay remained unresolved.

The trade union felt that comparisons with other employers within the industry, and the disruptive effects of shift working on employees' personal lives, justified higher rates of pay than the company was offering.

However, the company held the view that its rates, when considered as an overall 'package', were competitive and also realistic given its financial position.'

Source: *ACAS Annual Report*, 1986

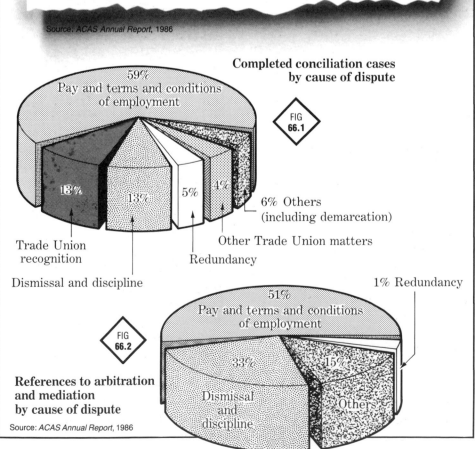

Completed conciliation cases by cause of dispute

FIG **66.1**

- 59% Pay and terms and conditions of employment
- 13% Trade Union recognition
- 13% Dismissal and discipline
- 5% Redundancy
- 4% Other Trade Union matters
- 6% Others (including demarcation)

References to arbitration and mediation by cause of dispute

FIG **66.2**

- 51% Pay and terms and conditions of employment
- 33% Dismissal and discipline
- 15% Others
- 1% Redundancy

Source: *ACAS Annual Report*, 1986

ACAS

Every year, hundreds of industrial disputes are settled peacefully through the work of **ACAS**, the Advisory, Conciliation and Arbitration Service. ACAS is an independent body with a high reputation on both sides of industry for its professional skills and practical approaches. Some of its main functions are:

- to settle collective disputes between unions and employers by **CONCILIATION**. ACAS can take action on its own behalf or at the request of one or more parties to the dispute.
- to refer unsettled disputes to **ARBITRATION** with the agreement of all the parties involved.
- to conciliate in cases of complaints by individuals.
- to advise on ways of improving industrial relations.

ACAS's services are provided free to employers, trade unions, employers' associations and employees.

ACAS gets most publicity from big industrial disputes, such as those involving printers and teachers in recent years. Normally ACAS will only become involved when all the other agreed procedures for settling disputes have failed. Its officials try to reach agreement between the two sides by talking separately to each to see how far they will change their demands, and trying to bring them together.

The work takes much time, skill and patience. The ACAS success rate is so high – 86 per cent of cases completed in 1986 were settled without industrial action taking place – that both employers and unions turn increasingly to ACAS. In 1986, half of the 1,457 requests for ACAS to conciliate were joint requests by employers and unions.

If ACAS fails to sort out a dispute, there is one last resort. With the consent of all parties involved, ACAS can refer the dispute to arbitration. The arbitrator works alone, though in big disputes there may be more than one. Each is a highly-qualified, independent person with experience of industrial affairs. Their judgements are not legally binding, but are usually accepted by both sides.

Industrial tribunals

ACAS also deals with thousands of individual conciliation cases each year. In 1986, it handled over 50,000. The vast majority concerned claims for unfair dismissal [see Unit 76]. Either the employer or the employee may ask ACAS for help. This may be done either before or after a formal complaint has been made to an **INDUSTRIAL TRIBUNAL**. In 1986, ACAS settled over half of the cases referred to it and nearly another quarter were withdrawn. Just over a quarter of the cases went on to an industrial tribunal for settlement.

BUSINESS TECHNIQUES
Employment policies

Discipline

> Is there a disciplinary procedure? E.g. who has the authority to discipline? Do employees have an opportunity to put their side of the case?

Written procedure
Authority/responsibility

FIG 66.3

Levels in procedure:
☐ number of warnings
☐ type of warning (oral, written).

Treatment of:
☐ first offences
☐ misconduct while on final warning
☐ trade union representatives.

Suspension:
☐ paid
☐ unpaid.

Opportunity to state case

Representation at disciplinary interviews:
☐ role of trade union officials
☐ other representatives.

Appeal arrangements:
☐ final appeal, to whom
☐ timescales.

Source: ACAS, Employment policies

Much trouble can be avoided in the workplace, without the need for help from ACAS or going to an industrial tribunal, if the firm has an employment policy which is effective and fair. One of the most important aspects is discipline.

You are the personnel officer in a medium-sized engineering company. Using the ACAS checklist in Figure 66.3, construct a complete code of discipline. For each point in the checklist, state what procedures you would adopt. For example:

> *Checklist point:* Number of warnings
>
> *Code of discipline:* 3 warnings will be given to an employee and after the final warning, disciplinary action will be taken.

Industrial tribunals are independent bodies, whose verdicts are legally binding. The chairperson is a lawyer and there is also one employers' representative and one trade union representative. The tribunal has powers to award financial compensation to an employee or to order a firm to re-employ them.

ACAS also provides advice to both sides of industry on improving industrial relations. It does this by a variety of means, including:
● answering over a quarter of a million individual enquiries a year
● publishing a series of booklets on many aspects of industrial relations
● advising on actual problems in the workplace concerned.

In 1986, ACAS's officials made nearly 9,000 visits to individual firms to advise them.

CHECKPOINTS

1 **What are the four main functions of ACAS?**
2 **Why does it have such a high success rate?**
3 **What can ACAS do if its attempts at collective conciliation fail?**
4 **What is the main cause of individual conciliation cases?**
5 **Describe the work of an industrial tribunal.**

KEY TERMS

ACAS or the Advisory, Conciliation and Arbitration Service – An independent body set up in 1974 which plays the leading part in attempts to settle industrial disputes peacefully and to improve industrial relations.

CONCILIATION Talking to both sides in an industrial dispute and trying to bring them together before attitudes have had time to harden, so that a strike or a lock out, where employers lock the employees out of the work premises until they agree to their terms, can be avoided.

ARBITRATION A voluntary settlement of a dispute by an independent person, the arbitrator, whose decision all parties have agreed to accept.

INDUSTRIAL TRIBUNAL An independent body dealing mainly with claims for unfair dismissal and other alleged breaches of employees' rights.

UNIT 67
Informal Groups

Two years ago, Varsha and Sarah set up their own business as hand-loom weavers in a small studio/workshop. They specialised in making colourful table place settings sold mainly in the local area. Although they were very good friends, they had heard about all the problems which could occur in partnerships [see Unit 14], so they got their solicitor to draw up a formal partnership agreement.

The business went well from the start. They both worked at the looms, but Sarah went out from time to time to do the selling. One day, Sarah came back very excited. She had just obtained a big order from a famous London store. The extra work meant that they would have to take on another worker.

Of all the applicants, they both liked Janice best. They decided to employ her. For several months, they all worked together in harmony, but then things started to change.

STUDY POINTS

1 Why did Varsha and Sarah decide to have a partnership agreement?

2 Describe in detail all the stages and procedures they would have gone through before they decided to employ Janice.

3 Why was there trouble after Janice arrived?

4 What actions should Varsha have taken when the trouble started?

5 What would be likely to happen if the situation went on unchecked?

In addition to formal groups in the workplace [see Unit 23], there are always **INFORMAL GROUPS** as well. This is true of all organisations. Look at any class in a school. Everyone is a member of the same form, or set – the formal group. Yet, there will always be smaller groups, or pairs, who share attitudes or ideas which are different from the others'.

These informal groups may not always be popular with the rest of the organisation. Opposition will, however, often make them stick together more. These groups may be doing good – working hard and creating a pleasant atmosphere, or they may be a source of constant trouble – doing little work and always complaining or behaving badly.

Why informal groups?

Large organisations, such as a school or a big company, expect their members to behave in a certain way. However, each person is an individual, with different needs. People will get together with others who are similar to themselves and form a group which has the same patterns of behaviour.

Informal groups may occur because of dissatisfaction at work. For example, in the Study Points, two partners took on a new employee, who caused trouble between the partners by siding with one of them. An informal group was set up between the employee and one of the partners which might have been stronger than the formal group of the partnership.

Similarly, on the shop floor, informal groups may be set up where workers are dissatisfied with the amount of pay they are receiving. These groups can decide to slow down the speed at which they work so that the rate of production will slow down too.

Informal groups are found among white collar workers too. For example, if a firm was taken over, many of the management made redundant and new workers recruited to replace them, the existing employees might feel isolated. They would have their own ways of doing things and they might not fit easily

into the new system. They might create informal groups opposed to changes in the way they work.

Informal groups do not always cause trouble. Groups which have worked happily together for a long time, and have shared – and overcome – many common problems, may be highly efficient, particularly if they feel they have a special place in the firm.

Managers who have worked for the same firm for a long time may be members of an informal group. Often, they can get a job done much more quickly by using their personal contacts rather than going through formal channels. Employees who share a common interest in the workplace, such as being members of the same sports club, may also form an informal group. They are more likely to help other members of the group in work situations. People who go to the same church, or who have lived in the same foreign country for a long time, may also find their informal contacts useful at work.

Different approaches

Managers have to learn to deal with informal groups. Some managers think the best approach is to try to bring them more into the formal organisation. They encourage as many workers as possible to join in the affairs of the firm. Some common means are:

- *Suggestion schemes* which encourage workers to make suggestions for improving efficiency. This makes them feel that they have a say and are not just a cog in the machine.

- *Small meetings* of employees from different departments, which encourages work-directed informal groups. These quality circles are

increasingly common in business. They bring workers and managers together in an informal meeting to discuss and analyse any work-related problems.

- *Joint consultation* which gives elected committees a chance to bring up grievances which have not gone through formal channels.

- *Improved communications* so that employees know what is going on and feel part of the firm.

Other managers feel it is better to encourage competition between individuals in an atmosphere of constant change, so that informal groups have less time to develop.

There is no right answer. Each manager has to make his or her own choice.

Communications

Part of your job is editing the company's news sheet. Rumours are sweeping the firm that there will be massive redundancies in the stores department. You have heard the same rumours on the grapevine; but you also know the true facts – that there will be a small number of redundancies in four months' time. Would you:

a) Say nothing in the news sheet?
b) Deny the rumours and give no further information?
c) Give the full facts now?

If you have chosen b) or c) write a report for the news sheet. If you have chosen a) give reasons for your choice.

KEY TERM

INFORMAL GROUPS Loose associations of people sharing common attitudes, interests or views, which exist outside the formal structure of the organisation.

CHECKPOINTS

1 What is an informal group?
2 How does it differ from a formal group?
3 Give two examples each of the good and bad effects of informal groups in firms.
4 If you were a manager would you encourage participation or individual competition? Give full reasons for your choice.

Activities

■ Review points

1 What is the CBI? What is its full name? Describe its main objectives.

2 What are the functions of employers' organisations?

3 Describe the main types of trade unions. What are the main functions of all unions?

4 Why are shop stewards important for both union members and the firm that employs them?

5 What is collective bargaining? What does it deal with at national and local levels?

6 Describe the different kinds of industrial action and state their objectives.

7 What outside bodies help in resolving industrial disputes? Explain their importance.

■ Essay questions

1 The workers in your firm are threatening to go on strike for higher pay. Describe in detail the steps you would take to resolve the problem.

2 A new computer unit has been set up in your firm staffed by members from the company's headquarters. State what actions you would take in relation to:
a) the new staff
b) the existing staff
to ensure that they worked together peacefully.

We will not

At the Trades Union Congress (TUC) conference in Blackpool, electricians' leader Eric Hammond yesterday launched a passionate defence of his union's controversial no-strike deals, claiming: 'Our case is freedom, we are the future and we are not going to go away.'

Opponents among the 1,065 delegates vainly tried to shout him down, but he went on to say the new-style deals were needed as the only way forward for a movement which has lost three million members since 1979.

His moderate union was under attack simply for trying to improve workers' status and to end the 'industrial apartheid' which had affected the country.

Left-winger Ron Todd of the giant Transport & General Workers' Union, said trade unionists should never commit industrial suicide by giving up the basic right to strike. And Bill Freeman of the print union SOGAT 82, whose sacked members on Rupert Murdoch's newspapers were replaced by those belonging to Mr Hammond's organisation, said: 'They are snakes in the grass – vipers in the nest of the union movement.'

Clive Jenkins, general secretary of the white collar workers' union ASTMS, in another swipe at Mr Hammond, said unions with no-strike deals were losing members. 'We organise 40 disputes every month,' he said. 'We don't have to carry them out because managements know we are serious. We are making net gains in membership every month as well. So it works.'

Rodney Bickerstaff, general secretary of the National Union of Public Employees and chairman of the TUC economic committee, launched a drive for a new-look trade union organisation by calling for steps to counter the misrepresentation of unions as 'bullying, threatening and undemocratic'.

He added: 'I'm getting a little bit tired of some of the people in our own movement who say we are in a crisis and going down the pan.'

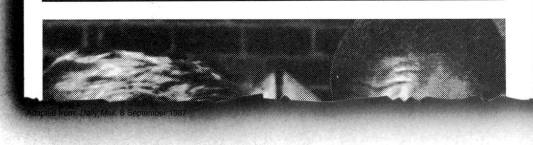

Adapted from: *Daily Mail*, 8 September 1987

go away!

Recruit more women urges Brenda Dean

PRINT union leader Brenda Dean urged the TUC to shed its male-dominated image.

She said its recruiting campaign should be aimed at more women, who now represent half the country's workforce compared with a third in 1960.

She told the TUC conference: 'It is possible that by the end of this century the majority of the workforce will be women, yet we still have the image as a movement which is male-dominated, treating women's issues as a fringe.

Brenda Dean

Our arrogant image, by engineers' chief

Many people regard trade unions as arrogant, warned John Lyons, general secretary of the Engineers and Managers Association.

He said: 'The British people do understand unions and they don't greatly like what they see.'

Mr Lyons went on: 'We are too busy recruiting from the public sector, but we must recruit more people from the private sector.'

John Lyons

Bullies out, says Fowler

EMPLOYMENT Secretary Norman Fowler yesterday warned union bully-boys that there will be no room for them in the new industrial Britain.

New laws due before Parliament will mean compulsory elections for all union officials.

And unions will not be able to discipline members who refuse to go on strike.

Mr Fowler said: "There is no place for the old-style bully-boy, narrow-minded and short-sighted trade unionism of yesterday.

"If unions are to make a positive contribution they must move away from their old traditions of confrontation and conflict."

1 How does the government propose to restrict trade union power?

2 What would be the effects of these changes on unions?

3 What did the Employment Secretary mean by 'the old-style bully-boy, narrow-minded and short-sighted trade unionism' of yesterday?

4 Do you think that is a fair judgment?

5 What kinds of trade unions would the government like to see.

1 What is a no-strike agreement? Describe the items it usually contains.

2 According to Mr Eric Hammond, what is the main purpose of no-strike agreements?

3 Why do some other union leaders oppose his views? Which, in your opinion is the right view? State the reasons for your choice.

4 What is the main argument for recruiting more women to trade unions? What may be one of the difficulties in doing so?

5 Why, according to Mr John Lyons, do many people think that unions are arrogant?

NHS pays for cut-price screening

A LONDON NHS hospital is to offer cut price private breast cancer screening to city businesswomen.

The scheme is the latest money-making plan by cash-starved St Bartholomew's Hospital. Savings of £1.25 million are being sought this year.

The scheme, using NHS staff and equipment, hopes to compete with private clinics run by BUPA. The hospital has already negotiated a contract with one large city firm.

The clinics will be held on two evenings a week from October.

The National and Local Government Officers Association (NALGO) wants to know why the general public can't have access to the NHS service.

NALGO officer Ada Maddocks said: 'The service must be determined by the needs of the public not by the ability to raise money from private health schemes.'

'The danger is that the more savings a health authority makes the less funding they will get from central government,' she said.

Dr Ken Grant, general manager for the City and Hackney district health authority, said the purpose of the scheme was to raise money. 'We have machines that are lying empty because we do not have the funds to run the department in the evenings,' he added.

Part of the money raised will go towards the cost of a screening service for hospital staff, he said.

The plans have not been discussed with staff or NALGO.

The first in a programme of NHS breast cancer screening clinics will not begin operating until next year. Then they will only screen women over 50.

Source: *Public Service*, September 1987

1 Why has St Bartholomew's Hospital introduced private screening?

2 What are the NALGO objections to the scheme? What do they fear will happen if such schemes multiply?

3 How does the district health authority defend the scheme?

4 Who, in your opinion, has the best case? Explain your reasons in detail.

■ Coursework

1 Collect as many newspaper cuttings as you can about a big local or national industrial dispute which is likely to continue for some time. Construct a table of the dispute showing, in date order, the actions that were taken by both sides and the reasons for them. Analyse some of the statements made by both sides, distinguishing between well-supported argument and opinion. Evaluate the merits of the case presented by each side and state how you would have solved the dispute if you had been an arbitrator.

2 Find out from a local trade union branch what benefits they offer workers, particularly young people. Draw up a marketing plan for attracting young recruits to the union. Design a recruitment advertisement for the local press.

3 Take any organisation you know well, such as a club or your school. Write a report describing the informal groups that exist within the organisation and whether they are harmful or beneficial. Explain how a manager might use these groups for the benefit of the organisation.

4 Contact a local chamber of commerce, industry or trade and find out what help they provide for various types of business. Interview some local business persons in those categories to discover what help they receive from their local chamber of commerce. State the number, kind and location of other firms you would have needed to interview to gain a more representative view.

5 Look at the CBI's *Guidelines for government* again in Unit 62. Visit the reference section of a public library and find out in newspapers and magazines how much notice the government has taken of the CBI requests. Write a report describing the suggestions which have been accepted and their effects, and suggest reasons why no action has been taken over the other suggestions.

■ Groupwork

As a class, or a large group, design a market research questionnaire about attitudes to trade unions. Make a quota of the people you want to interview. Arrange for each student to interview two people from the sample quota. When all the interviews have been completed, analyse the results as a class or a group. Select a smaller team to write a report describing the findings, which could be illustrated with charts and graphs.

Aiding and Controlling Business Activity

Government Help

ENTERPRISE

Enterprise Allowance Scheme

Want to start a new small business or work for yourself but can't afford to lose out on benefits until you get off the ground?

The Enterprise Allowance Scheme will provide financial help during the first 12 months that you are working for yourself.

Plenty of unemployed people would like to become self-employed or start their own small business, and many thousands have already done so — thanks to the Enterprise Allowance Scheme. The scheme is intended to help unemployed people who have a business venture in mind but who may be put off from working for themselves because they would lose their entitlement to State benefits. EAS helps to overcome this problem by paying them a regular allowance for one year.

Many different businesses are being supported, from plumbers, mechanics, retailers and dressmakers to computer software designers. Successful businesses may well go on to create new jobs for other unemployed people.

Those interested first attend an information session to find out how EAS operates and to get advice on setting up a new business. Once they have joined the scheme, participants are entitled to further free advisory sessions.

Financial help

£40 a week for 52 weeks will be paid to supplement the receipts of the new business while it is being established. The business may also qualify for help under other Government and local authority schemes. The Small Firms Service can advise.

Who is eligible?

Anyone between 18 and State retirement age receiving unemployment or supplementary benefit and who has been out of work for eight weeks.

Applicants must also have at least £1,000 to invest in their business — or be able to raise it by loan or overdraft. It is not necessary to produce it at the application stage.

Contact
Your local Jobcentre before start-up.

Source: *Action for Jobs*

STUDY POINTS

1 Who is the Enterprise Allowance Scheme (EAS) for?

2 How much money of your own do you need before you can apply for the scheme?

3 Describe in your own words what the EAS offers.

4 Why was the EAS set up?

5 Make a list of some of the questions you might find on an application form for the EAS.

Help for small businesses

There are now far more government schemes to help small businesses than ever before. One example is seen in the Study Points. Another example is the Business Expansion Scheme, which encourages investment in small businesses by giving tax relief on the money put in by investors. The Loan Guarantee Scheme is one where the government guarantees 70 per cent of a loan, thus encouraging banks to lend money to businesses which have no security, or no credit history.

A large amount of help and information is now available from the Small Firms Service on finance, premises, marketing and many other matters. It also provides advice and support from experienced business men and women and some very useful publications for anyone who is thinking of starting their own business, however small. (There is a brochure, *Employing People*, written especially for small firms by ACAS (Advisory, Conciliation and Arbitration Service), which is an excellent guide to avoiding pitfalls in all employment matters.)

The government has tried to create a more encouraging climate for small firms (i.e. those employing fewer than 200 workers). It has done this by cutting the time taken for making decisions, particularly in planning applications; reducing taxes; curbing union power [see Unit 63]; and making it easier for worthwhile schemes to obtain finance. The government hopes that its policies will encourage enterprise, and reduce unemployment as small firms expand and take on employees.

To a certain extent, this has already happened. There has been an increase in the number of small firms. The growth of employment among really small firms employing less than 20 people has been greater than for any other size of firm.

Although some of these jobs have been created in the hi-tech industries, many of them are part-time, low-paid jobs in poor working conditions. Moreover, little attempt has been made to control the quality of work provided by small firms, particularly in such sectors as house repairs.

Industry as a whole

The government has favoured this policy of helping small businesses partly because the amount of public investment is relatively small. Its policies towards industry as a whole, however, have been very different. Apart from grants for science and technology, public expenditure on regional aid [see Unit 69] and on individual industries has been reduced in the last few years.

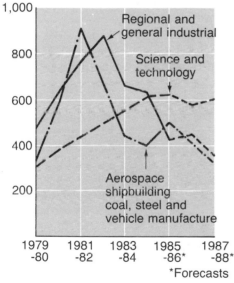

Public expenditure on industry support
(£ million)

Source: *Economist*, 26 October 1985

Even so, the amounts involved are still enormous. According to Treasury estimates, quoted in the *Economist*, the total amounts spent between 1979 and 1985 were:

● Regional and general industrial support, £4.2 billion;

● Scientific and technical assistance, £2.9 billion;

● Support for aerospace, ship-building, coal, steel and vehicle manufacture, £3.4 billion.

The government has demanded a heavy price for its continued support of industries such as steel,

shipbuilding and mining. Thousands of people have lost their jobs as plants, yards and mines have been closed in the interests of greater efficiency. Productivity has increased by concentrating investment in the most profitable units, which is a **SOCIAL BENEFIT**. However, there has also been a great **SOCIAL COST** as people have lost their jobs and whole areas of former industrial importance have been laid to waste. The government has then had to provide regional aid for these areas in the hope of attracting new industries [see Unit 69].

What industry wants

Although business likes some of the changes that have been made [see Unit 62], there are many others which would have been of even greater importance. These include:

● Greater government support for British exporters. British companies commonly lose overseas orders, because their foreign rivals can offer cheap long-term loans from their governments to foreign customers.

● Stable exchange and interest rates. These allow business to make definite plans for the future, as they know that they will not suddenly have to pay more interest for the money they have borrowed, or that the price of imported raw materials or semi-manufactured goods will not suddenly increase because of a fall in the value of the pound.

● Improvements in the physical infrastructure such as roads. This would enable business to move its goods around more easily.

An example of improved infrastructure – the M25 motorway was completed in 1986

Loan applications

You are setting up a small business for which you need a loan of £5,000. You have no capital of your own, but an uncle has agreed to provide security for a bank loan of £1,500. You hope that you can get the rest of the money you need under the Loan Guarantee Scheme.

Write a letter to a bank manager asking for a loan along these lines. Describe what kind of business you want to set up, what you need the capital for, and any other relevant information. Enclose a business plan to strengthen your case for getting a loan.

KEY TERMS

SOCIAL BENEFITS The benefits to society as a whole which business or government actions might bring, e.g. greater productivity.

SOCIAL COST The losses that a community might suffer as a result of business or government actions, e.g. unemployment, pollution.

CHECKPOINTS

1 **What help has the government provided for small firms?**
2 **What might be some of the drawbacks of the aid provided?**
3 **What was the total amount of aid to industry between 1979 and 1985? Which area of industry got the largest share?**
4 **What other forms of aid would business like and for what reasons?**

Regional Aid

Ministers propose regional aid shake-up

DEPARTMENT of Trade and Industry (DTI) ministers yesterday began a two-day session on their future role in government, which could lead to a shake-up in the way regional aid is distributed to business.

The centre of the discussion will be the department's £350 million a year budget in regional aid and how best to redirect this so that it has maximum impact on the inner cities.

Ministers have long been dissatisfied with the way regional aid is directed, believing it often ends up in the hands of large, profitable companies which qualify simply because they have a plant which is in an area eligible for aid.

To qualify for a regional development grant a company has to be in a development area. In an intermediate area, businesses can apply only for regional selective assistance which is not always given. Outside these areas there is no aid at all.

Some of the inner city areas in which the DTI has set up task forces to deal with longstanding problems, such as Notting Hill and North Peckham in London, do not qualify for any form of regional aid and others, such as Handsworth in Birmingham, only fall into the intermediate area category.

One choice is to abolish automatic grants and use the money instead to employ private consultants to advise firms on how to expand. The idea would be to target regional aid more carefully towards fostering enterprise and away from already profitable companies.

Adapted from: *Independent*, 12 September 1987

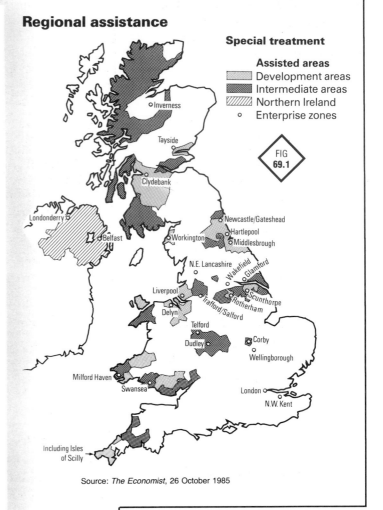

Regional assistance

Special treatment

Assisted areas
- Development areas
- Intermediate areas
- Northern Ireland
- Enterprise zones

FIG 69.1

Source: *The Economist*, 26 October 1985

Since the 1930s, all UK governments have provided some form of **REGIONAL AID** for business. This aid is usually given in the form of grants, loans or tax relief. It is designed to attract firms to areas of the country which have high unemployment, so that more jobs will be created.

Changes in distribution of grants

In the past, too much of the aid has gone to firms who didn't really need it. Oil companies who set up plants along the east coast of Scotland and England have received millions of pounds in regional aid. However, they would have had to locate their plants there, anyway, to be near the North Sea rigs; and they were rich enough to build their own plants. Moreover, not

STUDY POINTS

1 Look at the map in Figure 69.1. What is an enterprise zone? Give three examples from different parts of the country.

2 Where are the development areas situated?

3 Why is the Department of Trade and Industry not happy with the way in which regional aid is distributed at present?

4 Who will benefit from the proposed changes and who will lose?

many new jobs were created, once the construction work was done.

Since the Conservative government came to power, the total amount of regional aid has been reduced from over £900 million in 1982 to £350 million in 1987. In 1984, the way in which aid was given was altered. Instead of giving an automatic grant to any firm who set up in a development area, grants were provided only if new jobs had been created.

In the development areas, firms can now get a job-creation grant of £3,000 for each job created, or a capital expenditure grant of up to £10,000. (Small firms can get more.) At the same time, service industries, which had previously been excluded, became eligible for grants. In the intermediate areas, firms may or may not get grants depending on how much financial assistance they need to create jobs.

Now, the government is proposing an even bigger change in line with its policy of supporting small, rather than big, firms [see Unit 68]. Instead of giving automatic grants to firms who create jobs in development areas, however rich the firms may be, the aid may be given instead to small firms in inner city areas.

Enterprise zones

In addition, the government has also set up new enterprise zones [see Unit 6]. There are 25 enterprise zones in various parts of the country, such as the Isle of Dogs in London. The government provides money to create a better infrastructure and valuable incentives for firms in the hope that private investment will be attracted to the area. The incentives include not having to pay rates for 10 years and capital allowances of up to 100 per cent for building industrial or commercial premises, whether they are for the firm's own use or for letting.

Sony UK received an EC grant of £173,000 towards the cost of a new television tube plant at Bridgend.

Grants of £37 million from the EC were used to help finance the Kielder Reservoir scheme in Northumberland, to improve the water supply to the North East.

Although the enterprise zones have created some jobs, not all of them have been new jobs, as firms have moved in from neighbouring areas to take advantage of these concessions. Relatively few jobs in enterprise zones have gone to local people.

European Community grants

Firms and public and local authorities can also get regional grants from the European Community (EC). In 1985, the United Kingdom received £245 million pounds from the European Regional Development Fund. The EC also provides grants and loans to the private and public sectors for such items as:

● training, resettlement and job creation schemes
● developing energy supplies
● improving the economic and social conditions in coal and steel producing regions
● research and development
● economic development.

BUSINESS TECHNIQUES

Building costs

The cost of building a hi-tech industrial building with raised floors, air conditioning and suspended ceilings is £460 per square metre. Calculate the total cost of building a 1000 square metre property of this kind.

If you decided to build the factory in an enterprise zone, you would get a 100 per cent allowance against tax. This means that you will not pay tax on the money you spend on building the factory. If corporation tax is 35 per cent, work out how much you will save by building in the enterprise zone.

CHECKPOINTS

1 What is regional aid?
2 Who gives regional aid to businesses?
3 Which other organisations can receive regional aid and from what source?
4 Name three types of grants or loans which the European Community gives to Britain.

KEY TERM

REGIONAL AID Grants or loans given to firms and local authorities to create jobs or to improve the infrastructure in areas of high unemployment and poor physical or social conditions.

Export Promotion

Kozy Kitchens produces up-market kitchen units mainly for the domestic market. Over the last few years, it has had short order books. To make full use of the spare space in its factory, the firm has decided to try to build up its small export trade to 15 per cent of the total.

Preliminary desk research, and visits to the country itself, have shown that Canada presents the best opportunities for exports. If a secure foothold could be established there, the firm might then investigate the chances of expanding across the border into the United States.

The firm has taken a small stand at a big, trade furniture fair in Montreal. It hopes to get some direct orders from Canadian furniture retailers and, possibly, to find an agent who would handle all the imports – if the terms were right.

You have been asked to produce a four-page brochure which will be available on the stand. You have produced a draft of the front page, but the managing director doesn't like it at all.

kozy kitchens

proudly presents . . .

its range of hand-crafted fitted kitchens

'A touch of the old home country'

The Old Farmhouse built of solid oak

Edwardian Elegance in high-quality beech (illustrated above)

Victorian Dream built of fabulous mahogany

S T U D Y P O I N T S

1 Study the draft front page above. What do you think the managing director might have disliked about the layout, the drawing, the appeal to up-market consumers or the suitability for the Canadian market?

2 Design a new front page for the brochure, based on what you think the managing director's comments would have been. Include any other information you think should be given.

Finding the market

Before firms enter export markets, they have to carry out just the same kind of research as they do in the home market [see Unit 30]. First of all, they have to do their desk research – finding out from printed material everything they can about the proposed overseas market. For example: what gaps home producers have left unfilled; what the size of the market segment is; whether the firm's prices would be competitive; whether there are any special regulations about imports.

Some ideas can be dismissed immediately. It probably wouldn't be much use trying to export Union Jacks to Russia or alcoholic drinks to Saudi Arabia. However, every possibility should be considered. Some firms have done well by exporting goods to unlikely places: sand – of a special kind – to Saudi Arabia; peanut butter to the United States. Market gaps like these can provide small firms with profitable opportunities.

Information and statistics

Government departments, such as the Department of Trade and Industry, and other official bodies, such as the Central Statistical Office, can provide exporters with masses of valuable information and statistics. Trade and employers' organisations can also give much detailed help [see Unit 62]. The information departments of the foreign country's own embassy or high commission are another source of background information.

Once the desk research has been done, a member of the firm, or a team, needs to visit the country to do more detailed research. The commercial section of the British embassy in the country may help the firm's representatives during the visit.

British Overseas Trade Board

When the firm has decided to go ahead and export its products, the government offers more direct help to firms in promoting their goods overseas. This is done mainly through the **BRITISH OVERSEAS TRADE BOARD (BOTB)**. In 1986, the BOTB provided help for nearly 7,000 firms exhibiting at trade fairs in 40 countries. It also sponsored over 2,000 firms in trade missions to foreign countries to assess the prospects for exports or to sell their goods.

The main forms of BOTB help include:

- Joint ventures – reduced costs for a group display sponsored by a trade association or similar body at an overseas trade fair. Firms exhibiting for the first time pay only 40 per cent of the BOTB's direct costs. Help with travel costs for up to two representatives at fairs outside Western Europe may also be given.

- British pavilions – at fairs where many British exporters are taking part, the BOTB may organise a British pavilion. Reduced prices and help with travel costs outside Western Europe can sometimes be offered.

- UK trade fairs – financial help may be available to organisers for costs of advertising the fairs overseas.

- Inward missions – financial aid offered to trade associations who arrange visits by groups of foreign buyers to Britain.

- Store promotions – financial help given to overseas department stores who arrange special promotions of British goods.

The BOTB advises British firms taking part in store promotions

When there are a number of British exporters at an overseas trade fair, the BOTB may organise a British pavilion, grouping all the British exporters together. The pavilion here is at an information technology fair in Hanover.

overseas to write to the store in the country's language giving details of price and delivery, and to send samples where possible.

Another government organisation – the Central Office of Information (COI) – can also be of help to British exporters. It distributes press releases and photographs to the overseas media about British achievements, including business achievements. This can provide a firm with valuable publicity overseas.

The Queen's Award for Industry is awarded annually on the Queen's birthday, 6 April, to firms who have increased their exports greatly or have broken into difficult markets. The firms can display a drawing of the award on their letters and packaging.

Store promotions

Your firm is taking part in its first overseas store promotion. Write a letter to the store in accordance with BOTB advice. The store could be in the United States; but preferably should be in a country whose language is not English.

CHECKPOINTS

1 Describe the main stages of research that a firm would undertake before it decided to enter an export market.
2 What kinds of help does the BOTB provide for exporters?
3 What is the Queen's Award for Industry?
4 Find one firm which has been given the Queen's Award for exporting and describe what its achievement was.

KEY TERM

BRITISH OVERSEAS TRADE BOARD (BOTB) A government organisation whose Fairs and Promotions branch provides financial help and advice for exporters. The BOTB is also concerned with export market research and aid to British firms operating abroad.

Private Sector Help

EXPORT NETWORK

The key to Export Success

Export Network has produced the world's most advanced information service for exporters, by using the knowledge and experience of many successful exporters, in order to avoid the bother of having to get information from many different sources.

Export Network collects, collates, edits, stores — and constantly updates — the information that would otherwise occupy a large research department.

The Export Network computers sort out and select the data and within seconds produce facts, figures and key contacts to meet specific requirements.

The information is there at the touch of a button for those who subscribe to the service. Information can be searched by product or by country. All you need to do is to connect any computer terminal to Export Network through a telephone line, at local call charges.

Electronic Data Interchange (EDI), or 'paperless trading' as it is known, is the fastest growing industry in the world. It reduces administration, cuts costs and cuts out expensive errors in paper documents. It allows you to communicate with other users, or with service companies, to obtain quotations, place orders, send telexes and transmit documents.

For less than £3 per day Export Network keeps you in touch with what is happening in nearly 200 markets around the world.

E N

Adapted from: Export Network

STUDY POINTS

1 Describe Export Network in your own words.

2 What kinds of exporters would Export Network be especially suitable for?

3 Would you rely on Export Network alone if:

a) you were running a small firm?
b) you were in charge of exports in a large company?
Explain your reasons in full.

4 Find out what other kinds of business are now done by EDI? What are the main advantages and disadvantages?

Businesses don't have to rely solely on the government for help. There are many private firms and organisations offering advice, information and financial aid. New firms with new ideas – like Export Network – are springing up all the time. Trade associations play an important part, too. These associations help to organise the British exhibitions at overseas trade fairs [see Unit 70]. In addition, associations – and private exhibition organisers – help to arrange trade fairs and exhibitions in this country, e.g. the annual London Motor Show, as seen below. Some trade associations also carry out research for the whole industry. All of them provide invaluable advice and information to their members.

British cars on show at the London Motor Show

Chambers of commerce

Chambers of commerce are another source of aid. These voluntary associations of business people are situated in big industrial and commercial cities throughout the country. Their members come from a wide range of businesses: finance, manufacturing, commerce, transport. They help to develop and to expand trade and industry in the locality and also keep an eye on their members'

interests in the area. They have much more important functions, too. Over the years, they have forged links with British chambers of commerce abroad and with many foreign countries. They can provide much information and useful contacts for businesses both at home and abroad. Many of them also take a great interest in education and training for jobs, particularly the London Chamber of Commerce and Industry, founded in 1881, which has long been a pioneer in this field.

Aid from banks

For most businesses, large or small, the most important institutions are the merchant banks and the clearing banks – the Big Four high street banks (Barclays, Lloyds, Midland and NatWest). Without their cheque system and their loans service, business would soon grind to a halt.

The Big Four banks have always provided many other services for business customers, such as overdrafts, help in setting up businesses, foreign exchange transactions, advice on taxation etc. During the last few years, the range of their services has expanded greatly – particularly for small firms, which, at one time, could not get all the help they needed. NatWest, for example, publishes a regular *Small Business Digest* with useful advice on such matters as training, VAT and exporting.

NatWest offers a wide range of services for small, or first-time, exporters. The bank's economic analysis department can provide much time-saving information for small firms' basic desk research. Information on economic and political developments in some 75 overseas countries is also provided regularly.

NatWest's Trade Promotion Section in London is able to make enquiries about export opportunities in most countries of the world. The section also receives many overseas inquiries from foreign customers seeking British suppliers. A bulletin of trading opportunities is published weekly, and details of export opportunities are

listed in the bank's monthly *Exporters' Bulletin*.

Banks can also help with that important first visit to the chosen market. A letter of introduction puts the firm's representative in touch with a foreign bank manager, who can provide useful contacts and local knowledge about the business environment in the country.

Valuable advice is also available on all export documents – invoices, contracts of sale, certificates of origin etc. Obtaining payment for your goods is obviously very important and banks, again, can advise on which method is the most suitable and the safest. Finance for exports, by overdrafts or other means, is also available from banks.

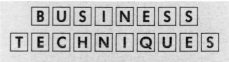

BUSINESS TECHNIQUES

Letters of introduction

You are working as a manager in a small branch of a high street bank. One of your customers is Mr John Smith of Bags and Bits – a small firm making plastic carrier bags for retail stores, which can be printed with the customer's own name, logo and advertising slogan. Mr Smith is trying to expand his business into mainland Europe. His first visit is to the Netherlands. Write a letter of introduction to the manager of your group's bank in Amsterdam.

What other services might you offer Mr Smith for his trip?

CHECKPOINTS

1 What are the main functions of chambers of commerce?
2 What help can trade associations provide for business?
3 Describe the main forms of aid that NatWest offers to small firms who are trying to export their goods.

Local Authorities

Nightspots and a fishy smell

HULL COUNCIL is transforming the city's disused docks from grimy eyesores into attractive assets.

Without the financial input of the development corporations which have speeded up the redevelopment of Liverpool and London's docklands, Hull City Council made a start by converting the central Humber Dock and Railway Dock into a marina, as part of its plans to revive the historic town centre.

At St Andrew's Docks, Grosvenor Square Properties are due to start work this year on 250,000 square feet of retail warehousing, plus a leisure complex, cinema, bowling alley and, possibly, a marina.

Albert Dock, in contrast, has seen a revival of Hull's dying fishing industry after some not so good years. Local trawler firms Boyd and Marr have invested £3 million between them in new trawler and freezing vessels—a welcome sign for the future. Albert Dock houses a successful wholesale fish market and is the centre of the city's fishing industry. There are, however, hopes that a former paddle steamer may be moored near the dock entrance as a floating nightclub.

A scheme already under construction, by Beazer Homes, will provide 175 town houses grouped in a courtyard beside the marina created from the other two old town docks, Humber Dock and Railway Dock. The new homes will sell for under £30,000.

Adapted from: *Daily Telegraph,* 29 March 1988

Albert Dock, Hull (top) and Hull Marina (bottom)

STUDY POINTS

1 What changes are being made at St Andrew's Docks?

2 Look at the Study Points in Unit 6. Describe any differences between the docklands developments in London and in Hull.

3 Why are docklands being redeveloped in many parts of the country?

4 Choose any derelict site, big or small, in your area. Work out a plan for how it might be redeveloped. Write to your local council proposing a joint redevelopment. Include any maps, plans, drawings or financial information which would support your case.

Local authorities get their money from three main sources:
● government grants (about half of the total amount)
● domestic ratepayers (just under a quarter of the total amount)
● non-domestic ratepayers such as owners of shops, factories and warehouses (just over a quarter of the total amount)

They use this money to provide services – such as schools, colleges, fire brigades, meals-on-wheels – for the whole community.

Changes to the rates system

In the past, businesses have made

many protests about RATES [see Unit 62]. They claim the present system is unfair because:

● The rates are too high.
● They are paying for services they do not use, like the councils' social services.
● They have no vote in council elections and, therefore, no control over how the money is spent.

From 1990, the Conservative government plans to change the whole rating system. Under their present plans, a uniform rate POUNDAGE would be set for businesses throughout England, and separately for Wales. Business premises would be revalued at present day values and future increases in the rates would be limited to increases in the cost of living. At the same time, domestic rates would be got rid of and replaced by a community charge. This will be a flat-rate payment (i.e. one where everyone pays the same) to the local council paid by practically all persons over 18 living in the area.

The government's plan would make business rates more stable; but some firms would have to pay much more than they do now. The Confederation of British Industry (CBI) is not in favour of the scheme because it wants a general reduction in the amount that businesses have to pay in rates to local councils.

The way in which a council spends its income has a big effect on business in the town or city. If the city is attractive and pleasant to live in, with good facilities such as parks and leisure centres and schools which provide a good education, more firms will want to move into the area [see Unit 26]. This will help to make the place even more prosperous than it

was before. On the other hand if the city is poor and neglected, with run-down inner city areas, few investors will be attracted, and the place will decline even more.

Planning permission

In the past, PLANNING PERMISSION has been one of the main sources of dispute between business and local councils. If a business wants to build an office or a factory or a supermarket it has to obtain permission from the council which deals with local planning applications. A business has to do the same if it wants to change the use of its premises, say, from a dress shop to a restaurant.

At one time, there were often long delays in dealing with planning applications and many were rejected. Councils now co-operate much more with business. Delays in dealing with planning applications have been reduced and nearly 90 per cent are approved in the end. Councils have learnt that they can benefit from business needs by:

● selling surplus council land for business development

● entering into joint development schemes so that, for example, the developer gets a supermarket and offices and the council gets the flats above

● taking shares in a development so that the council gets a profit in the future

● leasing land to the developer which provides the council with an income.

Providing jobs

As unemployment has increased, practically all councils have become aware of the need to provide jobs in their area. For this reason, they now turn down very few planning applications which would create long-term jobs. Many cities go much further. They make big efforts themselves to attract more firms to the area by providing industrial sites and financial incentives [see Unit 26]. Practically all councils also try to help small businesses by providing workshops and studios at reasonable rents. Some go even further by providing grants and loans for worthwhile schemes which will provide new jobs that will last for at least two years.

B U S I N E S S
T E C H N I Q U E S

Planning applications

You want to start a scrap metal yard in your back garden; but your neighbours have told you that you must get planning permission from the local council first. Find out the name and address of the council which deals with planning applications in your area. Write a letter to the department concerned asking for any information about planning permission and any necessary forms.

C H E C K P O I N T S

1 **What is the community charge? What will it replace?**
2 **What is planning permission? Why is it important for business?**
3 **How will the proposed business rating system affect businesses? What are the CBI's objections to the scheme?**
4 **Why have councils started to be more co-operative with business?**

K E Y   T E R M S

RATES Charges made by local councils on businesses and house owners, which are based on the value of their property.

POUNDAGE The way in which rates are assessed. Property is valued at the price for which it would be let and the rates are calculated at so many pence for each pound of the value, e.g. 181p in the pound.

PLANNING PERMISSION Council approval of a new business development or of a change of use for business premises.

Activities

■ Review points

1 Explain how the government's regional aid helps business. Why is this aid provided?

2 What is an enterprise zone? Give two examples.

3 Describe how commercial banks help a) exporters, and b) small businesses.

4 Why have local authority attitudes to business changed in recent years? Describe some of the changes that have been made and give examples.

5 Explain how government promotional services help business.

6 What kinds of information, which are useful to business, can be obtained from government departments?

7 What kind of help does the government provide for people who want to set up their own small business?

TEACH ALL KIDS TO BE TYCOONS

PUPILS should learn at school how to set up and run businesses, said industry secretary Lord Young at the launch of the second schools' mini-enterprise scheme.

The second phase of the scheme, which has involved nearly 90 per cent of secondary schools, aims to set up a mini-enterprise in every middle or secondary school.

The idea is for pupils to think up business ideas and then to carry them out.

Phase two of the scheme, backed by £500,000 from the government and £300,000 from the National Westminster Bank, also aims to set up teacher training courses on enterprise education.

Source: *Today*, 24 September 1987

Fashioning a British success

BRITAIN'S fashion industry is attacking home and export markets and taking the trade near to its all-time high 1979 production figures.

The industry is a major British employer, with over 200,000 actively involved – over 75 per cent of whom are women. The flair and inventiveness of the country's young designers is making the 'made in Britain' label a sign of retail success on the world's fashion stage.

The past week has seen buyers, designers and manufacturers from all over the world flocking to London for the London Designer Week.

Highpoint of the week is the British Designer Show at Olympia where, with the support of the British Overseas Trade Board, exhibitors reported soaring sales.

The government has been supporting the events, confirming the importance attached to the industry. At the close of the latest event, a reception was held at London's Whitehall government banqueting centre, where Secretary of State for Trade and Industry Lord Young presented the British Fashion Council's award to the British Designer of the Year, John Galliano.

The Department of Trade and Industry (DTI), recognising the importance and potential of fashion and design, has supported a number of plans in the clothing sector.

The Young Designers into Industry scheme meant that in 1985–86 12 designers benefited from planned work ex-

A John Galliano design

perience. In 1986–87, 26 students were placed, and in 1987–88 there are to be 68 places.

In 1985 the DTI introduced a £4½ million scheme providing 50 per cent grants to help colleges and universities buy equipment. Over 30 colleges have benefited from this.

Adapted from: *British Business*, 16 October 1987

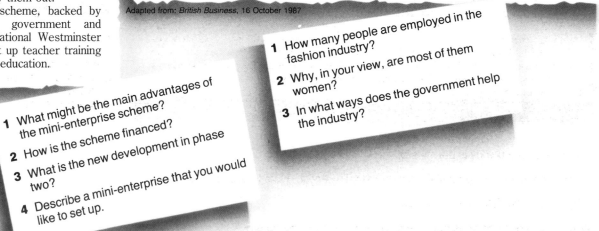

1 What might be the main advantages of the mini-enterprise scheme?

2 How is the scheme financed?

3 What is the new development in phase two?

4 Describe a mini-enterprise that you would like to set up.

1 How many people are employed in the fashion industry?

2 Why, in your view, are most of them women?

3 In what ways does the government help the industry?

Cut-price house lure

ROCKETING house prices in the Home Counties have forced a council to offer up to £5,000 to help with mortgages to attract the best staff.

Applicants from the North are turning down jobs with Berkshire County Council when they realise the cost of homes in the area.

The council is saving so much money in salaries from unfilled jobs that it is now able to offer cut-price mortgages.

An investigation showed that a £14,000 vacancy was turned down by four applicants because of the high cost of housing.

Jobs move can cost a wage packet

WORKERS wanting to move South from the North need pay rises of up to 30 per cent to keep the same standard of living.

A company director on £62,099 in the North needs an extra £17,913 to enjoy the same life-style in London, says the Regional Rewards Survey. Similarly a junior manager on £18,547 needs an extra £5,454 and middle managers on £23,816 need an extra £8,108.

And, the report says, this gap is widening.

Source: *Today*, 24 September 1987

1 What is the main factor that stops workers in the North taking jobs in the South?

2 How much more would a northern worker need to be paid to have the same standard of living in the South?

3 Suggest how different regional policies might help to iron out the differences between the North and the South.

Uniform business rate will 'throw up big losers'

THE FAILURE of the government to fulfil the promise of reduced rates for industry in its proposed reforms was strongly criticised by the Confederation of British Industry (CBI) conference.

A vote calling for the proposed uniform business rate to be abandoned was passed by a large majority.

The CBI dropped its support for a uniform business rate when Ministers refused to give, in addition, a 25 per cent reduction in the present total of £8 billion paid by industry.

Speakers from the regions spoke of fears that the proposed changes would do nothing to put right the fact that they were paying higher rates than similar businesses in the South East.

Adapted from: *Daily Telegraph*, 3 November 1987

1 How much does business pay in rates each year?

2 What is the major change that the government is going to make to business rates?

3 Why doesn't the CBI like this change?

4 Why are business persons from the regions opposed to the scheme?

■ Coursework

1 Find out from your local council and from your local job centre what kind of help is available for small businesses. Explain how it would be useful for:
   a) three people who wanted to set up a restaurant which would be run as a co-operative
   b) a carpenter who wanted to set up his own business making kitchen and dining room furniture
   c) someone who wanted to start an import/export agency.
   Discuss whether the local or the national authorities offer the most valuable aid. Describe what other kinds of help could be provided by either source which would be of benefit to these three small businesses.

2 Visit an occupied workshop/studio site for small businesses. Find out who runs it and what the rents and other costs are. Draw a plan showing the location of businesses on the site indicating the kinds of production they are engaged in. Explain how the firms reflect consumer demands in the area. Describe what kinds of small businesses you would expect to find on a similar site in a totally different kind of area.

3 Find out what kinds of financial aid for businesses are available in your region. Collect other information about the region's advantages for business in such matters as communications, higher education, infrastructure, nearness to markets etc. Design and write an advertisement which would persuade Japanese manufacturers to set up in the region.

4 You have been given the task of designing the British pavilion for a fashion week in Paris. Collect some photographs of the work of leading British designers. Use these to construct a plan for the layout of the backcloth to the pavilion and include suitable slogans which will attract the attention of foreign buyers.

■ Essay question

A small toy-making firm is considering exporting to the Continent. Explain what aid it might receive from:
a) a high street bank
b) a chamber of commerce
c) the government.

Government Constraints

A satellite with wide angle television camera

Daily Blast, 30 October 1987

Pound rises in chaotic trading

James Dunn City Editor

Following the stock markets crash, the dollar went into a nose dive on the international money markets yesterday. It was down against all the major currencies including the pound.

Last night, the pound stood at $1.75, up 1.45 cents on the day. This is the highest value of the pound against the dollar for five years.

Daily Blast, 5 November 1987

Base rate down again by ½%

James Dunn City Editor

To halt the rise of the pound against the sliding dollar, the Bank of England slashed ½ per cent off interest rates yesterday – to 8 per cent. NatWest and Barclays immediately dropped their interest rates by ½ per cent and the Midland and Lloyds are expected to follow today.

On 20 August, Space Systems plc put in an offer for an American defence contract in competition with other American and European companies. Their bid of $35 million was made when the pound was worth 1.4 dollars. If it got the contract, the firm would have to borrow £20 million for a year for the costs of the work. Interest charges in August were 12%.

Before the firm had received a reply to their bid from the Pentagon, there were changes in the exchange rate and British interest rates.

STUDY POINTS

1 How much would the contract have been worth to Space Systems plc in pounds on 20 August?

2 How much was it worth in pounds on 30 October?

3 What would the firm have had to pay in interest charges for a year when it made its bid?

4 What would the interest charges have been for a year after 5 November?

5 If you were in charge of the contract, would you withdraw the offer or keep it in? What estimates of future changes in exchange and interest rates would influence your decision?

Controlling taxation

The government's financial policies have a great impact on all businesses, large or small. One of the main ways the government controls the economy is by its **FISCAL POLICY** on taxation and public spending. An increase in any tax will slow down business activity in different ways. For instance:

- An increase in income tax will reduce the amount that consumers have to spend as they will have to pay more tax to the government.
- An increase in VAT will also reduce consumer demand as goods and services will become more expensive.
- An increase in corporation tax, which is paid by businesses, will force them to reduce investment, pay lower dividends, cut costs or increase prices.
- An increase in National Insurance contributions will reduce consumer spending as employees will have less money to spend. It will increase firms' costs as they will have to pay out more money to the government to cover their share of the National Insurance contributions. It will also discourage them from taking on more employees.

Public spending

The amount the government itself spends also affects the business world. Usually more money is spent than is received in taxes, and the difference is made up by borrowing money – the public sector borrowing requirement or PSBR. If the government decides to cut its PSBR, it will spend less money and the private sector will receive fewer government orders. For example, if the government decided to cut defence spending, firms who supply the armed forces with goods and services would receive fewer orders. A reduction in the PSBR, however, may allow the government to reduce taxes, because it needs less money itself. This would boost the economy, as firms and consumers would have more money to spend, so the total effect might be better for business.

Controlling the money supply

The government can also try to control the economy through its MONETARY POLICY. It can try to control the money supply – the total amount of coins and notes in circulation and money deposited with banks and building societies – and the amount of money borrowed. There are direct ways of doing this. The Bank of England, acting for the government, can order the high street banks to deposit a certain proportion of their money with it, or it can tell the banks not to lend more than a certain amount. The government can also increase the amount of deposits for goods bought on hire purchase or by other forms of credit.

Alternatively, an indirect approach may be used. The Bank of England can put up interest rates – the amount charged for borrowing money. The high street banks will then usually do the same. If interest rates rise, firms will think twice about new investments because it will cost them more to borrow the money. Consumers might delay buying goods on credit because the interest payments will be higher. The general effects of these measures will be to slow down business activity and to reduce the money supply.

Some economists believe that if the money supply is reduced, INFLATION will fall. Other economists believe that inflation is caused by increases in

production costs, such as high wages or profits, or by increased demand for goods or services at existing prices.

It is far more difficult for the government to make its monetary policy work than to make its fiscal policy work, as interest rates and money supply are affected by market forces, over which the government has little real control.

Exchange rates

Another important effect of interest rates (in the short term, at least) is on EXCHANGE RATES. The exchange rate is the price that you have to pay to buy another currency. At any one time, the pound will buy so many American dollars, so many German marks, so many French francs. The value of the pound – and of all other currencies – is decided by the forces of supply and demand in the international money markets. If foreigners want to buy pounds, the price of the pound will rise. One factor which will make them want to do so is if the interest rate in Britain is higher than in other countries. This means that they will get a better return on their money by investing it in Britain. As the demand for the pound increases, so the value of the pound will rise.

Other factors also influence the demand for currencies. Investors are also interested in the strength of the economy – whether the country's balance of payments is in the red or the black [see Unit 4]. If the big institutional investors – like banks, insurance companies, pension funds – believe that the long-term prospects for a country's economy are poor, then investors will be less likely to invest their money there, even if the interest

rates are high. These investors control the billions of dollars, pounds and other currencies whirling in the international money markets each day. Their decisions have a much greater effect on exchange rates in the long term than the efforts of individual governments to control exchange rates.

Governments can only try to control the economy. Their policies can be blown off course by events over which they have no control – like the rise in oil prices in 1974 or the great crash in stock market values in 1987. Business has to pick up the pieces and deal with them as best as it can.

B U S I N E S S T E C H N I Q U E S

Public relations

Business has to make its voice heard. One way of doing this is by writing letters to newspapers.

Interest rates have been at a high level for a long time, which has affected the export side of your business. Write a letter to a national newspaper of your choice describing the effects and suggesting what actions the government should take.

C H E C K P O I N T S

1 **What is fiscal policy?**
2 **Describe two ways in which the government can try to control the money supply and the amount of money borrowed.**
3 **Explain why the government can exercise less control over its monetary than its fiscal policy.**
4 **Describe how changes in a country's interest rates can affect exchange rates.**
5 **Explain all the effects that a general increase in taxes might have on a small manufacturing company.**

K E Y T E R M S

FISCAL POLICY Government decisions about taxes and public spending.

MONETARY POLICY Government decisions over money supply and rates of interest.

INFLATION A rise in the general level of prices over a period of time, which reduces the buying power of money and creates economic uncertainty.

EXCHANGE RATES The price at which one currency is bought and sold for another currency, e.g. the pound will buy 1.46 dollars.

Legal Controls and Voluntary Codes

Free book
(Send only £3 for post and packing)

GUARANTEED TO CURE BALDNESS OVERNIGHT

Your mum will never forgive you – if you forget MOTHER'S DAY

YOU COULD MAKE **££££**s
SIMPLE HOMEWORK
SEND FOR FREE BROCHURE

Jobs galore!
Registration fee: £3

Do you want to leave your wife penniless? See us for the best insurance

SALES REP REQUIRED. No women or timewasters. – Box 3487

If you want to be **SLIM** *drink our herbal tea*

OUR LIGHT BULBS WILL NEVER WEAR OUT

Business and the law

There are hundreds of laws controlling business. Every year, parliament makes many more. Their main purposes are:

● to make sure that there is free competition between businesses so that they do not gain unfair advantages over their rivals [see Unit 75]

● to improve working conditions and terms of employment [see Unit 76]

● to protect consumers [see Unit 77].

Look at Figure 74.1, which shows some of the major laws affecting business which have been passed in the last twenty-five years. Which of the three categories described above does each law fit into? Some of the laws – like the Sex Discrimination Act and the Race Relations Act – have a much wider scope. Their aim is to create a society which provides equal opportunities for all, regardless of sex or race. To what extent has this been achieved?

Business persons who break these laws can be fined or imprisoned or be ordered to pay compensation by an industrial tribunal, i.e. a body set up to ensure fairness in industrial situations. In addition, they can also be sued for damages in the civil courts. For instance, if a drugs company's products had dangerous side effects, it might have to pay out millions of pounds in damages to those who had been injured.

The European Community (EC)

In addition, British business has to obey the laws and regulations of the European Community (EC), of which Britain is a member. The EC, which supports free competition, has very strict laws against price-fixing, restrictions on production and other unfair agreements between firms. It

FIG 74.1

Laws affecting businesses

Resale Prices Act 1964 makes it illegal, with a few exceptions, for manufacturers to fix a minimum price at which their goods can be sold in shops.

Trade Descriptions Acts 1968 and 1972 stop traders giving a false or misleading description of goods or services [see Unit 77].

Fair Trading Act 1973 set up an Office of Fair Trading with a Director General of Fair Trading to keep an eye on unfair business practices [see Unit 75].

Consumer Credit Act 1974 introduced licences for businesses which give credit or hire facilities to consumers. The Act made it compulsory to give full details of the charges for credit and regulated advertisements, contracts and doorstep selling [see Unit 77].

Health and Safety at Work Act 1974 requires employers to maintain high standards of health and safety in all working places – except for domestic servants in private households [see Unit 76].

Sex Discrimination Act 1975 makes sex discrimination illegal in employment, training, education and the provision of goods, facilities and services. It established an Equal Opportunities Commission to enforce the law [see Unit 76].

Restrictive Trade Practices Act 1976 prevents businesses fixing prices, restricting output or dividing up the market between them, unless permission has been obtained from the Restrictive Practices Court. It will only give approval if the practices appear to be in the public interest.

Race Relations Act 1976 makes racial discrimination illegal in employment, housing, education, clubs and in all consumer affairs. It established a Commission for Racial Equality [see Unit 76].

Competition Act 1980 is designed to stop anti-competitive practices [see Unit 75].

Supply of Goods and Services Act 1982 specifies that goods and services must serve their intended purpose [see Unit 77].

Equal Pay Act 1984 provides for equal treatment of men and women in pay and terms of employment for the same work or work of equal value [see Unit 76].

Data Protection Act 1984 gives people the right – with some exceptions – to see information about them which is stored on computers [see Unit 77].

also provides for the free flow of capital and labour between member countries. It is planned to abolish all trade barriers between member countries in 1992, so that there is a single European market.

The EC already exercises great control over many aspects of business life. For example, the total output of steel and coal in the EC (including Britain) is decided in Brussels by the EC as a whole. The price that farmers get for their products, and even the number of cows they can keep, is also decided in Brussels – not in Britain. The EC increasingly governs more and more aspects of our daily and business life, right down to the smallest detail. For instance, additives in packaged foods, which begin with the letter E, show that they have been approved by the EC, just as E3 on detergents shows a standard EC size of package.

Voluntary codes

Many businesses are subject not only to the law, but also to **VOLUNTARY**

CODES which have been established for their industry. These codes set a standard of business practice which all members of the industry are expected to follow. Some of the industries which have their own codes are the Stock Exchange, the Press and advertising.

One of the most successful has been the British Code of Advertising Practice for all print and cinema advertising. The main reason for its success, is that it is run by an independent body – the Advertising Standards Authority – which was set up in 1962. The Authority – unlike the Press Council – has considerable influence and power. If it bans an advertisement, practically no newspaper or magazine will publish it.

KEY TERM

VOLUNTARY CODES Standards of business behaviour which are established freely by industries for all their members to follow.

Under the code, all advertisements must be 'legal, decent, honest and truthful'. The code is continuously reviewed to keep it in step with changing public attitudes. It is also extremely detailed.

None of the advertisements in the Study Points would have found much favour with the Advertising Standards Authority. Goods cannot be described as 'free' if the costs of acquiring them are greater than they would normally be, for example, 'free gifts' which have to be sent for by post. No advertiser is allowed to claim to cure any ailment or disease, and only slimming aids which can be proved may be advertised. No advertisement for children should suggest they will be failing in their duty if they do not buy, and no advertisement of any kind should prey upon fear without a good reason. Employment opportunities should not be accompanied by a request for money, and homeworkers should be told what they might earn. Advertisements which discriminate against race or sex would be banned by the Authority.

BUSINESS TECHNIQUES

Voluntary codes

Write a voluntary code for football clubs suggesting ways of behaviour for fans which will help prevent hooliganism.

CHECKPOINTS

1 State the three main purposes of laws governing business.
2 What is a voluntary code? Describe how it works in the advertising industry.
3 Describe the effect that EC law has on British business.
4 Study the laws in Figure 74.1. What effects have they had on a) traders, b) manufacturers and c) black women?

Monopolies and Mergers

The Competition Act 1980 is designed to encourage and protect free competition in business.

Any policy or practice which is 'likely to have the effect of restricting, distorting or preventing competition' in the production, supply or acquisition of goods or services can be investigated. The inquiry is carried out by the Director General of Fair Trading. Study these brief summaries of three investigations.

Arthur Sanderson & Sons Ltd

The investigation was concerned with the manufacture and retailing of furnishing fabrics. The firm was using a selective distribution policy and had refused to supply a number of retailers who had to use other brands of furnishing fabric instead. The Director General concluded that the firm was not behaving in an anti-competitive way.

(27.8.81)

Scottish and Universal Newspapers Ltd (SUNL)

The investigation concerned newspapers in the Lanarkshire region. To compete with a new free-sheet SUNL launched one of its own. Free advertising space was provided for the first period, and then at a rate much below cost. The initial offer of free space was on the condition that the advertiser should not use any other free newspaper in the region. The Director General found that the behaviour of SUNL was anti-competitive. The firm agreed to alter its advertising terms and conditions.

(11.1.83)

British Railways Board (BRB): Brighton Central Railway Station

The investigation concerned taxi services to and from the station. BRB had made an arrangement with an association of taxi owners to provide a service from the station, other taxi owners being prevented from trying to pick up customers there. The Director General concluded that the arrangement was anti-competitive. BRB agreed to make suitable changes in its arrangements.

(24.11.82)

STUDY POINTS

1 In which of the above cases did the Director General decide that the effects were anti-competitive?

2 Explain in your own words what each of the businesses was doing that was found to be anti-competitive.

3 Why do you think the Director General's decision was different in the remaining case?

4 If you had carried out the investigations, would you have come to any different decisions? Explain your reasons.

Source: Office of Fair Trading, *Anti-Competitive Practices*, 1986

Free competition

Business in the western world is based upon the idea of free competition. Firms do not have the right to compete unfairly with their rivals. They have to operate within a framework of law. These laws are designed to stop them:

- taking unfair advantage of other firms
- creating a **MONOPOLY SITUATION**
- making **MERGERS** which are against the public interest.

If a firm's actions are shown to be unlawful, the Secretary of State for Trade and Industry can either order them to stop the unfair practice or ban a proposed merger. As the Secretary of State has the final power, the way in which the laws are applied will vary from time to time, according to which political party is in power. One party might be strongly against mergers of almost any kind. The other party might take a more tolerant, or relaxed view of them. The government (and the EC) is mainly responsible for how much free competition there is in the business world.

When the Director General of Fair Trading carries out an investigation under the Competition Act, his first task is to assess the market power of the firm concerned. If a firm has a very small market share, then it is unlikely that anything it does can have much effect on competition. If, for example, a builders' merchant refused to supply a particular builder, it wouldn't be anti-competitive as the builder could easily obtain his supplies elsewhere. However, the action of a firm which had a lot of power in a local market might be anti-competitive, because it could have a great impact on its rivals.

Anti-competitive practices

Some business practices which might be considered anti-competitive are:

- getting rid of competition
- preventing the emergence of new firms
- exclusive purchasing contracts, i.e. where a customer agrees to buy from a single supplier
- selective distributive systems, where a supplier will deal only with distributors who keep a certain level of stock or provide specified before and after sales services
- tie-ins, where a supplier of a product insists that customers must buy all, or part, of another product from him as well
- restrictions on supply of parts to competitors.

Not all of these practices are necessarily anti-competitive. It is the *effects*, not the practice itself, which are important.

If the Director General finds that the practice is anti-competitive, he can accept an undertaking, or promise, from the firm that they will stop or change the practice. If such an undertaking is not given, he may refer the matter to the **MONOPOLIES AND MERGERS COMMISSION**. The Commission will decide whether the practice is anti-competitive and, if this is so, whether it is against the public interest. If it is, the Secretary of State can ask the Director General to seek an undertaking from the firm, or he can ban the practice himself.

In addition to this task, the Commission has two other important functions. The Director General or the Secretary of State can ask the Commission to see if a monopoly situation exists in the supply of goods or services. If the Commission decides that the monopoly does exist, and that it is against the public interest, the government may decide to break it up.

The Secretary of State can also ask the Commission to investigate any proposed merger between two firms to see if it is against the public interest. On average ten proposed mergers are investigated every year, all concerned with big mergers, where the assets being acquired are worth more than £15 million. The Commission has no power to stop a merger, only the Secretary of State can decide that a merger should not go ahead.

Mergers

Collect some newspaper cuttings about a proposed merger where the value of the assets to be acquired is more than £15 million. Write a report to the Secretary of State for Trade and Industry recommending whether the Monopolies and Mergers Commission should investigate it or not.

C H E C K P O I N T S

1 Who is mainly responsible for ensuring that there is free competition?
2 Give three examples of business practices which might be considered anti-competitive.
3 What would be the main test of whether the practices are anti-competitive?
4 Describe the functions of the Monopolies and Mergers Commission.
5 Why did the Commission have to be set up?

K E Y   T E R M S

MONOPOLY SITUATION A situation in which a firm or person controls 25 per cent or more of the total supply of a particular product or service.

MERGER The acquisition of one company by another or the joining together of two firms.

MONOPOLIES AND MERGERS COMMISSION An independent body set up under the Fair Trading Act of 1973 to investigate monopoly situations and mergers to see if they are against the public interest. It has no powers of its own; only the Secretary of State for Trade and Industry can order the monopoly to be broken up or the merger to be stopped.

Employees' Rights

Employers cannot treat their workers in any way they like. There are dozens of laws protecting employees' rights. If employers break some of these laws, they may be taken before an industrial tribunal and ordered to pay compensation. This can be very expensive. In one recent case, an employee was awarded £40,000. The wise employer will, of course, take out insurance to cover the risks [see Unit 19]. A premium of about £50 will provide insurance cover for a gross pay roll of £100,000. If employers break some of the other laws, such as the Health and Safety at Work Act, they may be prosecuted, and fined if they are found guilty. So it is essential for employers, big or small, to know about employees' rights if they want to avoid financial loss or prosecution.

Things an employer must do

Some of the things an employer *must* do are:

● Provide employees with a written **CONTRACT OF EMPLOYMENT** within 13 weeks of starting work, unless they work for less than 16 hours a week. The contract must include:
  – the employer's name
  – the employee's name
  – the date employment began
  – the job title

– the amount of pay and the intervals between payments
– hours of work
– holiday entitlement and pay
– sick pay arrangements
– pensions arrangements
– notice periods
– disciplinary, grievance and appeal arrangements [see Unit 66].
● Provide an itemised pay statement, showing statutory deductions for income tax, National Insurance contributions and pensions (where these apply) and voluntary deductions [see Unit 57].
● Give members of the opposite sex equal pay if they are doing similar work or work of equal value [see Unit 74].
● Pay the minimum wage to employees over 21 in industries covered by a **WAGES COUNCIL**.
● Continue to pay an employee who is laid off through shortage of work – for up to five days in any three-month period.
● Observe the Health and Safety at Work Act, 1974, by maintaining safe plant, premises and working systems, and ensuring that the health of employees is not affected by their work.
● Give written reasons for dismissal to employees who have at least six months' service.
● Provide proper notice of termination of employment. Employees are entitled to receive at least one week's notice (or pay *in lieu*, i.e. instead of) after one month's service and an extra week's pay for each year of service up to a maximum of 12.
● Give redundancy pay to employees with at least two years' service. This ranges, according to age, from half a week's pay to one and a half weeks' pay for each year of service.

Things an employer must not do

An employer *must not*:
● Discriminate against employees on the grounds of sex or race [see Unit 74]. The Sex Discrimination Act, however, does not apply to firms which employ fewer than six people. Complaints by individuals can be made to an industrial tribunal.
● Make deductions from pay, except for statutory or voluntary deductions, unless they are specified in the contract of employment.
● Stop an employee joining a trade union.
● Stop an employee taking time off work for public duties. For example, as a magistrate or a member of a jury.
● Dismiss an employee unfairly.

Dismissals

The main reasons for which an employer can dismiss an employee are:
● misconduct
● inability to do the job
● redundancy, if the employee's labour is no longer needed.
Even then, the employer can't just tell a worker to go. The employer must also be able to show that he or she acted reasonably in the particular circumstances.

If the dismissal was for misconduct, the employee must know that she or he was committing an offence, and a warning has to be given so that the employee has a chance to put his or her case, or to put right his or her behaviour.

If it was for inability to do the job, it must be shown that adequate training and supervision were provided and that a more suitable job was offered instead.

If it was for redundancy, the employer needs to show that he or she gave as much notice as possible and that the method of selection was fair.

Every dismissal must be judged on its individual situation. If the employee feels that it is unfair, he or she can complain to an industrial tribunal, provided that he or she has been working for the same firm for two years. The officers of the Advisory Conciliation and Arbitration Service (ACAS) may be able to help the employer and employee to reach an agreement before the tribunal hearing [see Unit 66].

However it is always unfair to dismiss employees for belonging to a trade union or taking part in its activities, regardless of how long they have worked for the firm.

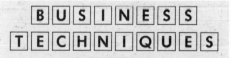

BUSINESS TECHNIQUES

Contracts of employment

Write a contract of employment for the waitress in the study points, using the information in the text. Make up the individual details yourself, and include points which cover the problems which arise in the Study Points cartoons.

CHECKPOINTS

1 What is a contract of employment?
2 What is a wages council?
3 Explain what is meant by unfair dismissal and give examples.
4 What can employees do if they believe they have been unfairly dismissed?
5 Give two examples each of race and sex discrimination. What actions can employees take?

KEY TERMS

CONTRACT OF EMPLOYMENT A legal agreement concerning the rights and duties of an employer and an employee. It comes into force as soon as an offer of employment is accepted. By law, employers have to provide full-time employees with a written contract within 13 weeks.

WAGES COUNCIL A body which sets legal minimum rates of pay for workers over 21 years of age in some low-paid industries. There are 26 wages councils covering about 3 million employees.

Activities

■ Review points

1 What are the main points covered by the Health and Safety at Work Act 1974?

2 What are the main points which must be included in a contract of employment?

3 Explain the work of the Advertising Standards Authority.

4 Describe the main features of recent laws concerning race and sex equality and show how they operate.

5 Describe the work of industrial tribunals. What is their importance in protecting employees' rights?

6 What are the main grounds on which employees can be fairly dismissed? Give an example of each.

7 Describe the work of the Monopolies and Mergers Commission.

8 Explain how the government tries to control the economy by its fiscal policy.

9 How far can the government exercise control through its monetary policy?

■ Essay question

At any one time, a firm which employs 200 people has an average of two people on maternity leave, 17 people off sick and one person being subject to disciplinary procedures. Explain what effects this might have on:
a) the firm's finances
b) the other employees?

Inquiry halts WH Smith book club disposal

W.H. SMITH'S £69 million sale of its book club stopped yesterday when the Government announced it was launching a Monopolies and Mergers Commission investigation into the deal.

The immediate effect will be to freeze the first £35 million payment which was due to be made to W.H. Smith on Tuesday.

The surprise decision throws the £100 million turnover book club industry into uncertainty. The investigation will focus on a series of transactions which, if allowed to go ahead, would give two European companies, Bertelsmann and Les Presses de la Cite, joint control of the two largest book club companies in Britain and a dominant 75 per cent market share.

The two British companies are Book Club Associates, easily Britain's largest with about 1.7 million members and Leisure Circle, with 350,000 members. The rest of the industry together probably has fewer than 500,000 members.

At the request of the Office of Fair Trading, W.H. Smith agreed yesterday not to proceed with the sale. Malcolm Field, group managing director, said: 'We are obviously disappointed'. But he added that he thought it extremely unlikely that the commission would prevent the sale.

Adapted from: *Daily Express*, 9 September 1987

1 What is the turnover of the book club industry in Britain?

2 Which is the largest book club?

3 Explain the reasons why the proposed sale was being investigated.

WOMEN FIGHT FOR TOP JOBS

SIR Bryan Nicholson, in his last major speech as Manpower Services Commission chairman, said that much should be done to improve the situation for women. But he warned a fair deal would not just fall into their laps.

Speaking about Britain's industrial fortunes, he said: 'We are starting to fight back, but it will be a one-sided fight if we continue to treat women as second class workers.'

He told delegates at the Women's National Commission Conference in London: 'There is much, much more that can be done to improve the opportunities open to women.'

Sir Bryan, who is to become the new Post Office chairman, said women's earnings were 25% less than men's and only 3% of companies had women leading them.

'Unless employers start to use the full potential of women across all types of job they may find skill shortages can hurt much more than they do at present.'

1 What percentage of companies have a woman in charge?

2 How much less do women earn than men?

3 In Sir Bryan Nicholson's view, what will happen if we continue to treat women as 'second class workers'?

4 Which laws should prevent this state of affairs continuing?

5 What can women do about not having top jobs a) individually and b) together as a group?

WHAT A SNIP-OFF!

Posh salons pay hairdressers a poverty wage

The unkindest cut of all for Britain's 100,000 hairdressers is when they get their pay packet at the end of the week. Nineteen out of every twenty earn poverty wages, according to a report out today.

At some top salons customers pay more for one hair-do than the hairdresser earns for a whole week's work. Salons, even in posh Knightsbridge and Bond Street, start trainees on only £33 a week. A qualified hairdresser was offered £70 a week by an Oxford Circus shop while a stylist took home £58 a week for 46 hours work.

Average earnings in the industry last year were £78.60 – and that included commission. The new legal minimum wage is £78 a week for

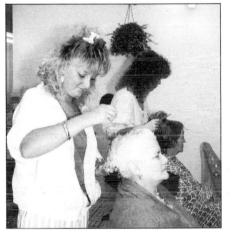

adults working full time. But a Low Pay Unit survey found that more than one in three hairdressing firms checked were caught underpaying.

1 How many hairdressers are there in Britain?

2 What is the average adult wage in the industry?

3 What is the legal minimum wage?

4 How many salons which were checked were underpaying their employees?

5 Why, in your view, do hairdressers get low pay?

6 a) What other jobs are also low paid?
b) What effect does this have on the economy?

■ Coursework

1 Collect newspaper cuttings on a proposed merger which has been referred to the Monopolies and Mergers Commission. Write a report explaining why it was referred to the Commission, the reasons for the Commission's decision and what action was taken as a result by the Secretary of State. Analyse the effects on the market if he had taken a different decision.

2 Contact a local trade union branch and find out what actions they are currently involved in concerning employees' rights. Explain why these issues are of concern in the area at the present time. Assess the chances of the union achieving a successful outcome.

3 Part-time workers and workers in small firms do not have the same degree of employment protection as full-time workers in larger firms. What are the main differences? Interview some part-time workers and find out whether this lack of rights has affected them and in what way. Write a charter for part-time workers based on the information you have acquired. To what extent could this be applied nationally?

4 Find out about the work of the Press Council and examine whether it has been successful in controlling newspapers effectively and efficiently. Describe what changes might be made to its organisation and powers to increase its control. Explain how your proposed changes would affect newspaper owners, and business in general.

5 Keep a record of changes in British interest rates over a period of time. Use graphs to show the effects of these changes on borrowing, the exchange rate and consumer spending. Evaluate how successful the Chancellor and the Bank of England have been in achieving their financial objectives. Was there any other course of action which might have been more effective?

Consumer Protection

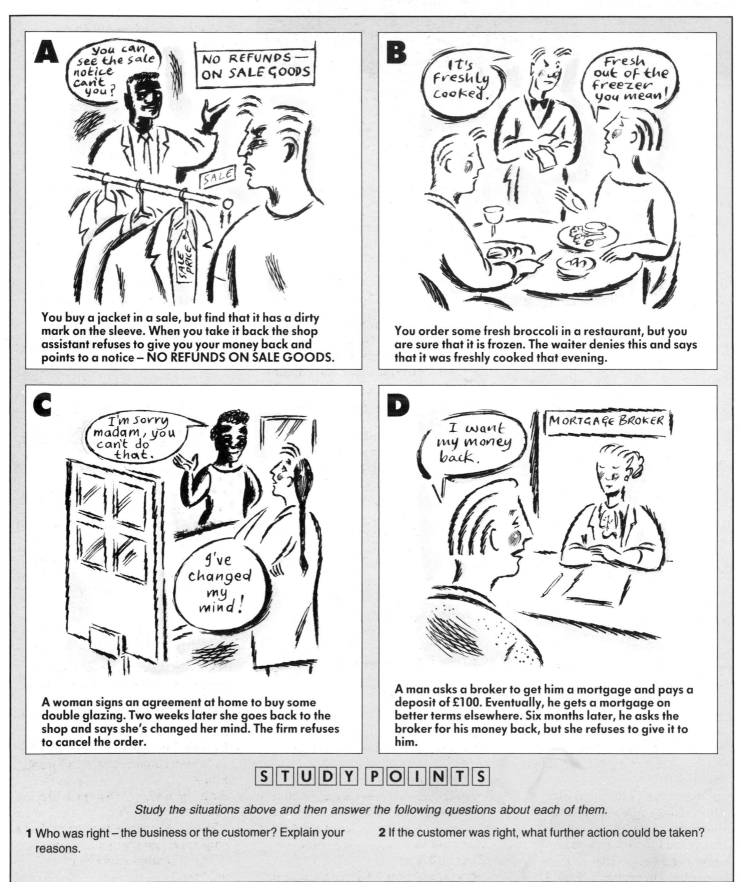

A

You buy a jacket in a sale, but find that it has a dirty mark on the sleeve. When you take it back the shop assistant refuses to give you your money back and points to a notice – **NO REFUNDS ON SALE GOODS.**

B

You order some fresh broccoli in a restaurant, but you are sure that it is frozen. The waiter denies this and says that it was freshly cooked that evening.

C

A woman signs an agreement at home to buy some double glazing. Two weeks later she goes back to the shop and says she's changed her mind. The firm refuses to cancel the order.

D

A man asks a broker to get him a mortgage and pays a deposit of £100. Eventually, he gets a mortgage on better terms elsewhere. Six months later, he asks the broker for his money back, but she refuses to give it to him.

STUDY POINTS

Study the situations above and then answer the following questions about each of them.

1 Who was right – the business or the customer? Explain your reasons.

2 If the customer was right, what further action could be taken?

Consumer rights

Consumers now have almost as many rights as employees. The business person must know something about the law to stay out of trouble. Firms can be prosecuted if they break the law. A court appearance can affect business, so it is best to take precautions. If you make a mistake, try to settle before the case comes to court.

Protection by law

One of the main laws protecting consumers is the Supply of Goods and Services Act 1982. Under this Act, goods must be:

● 'of merchantable quality' – that is, fit to be sold, e.g. matches must light not explode

● 'as described' – if a label states that a jacket is real leather, it must not be imitation

● 'fit for their purpose' – that is, capable of being used in a normal way, e.g. shoes must not leak in the rain.

If any of these conditions are not met, the customer can get his or her money back, even on sale goods. In situation A in the Study Points, the goods were not of merchantable quality, so the customer was right.

The Trade Descriptions Acts of 1968 and 1972 stop business persons giving false or misleading descriptions of goods or services. In situation B, 'feshly cooked' is not the same as 'fresh' vegetables, so the customer was right.

The Consumer Credit Act 1974 gave greater protection to consumers when they borrowed money or bought on credit. This Act:

● introduced licences for firms who give credit

● forced firms offering credit to state the annual percentage rate of charge or APR (see Unit 42)

● prevented firms inviting people under 18 to borrow money or buy on credit

● gave a cooling-off period (time to think) for people signing hire-purchase agreements at home

● restricted brokers' charges for mortgages not taken up.

The cooling-off period in which

Some covers of *Which?* magazine, produced by the Consumers' Association

customers can change their minds lasts only for a few days – not two weeks. In situation C, the firm is right. If the agreement is signed on the firm's premises, there is no cooling-off period.

If a mortgage offer is not taken up within six months, the broker can charge only £1 for his or her services. Therefore, in situation D, the broker was wrong.

The Weights and Measures Act 1963 made it an offence to give short weight or measure of any goods on sale. Some goods, like beers and spirits, must be sold in standard measures, and by law a half pint must mean just that. There is no fixed measure yet for wine.

The Data Protection Act 1984 gave everybody the right to see what information is held about them on computers. This already applied to information supplied by credit agencies, and is now extended to many other kinds of computer information. There are exemptions, e.g. if national security is involved.

Watchdogs

In addition to these laws, there are many official and unofficial watchdogs protecting consumers' rights.

The Consumers' Association investigates many goods and services in its magazine, *Which?*, and there are newspapers, and television and radio programmes which do the same, e.g. 'That's Life'.

Local Consumer Advice Centres or

Citizens' Advice Bureaux provide general help and advice for consumers on all topics. The local Trading Standards Officer deals with weights and measures, false descriptions and other matters. Government-funded councils, like the Post Office Users National Council, deal with complaints about public services. Government-appointed ombudsmen (or commissionaries) investigate and report on complaints against public bodies, such as the National Health Service, local councils etc.

The new small claims courts allow consumers to take legal action against firms for claims for less than £500. They are cheaper and easier than using a solicitor in a county court.

A business, however, still has rights too. Once a customer agrees to buy something a contract is made, and it cannot generally be broken. The business is entitled to get back any money lost due to a customer's change of mind.

BUSINESS TECHNIQUES

Complaints

Work in pairs. One person should take the role of a shopkeeper and the other that of a customer who has come back to complain about an article. Use your knowledge of the law to try to reach a reasonable agreement for both parties.

CHECKPOINTS

1 What are the main provisions of the Supply of Goods and Services Act?

2 What is the main effect of the Trade Descriptions Acts?

3 Explain how the Consumer Credit Acts affect businesses of different kinds.

4 State the main provisions of the Data Protection Act.

5 What are the main ways in which a consumer can try to make sure he or she is treated fairly by a business?

Pressure Groups

Anti-Apartheid Movement ends Barclays boycott

THE ANTI-APARTHEID MOVEMENT has formally ended its 17-year campaign to boycott (or have no dealings with) Barclays Bank, following Barclays' withdrawal from South Africa last November.

A spokesman for Barclays Bank said yesterday: 'We are delighted that our critics have recognised that our pulling out from South Africa is real and not just for show, and we expect to see the boycott totally removed, particularly among students.'

Mike Terry, the secretary of the Movement, said that it had waited to make sure that the withdrawal was real, that there would be no credit lines available to Barclays' corresponding bank in South Africa and that technical and training co-operation with South Africa would be minimal. 'They have satisfied our criteria,' he said.

Barclays announced its decision last November; the bank had lost a number of commercial accounts, mainly among students, as a result of the Movement's activities.

Barclays' share of the student account market fell from 27 per cent to 16 per cent because of the campaign.

The withdrawal of Barclays was the single biggest blow to overseas companies operating in South Africa.

Adapted from: *Independent*, 11 May 1987

An anti-apartheid demonstration

S T U D Y P O I N T S

1 How long did the campaign by the Anti-Apartheid Movement against Barclays Bank last?

2 What was the chief method it used to achieve its objective?

3 Which three factors persuaded the movement to end its campaign?

4 Write a leaflet for distribution to students explaining the Movement's case for a boycott.

5 If you had been in charge of Barclays Bank, suggest what steps you might have taken to counter the Anti-Apartheid Movement's campaign.

It is much easier for a firm to deal with a complaint by an individual than a campaign by a **PRESSURE GROUP**. In the same way as a trade union has much greater strength than isolated workers, a pressure group has greater power than its individual members. Unlike a trade union, however, pressure groups usually concentrate on only one issue – persuading people to give up smoking, stopping the building of an airport, trying to end apartheid in South Africa as seen in the Study Points. All of these campaigns have had a great influence on the businesses involved. Cigarette smoking has declined; a number of places have successfully resisted the building of airports; many firms have stopped trading with South Africa.

Long history

Pressure groups have a long history. Some of the older ones, like the Lord's Day Observance Society, formed in 1831, and temperance societies, which try to stop people drinking, still have a significant influence on government and business today. In 1987, the government introduced a Bill to allow pubs to open from 11am to 11pm on weekdays, but not on Sundays. It feared that Sunday afternoon opening might cause the Bill to be defeated – just as its earlier proposal to reform the Sunday Trading Laws had been. Even so, the Bill ran into great opposition.

The number of pressure groups has increased greatly in recent times. Some of them are international like the Anti-Apartheid Movement; others are national like ASH (Action on Smoking and Health); and many are purely local. An increasing number are concerned with environmental issues such as pollution, noise, energy conservation, or nuclear power [see Unit 79].

Campaign methods

Pressure groups use a variety of methods to achieve their objectives. They may use constitutional means

Information leaflets from various pressure groups

such as lobbying (or meeting) MPs and Ministers in Parliament to try to persuade them to introduce laws which will bring about the desired change. If a local issue is involved, such as the building of a superstore in the Green Belt, the group will also contact their local councillors to see if they can obtain their help. In addition, they may try to contact the chairperson or the managing director of the firm involved, in person or by writing to them.

Pressure groups also use many kinds of publicity to achieve their objectives [see Unit 35]. These include:

● writing letters to newspapers and magazines
● holding public meetings
● publishing advertisements
● distributing leaflets
● organising marches and demonstrations.

Direct action

Some pressure groups also use **DIRECT ACTION**. One of the oldest methods is the **BOYCOTT** which was used by the

Anti-Apartheid Movement against Barclays Bank. It was first used in 1880 against Captain Charles Boycott, a land agent in Ireland, to stop him evicting tenants from the estates he managed. That is how this kind of action got its name.

Many other forms of direct action – both violent and non-violent   have been used by other pressure groups.

● Protesters have occupied sites to try to stop an airport from being built.

● Workers have staged sit-ins at factories to stop them from being closed.

● Mothers have halted traffic at accident 'black spots' by forming a human chain across the road.

● Animals, used to test drugs or cosmetics, have been released from their cages.

● Scientists involved in nuclear weapons research have been harassed by the repeated phoning of their home late at night.

● Wealthy business men have been

murdered or held to ransom by terrorist groups.

A threatening letter

You run a small fur shop which has been in the family for almost a century. Trade has been declining in the last few years, as fewer women are willing to wear fur coats, so that the shop only provides a bare living. However, you own the freehold of the shop – a valuable asset worth £250,000.

You have been somewhat undecided about your future for some time. Then, one morning you receive a letter which makes you realise that you have to come to a decision. The letter threatens to burn down the shop if you do not stop selling furs.

Would you,

a) Just report the letter to the police and try to forget it?
b) Tighten security at the shop?
c) Ignore the threat entirely and just go on trading?
d) Change the nature of your business?
e) Sell the shop and retire?

Explain your reasons in full.

CHECKPOINTS

1 What is a pressure group?
2 Why can it have a bigger impact on business than an individual complaint?
3 Explain how a boycott is organised and its likely effects on a firm.
4 What are the normal means of persuasion used by pressure groups?
5 Explain the meaning of direct action and give two examples of your own.

KEY TERMS

PRESSURE GROUP A group of persons who band together to try to bring about a change of policy by a firm or a public body.

DIRECT ACTION Campaigns that will have a direct impact on an organisation – such as a sit-in. They are used when normal means of persuasion appear to have failed.

BOYCOTT To join with others to exclude a product from the market or to refuse to have any dealings with an individual, a firm or an organisation.

The Environmental Lobby

Daily Blast

The dearest hole in Britain

DRILLING A HOLE in West-shire's Stag Forest will cost the Ringoil Corporation £50 million – making it the dearest and the deepest oil drilling exploration ever in Britain. And the company could fail to get a penny back if oil is not present in commercial quantities.

Or they could have hit upon a site which will produce millions of barrels a year until the year 2020 – and make the company a profit of £700 million. A company spokesman said yesterday that they were convinced it was right to take the risk, not only for the sake of the company but for the whole of Britain.

City Voice

Ringoil up 25p

Ringoil shares rose 25p to a new high of 315p yesterday following the announcement that the government had given the go-ahead for exploratory drilling in the Stag Forest.

Car stickers, like those above, show how strongly many people feel about taking care of the environment.

Daily Bugle

'Sacrilege' – Westshire MP

IN A SAVAGE ATTACK on the government yesterday, Bill Fross, Labour MP for Westshire, described the planned oil drilling in the Stag Forest as 'sacrilege'. The government should never have given permission, he said.

It was one of the last few remaining areas of natural beauty entirely in private hands. It was scandalous that the private profits of the owner should have been given greater importance than the interests of the whole nation. Would the government state publicly how much the owner had received from the oil company?

Hundreds of thousands of people visited the area each year and walked the footpaths through the Forest. 'What profit would there be for them, or for the residents in the area?' he asked.

Daily Bugle

3 Injured in Stag Forest crash

A young couple and their baby were seriously injured last night in West-shire's Stag Forest when their car was in collision with a lorry from Ringoil's new oil drilling site.

□S□T□U□D□Y□ □P□O□I□N□T□S

Study the fictional articles above.

1 Describe in detail how you would set up a pressure group to stop the proposed development in Stag Forest, mentioning the people, organisations and other pressure groups you might contact.

2 Explain how you would get the greatest publicity for your cause.

3 Prepare a leaflet for door-to-door delivery, opposing the scheme planned by Ringoil and the government.

Pesticides Banned

AIRPORT PROTEST

Rain Forest Threat

Almost everyday there are headlines like these in the newspapers about similar topics. There are also television programmes about wildlife, endangered species and conservation which attract millions of viewers. Everyone, it seems, is concerned with the environment now. It is a force that governments and business find increasingly difficult to ignore.

What has brought about this dramatic change in attitudes? Pressure groups are mainly responsible. Greenpeace has attracted great attention with its small-boat protests against ships dumping nuclear waste at sea and its underwater missions off the British coasts to measure nuclear radiation levels.

Friends of the Earth

Since it was set up in Britain in 1971, Friends of the Earth has also mounted many campaigns, including those against:
- the sale of whale products
- a new nuclear waste reprocessing plant at Sellafield
- emissions from power stations and car exhausts which produce acid rain
- the use of dangerous pesticides
- the pollution of cities by motor cars and lorries.

There have also been many other campaigns by other pressure groups for animal rights, lead-free petrol, quieter aircraft etc. It is an almost endless list, as independent scientists and researchers discover the harmful effects of many scientific and technological 'advances' made in the last 20 or 30 years. As Jonathon Porritt, Director of the Friends of the Earth, writes in the Annual Report for 1985–86:

'Despite a significant shift in attitudes towards the environment, the damage still goes on. For every problem solved, it seems there is always another looming large on the horizon.'

Environmentalists have had many setbacks, but have been responsible for some notable achievements, including:
- a ban on commercial whaling
- a gradual introduction of lead-free petrol
- steps to stop acid rain
- the banning of some dangerous chemicals and pesticides.

Above all, there has been a marked increase in public awareness of the problems. Green parties have become a significant political force in many European countries. It was decided that 1987 should be the Year of the Environment. The whole pattern of modern farming, based upon the extensive use of chemicals, has come under close examination and increasing attack.

Private costs and benefits

The environmentalists have made us see our world in a different way. In the past, business decisions have been made almost entirely on the basis of **PRIVATE COSTS** and **PRIVATE BENEFITS**. For example, if an airport was being extended, some of the private costs would be:
- the cost of the land
- building costs
- interest charges
- depreciation
- running costs.

Some of the private benefits would be:
- greater turnover
- bigger profits
- lower unit costs.

Social costs and benefits

The private costs and benefits would all be itemised in the firm's accounts; but they would not include the **SOCIAL COSTS** and **SOCIAL BENEFITS**. Some of the social costs might be:
- greater noise
- more traffic congestion
- reduction in business at other airports.

Some of the social benefits might be:
- greater British share of air traffic
- more employment
- cheaper air fares.

The environmentalists have made us far more conscious of the social costs and benefits of business or government decisions. Sometimes, these are not easy to measure in financial terms, but this is not always the case.

Let's look at the issue of acid rain again. It is fairly easy to assess how much it would cost to stop emissions from factories, power stations and car exhausts which result in acid rain. It is not much more difficult to calculate the social costs of this in the destruction of forests, fisheries and crops. If it cost a billion pounds to stop acid rain for good, and it resulted in a saving every year of £500 million in trees, fish and crops, it would be a great bargain.

International co-operation

There is another problem. Emissions from Britain have their greatest impact in Scandinavia and Germany. So there would need to be much greater international co-operation if acid rain were to be stopped. Environmentalists have also made us far more conscious of the need for international co-operation. We all live in one world. The accident at the Chernobyl nuclear power plant in Russia did not respect national boundaries. British sheep were contaminated, as some of them still are.

Some social costs are more difficult to assess. Chemical emissions from factories may cause cancer as well as acid rain; if even one person died as a result, how would we measure the social cost in money terms?

Social costs and benefits

Describe the social costs and benefits of the oil exploration on the opposite page.

CHECKPOINTS

1 Describe the campaigns of the Friends of the Earth.
2 How have environmentalists altered people's views of the world?
3 What impact have environmentalists had on business?
4 Why is it difficult to measure social costs and benefits?

KEY TERMS

PRIVATE COSTS AND BENEFITS The financial effects of a business decision for an individual or a firm.

SOCIAL COSTS AND BENEFITS The consequences for the whole of society of an individual business decision.

Alternatives

Designs for the shape of things to come

Living in the future is a challenge most of us will have to face up to. Andrew Page has designed a new style of community which will use the benefits of technology to produce a more satisfying way of life. The village would have 2,000 inhabitants.

It is the development of information technology which Andrew sees as being the most important factor in deciding what kind of community to build for a society in which only 10 per cent of the population are likely to be involved in the production industries.

The physical structure reflecting this way of life would be a complex of small scale, with separate buildings into which are built cottage offices and workshops. It would be self-supporting in energy from local renewable sources, surrounded by countryside and dotted with private and collective gardens and farms.

Housing would be in blocks, with a maximum of four storeys, built of modular components (or parts) but with the details designed by the occupier. The homes would be small, but with enough privacy, designed to save energy, and with built-in

solar panels and conservatories.

Village facilities would include a market place as a centre for community life, a cafe pub open 24 hours a day, a multi-purpose village hall and a health centre with swimming baths.

There would also be a cottage office, a resource centre offering computer facilities, public telephone, post office, village bank, printing press for the village newspaper, CB radio station and a centre for checking the energy used by the community and for the maintenance of public services by the residents.

The village would have its own transport centre and cars would be banned from the streets. Much use would be made of bicycle, carts and of horses. High tech would meet low tech in an attempt to design a town which human beings would enjoy living in.

Adapted from: *Town and Country Planning*, February 1984

STUDY POINTS

1 Describe in your own words Andrew Page's village of the future.

2 What would be the main differences from life today?

3 Would you personally like to live in such a community? Give your reasons.

4 Do you think such communities are more likely to be built through choice or through some disaster which forces people to create them to survive? Explain the reasons for your answer.

The success of business in the post-war world has been remarkable. It has brought about a great increase in personal and national wealth. It has produced an astonishingly wide range of consumer goods. It has provided much greater job opportunities for millions of ordinary people. It has made gigantic strides in science and technology. These achievements have been made mainly by big business, the huge conglomerates whose commercial and financial empires stretch out to every corner of the world.

Worldwide effects of big business

The power and wealth of these huge corporations is enormous. The turnover of some of the oil corporations is bigger than the gross national product of some small countries. Their decisions, made in remote boardrooms, can have great effects that ripple through the world.

For example, let's say that a big car manufacturer decides to reduce its range of cars so that it can compete more effectively in the middle price range of £9,000 to £14,000. It decides to stop production of two models made in Country A and close its factory there. Figure 80.1 shows the effects of this decision at different levels of the business world.

Faults of the present system

Has big business got too much influence and power? Many people think that it has, including some members of the Conservative party who see entrepreneurs and small firms as one of the main ways forward. Few people would deny that the present business world, dominated by big corporations and financial institutions, has some defects. Critics of the present system point to the following faults:

● Instability, shown by the stock markets crash of 1987 when shares

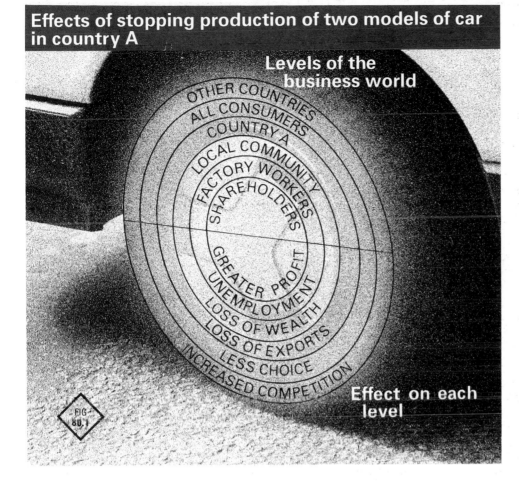

Effects of stopping production of two models of car in country A

Levels of the business world

OTHER COUNTRIES
ALL CONSUMERS
COUNTRY A
LOCAL COMMUNITY
FACTORY WORKERS
SHAREHOLDERS
GREATER PROFIT
UNEMPLOYMENT
LOSS OF WEALTH
LOSS OF EXPORTS
LESS CHOICE
INCREASED COMPETITION

Effect on each level

FIG 80.1

effects and the doubts and uncertainties may linger on for many months. Other changes are far more gradual, like the increasing awareness of how important the environment is. None of the changes, however, have altered the system itself.

History shows that no system lasts for ever. The world will be a vastly different place in 20 years' time, as it will be again in 50 or a hundred years. Shall we still have the same system of business, or of government? Or will there be something completely different?

Are there any real alternatives to the present system, anyway? Some people think that there are. One influential book in recent times has been Ernst Schumacher's *Small is Beautiful*. In it, he spelt out his vision of an alternative way of life based on organisations and technologies which are:

- small and suited to the scale of human beings

- simple and not too highly specialised

- non-violent so that we use the resources of Nature instead of trying to work against them.

The essential element in most alternatives is that people should stop concentrating on just one aspect of life – the scientific/material – and instead view themselves, and the universe, as a whole.

In the end, it will be society as a whole which decides if these new ways of life are adopted. Whether they are or not, the business person will still be there – but in a different form. The primary wants, which he or she satisfies, are never ending, whether they are provided by a big corporation, a co-operative or an individual.

plunged by 20 to 30 per cent on the world financial markets leading to fears of a **RECESSION**.

- Lack of international co-operation, which might have prevented the crash taking place.

- General emphasis on competition at the expense of greater co-operation.

- Inability to solve the problem of unemployment.

- Failure to divide wealth more fairly; both nationally, so that the rich in Britain have become much richer and the poor, much poorer; and internationally, so that the West is increasingly rich and the Third World is debt-ridden and increasingly poor.

- Concentration on private benefits at the expense of social costs.

- Maintenance of a centralised power structure and a hierarchical system of business management.

- Neglect of the environment and the ecological system, i.e. the community of all living things.

- Paying too much attention to materialism at the expense of the spiritual.

Changes

Some of these alleged defects are being remedied. The business world, like society as a whole, is always in a state of movement and change. Some events, like the stock markets crash, are sudden and dramatic, though the

K E Y T E R M

RECESSION When business goes into decline in an area; production is reduced, unemployment increases and wages and profit, and therefore investment and spending, all decrease.

C H E C K P O I N T S

1 Describe the main achievements of big business since the last war.
2 What are the main defects of the present business system?
3 What is the main philosophy of all alternatives?
4 Describe in your own words the main message of *Small is Beautiful*.

Activities

■ Review points

1 Explain how pressure groups operate. Describe the objectives and methods of any one pressure group.

2 What are social costs and benefits? Explain what they might be in relation to the opening of a) a nuclear power station, b) a supermarket and c) a disco.

3 What is the environmental lobby? What effects has it had on businesses?

4 Why do consumers need to be protected? Describe some of the main laws which have been passed in recent times to protect them and state how effective they have been.

5 What official and unofficial agencies exist to help the consumer?

■ Essay questions

1 You have been put in charge of local community relations at a 20-year-old nuclear plant which has been getting some bad publicity lately. Explain in full how you would try to gain the goodwill of the public through
   a) conducted tours
   b) local sponsorship schemes
   c) newspaper publicity.

2 You work in a Citizens' Advice Bureau. What advice would you give to the following people?
   a) A woman who complains that the glass of wine she ordered in a local pub was only half-full.
   b) A business man who says that many of the first-class letters he receives have taken two or three days to arrive.
   c) A shopkeeper who has been trying for two years to get permission from the local council to put up a sign, but still hasn't been given a decision.
   In each case explain your reasons fully.

ROME

PISA

Decline and fall of the Italian holiday empire

Families thinking of taking a holiday in Italy are warned today to expect the worst. They could face shoddy hotels, dull but expensive food, dirty beaches and the unwelcome attention of muggers.

Anyone looking forward to breakfast at their hotel will be disappointed. The meal 'is not so much a problem as a non-event, with watery coffee to accompany a papery roll', says a new *Which?* guide.

In an attack on the Italian tourist industry, the guide also criticises arrogant locals who resent holidaymakers and a lack of welcome at 'family' hotels.

'The Italians do not feel the need to put themselves out for the tourist. Towns close down for a three hour siesta and if you want to visit museums in the middle of the day, so much the worse for you.'

Guide editor, Ingrid Morgan, who regularly goes to Italy says: 'We feel people need to be warned before they go. We have had professional inspectors touring Italy and there was an awful lot they did not like.

'We all love Italy and its art and historic buildings. But we found damp bathrooms, peeling wallpaper, old sheets, poor quality furniture, and were often surprised at the prices.'

Adapted from: *Daily Mail*, 2 November 1987

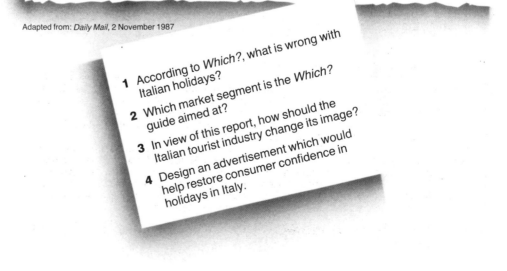

1 According to *Which?*, what is wrong with Italian holidays?

2 Which market segment is the *Which?* guide aimed at?

3 In view of this report, how should the Italian tourist industry change its image?

4 Design an advertisement which would help restore consumer confidence in holidays in Italy.

The second class post

Sending a letter has become a completely hit-and-miss affair, a watchdog group claims today.

And Post Office chiefs are masking the truth about the 'appalling' services by claiming deliveries are 30 per cent better than they really are, says the Government-funded Post Office Users National Council.

The Council says years of under-investment, not enough staffing and poor industrial relations mean the service cannot cope with the growing volume of mail.

The Council conducted two national surveys to test the system.

In the first, more than 38 out of 100 first-class letters failed to reach their destination by the next working day. In the second test the figure was 32 out of 100.

'Against a first-class target of 90 per cent next working day delivery these results are very disappointing indeed,' Council chairman Tom Corrigan said yesterday.

Research showed the performance of the first-class mail posted on Friday was particularly bad, he added.

Mr Corrigan claimed the survey confirmed what customers already knew – that their idea of the service differed greatly from Post Office claims.

The Post Office figures are based on the time it takes from collecting the letters from post boxes to when they are ready for delivery. The council considers the time when the letters are actually posted to when they reach their destination.

The official statistics, therefore, tell customers 'little about the service they can reasonably expect to get'.

Source: *Daily Mail*, 2 November 1987

1 Which body made the report?

2 According to the report, how many first-class letters reach their destinations by the next working day?

3 Which is the worst day for posting letters?

4 Whom does the report blame for slow deliveries?

5 What is the main difference in the methods used by the watchdog and the Post Office for assessing the length of time taken to deliver a letter?

Defect fears ban spray

A PESTICIDE widely used on fruit farms was banned yesterday by the Ministry of Agriculture, three months after evidence from the United States linked it with birth defects.

The ministry said the pesticide, sold under the trade name Plictran, had been withdrawn because it was 'a potential risk to female workers'.

The Agricultural Workers Union believe at least 5,000 women work on farms where the pesticide is sprayed on apples, pears, strawberries, tomatoes and hops to control mites.

Sir Richard Body, the Conservative MP and former chairman of the Commons agricultural select committee, accused the ministry of taking too long over the ban: 'If it wanted to it could act much more swiftly.'

This group of pesticides has been sold in the UK for 15 years. It is the first group of pesticides to be banned for human health reasons under the Food and Environment Protection Act which came into force last year.

Source: *The Guardian*, 11 November 1987

1 What are the possible dangers of the pesticide?

2 How long has it been sold in Britain?

3 How many women are thought to be at risk?

4 Why, according to Sir Richard Body, was it not banned before?

5 What might be some of the social costs and benefits of banning more pesticides?

■ Coursework

1 Collect advertisements from charities which help the developing world. Write a report, illustrated with charts and diagrams, describing the kind of aid they offer. Analyse which kind of aid is most valuable to the developing countries and explain what effects it might have on them.

2 Visit a Citizens' Advice Bureau or a Consumer Advice Centre and find out what kinds of consumer problems they deal with, the percentage of each kind of problem and how these percentages have changed over the years. Write a report on your findings, illustrated with graphs or charts, analysing the likely reasons for any changes that have occurred over the years.

The sign on the door of a local Citizens' Advice Bureau

3 Contact any pressure group in your area which is opposed to business interests, e.g. an environmental group, a pressure group which is resisting some business development etc. Find out how the group operates, why it is opposed, and what successes, if any, it has had. Contact any of the businesses involved to find out their views. Write a balanced article for a local newspaper giving the points of views of both sides.

Index

Entries are in word-by-word alphabetical order (in which a word (or a group of letters) followed by a space (as when part of a phrase) comes before the same group of letters followed by another letter); so 'work to rule' comes before 'workers'.

References which include definitions in the 'Key Terms' boxes are indicated by an asterisk, e.g. bad debts 125*.

Topics appearing only in the Activities sections are not indexed, nor are those featuring only in press extracts or other copyright material.

A

ACAS (Advisory, Conciliation and Arbitration
 Service) 168–169*
accounting, management 104–105*
accounts,
 annual 128
 final 130–131
 profit and loss 124–125*
 trading 122–123*
acid rain 203
administration, measuring efficiency of 131
advertisements 154
 classified 91
 display 91*
 newspaper 83
advertising 90–91 (see also promotion)
advertising agencies 91*
advertising media 91
Advertising Standards Authority 191
Advisory, Conciliation and Arbitration Service
 (ACAS) 168–169*
affiliation 146–147*
age, as market factor 79
age groups in population 16–17
AGMs (annual general meetings) 43
aid,
 government 176–177
 regional 178–179*
air freight 101
alternatives 204–205
annual accounts 128
annual general meetings (AGMs) 43
annual percentage rate (APR) 109*
annual report 128
Anti-Apartheid Movement 200, 201
anti-competitive practices 193
application forms 155*
appraisal 151*
APR (annual percentage rate) 109*
arbitration 168–169*
 binding 163
articles of association 43
assets 126–127*
 leasing 107
 selling 106
auditors 128, 129*
authorised capital 129*
authority 57*
automation 74–75*

B

baby boom 19
bad debts 125*
balance of payments 9*
balance of trade 8, 9*
balance sheets 126–129*
Bank of England 189
banks 106–107
 aid from 183
bar charts 3
bargaining, collective 164–165
basic needs 2, 3*
basic wage 148–149
batch production 70–71*
bears (speculators) 131*
benefits see fringe benefits; private benefits;
 social benefits

better value offers 33
big business see conglomerates
bills of exchange 107
binding arbitration 163
bonuses 149, 151
borrowing 108–109
BOTB (British Overseas Trade Board) 181*
boycotts (industrial action) 166, 201*
brand names 88–89*
branded goods, life cycles 95
branding 88–89
break bulk 99*
break-even 114–115*
break-even chart 114–115*
break-even point 114–115*
British Code of Advertising Practice 191
British Overseas Trade Board (BOTB) 181*
British pavilions 181
budgetary control 116–117*
budgets 117*
 for production 67*
bulls (speculators) 131*
business, social responsibilities 30–31*
Business Expansion Scheme 176
business format franchising 40–41*
business location 68–69
business objectives 24–25
business opportunities 2–3
buyers 4 (see also consumers)

C

CABs (Citizens' Advice Bureaux) 199
CAD (computer-aided design) 75
CAM (computer-aided manufacturing) 74–75
campaign methods, pressure groups 200–201
capital 3*, 126, 127*
 authorised 129*
 as factor of production 11
 issued 129*
 nominal 43*
capital expenditure 113*
case study (training method) 157
cash flow 118–119*
cash-flow forecasts 118*
cash-flow plans 35
CBI (Confederation of British Industry) 11, 160–
 161*
CDA (Co-operative Development Agency) 39*
CEGB see Central Electricity Generating Board
cellular phones 140
 use in road transport 100
Central Electricity Generating Board (CEGB) 50,
 51, 60–61
Central Office of Information (COI) 181
centralisation 60–61*
chain of command 57*
chain of production 6–7*
chambers of commerce 183
change, management of 105*
channel of distribution 99*
charts,
 bar 3
 break-even 115*
 organisation 56, 57, 58, 61
 pie 7, 75
 work study 67
children in population 17
CIM (computer-integrated manufacturing) 75*

circulating assets 127*
Citizens' Advice Bureaux (CABs) 199
clashes of interests 31
classified advertisements 91*
closed shops 162–163*
coastal shipping 101
COI (Central Office of Information) 181
collective bargaining 164–165*
commission 151
communications 136–139
Communist societies 13
community charge 185
companies,
 limited 42–43*
 registered 28–29, 42
Companies Registration Office 43
company balance sheets 128–129
company liquidations 42
company logos 25
competition 193
 branded goods 89
Competition Act (1980) 191, 192
competitions 93
compound interest 107
computer-aided design (CAD) 75
computer-aided manufacturing (CAM) 74–75
computer-integrated manufacturing (CIM) 75*
computers,
 mainframe 141*
 personal 140
 for road transport mapping 100
conciliation 168–169*
conditions of employment 165
Confederation of British Industry (CBI) 11, 160–
 161*, 185
Confravision 140
conglomerates 25*, 27 (see also multinationals)
 world-wide effects 204–205
consumer advice centres 199
consumer co-operatives 39*
Consumer Credit Act (1974) 191, 199
consumer durable market 4–5
consumer protection 198–199
consumer rights 199
consumer spending 2
consumers 3* (see also buyers)
Consumers' Association 199
containers 100
contingency planning 105
contract hire 101*
contracts of employment, 194–195*
contribution 133*
control span 59*
controls, legal 190–191
co-operation 29, 203
Co-operative Development Agency (CDA) 39*
co-operative societies 39
Co-operative Wholesale Society (CWS) 39
co-operatives 38–39*
corporations, public 51*

D

database 140–141*
demand 5*, 87
demarcation 165*
demographic change, effect on employment 19
demography 17*
depreciation 125*

Y